Also by Sally Jenkins Available from Random House Large Print

The Real All Americans

THE STATE OF JONES

The Small Southern County That Seceded from the Confederacy

Sally Jenkins and John Stauffer

RANDOM HOUSE
LARGE PRINT

Cover design by Greg Mollica
Cover illustration (flags) by Dual Identity

Insert credits appear on pages 590–591.

The Library of Congress has established a
Cataloging-in-Publication record for this title.

ISBN: 978-0-7393-2858-3

www.randomhouse.com/largeprint

FIRST LARGE PRINT EDITION

10 9 8 7 6 5 4 3 2 1

This Large Print edition published in accord
with the standards of the N.A.V.H.

For Gary Ross, Phyllis Grann, and
Jim Kelly, the three great minds
who brought us together, with
enormous gratitude and affection

I see a book kissed here which I suppose to be the Bible, or at least the New Testament. That teaches me that all things whatsoever I would that men should do to me, I should do even so to them. It teaches me, further, to "remember them that are in bonds, as bound with them." I endeavored to act up to that instruction. I say, I am yet too young to understand that God is any respecter of persons. I believe that to have interfered as I have done—in behalf of his despised poor, was not wrong, but right.

—John Brown, "Last Address to the Virginia Court," 1859

CONTENTS

PROLOGUE

The South's Strangest Soldier

1921, Border of Jones and Jasper Counties, Mississippi

The newspaperman drove his big city car along a rutted red-clay country road, sending up garlands of Mississippi backwoods dust. Newton Knight was hard enough to find when he was living. Dead, he would always be a fugitive, the newspaperman supposed. The old Civil War guerrilla was said to be nearing ninety years of age, and it wouldn't be long before he escaped his worldly pursuers and went to the grave—and plunged straight to hell, his enemies hoped. But before he did, the newspaperman intended to take down his story with an honest pen.

The chance to interview Knight was an irresistible summons to Meigs O. Frost. An Andover- and

Harvard-educated correspondent for the **New Or-leans Item,** Frost, thirty-eight, was always on the lookout for a rich subject. He'd made a career out of exploring the queer angle, the surprising complication, and the buried secret. Newton Knight qualified on all of these counts; there wasn't a more controversial—or reclusive—Civil War figure in the South. He'd still be debated long after the last headstone of the oldest combatant was covered with moss, Frost guessed.

Frost pressed the gas of his black Model T and en-dured the jouncing of his wheels, the rattling of the shutter hood, and laboring of the crankshaft. The rough road, littered with stones and pine boughs, wound through steep, wooded fields and across the crest of a lonesome timber-covered ridge. At last, a clearing opened up. Frost braked to a stop, with a sound of **ahooga** from the brass horn. He sat on the cape of a remote hill, with a sentinel-like view of the surrounding ridges. It was a place that suggested guardedness rather than peace.

Before him was a weather-beaten cabin, sheltered by lofty pines and crooked oaks, the sort the Confederate cavalry had hung traitors from. Frost got out of the car, and as the dust swirled around his cuffed pants and city shoes, he felt a stir of anticipation. He just might get the answers to some long-asked questions. Everyone had an opinion about the man whose loy-alty to the Union had caused him to betray the South. But no one had ever heard the opinions of Newton Knight himself.

Knight's role in Civil War Mississippi had been argued over ever since the surrender. The debate as to who he was and what he meant by his actions raged on, in old letters in school-taught hands, overlooked depositions, and wartime documents. Only one characteristic of the man did they all agree on.

"Just a fightin' fool when he got started," a friend described him.

From 1863 to 1865, Knight, an antislavery farmer in Jones County, Mississippi, led an insurrection against the Confederacy. For two long years he fought a war from within, successfully evading every bloodhound and tough-booted rebel that came after him. Working side by side with blacks and fellow fugitives, he raised the American flag in the marrow of the South, Confederate president Jefferson Davis's home state, and became such an effective opponent that in the last year of the war exaggerated reports circulated that he and his compatriots seceded from the Confederacy and formed a separate government. The phrase "The Free State of Jones" earned a storied if apocryphal place in Mississippi, and in the American imagination.

For all of that, "Captain" Newton Knight remained one of the less known and most poorly understood warriors of the Civil War. An expert in the art of disappearance, he had faded into the weeds of time the way he once faded into the canebrake of the Mississippi Piney Woods region. Virtually every local account of him was bent by lore or bitter memory. Depending on who told the story, he was called a hero, outlaw, soldier, or murderer.

"I believe in giving the devil his due, Newt was

a mighty sorry man," declared his old Confederate neighbor, Ben Graves.

Yet, to one local boy named Monroe Johnson, Knight left the indelible impression of a patriot. He looked, Johnson said, "like George Washington, with his long white hair."

Who was he, really?

He was a slave owner's grandson who never owned slaves; a dead-eyed shot who could reload a shotgun before the smoke cleared; a father and husband who after the war had two families, one white, the other black; a white man who in his later years was called a Negro. He fought for racial equality during the war and after, and he envisioned a world that would only begin to be implemented a century later.

Those were the facts. The full story was even more complicated.

That Newton Knight deserted and fought against the Confederate army was well known. Less well known, and seldom publicly acknowledged was Newton's long alliance with a woman named Rachel, a slave owned by his family, a woman of manifest strength and arresting appearance whom he was rumored to have loved, and even married. Rachel aided and protected Newton during the Civil War and after it bore his children. Newton shared his homestead with her until her death in 1889, and perhaps breaking the biggest taboo of all, he had acknowledged their children and grandchildren as his own. "What he did after the war was worse than deserting," old Ben Graves said.

The recovery of the life of this poor Mississippi farmer who fought for the Union was an important story, Frost believed. For one thing, Knight contradicted the romantic vision of the Southern past as a glorious Lost Cause. In this view, the Confederacy was a noble but failed attempt to declare independence from Northern aggressors—and slavery was ignored. One would never know, based on this Lost Cause mythology, that countless gallant Confederate heroes had committed treason, in defense of a still deeper crime. Or that the majority of white Southerners had **opposed** secession, that many Southern whites fought **for** the Union, and that a few of them, like Knight, burst free of racial barriers and forged bonds of alliance with blacks that were unmatched even by Northern abolitionists, and remained loyal against all odds.

Newton Knight was a spectacular reminder to Meigs Frost that the South was plagued by bloody internal estrangements. In fact, a major reason for the South's defeat stemmed from its enemies within, blacks and whites. In Jones County, fifty-three men had not only fought as anti-Confederate guerrillas, but formally enlisted in the Union army in New Orleans.

Definitive statements about Knight's career were perilous, given the scantiness of the record and the competing agendas of the witnesses. But this much Frost was sure of: for two long years Knight and his band "remained unconquered though surrounded by Confederate Armies from start to finish." Their resistance had hampered the Confederate army's ability to do battle against the North, forced it to conduct a third-front war at home, and eroded its fierce will to fight.

Not that anyone had ever thanked him for it. Newton Knight remained such a sore subject that many Mississippians refused to say his name, except to cuss him, and some of his own relatives even denied kinship with him. To them, he was a criminal.

"No romance about it at all, sir," an old Confederate said to Frost. "Just a bunch of deserters hidin' out and bushwhackin'."

To an extent, Knight's personal reticence had allowed others their opinions of him over the years. Knight never talked about the war. He gave only a few firsthand accounts of himself, even to his white son, Thomas Jefferson Knight. "One of the strange things about my father's activities was that he would never tell anyone how many men they killed or wounded," Tom Knight observed.

Newton believed it did no good to talk about the war and stir up the old bitterness. He made exceptions on five occasions between 1870 and 1900, when he filed claims through Congress seeking compensation for his service to the Union army. The claims were denied—Northern politicians were skeptical that any Southerners could have been loyal to the federal side. The rejection reinforced Newton's predisposition toward silence on the subject.

But he was reaching the end of his life, and he was tired of being misunderstood. In 1920, the white-haired

old man had sent out a missive from his hilltop property. He wished to tell his story to an independent
historian. He had heard too many "lies of the times,"
he said. He wanted to correct them.

An Ellisville attorney named J. M. Arnold wrote
a note to Dunbar Rowland, Mississippi's preeminent
military historian and archivist:

> One Newton Knight of war fame and leader of the
> Jones County deserters is still living. He is very old
> and has sent out word that he desire to have some
> person come with a stenographer and let him make
> a statement of the true conditions &c. of those
> times . . . This old man is liable to die any time and
> the chance to get the truth, men, facts and events
> will be lost if this statement is not obtained . . . I
> suggest you get some person he know to go with
> the stenographer as the old man will talk freer . . .
> I give you this information because I know you are
> interested in getting first hand knowledge and this
> is the first chance that has been had to get the true
> facts about Jones County during the war.

That was how Newton had come, on that spring
day in 1921, to grant an audience to the journalist
Frost. Yet even with an invitation, Frost was warned,
it might be difficult to get Knight to talk much about
the old days. The war still rankled in him, as it did
in his enemies in Jones and the surrounding counties. "Watch out you don't come back with a charge of

birdshot in your legs, if Uncle Newt ain't feelin right," a local told Frost.

Frost approached the weathered old cabin, in the shade of the long-straw pines. As he opened the gate of a hand-hewn split rail fence, a hound bayed, and a young couple wandered out to the front porch. Knight's daughter, Cora, wore an old-fashioned calico dress; her husband was in overalls.

"Uncle Newt home?"

"No, suh. He's oveh at the otheh place, bout three miles off."

She gestured into the woods, a direction that presumably led to the home of Knight's black family. Frost surveyed the rough, uneven ground with dismay; the thickets and tangled underbrush made it impossible to go any farther by car. He would have to hike. The man in overalls pointed to a narrow dirt footpath that wound into the woods. "Over yonder, past that naked pine."

Frost had just started up the undulating path into the dense woods when a figure loomed ahead, trudging through the brush. The tall, gaunt form that mounted the hill was a trifle stooped, but even with an old man's hunch in his back, Newton Knight was still formidably built. Frost surveyed a frame that was perhaps six-foot-four or taller, in an age when the average male height was about five feet seven. He was clad in a suit of dark homespun, heavily booted, and topped by a great-brimmed slouch hat of light-colored felt, which only made him seem larger.

The face that peered from beneath the hat was eagle-like. "A mighty beak of a nose jutted out like a promontory," Frost noted. "The jaw was seen through a sparse white beard. The white hair, uncut for years, hung about his shoulders." But it was the eyes that made the impression on Frost: they were the pale blue color of the winter sea, and they suggested all of the isolation and self-sufficiency of a survivalist who was willing to do whatever it took to endure. To Frost, they were the eyes of a gunfighter. "They were that cold, clear, blue-grey eyes of the killer now vanishing from the west," he wrote. "They looked clear through you. And by some peculiarity of control, hawk-like, the lower lids never moved."

The gaze was unnerving enough in peacetime, Frost thought. In fighting times—well.

"Glad to see you sir," Knight said, offering a handshake. The outstretched hand was a great slab of a thing, palm toughened and heavily muscled from a lifetime of hefting axes, wrestling livestock, and wielding firearms.

His accent was pure backwoods Mississippi, soft on the A's and hard on the E's. For emphasis, he used phrases like "right smart" or "right peart." The words came out "raht smahrt" or "raht peert." Knight suggested they move into the house to get out of the raw spring weather and warm themselves next to the hearth. "I'm feeling right peart this morning but I reckon a fire would feel good, don't you?" he said.

As Frost followed Knight along the path, the old man

covered the uphill ground like an athlete. He had once been a king of backwoods fighters, a bare-knuckled, crotch-kicking, ear-biting hellion. "He used to have the biggest, longest teeth you ever saw," one friend remarked.

They crossed the porch of the cabin, stamping dirt from their boots on the threshold. Knight's living room was a plain, barnlike space of rough plank floors and matchboard walls. A giant whitewashed stone hearth took up most of one side of the room. Above, mounted on a rack and gleaming, was a twin-hammered shotgun.

Frost wasn't intimidated by the weapon, or by the old soldier. The reporter had an air of the patrician about him—he was a Connecticut Yankee and a remote cousin of the poet Robert Frost—but he was also an ex-soldier himself and a former foreign war correspondent. As a young man he had once tried to chew buckshot, to build up his determination. Following Harvard and a brief stint as a reporter for the **New York Times,** Frost had enlisted in the Marines. He had chased Pancho Villa across Mexico and fought in the Great War. He still had a silver plate in his leg, which had been shredded by shrapnel. As a war correspondent he had covered a half a dozen Latin American revolutions and lost the sight in one eye from an infection contracted crawling through a jungle. He had finally settled down in New Orleans, where he wrote about everything from ghosts to corruption. But he remained a notoriously tough reporter, who would help bring down Louisiana governor Huey Long by exposing his scandal-ridden administration.

As they stood by the fire, Frost forthrightly introduced the subject he had come to talk about: did Knight remember much about the war?

"Well I remember a right smart of it," Knight said.

"Memory still as good as your eyes?" Frost asked.

"Better," Knight shot back. "My memory's all right. 'Bout my eyes, I've worn out three-four pair of spectacles. Don't think much of 'em. Quit 'em. I can see enough to shoot a bird on the wing or a rabbit on the run yet. That's good enough for me."

In fact, Knight's mind was as clear and keen as a man fifty years younger. He remembered all of it: the shell blasts that furrowed green fields, the nooses in the trees, the ravening hounds bursting through the brush. He remembered after the war, too, when it was just as dangerous, the years when he seemed to be forever defying the forces of a superior army from his hilltop retreat.

"We'll all die guerrillas, I reckon," Knight said. "Never could break through the rebels to jine the Union Army. The Johnny Rebs busted up the party they sent to swear us in. Always was unofficial. Well I reckon it don't make much difference now, anyhow."

Knight piled oak logs in the large mouth of the fireplace and then sat down heavily in an old splint rocker by the fire. He gestured to Frost to do the same. "Draw up a chair and make yourself comfortable," Knight said. He pronounced it "cheer." Frost sat down and took out his notebook and his pen.

"Now, sir," Newton said, as Frost settled in. "What is it you want me to tell you?"

ONE

Corinth

May 1862, Corinth, Mississippi

As far as the foot soldiers were concerned, the other side could have the damned town. The generals might have gladly given it up too, if not for the railroad junction. Corinth was pestilential. Even the Union's pitiless William Tecumseh Sherman said the place made him feel "quite unwell." Sherman's superior, Henry Halleck, had such a low opinion of it that when he fell ill with a bowel ailment, he sourly named it "the evacuation of Corinth."

It was wretched ground for a fight, with boggy fields, swarms of bugs clouding the fetid air, and a chronic shortage of decent drinking water. A Confederate colonel called it a "sickly, malarial spot, fit only for alligators and snakes." It left no better impression on a Yankee lieutenant from Minnesota, who found the locals "ignorant" and the women "she vipers" with the figures of "shad bellied bean poles," he wrote. As far as he could tell, the chief local produce consisted of "wood ticks, chiggers, fleas, and niggers."

But men on both sides understood, if reluctantly, that Corinth was one of the most vital strategic points in the South. It was "the vertebrae of the Confederacy," as one rebel official put it. In the middle of town, two sets of railway tracks crossed each other in a broad X: the Memphis and Charleston ran east-west, while the Mobile and Ohio ran north-south. The intersection was a working hive: locomotives screeched and huffed, while men on platforms loaded and offloaded downy bales of cotton, stacks of lumber, crates, barrels, sacks of provisions like salt beef, and other vital war materiel. Trains were the reason for Corinth's existence: the village was just seven years old and the streets were still raw dirt. The largest hotel in town, the Tishomingo Hotel, was a broad two-story affair with six chimneys that fronted directly on the tracks of the Memphis and Charleston, which ran just outside the front porch.

There were 80,000 Confederate troops under General Pierre G. T. Beauregard jammed into the brick and clapboard town, which normally housed just 2,800 inhabitants. Corinth was filled with rebel wounded from Beauregard's catastrophic encounter in April with U. S. Grant's Yankee troops at Shiloh, just a few miles away. The battle, so named for the log church where Grant's men had camped, was the worst bloodbath in the Western Hemisphere to date, with a toll of 20,000 in two days. "God grant that I may never be the partaker in such scenes again," one Confederate survivor wrote. "When released from this I shall ever be an advocate of peace."

Corinth was hardly an ideal place to recover. Contagion was inevitable with such a large army closely confined in pestiferous surroundings, the comings, goings, spewings, and brawlings of thousands of men, horses, mules, and oxen trod everything into mud, and their litter and foul runoff attracted hordes of fleas and mosquitoes. There were not enough rooms to accommodate the wounded, much less the sick. On the first floor of the Tishomingo, men lay on blood- and water-soaked carpets or blankets in the vestibule and hallways. On the second floor, the charnel-house vapors caused some of the doctors and nurses to pass out.

One of the wounded was a rugged thirty-year-old colonel in the 6th Mississippi Infantry, and a future governor of the state, named Robert Lowry. This peacetime lawyer had been raised in Smith County, one county over from Jones. He had taken wounds in the chest and another in the arm, as his company lost 310 men out of 425. The performance had earned his unit the nickname "The Bloody Sixth."

Those Confederates who survived Shiloh unharmed were as likely to get sick in Corinth. The rebels were preparing for a state of siege as a federal army of 120,000 under Union general Halleck encroached on the outskirts of town. Men labored constantly with shovels in the sweltering heat, as Beauregard ordered the defenses fortified with immense earthworks. The men dug until they were thirsty, then drank foul, swampy water. Diarrhea and dysentery became endemic. Soon, a quarter of the Southern troops were ill. "The water was bad enough to kill a dog much less a man," wrote a Mississippi cavalryman named William L. Nugent home to his wife.

Beauregard responded to the epidemic by trying to rally men with rhetoric: "We are about to meet in the shock of battle the invaders of our soil, the despoilers of our homes, the disturbers of our family ties," he wrote in a widely distributed letter. "Face to face, hand to hand, we are to decide whether we are to be freemen or the vile slaves of those who are free only in name . . . Let the impending battle decide our fate, and add one more illustrious page to the history of our Revolution, one to which our children will point with noble pride, saying, 'Our fathers were at the battle of Corinth.' "

But even as his letter circulated among the soldiers, Beauregard decided to evacuate the city. At the end of May, Beauregard hastily decamped his army and its provisions, mostly hunks of heavily salted meat, for the healthier environs of Tupelo to the west. Beauregard, too, had gotten sick. Suddenly, he did not feel his presence was required in such a swampland. He took an unauthorized leave to recuperate in comfort in Mobile.

With the Confederate withdrawal from Corinth, the Union forces moved in. They found the place a stinking pit. Abandoned foodstuffs and other detritus rotted on the roadsides. A soldier with the 81st Ohio, Joseph K. Nelson, noticed an odd glint in the earth that crunched under the soles of his boots. When he bent down to examine the dirt, he found it was literally moving with insects.

"The Johnnies left behind something for us to remember them by," he wrote in his diary. "The ground in places was alive with 'body guards'—lice—and was much littered in places with large chunks of very salt beef. The salt sparkled and glistened in it."

October 1862, Northern Mississippi, on the March

General Earl Van Dorn was a ringlet-tossing little Mississippian in search of a big reputation. Profligate with the lives of men and impossibly conceited, as suggested by his extravagant twists of auburn hair, Van Dorn openly aspired to "a burning name," as he put it. He was continually conceiving of schemes that could win him the flaming renown he sought, and his latest was typical.

As an Indian summer fell over Mississippi, Van Dorn about-faced the Confederate Army of the West and marched it back toward Corinth with the intention of retaking the town. His plan was a hurriedly drawn, surprise full frontal assault, and heedless of risk, but that only made it more infectious to some of his colleagues. He was after "great objects," and that justified the "unusual hazard" of the attack, according to his chief of staff, another overeager Mississippi cavalier general named Dabney H. Maury.

But Newton Knight, a young sergeant striding in Company F of the 7th Mississippi Battalion, felt none of the enthusiasm that the glory-seeking Van Dorn and Maury tried to summon with such verbal flourishes. He was neither free nor proud to be a Confederate soldier.

Company F, made up of sixty-nine men and four officers from Jones County, had been forcibly mustered into the ailing Confederate army after Beauregard's evacuation of Corinth in May. Now, just four months later, almost half the new men were ill. Fully two-thirds were absent or on leave, and six had died. At the last roll call, only twenty men and two officers had answered present, Knight among them. Men were sick with yellow fever, dysentery, malaria, and influenza. Or they were just plain sick and tired of marching around northern Mississippi as their vainglorious commanders ordered them to and fro across the sweltering countryside. It was a testament to Knight's sheer vigor that he was on his feet.

Newton was a long-limbed, shaggily handsome twenty-four- year-old accustomed to privation. His wavy black hair curled to his shoulders and was greased with sweat over a tall forehead. A rampant, untended mustache and beard fell below his chin into his shirt buttons. His large, pooling, blue-gray eyes seemed preternaturally sighted and were spaced far apart, which led some to accuse him of eccentricity. He had perpetually sunburned cheekbones and a large jaw clamped hard and slightly off center.

He was rawboned and muscular from habitual work and a lifelong diet of sweet potatoes, cornbread, and whatever wild game he brought down with his shotgun. "Big heavyset man, quick as a cat," a friend described him. Men from easier backgrounds found camp life a misery; the beds on wet ground, the foraging and scrabbling for decent victuals, the tramping in all weather with never a change of clothes. Not Newton: hard didn't bother him.

Newton suffered from a different complaint: he was an unwilling soldier. In April of 1862, the Confederacy, badly in need of reinforcements, had passed the first Conscription Act, drafting all men between the ages of eighteen and thirty-five. "They just come around with a squad of soldiers 'n took you," Newton remembered. On May 13, 1862, Newton and twenty-two of his closest relatives and friends, young men who hunted together, worshipped together, drank together, helped build one another's homes, and even married one another's sisters, had reluctantly enrolled in Company F together, "rather than be conscripted and be put into companies where we didn't want to go," another Jones Countian recalled.

As an inducement, those who volunteered rather than waited to be impressed received a fifty-dollar bounty. But those who hesitated were coerced or faced arrest. Under the threat of law, "they all came in," re-

called the major commander of the 7th Battalion, Joel
E. Welborn, who raised the troop. "I did organize the
men as conscripts." Welborn and the unit captain, his
relative J. G. Welborn, took down enrollments until
the battalion numbered 760 or so.

At least by joining up together, Newton and his
friends could be messmates. Eating together was the
strongest tie in the dreary life of the army other than
fighting together. Messmates were more than supper
companions; they foraged, cooked, groused, sang,
gambled, argued, smoked, and killed time together.
Over meals, they confided their daily thoughts and
fears to like-minded men who shared their wretched
experiences.

Mess was a small relief for Newton and his comrades as they moved toward Corinth on October 2,
1862. At the end of the day, the men unshouldered
their gear and dropped it heavily. They stacked their
muskets in triangles, barrels crossed and rifle butts in
the dirt, and sagged to the ground or low campstools,
a seedy lot in mismatched clothes and heavy beards.
They thrust pipes in their mouths or pulled out newspapers, while around fires, rank-smelling meat stew
began to simmer in a heavy black iron pot and coarse
cornbread roasted in a black skillet, which an assigned
man had carried, stuck handle first in his rifle barrel.

The men griped incessantly about their fare, the
dry cornbread cooked in bacon grease (wheat flour
was usually too precious to be wasted on infantrymen)
and the rancid beef they were issued. The blue-black

meat had a gluey texture, and they wondered if they threw it against a wall whether it would stick. "Buzzards would not eat it at any season of the year," one Mississippian claimed. They joked that the cattle supplying the army were so emaciated it took two soldiers to hold up one cow so it could be shot.

Depending on what the countryside offered, they would enhance their meal with foraged field peas or onions, or fruit plundered from orchards. A favorite recipe was "cush," a stew made of beef, bacon grease, water, crumbled cornbread, and mashed green apples. But sometimes they had nothing but dry bread and musky beef, which they roasted in strips on the ramrods from their guns. As one Mississippi captain in another regiment reported, "The discipline of the troop would be promoted by a more regular issue of rations."

None of their issue was regular. They wore sallow gray-brown tunics and cartridge belts, in which the best-armed men might have a pistol stuck one way and a knife the other. They were unevenly equipped with rifles; some had Springfields with barrels long as rails, others the shotguns they brought from home. In addition to their eighteen-pound firearms, they packed forty rounds in ammunition pouches, three days of rations in haversacks, clanking metal canteens, and mess kits, if they hadn't thrown them away to lighten the load. Sometimes when a man didn't have a plate to eat from, he exploded a cartridge in a canteen. The canteen would split open and flatten.

As they ate, the men of Company F commiserated and discussed their apprehensions about the coming battle. They once again debated, as men on both sides often did, the cause they had been drafted into. A few even openly expressed an unwillingness to fight: the outfit was unusually full of independent-minded men who resented conscription and felt no loyalty to the Confederacy, though they had to be careful saying so in front of officers.

A leading example was Jasper Collins, a thirty-four-year-old corporal with a face flat and leathered as a saddle who was one of Newton's closest lifelong friends. "When there was a fight on, he was right there with my father," wrote Newton's son. Collins was considered one of the most knowledgeable and politically informed men in the company, "He kept well posted on business . . . and read lots, on various matters that would come up." He was from a family of staunch Unionists, who were tough enough to be able to state their beliefs aloud and defend them. His father Stacy had spoken out vehemently against secession, and his six brothers were pro-Union as well; Jasper's older brother Riley had flatly refused to be conscripted.

Newton's own convictions about the war stemmed from a combination of politics and faith. He was a Unionist in principle, and he had opposed the state's Ordinance of Secession. He also questioned the fundamental religiosity of slavery and the underlying basis of the war. In his worship he was a Baptist, and some evidence suggests he was a Primitive, one who tended to believe in the equality of souls, including those in bondage. As he read in his Bible, Acts 17:26: "And God hath made of one blood all nations of men for to dwell on all the face of the earth."

Newton had resisted serving the Confederacy, to the point that he courted arrest. He declared to the conscription officers that he didn't want to fight and instead volunteered as a battalion hospital orderly. In that way, he hoped to avoid killing men and care for them instead, and to reconcile his conscience with his actions. "I told 'em I'd help nurse sick soldiers if they wanted," he remembered.

His defiance didn't sit well with the Welborns. At one point, according to a fellow soldier, "the captain threatened to have him shot."

Knight simply didn't feel any common interest with the merchants and planters who made up the officer class and who had pressed him into service. The man who had forced Newton into uniform, fifty-one-year-old Major Joel Welborn, was a moneyed, well-connected land speculator with a reputation for crooked dealing back home. Welborn was among the richest men in Jones, the owner of an ever-expanding empire of real estate with a personal worth of $36,000. A year earlier, he had been accused by his neighbors of fraud for abusing his position as swamp commissioner to seize as many as 25,000 acres of land and resell it.

Newton was a yeoman farmer who had left behind a homestead and acreage worth just $800, on which he struggled to feed his wife, Serena, and three infant sons. Yeoman farmers depended upon their own sweat and toil and took pride in their independence. But the planter-merchants were contemptuous of small farmers like Knight in civilian life. A prominent Mississippi attorney turned cavalryman, William L. Nugent of the 28th Mississippi, patronizingly described "the humble tiller of the bleak hillsides of the interior" who "eked out a miserable existence." General Dabney Maury more bluntly called them "the worst class in our population." Colonel Robert Lowry of the 6th Mississippi referred to them as "ignorant persons" despite the fact that he had grown up among them, as his neighbors.

These elites were just as infuriatingly arrogant in the military. Many of them seemed to view their officer status as a prerogative, and the men in the ranks as vassals. They could afford luxuries such as tents with flaps that closed, changes of underclothes, and lavish fare like wheat biscuits. "We are treated here worst than dogs," wrote J. B. Shows of Company C of the 7th Battalion angrily to his wife in Jones County. One enlisted man described Confederate officers ordering infantrymen around "as if they were a lot of negroes. I am in favor of discipline but not of tyranny." Still another wrote in his diary, "I only hope that a false patriotism will never again induce me to put myself at the mercy of such damnable despotism as governs the army."

The chronic hardship of camp life for the Confed-

erate private exacerbated his resentment at conscription. The pay was only eleven dollars a month—when
the men received it, which was seldom—not enough
to purchase a clean shirt. As their clothing tattered,
so did their morale. One angry Confederate soldier
"chafed from morning till night" at the "starvation,
rags, dirt and vermin" and the "insuperable obstacles
to decency by which I was surrounded" and blushed
with mortification at his own appearance.

Newton therefore felt little loyalty to his superiors.
The sinewy physical giant who wished to remain in
the rear frustrated his officers. But if they wanted to
shoot him, at the same time they needed him. Newton was popular and held sway over the men, enough
so that upon conscription Welborn had designated
him fourth sergeant of the company. In fact, Newton showed the makings of a good soldier: he had an
unbreakable constitution, an unerring eye through
a gun sight, and a capacity for hard marching. He
performed his duties well enough that he was shortly
promoted to third sergeant, though that may have
had as much to do with the sickness in the company.
As a sergeant, Knight was required to study Hardee's
Rifle and Light Infantry Tactics and learned how
to issue basic drill commands: "Attention, company!
Shoulder—arms!"

Knight's dual roles as sergeant and hospital orderly
kept him busy given the poor health of the unit as
it moved toward Corinth. Among his responsibilities
was dosing his comrades with the standard, crude

army remedies for their ills. "I went around giving the sick soldiers blue mass and calomel and castor oil and quinine," he said. "That was about all the medicine we had then."

At night, the field hospital staff pitched a small tent, about fourteen feet square with about eight cots. There wasn't much temptation for men to malinger with medical excuses, as there were no sheets or pillows, just rough-fibered army blankets, and no one had heard yet of sanitizing. Too long a stay on one of those cots was likely to give a man an infection if he didn't already have one.

The next morning, after reveille, the doctors determined who was fit to march. Newton distributed bitter-tasting drafts, made of various powders stirred into tepid water. Often, medicines were unavailable, owing to the Union blockade, and ether and chloroform were too expensive to use on common soldiers. An array of small bottles was lined on temporary shelving, holding herbs and home remedies. There was Dover's powder, quinine, rhubarb, Rochelle salts, castor oil, sugar of lead, tannin, sulphate of copper, sulphate of zinc, camphor, tincture of iron, camphorata, syrup of squills, simple syrup, and an assortment of alcohols—whiskey, brandy, port wine, and sherry. For those suffering with nervous disorders, there was the herb valerian, or perhaps some opium, to induce calm and sleep.

Newton changed bandages, read the Bible to men who requested it, and found water for the ailing. His disposition mattered more than medical knowledge. With death so common, doctors became calloused, and the soldiers resented them, believing they were butchers who "kills mores than they cour," as an Alabaman put it. Captain Walter A. Rorer of the 20th Mississippi, who had fought at Shiloh, flatly despised them. "There is nothing held by them so cheap as human life, and all seem to think if they do not murder men directly, they are not responsible," he wrote. A compassionate orderly was a wounded soldier's best friend.

But Newton knew he was going to have to fight eventually, whether he wanted to or not. The 7th Battalion was marching in a force of 22,000 men led by Van Dorn on a circuitous route to his great object, Corinth. As part of the 3rd Brigade, 1st Division, Newton was under the immediate command of General Sterling Price, another pugnacious staff officer who craved conflict. He had already led Newton into battle once, at Iuka two weeks earlier.

Price was a thickset Missourian who stood six foot two and weighed nearly three hundred pounds, with a face shaped like a lamb chop and swirls of white-gray hair at his temples that plunged downward into cottony sideburns. He struck one Mississippi lieutenant colonel as a "hale, hearty, handsome old farmer," and his Missouri soldiers called him "Old Pap," for his grandfatherly appearance. But he had a vehement temperament and was prone to grandiosity. A few months earlier, he had demanded preferment from Jefferson

Davis by slamming his fist down on the presidential desk, shouting, "I will surprise you, sir!" His sense of entitlement was based on a widely varied career as a lawyer, hotelier, tobacco planter, congressman, veteran of the Mexican War, and governor of Missouri. He was portentous. When shown the fortifications of Corinth built by Beauregard, he said, "I only saw anything like them but once and I took them." Although he initially opposed secession, he turned fanatic, and at the end of the war he would choose exile in Mexico over surrender.

In mid-September, Price had stormed his men into Iuka, swaggeringly advising his troops that if the Yankees had "the impudence to come near," to shoot at their knees. But the battle had been a near disaster: they had almost been trapped by federal pincers led by Grant and General William Rosecrans.

Newton and the 7th Mississippi Battalion had been among the last to arrive on the field, shortly before nightfall. The firing had subsided, but he witnessed the toll of it in the dim twilight, and heard it too, from the thousands of wailing wounded. The moon had been full that night, shining on pale corpses and dark humps of dead horses. Confederate losses were as high as 520 killed and 1,300 wounded, while the Union reported 141 killed and 613 wounded. Before dawn, the men had been shaken awake with orders to withdraw. Price, badly outnumbered, had been fortunate that an entire arm of the Union force under General Edward O. C. Ord had remained idle due to an acoustic topographical fluke, unable to hear the sounds of battle from behind a hill. Price seized the opportunity to escape down an open road, and the sleepy, unnerved men went tramping back the way they came.

Ever since then, they had been on a wearisome circular journey. Price had given his men just two days' rest before putting them on the rapid march again, this time to Ripley, twenty miles north, for a rendezvous with Van Dorn and the attack on Corinth. "Without waiting to fix things up and get together our old men we again started on a more foolhardy expedition than the last," said one staff officer.

Capricious weather and the pace of the march told on the men. At first, it rained as Newton and comrades trudged over the steep hills of northern Mississippi. They arrived at Ripley footsore and mud soaked, and with ill will toward their commanders after marching for seven hours at a stretch, "at night thru rain and darkness so black you could scarcely see your hand." They slept on wet ground, with no idea of why they were heading north with such urgency. "It is manifest that Gen Price is <u>fast losing</u> the <u>confidence</u> of all his soldiers," wrote Lieutenant Colonel Columbus Sykes, a cotton planter serving with the 43rd Mississippi in the same brigade as Newton, to his wife Pauline. Finally, the rain had cleared and a high, hot sun had dried the roads. By the evening of October 2, the trudging columns sent up swirls of choking dust that parched throats and made it hard to breathe.

Buck Van Dorn was a "harebrained" and "thick skulled" strategist, to borrow a description from historian Shelby Foote. He had been nearly thrown out of West Point before finishing fifty-second in his class of fifty-six, and he preferred horse racing to the drudgery of logistics, which made him ill suited to lead such a large coordinated attack. By the morning of October 3, 1862, his personal unevenness was catching up with him, and he would emerge from the impending battle facing charges of negligence. In Van Dorn's haste to get to Corinth, he failed to take into account the undulating, heavily wooded terrain and how fatiguing such a forced march was as a preamble to battle. In his hurry, he also failed to ensure the men had adequate food and drink.

After mess, Newton and the men fell into a short, exhausted sleep. At 4:00 a.m. on the morning of October 3, they were awoken for the final leg of the march. As they covered the last ten miles toward Corinth, the sun drew up in the sky and the temperature reached ninety degrees. The sandy roads were so hot that the men could feel the heat through their boot soles, and dust rose up like smoke. To make matters worse, it was almost completely dry for several miles around Corinth. There was no water for the men to refill their canteens. After a scorching hike, the footsore, dry-throated troops approached the town. The 7th Battalion moved across a broad triangle of ground between the two train tracks, pressing through heavy woods and undergrowth, broken by occasional pastures. Ahead, they could see the outer breastworks of Corinth, full of Yankees.

With a hoarse shout of orders and a jangle of equipment, Newton and the rest of Company F formed their line of battle.

October 3, 1862, 9:00 a.m., Corinth

The 25,000 Union troops garrisoned in Corinth were no happier or healthier than the rebels who had been there. General William Rosecrans, not satisfied with the already formidable defenses, put the men to work with axes and shovels, building a ring of batteries, large earthen bulwarks mounted with twenty-pound Parrott guns, around the circumference of town. The approaches were littered with felled timber, called "abatis," to slow attackers. The landscape was one of open desolation, fields of nothing but hacked-off tree stumps.

The northern men had suffered just as much from the heat and impure water of Corinth, with a sickness rate of 35 percent. Their rations were no better either; they existed on salt pork or beef unless they could supplement their diet from the surrounding countryside, already largely picked clean by the rebels. One Iowan who went foraging could find nothing but muscadine grapes. "Had grape pie for supper," he reported.

Once again, the Tishomingo Hotel became a hospital, and the federal infantrymen believed their doctors were just as incompetent as the rebels did. To Hugh Carlisle of the 81st Ohio, they were perpetrators of malpractice and dispensed the same ineffectual powders no matter what the ailment. He refused to take his medicine. "You must think I am a damn fool," the surgeon said to him.

"You must be a mind reader," Carlisle replied.

Many of the occupiers of Corinth were seeing the Deep South for the first time, and they examined it with curiosity. Corinth was a hub for seized cotton, and huge poofed bales sat on the train platforms in front of the Tishomingo, ready to send north. The town was also a destination for "contrabands," scores of slaves who fled or stole away from their plantations with the Yankee invasion of Mississippi and came to the Union lines seeking freedom. They staggered into Corinth in rags and on bare feet, or rode in bunches on mules and buckboards. "It is all humbug about Slaves liking to stay with their masters," an Ohio colonel discovered. "Men and women and children run off whenever they get a chance."

Some Northern soldiers were repulsed by contrabands, and many had, at best, mixed feelings about them. But they were unanimous in appreciation of the fact that they relieved white men of the hardest labor. Contrabands did the most punishing work on the fortifications; they worked as diggers, drivers, haulers and did the cooking, scrubbing, and laundering. An Illinois infantryman wrote from Corinth, "Every regt has nigger teamsters and cooks which puts that many more men back in the ranks . . . It will make a difference in the regt of not less than 75 men that will carry guns that did not before we got niggers."

Contrabands exposed northern soldiers to slavery

firsthand and frequently caused men to revise their views of it. Some slaves came to Corinth bearing livid marks and scars inflicted by owners. But external wounds only signified one kind of physical punishment. Joseph Nelson of the 81st Ohio Infantry wrote about a revelation he received on a visit to an area plantation: "We learned of one of the beauties of slavery of which we had not previously thought. A resident here owned a large strong muscular Negro whom he stood as men do a stallion, $100 to insure a live youngster to kick, yell, and suck. Slave women were brought to him and bred, that they might reproduce their kind."

Abolitionists and non-abolitionists alike among the soldiers were appalled by the condition many of the contrabands subsisted in. Yet their treatment by Union troops was often hardly better than that they received from Confederates, and sometimes worse. One Union soldier wrote in his diary wondering whether they were any better off. "They are quartered together in barracks, are filthy and diseased, the small pox are raging among them. If these Negroes cannot be treated better than they are, we ought to leave them with their masters, who can certainly take better care of them."

A close-up view of slavery, combined with the heat, stale camp food, incessant work, and tension of combat, cured Northern soldiers of any romance they may have had with antebellum Mississippi and its beguilingly beautiful plantation homes. One Iowa infantryman who went into the countryside outside of Corinth came to a large manor house, where a mistress supervised two Negroes as they killed hogs. The mistress complained that the flight of slaves had forced her own daughter into the kitchen. The girl "had never washed the dishes until the Yankees had come into the country," she bitterly informed the Northern soldiers.

By the end of September, the occupying Yankee troops had developed a sincere hostility toward their Mississippi hosts. When a Yankee transport on the Mississippi River came under sniper fire from the banks, infuriated troops leaped onto shore and burnt every single thing in sight. "All, all committed to the flames," a Union captain reported. He added, "They have met a just retribution."

As Van Dorn advanced on Corinth, he was convinced that the Yankees would not match the fierceness of the Southerners fighting for their home soil. But the Northern invaders were clearly in an ill temper, too.

October 3, 1862, 10:00 a.m., Corinth

Sharp musketry and the humps of cannon erupted as the 7th Mississippi Battalion surged through the woods in massed columns and began a slow but steady progress across a field toward the Union works. There was enough of a breeze to blow the dust and gun smoke away, so that the federals could clearly see the rebels approach; their lines were so long, it seemed they might overlap.

Newton and other men experiencing battle for

the first time were stunned to realize they could actually **hear** the Minié balls flying around them. The thumb-shaped lead bullets weighed an ounce or more, and their buzzing whine gave the illusion that they could be dodged. But that was "as impossible as dodging chain lightning," remarked an Iowa infantryman named Lewis F. Phillips, "for the savage little 'zip' noise they made in passing could not be made 'til they were opposite the ear and gone." Still, some couldn't resist ducking. When a man put his hand to his ear, you knew one had just missed.

Those who were hit likened the feeling to being struck by a club, followed by scalding water. A Minié ball almost invariably shattered a bone and at best left a large, ugly perforation in the flesh, large enough to pass a handkerchief through. Which some surgeons did, to clean the wound.

The first shell and grapeshot tore into the neat Confederate lines and left sudden gaps, as if the hand of God had swiped men away. Musket fire punched into them and dropped them. Cannonballs ploughed through the woods, shearing off tree limbs and making bark fly. To John McKee of the 2nd Iowa, the man who'd eaten grape pie for supper, the rebels "only came on the faster" in the face of the fire, their colonels in front rallying them onward.

As the 7th Mississippi Battalion pushed ahead into the open field, climbing through the abatis, two Yankee batteries on a distant hill, eight guns in all, roared to life and further cut them up. Their brigade commander, General Martin E. Green, brought up some artillery to answer, and the sound of orders rang out: "Caisson limbers forward!" Newton and the other infantrymen dropped down and hid behind logs, hugging the ground close, while for the next forty-five minutes the two sides exchanged cannon fire.

Men were injured almost randomly in the artillery duel. Hugh Carlisle of the 81st Ohio lay facedown in the dirt next to a boy named John, who lifted his head and wiped a drop of blood away from the end of his nose.

"John, are you hurt?" Carlisle asked.

"No, I scratched my face when we laid down."

A lieutenant said, "John you're hurt, you better go to the rear."

"No, I'm not hurt. I can stay as long as the rest of you."

He pushed back his cap, and more blood trickled down his head. He drew a hand across his brow, and a handful of brains came away in his hand.

"I believe I'm hurt after all," he said. He went to the rear.

Shelling did freakish things. An Ohioan lucked out when a shell struck the visor of his cap, knocking him into a daze and turning half his face black, but leaving him otherwise unhurt. Two Iowa companies were lying under a tree when a cannonball blasted into it and sailed clear through the center of the trunk, showering them with splinters but sparing their lives.

As Newton and the men of the 7th Mississippi Battalion hugged the ground under the artillery fire, the outfit's lieutenant colonel, James Terral, organized a charge against the Union batteries that had them pinned. He collected a group of men from Jones and surrounding counties and led them in a rush toward the gun barrels. The men scrambled over obstacles of every kind—fencing, heavy timber, and thick brush— under fire.

As the rebels came on, the Yankees cut the fuses down progressively, until shells exploded just three-fourths of a second after leaving the mouth of the cannon. Still Terral urged the Mississippians on. The officer, on horseback, surged twenty yards ahead of his men—straight into a blast of fire. A ruddy-cheeked, sleepy-lidded boy from Jasper County named William Denson Evans watched as Terral was rag-dolled by bullets and fell from his horse.

Evans reached Terral and lifted him up. "Knock them off of their guns, boys, for I cain't do any more," Terral said.

Evans helped carry Terral to the rear. "He was shot all to peaces," Evans wrote. "Boath leges were broke boath arms was broke and 4 or five bullits were shot in his boddy."

Evans himself lost his left eye and was wounded in the arm, but "we done what he told us to do and spiked the big guns."

The Yankees would fight, fall back, regroup, and reinforce. The 7th Mississippi Battalion advanced only a few yards at a time. "We would fight them in one position until flanked then take another, only to repeat the operation," recorded Hugh Carlisle of the 81st Ohio. After hours of continuous fighting, all that lay between the rebels and Corinth was a last semi-circle of earthen batteries. But by then the Yankees were "trebled by reinforcements," observed the rebel commanders, and not only did they have fresh men, they had food and water. The rebels, though they were within six hundred yards of the town, had gone several hours without anything to eat or drink and were utterly played out.

As sundown came, their firing diminished, then ceased altogether. Van Dorn watched the light fade with regret: "One hour more of daylight and victory would have soothed our grief for the loss of the gallant dead who sleep on that lost but not dishonored field," he insisted. But he also had to admit that the ten-mile march, lack of water, difficulty of getting into the battle through forests of undergrowth, and the resistance of the enemy had been more than his men could overcome in a single day.

The men of the 7th Battalion had fought for eight hours in ninety- to one-hundred-degree heat, with scarcely a drop of liquid. The hands of their brigade commander, General Martin E. Green, were black with gunpowder. Soldiers sank down on one knee, supporting themselves on their rifle butts. As the sun set, a chill set in, and men who had been soaked in their own sweat all day were suddenly cold.

For the first time, Newton and the other orderlies could ferry the wounded to the field hospital without being shelled. The orderlies stanched blood and applied emergency bandages from out of knapsacks, and helped load men into the ambulance, a covered, horse-drawn, four-wheeled wagon with a hinged rear gate that could be lowered for the most severely injured.

Newton sorted through the bodies, listening for moans and looking for writhing movement. The swampy battlefield attracted the attention of hogs, scavenging for food. Newton had heard numerous reports of hogs eating the guts out of men. He knew what was happening when a hog lifted its head from a body and revealed a crimson muzzle. If the man's eyes were filled with blood, then peace would come soon. Once a hog made a meal out of a man, there was little Newton or anyone else could do to keep him alive.

The survivors were lifted onto the rickety wagon and carried back to the field hospital. Newton assisted Dr. John M. Baylis, another wealthy officer from back home who was the battalion surgeon, as he worked frantically, examining and dressing wounds, digging out Minié balls with forceps, stitching up flesh with silk thread, and amputating countless limbs. There was no such thing as antiseptic, and it never occurred to anyone to wash his hands or scrub under his nails. Surgeons ran their dirty index fingers and bloody implements in and out of wounds, which almost invariably suppurated.

The key to a successful amputation hinged on doing it quickly to prevent shock and excessive bleeding. But inexperienced battle surgeons like Baylis, not knowing this, often prolonged the process and sometimes stopped sawing to gaze at the twitching nerves and muscles. The soldiers were remarkable in their restraint. To scream was considered cowardly and dishonorable. Those who sobbed were usually delirious in their pleas for help. The severed arms and legs were stacked against the side of the barn like firewood. The limbs signified the pain and suffering of a war that Newton had opposed from the outset, and they must have made the pretty, abstract words of the Van Dorns and Maurys sound not only hollow, but obscene.

Conditions were just as horrifying for the Union wounded at the Tishomingo Hotel, where nurses in aprons seemed to Hugh Carlisle of the 81st Ohio to be "colored in blood from their necks to their hems." Carlisle was fortunate; a Minié ball had struck his bayonet before ricocheting into his thigh. His bayonet was bent into a circle, but his thighbone was undamaged. A surgeon fingered the wound, stuffed some cloth into it, and poured cold water on it. It was all the treatment he got—three days later, he would pull the dressing out himself.

After the battle, Carlisle lay on the floor of the hotel near the amputating table and watched the surgeons operate through the night.

"They would cut off an arm or leg, take it by the thumb or toe, and pitch it over the porch into the street," he wrote.

October 4, 1862, 4:00 a.m., Corinth

In the Confederate fields, men hardly slept. While the surgeons worked and the wounded groaned, Van Dorn and his generals plotted their movements for the following day. The rebels listened to the faint noises coming from the Union fortifications just a few hundred yards away—muffled voices, the creaking of wheels, hammering, the clanking of gear—and wondered what they meant.

The ever-confident Buck Van Dorn was sure that the noise meant the Yankees were evacuating. But his officers weren't convinced. The man in charge of the brigade to which the 7th Battalion belonged, General Green, had a more sensible impression. "What made me doubt they were evacuating was the chopping of timber," Green said. "There was a difference of opinion among the officers with whom I discussed the matter. I also doubted they were evacuating because I heard the cars coming in twice and a shout on their arrival." In fact, the Yankees were digging deeper rifle pits, piling more obstacles in front of the batteries, and shifting men as reinforcements arrived via train.

Van Dorn, however, was certain he could take the town with a swift early-morning assault before it was fully reinforced. He ordered a coordinated wave of attack on the city's irregularly shaped horseshoe of inner batteries. The main thrust would be a sweeping roundhouse charge from the right, led by Newton's divisional commander, General Louis Hébert, who was to launch the 1st Division at daylight in force, including the 7th Mississippi Battalion. The left would be led by Dabney Maury, whose troops would make a shorter, more straightforward thrust toward the town as soon as he heard rolling fire from Hébert's men. As a prelude, there would be an intense predawn artillery bombardment.

At 4:00 a.m., under a waning moon, the rebels opened up their guns. Fire blossomed from the cannon muzzles, and for a few moments, paralyzed with awe, men followed the courses of the cannonballs by their flaring, hissing fuses. Blasts of color irradiated the black sky with an eerie beauty. "A more pleasant sight one cannot imagine," wrote a Missouri volunteer named Nehemiah Davis Starr. "We could see the flash of their cannon . . . then hear the report and trace the coming shell by their light over the tops of the trees until they exploded." To a Union brigadier, "The different calibers, metals, shapes, and distances of the guns caused the sounds to resemble the chimes of old Rome when all her bells rang out."

But the stargazing turned to fatal horror as the artillery found its range, guided by the Yankee campfires. Messmates were just cooking their breakfasts, frying salt pork or hanging kettles of coffee to boil by baling wire, as the shells began to keen. Seconds later explosions gouged bloody potholes in their midst. Men frantically doused the fires, and cooks and teamsters panicked and scrambled toward shelter. There was none—the artillery was also firing at the lights in the village. A shell exploded through the doorway of the

Tishomingo Hotel, killing a man and wounding two more.

"The scene soon changed and you may believe was less pleasant," Starr scribbled,

as they noticed the fires which cooked our breakfast and directed their aim on them which was done very accurately the shell commenced exploding amongst us one solid ball struck a man close by me and killed him I heard the ball coming. through the air rattling in the branches of the trees and knew that it must fall very near us . . . by this time we had put out the fires which made it much darker than it was before, two men were wounded on the right of our breakfast table; I was almost persuaded to be a Christian Coward and run, but seeing all our contraband Negroes had run away from their duty, and not wishing to be likened unto a contraband I remained, and had part of their work to do in loading our desks, boxes, mess chests, etc. on the wagons.

The Union's siege guns began to return fire, the batteries opening up with such concerted force it seemed to cause the ground to shift. Lewis Phillips of the 4th Iowa "actually believed the earth to be dropping from under our feet."

Newton had been awakened by the thunder of the artillery duel, and in this unholy noise he and the rest of the 7th Mississippi Battalion fell back under the cover of a hill to cook some rations, along with their general, Martin Green. But just as they dug into their breakfasts, Union guns found them and shellfire rained down, plowing up dirt. It would be another long, hungry, thirsty day.

As the sky brightened, Van Dorn waited for Hébert's infantry attack to launch. But only silence came from the battlefield. Eventually, light musket fire began to ripple from Dabney Maury's side of the line; his skirmishers were engaged. But Hébert's attack had not begun. He failed to respond to three separate inquiries. Van Dorn was at a loss. Where was he?

At last, at 7:00 a.m., Hébert appeared, pale, to report that he was sick and could not take the field. His inexplicable behavior was later variously rumored to be the result of drunkenness, or cowardice, but it was irrelevant. In either case, he left the Confederate assault in chaos. "I regretted to observe that my whole plan of attack was by this unfortunate delay disarranged," Van Dorn reported, in an understatement. Van Dorn speedily revised the order of command: the next senior officer, Martin Green, would take charge of the attack.

Green was still covering his head and trying to eat under shellfire when a message arrived informing him Hébert was ill and he was now in command of the entire division. The message left Green "hopelessly bewildered," another officer observed. Hébert may not have been drunk or cowardly, but he was surely sloppy: he had failed to give his subordinates any information, preparation, direction, or even orders.

Green was unprepared to assume command of the division. He looked like what he was, a businessman, who at the outbreak of war operated a sawmill in Lewis County, Missouri. "A kind-hearted, unostentatious man," Lieutenant Colonel Columbus Sykes of the 43rd Mississippi described him. He had a long, bony face, elongated further by a split, gauzy white beard. As he tried to cope with the sudden pressure of organizing five brigades comprised of several thousand men into a massive attack, he radiated uncertainty. Two hours passed as he hesitantly realigned his troops—a feat, given the flaming leaden debris that was raining down on them.

Newton and the men of the 7th Mississippi Battalion found their places in the line. They would advance across the triangle of ground formed by the two intersecting railroad lines and form the innermost muscle of the sweeping Confederate roundhouse punch, aimed at the crossroads in town. Their path would take them between two of the largest Union gun fortifications, one named Battery Powell and the other Battery Robinett. Ahead, the men could see the Union positions, "bristling with artillery and strongly supported by infantry," Green reported.

Green ordered the men forward. "With a wild shout," the Mississippians leaped across a railroad cut with the rest of the brigade. A command came to charge at the "double-quick."

It was the last order that could be heard, as at least fifty federal guns opened fire on them. The trembling thunder of artillery was joined by the shrieking, concussive outbursts of shells and the short, almost muffled **spat-spat-spat** of Springfield rifles, hammers hitting soft gunpowder, followed by the metallic raking of ramrods. "The very atmosphere seemed filled with shot, shell, grape and canister," Green reported.

Suddenly it seemed as if they were in a rainstorm of blood. Horses plunged and caterwauled, and men screamed incoherently. There was something about such a charge that forced the breath from men's throats, almost reflexively, without their even knowing it. As one Mississippi soldier recorded in his diary, "I always said, if I ever went into a charge, I wouldn't holler. But the very first time I fired off my gun, I hollered as loud as I could, and I hollered every breath until I stopped!"

The Confederates sprinted heedlessly forward, over logs and fallen timber toward the Union lines that belched flame and smoke. "Not for a moment did they halt," observed a horrified Union soldier watching the approaching slaughter. "Every instant death smote. It came in a hundred shapes, every shape a separate horror. Here a shell, short-fused, exploding in the thinning ranks, would rend its victims and splatter their comrades with brains, flesh and blood. Men's heads were blown to atoms. Fragments of human flesh still quivering with life would slap other men in the face, or fall to earth to be trampled underfoot."

One of Newton's oldest friends, John Harper, fell wounded in both feet. Another Jones County man, James Reddoch, was shot through the jaw.

But the Union artillery simply couldn't fire rapidly

enough to slow the onslaught. As the rebels charged over the killing field, some Northerners flinched and broke even before their lines were struck. Horses stampeded with their limbers on, dragging heavy cannon over and crushing infantrymen. Others dodged out of the way but caught the panic of the animals and dashed to the rear through the columns. "Then a few men followed the horses," Joseph Nelson of the 81st Ohio wrote. "Then a few more. And still more." General Rosecrans rode among them, livid, swearing that they were "old women."

The Confederates overran Battery Powell and took possession of the large guns, nesting among bloody cadavers and horse carcasses. Surging just to the right of the earthworks, the 7th Mississippi Battalion roared through a line of Iowans and Illinoisans and straight on into town.

In Corinth, they fought from house to house. Musket fire spattered against clapboards and made splinters and shards of masonry fly, until whole buildings were practically shot away. Years later, bullet holes still riddled the walls of homes. Some of the rebels, famished despite the battle howling around them, slipped into kitchens and wolfed down whatever they could find to eat, only to be set upon by Yankees. "Every one of them received either the hot lead or the cold steel," bragged one Iowan who stumbled upon them. More than one hundred Southern men were captured after the battle, "in the bakeries and stores," marveled another Iowan.

Steadily, the rebels worked their way toward the

Tishomingo Hotel. The Yankees used crates and barrels on the train platforms for cover to return fire. As
the action neared Rosecrans's headquarters, his staff
hastily evacuated, officers and contrabands alike almost rioting in alarm at the approach of the Southerners. "There was one of the greatest stampedes of
teams, teamsters, non combatants and Negroes that I
ever saw," Edward Dean of the 4th Wisconsin wrote
in his diary. "There were all of our Army wagons with
teams hitched up, loose horses and mules and Negroes
huddled close together, and they began to run and
shout; then they seemed to be frantic with fear. The
noise could be plainly heard above the din of battle."

But the Southerners had outrun their means. Just as
they reached the train crossroads, their brigade leader,
Colonel W. H. Moore of the 43rd Mississippi, was shot
down. Alone and unsupported in the town, against the
entire Federal reserves, the rebels began to run out of
ammunition. Yankees, mostly Iowans and Illinoisans,
now counterattacked: light artillery poured shot into
the melee, shells whizzing over the heads and backs of
the soldiers, while Iowa sharpshooters from a nearby
low rise picked off men in gray. In the face of such
an array of fire, the Confederates wavered, and then
began to fall back.

"Our lines melted under their fire like snow in
thaw," reported a rebel captain.

With no choice but to retreat men did so frantically,
companies dissolving into fragments. Some of them
grabbed at bridles of Yankee horses that were hitched

in front of the Tishomingo and swung themselves into the saddles. But whether on horseback or on foot, the retreat was more perilous than the advance. "No description is adequate to picture the gauntlet of death that these fugitives ran," an Iowan reported. "Very few reached the timber **alive . . .** they had been **cut to pieces** in the most intense meaning of that term."

All around, the same was happening to other rebel brigades. Just down the line, Confederates assailed Battery Robinett, the largest of the Union gun fortresses, with catastrophic results. Robinett was a stout earthen and log redan near the Memphis and Charleston rail line, with three Parrott guns atop it, masked by two enormous oak trees.

Almost 1,900 rebels attacked the battery three times, led by Colonel William P. Rogers of the 2nd Texas, astride his horse. On the third charge, the rebels screamed through a shallow ravine and came up the steep bank at a dead run. At fifty yards, the Yankees sprang up and fired, mowing them down in hundreds. The rebels still reached the base of the battery, where they clustered in a ditch at the foot of the bulwark and climbed upward in a hand-to-hand, musket-swinging death struggle. Men used their bayonets "like pitch forks," and stabbed each other through. Rogers spurred his black mare up the incline, but "he had no more than straightened up until he was full of bullet holes," according to one Iowan. He toppled backward into the ditch. In just a few minutes, 272 Southerners fell, killed or wounded around Robinett.

It was all over before noon. "My God, my boys are running!" Sterling Price cried, as the men retreated to the tree lines and railroad cuts, the same ones they had charged out of with a yell just two hours earlier.

Soon, the army was in full retreat. Some men ran heedlessly, others ignored orders and dropped to the ground exhausted, sitting where they were, sullenly, with their backs against tree trunks, to be taken prisoners later by Yankees. Others collapsed to their hands and knees and retched. It was a common occurrence after a charge and repulse: often men were ill from slaughter. A Mississippi private remembered that after one foray, he " 'vomited like a very dog' & . . . threw myself [down] completely prostrated, upon the ground, panting with the white slime running from my mouth."

As the Confederates withdrew back into the heavy woods, Union soldiers surveyed fields blanketed with casualties. "There was hardly a spot for a hundred acres but what there lay the dead of the Secesh," observed Alonzo Courtney of the 63rd Ohio. At Batteries Powell and Robinett, bodies lay crumpled, heaped, and tangled together on the ramparts, arms thrown over legs, legs over hips.

In the ditch before Robinett, Union soldiers found the corpse of Rogers. They propped him up for a photo, his eyes open and staring at the sky, his beard and face blacked with powder, his coat torn open, and his sleeves pushed up, businesslike, to his elbows. A young Iowa infantryman counted fifty-four other forms in the ditch with Rogers, including a regimental chaplain, a boy no older than fifteen, and Rogers's horse.

Soldiers wandering the fields came across odd, spectral images. A conical shell was embedded in the center of one of the huge oak trees sheltering Robinett; it had almost passed through the trunk, but not quite, its point just showing on the other side. In some sun-baked parts of the battlefield, bodies had turned black from the heat and gunpowder.

In another place, someone had lifted a stiff-dead Union soldier and braced him against a tree, his gun in hand, as at parade rest.

October 11, 1862, Holly Springs, Mississippi

The bloodied, beaten Confederates' trail away from Corinth could be followed by their discarded gear: gray coats, blankets, guns, canteens, knapsacks, broken wagons. To one federal, there was "evidence of great demoralization, in the way their arms and equipment were strewn upon the road. More and more was to be seen as we advanced. Finally their wagons were abandoned and much commissary stores were left, until one might think that everything they had" was thrown away. Troops patrolling through the surrounding thickets came across Southerners who simply sat, still, staring into space, and refused to move.

Van Dorn, distraught with the epic extent of his

failure and frantic to recover, considered turning around and trying another assault. His generals furiously argued him out of it. Price thought Van Dorn was almost crazed, his mind "rendered desperate by misfortune," and Maury accused him of loving danger for its own sake. As it was, the army was hard-pressed to recross the Hatchie River without getting cut off. Only the slowness of Rosecrans's pursuit allowed them to get away, and not before another 452 men were lost. The rebels worked desperately to lay planks over an old dam, and from there, they slogged disconsolately through rain, back toward their headquarters at Holly Springs.

The battle of Corinth was one of the most costly of the war for the South. A number of Confederate companies were "almost annihilated," and Van Dorn's army was "shattered." In two days of fighting, he had wrecked two of his three divisions and suffered a horrifying casualty rate of 35 percent. In some places "the dead bodies of Rebels were piled up . . . eight and ten deep," and in one spot two hundred bodies were arrayed as if in one long, thin coffin.

Strategically, the loss was "crushing" for the Confederacy, as General Grant put it, for it closed off Southern transportation lines, gave Grant control of northern Mississippi, and opened the way for his campaign against Vicksburg. General Sherman, nearby in western Tennessee, heard Southerners "openly admit that their cause had sustained a death-blow."

But to Newton and the other infantrymen who

trudged into Camp Rogers at Holly Springs, the loss was more personal. They were past endurance, done in with fatigue, disheartened, and filled with disgust at their officers. Van Dorn was to be court-martialed: there was talk that he had been drunk. Other commanders had been incompetent. During the retreat soldiers were marched in the wrong direction and then countermarched, and many were half-starved for want of food. Even when they reached camp at Holly Springs, there were shortages of everything, including tents. Worst of all, some of the wounded had been abandoned or lay uncared for.

A train, at least five cars long, was left overnight full of men with undressed wounds, some without blankets, and all of them with nothing to eat. They were unattended and no one could find an officer. A lieutenant discovered them at about ten or eleven at night by happenstance.

Van Dorn was acquitted in the court-martial, but it was obvious from testimony that he had treated his troops as if they were toy soldiers and that his slipshod logistical work had caused needless suffering. One of those who testified against him was Colonel Robert Lowry of the 6th Mississippi, the veteran of Shiloh, who described his efforts to feed his famished men. The rations were "insufficient," Lowry snapped. By the close of the first day's fight, "our commissary stores were exhausted," he said. As they fell back, they were given nothing except a single mangy live cow, without any salt with which to cure it. After consultation with his men, Lowry drove the poor beast away. His men went two more days without rations of any kind, his pleas to superiors ignored, before Lowry finally sent men out with wagons to purchase forty bushels of potatoes, which he and his officers paid for with their own money.

Hunger only deepened the acrimony. The 7th Mississippi Battalion had done some of the heaviest fighting and suffered fifty-nine casualties. Company F lost a quarter of its men, among them some of Newton's relatives, neighbors, and close friends. His favorite cousins Alpheus Knight, Ben Knight, and Dickie Knight were all hospitalized. His friend John H. Harper had almost lost both his feet, and Harper's brother was dead. Jimmie Reddoch, whose family owned land adjoining the Knights', had a hole in his jaw. It seemed like everyone he knew was in the hospital: Jim Ates, Tom Ates, Maddie Bush, Tapley Bynum, Jeff Collins, James Morgan Valentine, all of whom he had grown up with. When Company F mustered after the battle, Newton was the only noncommissioned officer who reported for duty.

Newton apparently behaved well at Corinth, because shortly afterward he was promoted to second sergeant and assigned as a provost guard, a kind of policing role. But his rank may have resulted from the fact that so few able-bodied men remained.

Once again, Newton nursed the sick; Major Joel E. Welborn recalled seeing him in the hospital at about this time. But in the days after Corinth, Newton and his friends in Company F became increasingly disaffected. It's possible that he and his comrades associated their battle ordeal with the ancient siege of Corinth: classical stories often circulated among the troops, and the tale of the Athenian general Iphicrates, a deserter and a traitor to his country who achieved fame in liberating the city, was an unmistakable connection. Perhaps they recited from Lord Byron's "Siege of Corinth":

He stood a foe, with all the zeal
Which young and fiery converts feel,
Within whose heated bosom throngs
The memory of a thousand wrongs.

Newton felt a thousand wrongs. But perhaps the most galling wrong of all came a week after the battle. On October 11, 1862, the Confederate legislature passed its infamous Twenty Negro Law. The edict exempted the richest men from military service: "One white man on every plantation with twenty or more slaves" was permitted to stay at home.

Wealthy planters had pressured the Confederacy to pass the Twenty Negro Law in response to anxiety about maintaining discipline on the plantation. Slaves constituted half the population in the Deep South, and fears of revolt ran deep. The law would discourage slaves from running off to Union troops and prevent wives and daughters from being left alone with a lot of Negroes. Also, if planters and overseers remained at home, they argued, they could better see to the crops that fed the Confederacy.

When word of the decree reached Company F, anger boiled over. Jasper Collins was in camp with Knight when he heard about it. "This law," he said, "makes it a rich man's war and a poor man's fight." The phrase would reverberate through the South for the rest of the war.

Collins threw down his rifle. "I'm through," he said. He told one of his officers, "I don't intend to shoot another gun here." The officer said, "Don't you know they will kill you?"

"They will have to catch me first, before they kill me," Collins replied.

Soon after, Collins deserted. As of October 31, 1862, he was reported absent without leave.

Throughout the ranks, the Twenty Negro Law was greeted with outrage. A farmer from Smith County (adjacent to Jones) wrote to Mississippi governor John J. Pettus: "We who have but little or nothing at stake but honor are called on to do the fighting and to do the hard drudgery and bear the burthen and brunt of the battle, while the rich and would-be rich are shirking and dodging in every way possible to shun the danger." This Twenty Negro Law "did more to injure the Southern case" than Lincoln's recently announced Emancipation Proclamation, he insisted.

Newton lived not on a plantation, but in the up-country; he wasn't a planter, he was a herder and farmer who owned no slaves. Yeomen made up the vast ranks of Confederate soldiers doing the bitterest fighting—and from this point onward, they would also make up the ranks of deserters and resisters. The Twenty Negro Law was written exclusively for the planter class, not for the infantrymen. As one Alabama yeoman farmer said, "All tha want is to git you . . . to fight for their infurnal negroes and after you do their fightin' you may kiss their hine parts for o tha care."

What little loyalty Newton had to the army was utterly gone. "He felt that the law was not fair," his neighbor Ben Graves said. "That it enabled the rich man to evade service and that it was not right to ask him to risk his life for people who rated themselves so far above him."

All told, in the months after Corinth about seven thousand men in southeastern Mississippi went absent without leave. Whole companies vanished into the woods. Some of them were merely frustrated and would eventually return to the ranks out of guilt, or loyalty. Others were captured and forced back.

With Jasper Collins already departed, Newton grappled with his own conscience. Desertion was an act of shame, according to traditional understandings of loyalty and honor. But he surely wondered if the dishonor of desertion could be any worse than the dishonor he suffered as a Confederate. He wasn't the only one who was thinking this way: between the battle of Corinth and the turning of the New Year, men from Company F deserted in droves. A muster roll for February 28, 1863, listed thirty-nine of them as AWOL.

There were also practical reasons for the massive desertions that fall and winter: 1862 was a horrible crop year, especially in the hill country, where a summer drought had destroyed much of the food in the fields. Rich planters could survive a bad year, but not poor farmers. Worries over crops, winter food stores, and the welfare of their families hastened soldiers home.

At the same time, the Confederacy passed yet another egregious law: a tax in kind. This gave officials the authority to enter farmers' storehouses and walk off with 10 percent of their provisions. Officers, or thieves masquerading as such, "roamed the state seizing slaves, horses, food, and even houses."

One month after Jasper Collins deserted, Newton received a letter from his wife, Serena. A Confederate cavalryman had come to their farm and seized their best horse, and mistreated her while he was at it. Serena cried and begged to be left the much-needed animal: it was several miles to the nearest mill and there were children to be fed. The cavalryman cursed her, caught the horse, and got on him.

"This was too much for my father," Tom Knight wrote.

Newton was done with the Confederacy. He did not intend to serve a new nation conceived in slavery and dedicated to the perpetuation of rich men's interests. Jasper Collins led him to the Rubicon, and perhaps the stories of courageous martyrs and deserters at the ancient Corinth gave him the faith to cross it. "I felt like if they had a right to conscript me when

I didn't want to fight the Union, I had a right to quit when I got ready," Newton said.

One day in early November, Newton deserted. The 7th Mississippi Battalion was on the retreat in early November of 1862, as it fell back under pressure from U. S. Grant, who was pressing down into Mississippi from Memphis. As the regiment evacuated a camp town called Abbeville, Newton was "lost on the retreat," according to his military record. Somewhere, in all the marching, Sergeant Newton Knight slipped away into the woods.

"While they were there they did their duty the best they could," Tom Knight wrote. ". . . They were poor men. They had no negroes to fight for, but the most of them had a dear wife and little children that needed their protection at home. They came home and did their duty here at home in Jones County."

Recollections of George Washington Albright, Holly Springs, Mississippi

We slaves knew very little about what was going on outside our plantations, for our owners aimed to keep us in darkness. But sometimes, by grapevine telegraph, we learned of great events. It was impossible to keep the news of John Brown's attack on Harpers Ferry from spreading. That attack threw a scare into the slave owners. One day not long after the arrest of Brown, a boy in a nearby orchard shot off a pop gun and my mistress ran in terror to the house, screaming that insurrectionists were coming.

Like many other slaves, my father ran away from his plantation in Texas and joined the Union forces. I found out later that he was killed fighting in the battle of Vicksburg.

When the Emancipation Proclamation was signed, the plantation owners tried to keep the news from us ... The slaves, themselves, had to carry the news to one another. That was my first job in the fight for the rights of my people—to tell the slaves that they were free, to keep them informed and in readiness to assist the Union armies whenever the opportunity came.

I was 15 years old when I became a runner for what we called the 4-Ls—Lincoln's Legal Loyal League. I traveled about the plantations within a certain range, and got together small meetings in the cabins to tell the slaves the great news. Some of these slaves in turn would find their way to still other plantations—and so the story spread. We had to work in dead secrecy; we had knocks and signs and passwords.

TWO

Home

December 1860, Jones County

To old Jackie Knight, secession was no cause for anthems. It meant the smoking destruction of all he had built, the country he had settled and the acreage he had cleared, planted, and colonized too, with eleven children and thirty-six grandchildren scattered across Jones County. There were Knights, too, among the slaves he owned.

"I am ruined," he said.

Forty-five years earlier, Jackie had ridden into the primeval wilderness of the Mississippi Territory and subdued it with a whip and an ax. Newton's grandfather was an archetypal pioneer, an imbiber of "Protestant scripture and boiled whiskey," as William Faulkner described his kind, "Bible and jug in one hand, and like as not an Indian tomahawk in the other, brawling, turbulent, uxorious, and polygamous."

The eighty-seven-year-old Knight family patriarch tilted backward in a chair on the long gallery of his pine-log home. He occupied the same shaded spot each day, with his chair leaned at an angle against the wall, so habitually that there was a sleek place where his resting head had worn away the pine. As Jackie lamented the secession crisis that gripped Mississippi, he tossed his head from side to side in agitation. He moaned again, "I am ruined." He said it so often that it sounded to a small slave child named Martha, who was playing in the yard, like a chant.

"I am ruined, I am ruined."

The old man had much to lose. By the end of 1860 as secession fever swept the state, Jackie Knight was one of the wealthiest men in the vicinity. From his porch, he commanded an overview of 680 acres, profitably planted with cotton and rice, and more than twenty slaves working in them. The field hands wore hats of woven palmetto leaves to keep the sun off their brows as they moved among the planted rows. Closer in, eight slave cabins formed a semicircular yard, where women labored over washing tubs and vats, tended chickens, or roasted bushels of potatoes in an outdoor oven. At the foot of the porch, a dozen or so slave children did menial tasks. One fed kindling into the oven. Another waved flies away from the porch with a brush. When Jackie wanted to smoke his pipe, he called out, "Fire, fire!" A child grabbed a burning cob from the oven and ran over to light "ole master's" tobacco.

The Knight family's wealth and holdings did not

end at his property line, either. Adjoining Jackie's land was the farm belonging to his daughter, Altimirah, and her forty-six-year-old husband George Brumfield, who owned eight slaves. Two farms over, Jackie's youngest and most prodigal son, Daniel, and his wife, Elizabeth, lived on a spread with ten slaves.

Jackie Knight grieved over the secession crisis for manifold reasons. He was ailing, with not long to live. He was a patriot who'd had his own experience with soldiering, in the Chickamauga Wars and again in the War of 1812, and he knew the toll of conflict. He could see it in his own family, which was deeply divided by the issues underlying the secession crisis.

Most of Jackie's children were aspiring planters with a stake in the slave economy. But there was a significant exception. Jackie's eldest son, Albert, declined to own slaves. Albert was a modest shoemaker and tanner who made his own way and his own living. What's more, none of Albert's twelve children would own slaves either. His modest, independent-minded son Newton would display a special disdain for slaveholding. Albert was the one child who would not be bequeathed a slave in Jackie's last will and testament.

If anyone might be expected to partner in and benefit from Jackie's slave owning, it would have been his eldest son. On the other hand, eldest sons might also be expected to reproach their fathers for their sins.

Jackie Knight was self-made: born in North Carolina in 1773, he had pushed his way westward looking for virgin land, first to Georgia, where according to family tradition he served as a light horse soldier in the Chickamauga Wars and an infantryman in the War of 1812, and then on to Mississippi. He and his wife Keziah and their wagonload of children had arrived sometime in 1815 or 1816 at the vast expanse known as the Piney Woods, where the land seemed to heave with rising and falling hills, timbered by towering pines and split by creeks and hollows. "Here's where we stop," he said. He had built a home out of felled logs and survived for years despite the lonesomeness and lack of civil government. In 1822, he was one of eighty-nine settlers who petitioned to form Jones County, which they named after John Paul Jones. By 1850, it was still a placc without a telegraph, newspaper, or railroad. Yet Jackie had made his fortune, thanks to two commodities also rare in Jones County: cotton and slaves.

Jackie's acreage qualified as a plantation, barely. It sprawled on either side of the eddying Leaf River, which curled like a fat brown mud snake through the low thickets between Jones and Covington counties. Twice yearly Jackie made trips to the busy seaport of Mobile, Alabama, to sell his goods, drawing wagons loaded with as much as 750 pounds of rice and twenty-five bales of cotton (bundles weighing 400 to 500 pounds each). He used the profits to buy more slaves.

Knight was merely a rich man in a state full of tycoons. The South's cotton trade was valued at $200 million annually by 1860, and Mississippi was the largest cotton producer of all, shipping 535.1 million pounds of it to market. It seemed as though entire portions of the state, especially the soil-rich delta, were covered by harrowed rows worked by hoe gangs, hunching over the green, foot-high plants that blossomed with bolls, the dauby, gauzy stuff that was the fiber of the South. A visitor to the state saw "nothing but fields of mimic snow."

Thanks to King Cotton, the slave population had exploded. Of the 4 million slaves in America on the eve of the war, 1 million had been sold south into Alabama, Mississippi, Louisiana, and Texas between 1820 and 1860, to the tune of half a billion dollars. The slave trade constituted a larger piece of the American economy than even the railroads or manufacturing. In Natchez the mansions were the size of villas, their walls lined with art by French masters. There were 436,631 human chattels toiling in Mississippi, and their prices rose with cotton. A single field hand in the 1850s was worth anywhere from $1,100 to $1,800—roughly $75,000 to $135,000 in today's value. "My grandfather had one he gave $10 a pound for," recalled Ben Graves. "Bought him by weight."

In the 1850s, Frederick Law Olmsted journeyed through Mississippi as part of an extended tour of the South and filed a series of roving reports for the **New York Times.** In one exchange, he asked a Woodville, Mississippi, innkeeper what sort of country it was.

"Big plantations, sir. Nothing else. Aristocrats."

Olmsted asked how rich were the people he spoke of.

"Why, sir, from a hundred thousand to ten million."

"Do you mean that between here and Natchez there are none worth less than a hundred thousand dollars?"

"No sir, not beyond the ferry. Why, any sort of plantation is worth a hundred thousand dollars. The niggers would sell for that."

Jackie's fortune had come in part through some light slave trading. In 1840, he was still just a pioneer homesteader with land valued at a few hundred dollars, but he rapidly amassed wealth over the next twenty years, until by 1860 his personal estate was worth more than $25,000 ($1.9 million in today's currency). According to Knight family slave Martha Wheeler, Jackie "never was a big slave owner but he made much money trafficking in slaves." His holdings were so considerable that when his children married, his traditional wedding gift to each of them was a **pair** of slaves. Chattels were the ultimate measure of a man's status in Mississippi. A common way of inquiring as to someone's worth and social standing was to ask, "Have they any Negroes?"

Jackie was status conscious: his home was sophisticated for the area, made of good timbers with plastered indoor walls, and had two large front parlors, the sign of someone interested in showing his gracious accommodations to the public. He kept his cash and valuable papers in an iron trunk that was apparently a family heirloom from England, and he also had linens, tablecloths of velvet and silk, tableware, china, and silverware, as well as a fine buggy. Most rare, he had two cases of books. He was a man of some education, and his children could read and write.

But Newton Knight grew up in a home much plainer than that of his grandfather, with his cutlery, books, and house slaves. His father Albert expressly chose to belong to the yeoman rather than planter class, supporting his family as a tanner and a single-handed farmer. Born in 1799 in Georgia, Albert was a grown man when his family arrived in the Piney Woods, and by 1822, he had established enough of a stake to sign his own name to the petition that led to the formation of Jones County. But he remained a modest dirt farmer whose acreage was worth just $900 by 1860. In contrast, his socially aspiring younger brother Jesse Davis Knight by the age of just thirty-nine had amassed acreage worth $3,000 and a personal estate worth $8,900.

While his siblings received gifts and deeds of chattel from Jackie, Albert did not. What explained the exception? Albert's wife, Mason Rainey, may have influenced her husband in his views on slavery. She was a woman of obscure background, said to be an orphan whose family had been neighbors of the Knights in North Carolina, taken in by them after her own people died of "flux." Mason supposedly went with the Knights when they migrated west and married Albert, ten years her elder, when she came of age in 1820. While there is no direct evidence of Mason's beliefs, it's worth noting that not one of her dozen offspring ever owned slaves, a striking departure from the rest of the Knight clan.

Martha Wheeler, the Knight family slave who as a child did chores in Jackie Knight's yard and lit his pipe, recalled that Mason was compassionate, "quite a doctor," who tended to the sick in "all the surrounding country." Mason was also literate; she taught her children to read and write, and she and Albert donated land to establish the first school in the area. All of her children received some education.

The Knight family schism was reflective of larger rifts taking place all across Jones County, and Mississippi as a whole, during the secession crisis. The most common division was between rich and poor: it was a state of stark economic differences. On the eve of the Civil War, Jones County was an island of poverty in a sea of cotton- and slave-based wealth. Economically, the Piney Woods was as stagnant as its swamp water: it had the poorest soil and poorest people in the state.

Residents and outsiders alike referred to it as "de po' folks' lan.'" A vast, dark, meandering cypress marsh ran through the region, known as the Dismal Swamp. The ground was sandy and the pine barrens were almost impossible to clear, which made it better suited for grazing than cultivating cotton. Planters sneeringly referred to it as "cow country" and joked that the land was "too poor to raise a fuss on."

But one of the many ballads sung by the local poor

whites reflected, if not their ear for poetry, then their sense of regional pride and independence:

**I'm de po' folks' lan' with my miles of sand,
and my cottonwoods moan and groan,
An' I'm gonna stay free from hills to the sea
and my forests are all my own.**

Locals also called the area "no man's land," because so many settlers picked up stakes and moved when the better-soiled Choctaw lands were opened for settlement in the 1830s. Jones County was just too hard to clear, with its swamps, thickets, and mighty pines, to lure many large planters or slaveholders.

In 1860, the entire output of cotton in Jones County was just 633 bales. There were only 407 slaves, and those were concentrated in the hands of a wealthy few, like Jackie Knight: just seventeen families owned half of them. The rare Jones County farmer who **did** have slaves tended to have just four or fewer. Most families owned none at all.

But if Jones County was poor, it had a primordial magnificence that the inhabitants cherished. The rolling and wavelike forests were full of ancient, colossal pines that shot sixty feet in the air, their trunks so broad it took six men to encircle one. Streams glinted under canopies of oaks, so clear that riders who crossed them could see perch playing around their stirrups. Luxuriant grasses grew three feet high, and pastures were studded with wildflowers, amid which ranged herds of red deer and flocks of turkey and partridge. It was a place of fearful solitude at night, when the tall armless pines looked "gaunt and spectral and fall sadly on the soul," according to one traveler. Nothing moved other "than the flapping of an owl, and fantastic shadows, like trooping apparitions, chase each other into settled gloom."

The country Newton grew up in was still frontier, so wild that wolves scratched on the doors of homesteads at night. The woods were dense and full of panthers and bears, and the farms were few, separated by as much as fifteen miles. No one traveled without a gun, in case they met with a predator or wild game for the table.

The social milieu was raw as the landscape, one of hardship, faith, whiskey, bare-knuckle fighting, hunting, and farming. Albert and Mason Knight were typical of the homesteaders who predominated in Jones County, scratching at the earth on hardscrabble farms of fifty acres or so. They bent their faces to the earth, built a home and raised crops with their own hands, and took pride in that self-sufficiency. They ate what they grew and used the rest for sale or barter. While rich planters owned purebred horses and four or five eight-oxen teams, yeomen were lucky if they owned a couple of mules and oxen and a single horse.

Albert raised hogs and planted corn, sweet potatoes, greens, and whatever else took root in order to feed his large family. He harvested fewer bushels of corn in one year than the livestock on a large plantation consumed in a month. The produce from their few acres of cotton, which they hoed themselves, was used to make homespun, or was sold for supplies.

Albert and Mason Knight's home sat atop a grassy rise near the Leaf River, a one-room cabin of square-hewn logs with a drop-roof gallery across the front and a kitchen connected by a breezeway. Large oaks shaded it, and in the back, a creek flowed almost at the doorstep; Albert named it Mason Creek for his wife, who deserved something in her honor. Their dozen children were born virtually every other year from 1821 to 1850; Newton was their eighth. The children slept in a heap of bodies in the loft of the cabin, the interior of which was of peeled logs, mud chinked and patched with pine board and clouded with wood smoke from the enormous clay-and-stick chimney, the hearth of which was so large that all of the children could crowd around it.

The Knights' nearest neighbors were three of Albert's younger brothers, William, James, and Benjamin, who by 1840 had established adjoining farms. Also nearby was William Reddoch, who operated a small ferry across the Leaf River, essentially a flat boat with oars and a pull-rope.

Despite the sparse population, there was no lack of company on his family's spread, which teemed with children and animals. The pigs outnumbered the humans by six to one in Jones County. In 1850, there were just 1,890 white citizens, but there were 2,539 milk cows, 4,324 other cattle, and more than anything, there were hogs, 12,686 of them. The razor-backs free-ranged in the swamps, where they fattened themselves on acorns, beech mast, tender pine roots, chinquapins, lily roots, and crawfish. There was always pork on the table, along with an unvarying diet of sweet potatoes, of which Newton must have gotten heartily sick; Jones Countians raised 32,615 bushels of them that year.

Newton received his education from his mother, or from the itinerant schoolmasters who passed through annually and taught for two or three months at a time, charging by the head. Passels of youngsters crowded into a log hut, studying a **Blue Back Speller** or McGuffey's reader, or **Dilworth's Spelling-Book,** which taught them how to construct a short sentence like: "No man may put off the law of God." The teacher kept order with a hickory rod about as long as a boy.

In the evenings, the family regularly read their Bible and occasionally recited a few lines from Shakespeare or Lord Byron, who were among the most popular authors of the era and read by all classes. Newton may have even tried reading **The Columbian Orator,** the popular elocution manual designed for young boys, which taught Frederick Douglass how to turn words into weapons. But if he did, he either didn't get very far or failed to learn the art of elocution. He was never a wordsmith; for him the gun would always be mightier than the mouth.

On Saturdays, Newton hunted with his brothers

and cousins. He stalked deer and hung the carcasses in the chimney to dry. He kept an eye on the thick reed brakes that lined the creeks and branches; if they trembled, it meant bear. He played thread the needle, which meant shooting a rifle ball through a small hole in a board at a hundred paces. And he learned to re-pack a muzzle-loaded, twin-hammered shotgun faster than any boy around.

On Sundays, he attended church, sitting on a rough-hewn bench with trestle legs. The Knights and the other families either walked, so as to rest the horses that had plowed all week, or hitched the steers to wagons and put chairs in the back.

Farming and faith united the poor whites of Jones County. House raisings and corn shuckings were, like baptisms, communal rituals. When a family moved into the area, or a newly married couple purchased their first small plot, neighbors gathered round to help them build the frame, floor, and roof of their new home. Corn shuckings were celebrations of the harvest, of man and God working together to create the kernels that sustained life. The shuckers sang as they worked, in a call-and-response melody:

Pull off the shucks boys, pull off the shucks.
Round up the corn boys, round up the corn.

Shuckings, land clearings, and house raisings were social occasions that drew families from miles around. Newton's family thought nothing of traveling ten or fifteen miles to a log rolling. "They would go out in the woods, cut their logs, and haul them up," Newton's son Tom recalled. "Then they would split those logs, and ask in a few hands and put the logs up. Then my father would hew them down on the inside, and when it was finished call it a fine house."

Women cooked the dinner and sat together and picked cotton off the seed or spun and quilted. A dozen women at their wheels made an ambient buzzing noise, and Mason and the other women could weave as much as five or six yards each of homespun in a day.

With the shucking done, and the moon rising over the piles of naked ears, they sat down to feast on fresh pork and sweet potato pie. In their minds, they were the chosen people of God, morally superior to slave owners, who did no work and depended on others for their livelihood. They were God's special children.

The Knights were Baptists of a plain sort. Later in his life, Newton was a devoted Primitive Baptist, and he may have grown up one. It was an aptly named denomination, suggesting the nature of the faith. While baptisms in Natchez took place in marble fonts surrounded by Italian stained glass, Primitive Baptists received the sacrament outdoors, under God's canopy. After confessing their faith, the candidates for baptism waded into the muddy, snake-infested swamps, with the preacher leading the way, his Bible raised high over his head. It was full immersion. The congregation stood at water's edge, singing, "High in the

Father's house above our mansion is prepared, there is the home, the rest I love, with Christ forever shared."

These Baptists of the Piney Woods practiced foot washing, lay preaching, and egalitarian worship in unadorned buildings. The central tenet of their faith was that all humans were equal in God's eyes and infused with God's spirit. "God is no respecter of persons" was one of their favorite passages from the Bible. Another was: "Remember them that are in bonds, as bound with them; and them which suffer adversity, as being yourselves also in the body."

Until about 1820, all Mississippi Baptists had acted on these egalitarian doctrines; blacks and whites worshipped together and prayed together. Lay preachers spoke informally, as the word of God came to them. But when cotton became king, and money talked louder than God, silver-tongued ministers yoked the word of God to the command of the slave owner. Increasingly, slaveholders and Southern evangelical ministers became one and the same: the voices of God's authority.

Primitive Baptists resisted such sophistry. For them, "the tongue of the learned" was a forked tongue, as one preacher said. In the 1840s, they formed a separate church in order to worship autonomously and in traditional ways, renouncing privilege and the pastimes of the rich. Indeed, they viewed the planter class as lazy and effeminate: the gentry had soft "fair hands covered with gloves," whereas their own hands were hard and rough, "exposed by reason of hard labor." They embraced the purity of simple living.

Initially, Albert and Mason Knight attended the Leaf River Baptist Church, which sat at the junction of Jones and Smith counties, and which Jackie and Keziah Knight had helped found. But in the 1830s, its influential gentrified pastor, Norvell Robertson, began to lead the congregation away from primitive practices such as foot washing and toward more mainstream worship. Robertson was a Virginia-born planter who owned seven slaves, and he was also the sort who paid as much attention to others' behavior as his own. He attempted to impose his morality on a flock full of unruly and unrepentant backwoodsmen, censuring various members for offenses such as drinking, dancing, fiddling, and fornicating. This did not sit well with the Knight men, who were enthusiastic drinkers and brawlers. Neighbor Ben Graves recalled, "The early Knights were considered tuff people." In 1838, Albert Knight was excluded from the church for "repeated intoxication." A problem with whiskey may have run in the family; Jackie's youngest son, Daniel, would steadily drink up his inheritance. Still, it may have seemed the height of hypocrisy to Albert to be called sinner by a slave owner like Robertson. As the pastor became increasingly intrusive and the worship less primitive, most of the Knights stopped attending Leaf River, including Jackie. Albert and Mason instead began attending a church called Old Union.

Newton didn't drink, but other Knights and their neighbors enjoyed drinking as a pastime, a solace, and relief from backbreaking work. There was a choice of saloons in the towns of Williamsburg or Mount Carmel over in Covington County, if they wanted to go that far, where the various shades of liquor were served with evocative names like John Silver, Old Morgan, or Ben Gun. But they didn't need to travel to drink: just about every household in the area had a ten-gallon keg of whiskey in the house, bought during their annual trips to Mobile to sell goods.

Once or twice a year Newton and the other men of the family drove their surplus crops to Mobile by ox wagon for exchange or sale. The trip was 125 miles and took ten days, following a trail that meandered parallel to the Leaf River. Teams of oxen yoked in fours and sixes lumbered in front of springboard wagons hauling upward of five thousand pounds of melons, bushels of corn, and bales of cotton, along a road so barely traceable that it "looked more like Indian path." Often they halted, water-bound by rising streams. They made the journey with other families, sharing campsites and relying on one another for mutual protection.

The trip was a high adventure for a young man, a moving caravan and menagerie. Newton and the other boys herded the livestock, using cowhide whips to force seventy or one hundred hogs into a begrudging trot. Flocks of turkeys and chickens fluttered and skittered down the road before them and roosted in the trees at night.

Mobile, the South's second largest seaport to New Orleans, was a stunning, multihued international business capital, a crescent of packed quays and warehouses set against the shimmering azure of the Gulf. It roared with commerce, roustabouts bustling along wharves, merchants dodging in and out of cotton presses and slave houses, and dusky outlanders dickering in what must have sounded to Newton's ear like strange pidgin languages. Away from the water, on the quieter residential lanes, gracious silence reined over mansions entwined by honeysuckle and roses and cloistered by large oaks. British journalist William Howard Russell in 1861 described the market city, "crowded with Negroes, mulattoes, quadroons, and mestizos of all sorts, Spanish, Italians, and French, speaking their own tongues, or a quaint lingua franca, and dressed in very striking and pretty costumes."

With cash in their pockets from the sale of their produce and livestock, the Knights and other Jones County farmers perused the goods for sale. The first things they bought were kegs of whiskey for themselves, at eighteen cents a gallon. Next was calico for the women; at fifty cents a yard, it took five dollars' worth to make a dress. Flour was precious at ten dollars a barrel. They bought syrup, steeped in kegs like tar, and salt, which came in two-hundred-pound sacks that cost a dollar. Iron bars were another oft-purchased commodity, for hammering into tools and farm implements.

The trip to Mobile and back took nearly three weeks, but it was highly instructive to the young Newton. It acquainted him with every narrow footpath and log bridge between Jones and the coast, the various shortcuts and dangers along the route. It taught him to travel vast distances easily and without fear, how to move across the backwoods landscape and use its resources to his advantage.

It taught him that the frontier could be remarkably fluid, for all of its privations. The Knights and other Piney Woods yeomen ranged far and wide; in addition to their journeys to Mobile, they regularly traipsed the dirt roads and traced local rivers to smaller market towns in their region. They used the spring-swollen Leaf River to float timber all the way to the Gulf. They built flat, shallow-keeled barges to transport goods to a shabby little market center in nearby Perry County named New Augusta, which one visitor described as no more than eight or ten "tenements" around a village square, with a grocery and a public trading house. Farther off was the Pearl River, which ran along the western edge of Covington County all the way to the Louisiana Gulf coast and offered irregular steam packet service up and down its banks. There was also the old military road forged by Andrew Jackson from Nashville to New Orleans, which passed directly through Jasper, Jones, and Covington counties.

Most frequently, they traveled to the small burg of Ellisville, the county seat of Jones established in 1842, which was constituted of "the remnant of a log courthouse, and two . . . grog shops." Nevertheless, it had its pretensions, evidence of which were some handsome homes built by rising merchants, with fine heart-pine lumber, bricks, hardware, and paint brought from Mobile. The village sat eighty miles southeast of Jackson and twenty miles north of Hattiesburg and was named for Judge Powhatan Ellis, who had worked as a circuit judge in the vicinity before going to the Senate and the Mississippi Supreme Court. Ellis was a frontier traditionalist, judging by his ruling that it was perfectly legal for a husband to chastise an obstreperous wife.

The distance to market meant that between trips, the Knights made do with what they had or did without. Shoes were precious commodities and had to be handmade by Albert. He taught Newton to tan hides for them: they cut down a pine and dug a ten-foot trough in it, which they filled with lime, water, and ashes to remove hair from the skins. They cut the cured hides into shapes and tacked the soles together with tiny wooden pegs. Ladies' shoes were made of deerskin, men's of cowhide, and one pair was all any member of the family could expect per year. Some Jones Countians walked barefoot to church, carrying their shoes in hand to protect the soles, and only put them on once they were inside. Then they'd pull them off again after the service was over.

They grew indigo and boiled bark for dye. They made their own soap from redwood ashes, collected grease and cracklings in a large dripper, and molded their own tallow candles. Newton and his father carved their own plow stocks; for harrows, they used the crotch of a forked hickory tree and made teeth by whittling pegs. They used home remedies of herbs and roots for medicines, because the nearest doctor was a day's ride away. And they wore their hair long, with whiskers, because there was no barber and shaving was too difficult. When Newton needed a haircut, he did it with a pair of farming shears.

The yeomen who practiced such hard-won self-reliance naturally resented any encroachment on their autonomy. During Newton's youth in the 1840s and 1850s, the county was without much in the way of formal authority, and in fact it became famous abroad for its citizens' tendency to do as they pleased and reject outside interference, which may have given rise to the appellation "The Free State of Jones." The place was said to be so free of social convention, and any form of civil rule, that the people were "wholly indifferent to the judgments of the courts, for they had no jail except a log-pen, without a lock to its door or a roof upon it, and as for pecuniary penalties, they defied them."

But as Newton entered adulthood, burgeoning gentry appeared in Jones County and so did officialdom. A circle of local merchants, emboldened by their success in commerce, began to impose themselves as moral, civil, and political arbiters much as Norvell Robertson at the Leaf River Baptist Church imposed himself as a religious authority.

A conspicuous member of the self-designated local aristocracy was Amos McLemore, a thirty-four-year-old Methodist-Episcopal minister, schoolteacher, and slave owner. McLemore preached on Sundays in the largest church in the county, a five-hundred-seat congregation. But on Mondays, he set aside piety and did business across three counties from Perry to Jones. By 1860, he was the leader of the local Masonic lodge, carrying the title of worshipful master. He was also a land speculator and owner of a half interest in a dry goods business with Dr. John M. Baylis, the physician who would soon be performing amputations on the Confederate wounded. McLemore had a lordly sense of lineage: his grandfather had served in the Revolutionary War, an uncle had served under Andrew Jackson in 1812. His kin had founded Meridian, the second-largest city in the state, where they owned a vast plantation. He had a high opinion of his own refinements and a low one of the local yeomanry, judging by a descendant's description of him. His great-grandson, Mississippi historian Rudy Leverett, claimed, "He was among the very first to bring some of the gentler influences of civilization to one of the most notoriously primitive areas of the state."

Another member of this select circle was fifty-four-year-old businessman Amos Deason, a merchant known for scoundrelly business dealings and owner of arguably the most handsome home in Ellisville. The elegant white manor gave the illusion of being built of expensive imported white marble, but the façade was actually of wood panels painted to look like stone. Tall paned windows framed a broad octagonal porch, and oaks draped the elegant peaked roof. Deason would eventually become the district representative to the Mississippi Confederate legislature.

McLemore, Deason, and Baylis were all close to the crooked, fat-walleted Joel E. Welborn. The fifty-one-year-old Welborn's adroit land trading made him huge profits, apparently by defrauding his neighbors. Welborn was continually in court over land deals for which he collected large sums yet failed to surrender titles. In 1859, the local board of police charged him with fraud. By then, he already owned his staggering $36,000 in real estate.

Other members of their informal society included a merchant and future tax collector named William Fairchild and Jones County sheriff Nat Kilgore. These men would become the local enforcers of Confederate authority in Jones County. Their Holy Trinity was God, Mammon, and Slavery.

The young Newton Knight couldn't have been further from these men socially or politically. He regarded the McLemores, Welborns, Deasons, and Kilgores as arrogant barons and minders of other people's business, and he surely thought of them when he heard Psalm 18:27: "For thou dost deliver a humble people; but the haughty eyes thou dost bring down."

Even before the war came to Jones County, class warfare and local feuding already existed between members of the Knight family and this clique. In 1858, when Newton was twenty-one, his hard-drinking uncle Daniel Knight assaulted Joel Welborn on three different occasions, for which he was hauled into court and fined. That same year, Sheriff Kilgore killed Daniel Knight's brother-in-law, Tom Coleman, after Coleman resisted arrest on a gambling charge. Kilgore horsewhipped Coleman and stabbed him in the neck in Jackie Knight's yard, where he had gone for protection.

The McLemores and Deasons in turn regarded Newton as poor white trash, an impression he didn't particularly contradict. In a portrait of him as a young man, Newton seems intentionally to repudiate the convention of white respectability, presenting himself as slightly slovenly and rebellious: his disheveled black hair curls around his ears, his beard is untrimmed, and his suit coat is bunched and wrinkled. What's unmistakable about him are his broad shoulders and outthrust chest and his straight, upright posture. He was one of the strongest men in Jones County—and the tallest—and proud of it. He could lift a three-hundred-pound hog to his shoulders, and one can imagine him, like Abraham Lincoln, picking up a heavy ax by the handle and holding it horizontally without a quiver.

The portrait captured the conflicting facets of his emerging personality: the maturing Newton was a mix of tough and straitlaced, a ruffian yet a devout Christian, a fierce combatant when riled, but with a reputation for tenderness, a loner yet a generous neighbor whom others could count on for help. While his relatives drank hard, he abstained and was moderate in his habits. Nor did he cuss. "Never did hear him swear an oath," his sister Martha said of him. "He always meant business. When he was to do anything he did it in a nice, smooth way."

Like his father, Newton aspired to be nothing more than a dirt farmer and a good provider for his family. In 1858, at the same time his uncle Daniel was feuding with Welborn, Newton courted and wed a plain farmer's daughter named Serena Turner, a poorer relation of the Welborns. Newton was not considered a catch. He was "no-account" because he didn't possess a single slave. "If a girl's parents owned negroes, she didn't recognize Newt Knight any more than she would a Negro," said Ben Graves.

Newton and Serena struck out on their own, moving a mile north of the Jones County line, into Jasper County. There, he built a small cabin with unpainted pine beams, cleared eight hundred dollars worth of land, and set about supporting his family, which grew quickly. Newton and Serena's oldest son, George Mathew "Mat" Knight, was born in 1859, and twin boys, Thomas Jefferson and William E., came in 1860. By that time, Newton's worldly wealth amounted to all of three hundred dollars. Planters would have described his home as "rigid in economy" if they were being polite, "impoverished" if not.

The joys of newlywed life were undercut by the constant concerns and drudgery of farming. According to his family, Newton was a gentle, conscientious father. But his marriage, though it eventually produced nine children, does not seem to have been a love affair, and his life with Serena would be difficult.

In photographs, Serena appears melancholic. She was angular, with a thin face, downturned mouth, and large ears that stood out asymmetrically on her head. She wore her hair center-parted and pulled back tightly into a bun, which accented her jug ears and long neck. She was grim faced and prematurely weary, no doubt from unrelieved toils in the fields, at the stove, and late into the night at the spinning wheel and loom. Altogether Serena resembled her house: she was "rigid in economy," a portrait of a woman who spent her entire life working.

It's impossible to say what Newton did, or didn't, feel for his wife. But what is certain is that at some point in these years of early adulthood, he met the woman whom by every account he did love, and for whom, in the blast of war, he developed an unrestrained intensity of feeling, so much so that he eventually broke every rule of decorum and abandoned all familiar society for her: Rachel.

He first saw her in the home of his grandfather, perhaps serving at the table during a family gathering. According to Knight family lore, she was a witchy, hazel-eyed creature who cast a spell over him. This may not have been pure exaggeration: there is no definitive picture of Rachel, but two separate branches of her family possess photographs they claim to be of her. Although each portrays a very different face, both suggest Rachel could well have had a mesmeric quality.

One depicts a slim-shouldered, fair-skinned young woman with long, center-parted curling hair bundled behind her neck. The other shows a somewhat darker woman who was also lustrous haired, copper hued, and blaze eyed, with pupils that radiated energy, including one that seems slightly askew. In either case, Rachel was clearly of mixed European, African, and American Indian descent, the latter influence strikingly evident in her children as well, who tended to be beautiful. Oral tradition passed down to her descendants has it that she was partly Creek or Choctaw.

She was a girl from Macon, Georgia, the daughter of a slave named Abram. When she entered Jackie's household in about 1855 or 1856, she was just sixteen or so, but she was already a mother. She brought with her an infant daughter named Georgeanne, and she was pregnant again; in 1857 she would deliver a boy whom she named Edmund. They were probably the result of the sexual attentions of a white master or young man in the Georgia household she came from.

According to one account, Jackie bought Rachel and her child at auction, in either Mobile or New Augusta. This seems improbable. By 1855 Jackie was more than eighty years old and surely too frail for an arduous springboard wagon trip. More likely, Rachel passed to Jackie Knight through his Georgia family connections, probably his brother James, who lived in the Macon area, a coincidence hard to ignore. According to Rachel's granddaughter Anna (daughter of Georgeanne), Rachel was "sold at auction to a man named Knight who was going to Mississippi to find virgin territory where he and his family could colonize."

Rachel was reputed to be a house slave, and a family favorite, which meant she was at the top of the enslaved social order. On the bottom rung were field hands, many of whom Jackie had bought at auction in Mobile, where the largest slave houses sold as many as seventy to one hundred human beings in a day. A "likely ploughboy" went for $850 to $1,050, the field girls cost $1,300, and mature men $1,500. The auction houses kept the chattel bound in leg irons and shackled to rings in the floor until they were dressed for exhibition, where they were advertised in various terms calculated to appeal to the wants of the buyer: there were "fancy girls" and "likely boys" and "bright mulattos" and "jet black negroes."

Rachel must have been apprehensive about being sold into Mississippi. She had heard horror stories of the treatment slaves could receive on larger Mississippi plantations, especially those in the fertile Black Belt, where field hands worked cotton for eighteen hours a day under the lash of bullwhips wielded by overseers and "slave breakers," white men hired to maximize labor and destroy the will of insolent blacks. A young antislavery Presbyterian minister named John Hill Aughey who preached in central Mississippi claimed he never met an overseer "that didn't travel with a whip, pistol and knife."

Frederick Law Olmsted witnessed slaves at their

labors on a sprawling Mississippi cotton plantation: "They are constantly and steadily driven up to their work, and the stupid, plodding, machine-like manner in which they labor, is painful to witness. This was especially the case with the hoe-gangs. One of them numbered nearly two hundred hands (for the force of two plantations was working together), moving across the field in parallel lines, with a considerable degree of precision. I repeatedly rode through the lines at a canter, without producing the smallest change or interruption in the dogged action of the laborers, or causing one of them, so far as I could see, to lift an eye from the ground . . . I think it told a more painful story than any I had ever heard, of the cruelty of slavery."

In Holly Springs, Mississippi, a planter punished his slaves by slitting the soles of their feet with his bowie knife. In Rankin County, a slave named Vinnie Busby watched her master, one Colonel Easterling, throw her mother across a barrel and whip her unmercifully. He also beat her father to a pulp on a regular basis for trying to visit his family from a neighboring plantation. "When he would ketch him he would beat him so hard 'till we could tell which way he went back by de blood. But pa, he would keep a comin to see us an a takin de beatins."

On one occasion, Easterling punished a slave by hitching him to a plow "and plowed him jes' lak a horse. He beat him an jerked him 'bout til he got all bloody an sore, but ole Marse he kept right on day after day. Marse kept on a plowin him till one day he died."

Often the treatment slaves received was visible from their brands, scars, and burn marks—which were used to identify them when they ran away. The Southern newspapers were full of advertisements placed by owners seeking their fugitive property. The **Memphis Daily Appeal** cited an Amos Timmons who was held in the city jail: he had a scar "running up and down the back of his neck, a scar on his left thumb, and one stiffened joint."

A Mississippi slave's quality of life depended entirely on whether he happened to be purchased by a humane owner or sold to a sadist. In either case, the element of random fortune only heightened the sense of bondage. "When you is a slave, you ain't got no mo' chance than a bullfrog," said Virginia Harris of Coahoma County.

Sadists existed right in the vicinity of Jones County. In one notorious local incident, an area slaveholder named Bryant Craft caught a man named Jessie giving whiskey to the other Negroes and flogged him until the cloth of his shirt was embedded in his back. Afterward the tortured man crawled away to die, and he was lying by the side of an old dirt road when a horseman named Duckworth happened by. Duckworth took the slave home and tended to his wounds, greasing them with warm tallow, and then took him back to the Craft place, hoping to "reconcile" the master. Instead, Craft was enraged by Duckworth's interference and struck Jesse down with a lethal blow. "Let that be an example to you," he said to Duckworth.

In Jackie Knight, Rachel fell into the hands of an owner who treated the slaves with decency, which is to say he didn't beat them without cause or work them half to death, or sell them away from their relations. He does not appear to have been arbitrarily cruel, and some of the men and women who worked for him may even have been fond of him. He made an effort to keep families together and to care decently for children, according to the young Martha Wheeler, who remembered him as quite elderly but "kind and good."

As a Knight slave, Rachel joined one of the largest and closest-knit black enclaves in the area, one with its own customs and social order. At least fifty-three men, women, and children labored on behalf of the various Knights, perhaps more. The Slave Schedule of the U.S. Federal Census for 1860 listed twenty-two slaves living on Jackie's place, but there may have been nearly twice that: Martha Wheeler remembered as many as forty when she was a child. Jackie may have understated his holdings to avoid paying taxes. At any rate, he was far and away one of the largest slaveholders for miles.

Rachel moved back and forth between the Knights' domestic circles. She appears to have spent some time in the home of Jackie's daughter Altimirah Brumfield, who lived on the adjoining property, and whom she may have been fond of—one of Rachel's granddaughters would be named Altimirah. Jackie frequently gave small slave children into the keeping of Altimirah and deeded three girls under the age of twelve to her. Perhaps Altimirah trained them as house servants, or perhaps she was simply kind.

Rachel was also in the household of Jackie's second youngest son, Jesse Davis Knight, the thirty-nine-year-old aspiring planter and a future Confederate soldier. Known in the family simply as Davis, he was the closest of the Knight sons to his father in status. He had married well, to a Baylis named Sarah Elizabeth, and his father-in-law and neighbor George Baylis was a preacher and large landowner with fifteen slaves, whose property sprawled along an area known as Big Creek. Jesse Davis had a thriving farm worth eight thousand dollars on which he harvested forty bales of cotton, a huge amount for the area, and tended a herd of eighteen horses. He was prosperous despite ten mouths to feed and comfortable enough to house the local schoolmaster. Although Jesse Davis listed just four slaves among his property, his son John Melton Knight remembered twice as many in their domestic establishment. "All my people owned slaves, both sides," John Melton recalled. "We had eight or ten of them when my grand-daddy was alive." Some of them likely were on loan from Jackie, perhaps including Rachel.

Newton could not have failed to notice Rachel as she moved among the households of his close relatives. At Jackie's place, she inhabited one of the cabins that sat just one hundred yards or so from the front porch. Newton and his cousins visited their grand-father, who was generous with them. On one occasion, he promised one of them a new colt when it was born. Newton was familiar with the servants, particularly those he had known as a child, such as an elderly couple named Lewis and Kate. He would have been fully aware of the striking newcomer, an unusually eye-catching young woman near to him in age.

Rachel was a young mother even by the standard of the day; slave women tended to have their first child around the age of nineteen. Her youthful pregnancy may suggest that she was unusually attractive. As the slave memoirist Harriet Jacobs wrote, beauty was a curse: "That which commands admiration in the white woman only hastens the degradation of the fe-male slave."

In any event, Rachel's childbearing was encour-aged because her Knight owners, like all slaveholders, wished to see their property increase. Pregnant, Rachel received additional clothing and food allowances, and had a somewhat lighter workload. Once she delivered, however, her responsibilities doubled; one of the few things we can be sure of about her was that she was a woman of immense physical stamina. She nursed and tended to her children between ceaseless duties and house chores, preparing breakfast for the Knights, do-ing their laundry, cooking their suppers and dinners, and making trips to the henhouse or storehouse. In the evenings she spun and wove and did all of the sewing for the household, enough to occupy several hands. In fact, her presence in the house defined the matron for whom she worked as a "mistress" rather than a farmwife. The whites who truly ruled Rachel's life were not men but women.

Rachel had precious little time to devote to her own children, who were looked after by one of the elderly slave women and brought to her at work for feedings, as she herself had been as a small baby. As Rachel's children grew old enough, they acquired their own chores: hauling water, picking up wood chips, sweeping the yard, and carrying food from the kitchen to the big house.

The Rachel whom Newton first knew was a carefully masked young woman whose outward subservience hid guile, a quality any slave had to possess in order to cope with the domination under which she lived. The Knight slave cabins constituted a separate society, the goings-on of which the whites were almost wholly unaware. The people who lived in them were far more self-determined and politically alert than the Knights could have guessed—as Newton would discover.

Deception was a necessary and ubiquitous tool with which Rachel avoided unpleasant work or whippings, or hid clandestine activities. One South Carolina bondsman testified that he belonged to no fewer than seven secret societies formed by slaves to help one another in distress. They prayed constantly for the "day of their deliverance," and the meek front they presented to their owners was a disguise: "One life they show their masters and another life they don't show," he said. A white planter remarked on a trait "often noticed" in his slaves, "that of pretending to misunderstand what was said to them when it suited their purpose to do so."

The cabin in which Rachel lived had one room, about sixteen by eighteen feet, with a homemade bed and clay-and-stick fireplace draped with strings of dried red peppers and other drying medicinal roots and leaves, such as mayapple roots and cyprus. Out back, there were small garden patches full of melons and potatoes, which she cultivated in her free time, on occasion bartering and selling her goods.

At night and on Sunday, Rachel had her autonomy. According to her descendants, she was unusually independent, virtually self-sufficient in her cabin and vegetable patch. In the cabins, Rachel traded folk remedies, recipes, superstitions, favors, and information. She knew how to treat fevers with mint and horehound teas, and aches and pains with a resin from crushed pine needles. There was a lingering hint in the Knight family that she conjured spells, and she seems to have had some knowledge as a folk doctor.

A fugitive slave from another plantation could tap lightly on Rachel's door and be sure of receiving aid, such as medicines, directions through the swamp, and food: some hoecake, a cornmeal patty cooked in grease and ashes and wrapped in a collard leaf, greens and dumplings, or boiled peppergrass with meat scraps, with lumps of cornmeal to stretch it.

A thriving grapevine was a source of the latest gossip, as well as reports from the larger world. Whites were often astonished to learn of the speed and distance which information traveled in the black communities. The stunning news of John Brown's 1859 attack on the federal armory at Harpers Ferry penetrated deep into the interior of Mississippi, where it circulated in Marshall County. John Adams once observed that the grapevine was "a wonderful art of communicating intelligence among themselves; it will run several hundred miles in a week or fortnight." Rachel was an especially good source of information as a house slave; she had ample opportunity to eavesdrop on the Knight masters and mistresses. Children also learned to pass on what they overheard from whites while frolicking in yards, kitchens, or under porches. "I'd play around the white folks and then hear what they'd say and then go tell the niggers," a slave from Monroe County remembered.

As the 1860 presidential election approached, Rachel and the other Knight slaves were well aware that a victory by Abraham Lincoln could mean potential deliverance from bondage. Slaves all across the South were. It was impossible not to overhear the heated discussion among whites over secession, as fire-breathers like Dr. John Baylis ranted against "Black Republicans" who wanted to overturn all of civilized society by freeing the Negroes. Abolitionist Yankees sought to "lord it over the South," and soldiers would "come down here" and commence "killing our children and ravishing our wives." It was impossible not to sense their anxiety and their outright fear of violent slave revolts.

In Holly Springs, a doctor's wife noticed a large congregation of slaves crowded into a meeting in a cabin. Suspicious, she slipped over to a window and eavesdropped, as inside, a slave exhorted his companions, "I tell you ladies and gentlemen, we's all gwine to be free before long. We's all going to enjoy liberty, mos' right away. We won't be slaves no longer and whipped an' cuffed by de white folks." The slave reported that he had listened to a speech given by Jeff Davis. "From what he said de people from de Norf is comin' down to set us free an' dey'll just mow dese southern people down as dey mows de grass. An he said de northern people believes in Negro 'quality, dat de white folks up dar was willing to marry our daughters and let us marry theirn. Jes be ready, as the hime says."

The woman fled and repeated what the slave said to her husband, who seized a whip and flogged him.

Rachel came from a part of the country in which slaves were particularly attuned to public affairs in the fall of 1860. In Macon, Georgia, that September, every political speech "attracted a number of Negroes, who, without entering the Hall, have managed to linger around and hear what the orators say," a Georgia newspaper reported. The slaves were so engaged in the politics of the day that the local police in Columbus, Georgia, had to chase them away from "the meetings and discussions of different political parties."

But Rachel learned to keep her thoughts, and her

political sentiments, carefully hidden from view. Even if she trusted a member of the white community in Jones County with her innermost feelings, she likely wasn't inclined to confide in a Knight male, no matter how sympathetic or antislavery he appeared. All white men wanted to do, it seemed, was put their hands on her. As a member of Jackie Knight's household Rachel may not have suffered whippings, but she did endure another form of abuse: sexual exploitation.

In 1859 or 1860, not yet twenty, Rachel gave birth to another child, a mulatto boy named Jeffrey Early Knight. The father was Jesse Davis Knight. It was an all too common transaction: a work-roughened man came in from the fields or slipped behind a door, reeking of farm sweat, boot leather, ash soap, and perhaps brown whiskey. Jesse Davis had availed himself of Rachel's bed, and Jeffrey was the issue.

Sometime after the birth of Jeffrey, old Jackie Knight made his last will and testament. In it, he bequeathed slaves to each of his children by name—except for Albert, who received five hundred dollars in cash. While Albert left no direct statement of his feelings about slavery or the Confederacy, the will is highly suggestive. But perhaps the best record of his beliefs is the conduct of his son Newton, who at about this time is said to have first become protective of Rachel. If so, he had good reason.

There was another bequest in Jackie Knight's will, one that would prove to be significant to the family. To his second-youngest son, Jesse Davis Knight,

Jackie specifically bequeathed "a certain negro woman named Rachel," as well as the infant boy Jeffrey, plus Rachel's "increase, if any." She was to belong to Jesse Davis in perpetuity, to do with as he pleased, and her children would belong to him, too. Before long, Rachel would be pregnant again by Jesse Davis, with a daughter named Fannie.

Jackie had willed Jesse Davis his own offspring, as cash property.

On December 20, 1860, men began arriving in Ellisville on every sort of mount, from head-lolling nags to lightly stepping saddlebreds. Livestock pulled rattling wagons to a halt and parked, as passengers hopped down from the buckboards. Citizens stood in groups arguing, trading news, and knocking back amber liquor. Some men used the occasion to play cards on a whiskey barrel; others amused themselves with bare-knuckle fighting, as occasional scuffles broke out. Amid the raucousness, various speakers hollered to be heard for, or against, secession.

They were there to choose a delegate to the secession convention. After Lincoln was elected in November 1860, Mississippi governor John Pettus, a fiery secessionist, instructed the state legislature to call the convention so that delegates could vote on an ordinance of secession. Pettus declared himself the Moses of his people, telling them to "go down into Egypt while Herod rules in Judea."

All over the state, secessionists were shouting down their more moderate opponents. Those who argued reasonably against severing from the Union were drowned out by a vehement cacophony, "the booming of cannon, the joyous greeting, the soul stirring music," which urged the state to war. Even churches were filled by martial and menacing airs, so much so that even the ardent secessionist Episcopal bishop William Mercer Green found it sacrilegious. After preaching in St. Andrew's Church in Jackson, Green "had good reason to fear that the effect of the sermon was utterly driven from the minds of the congregation by the unseemly manner in which the Organ was played at the close of the service; the harsh and martial style of the music being much better suited to a military parade than to the quiet solemnity of the House of God." He worried that the "warlike" airs sent worshippers marching out of their pews with anything but godliness. "From such Profanations of Thy Temple, Good Lord deliver us!"

In a northern Mississippi county, the young Presbyterian clergyman John Hill Aughey stood in a local grocery store and listened to a virulent anti-Union tirade by Colonel James Drane, a member of the state senate. Anyone who opposed secession was "a base, craven submissionist," Drane declared. He insisted on "the right to carry slavery into the common domain," even if it meant war with "the perfidious Yankees. I cordially hate a Yankee."

To Aughey and other Unionists it all sounded very

much like treason. Aughey listened, appalled, to the very essence of "fire-breathing" from another secessionist speaker, who seethed against "the abominable, white livered abolitionist" Lincoln and vowed "to butcher the villain if ever he sets foot on slave territory." Not only did the elocutionist threaten to assassinate the president-elect, but he also offered to hang any of his fellow citizens who favored union over dissolution. "I, for one, would prefer an hour of virtuous liberty to a whole eternity of bondage under Northern, Yankee, wooden-nutmeg rule," the orator fulminated. "The halter is the only argument that should be used against the submissionists, and I predict that it will soon, very soon, be in force."

The speaker continued: "Compromise! Let us have no such word in our vocabulary . . . Let the war come—I repeat it—let it come! The conflagration of their burning cities, the desolation of their country, and the slaughter of their inhabitants, will strike the nations of the earth dumb with astonishment, and serve as a warning to future ages that the slaveholding Cavaliers of the sunny South are terrible in their vengeance. I am in favor of immediate, independent, and eternal separation from the vile Union which has so long oppressed us . . . Cursed be the day when the South consented to the iniquitous league—the Federal Union—which has long dimmed her nascent glory."

Somehow, after listening to such railings, Aughey still found the courage to vote against secession. At his local precinct, he asked in a clear voice for a Union ticket. He was told there was none. Aughey wrote one out by hand and deposited it, amid glares and murmurs.

The yeomen of Jones County also weren't the sorts of men easily swayed by fiery oration; they voted their consciences. Newton's feelings were apparent to those who knew him. "He was strictly a union man, he lived and died a union," according to one of his oldest friends and neighbors, George Ellzey. Most of his relatives and neighbors felt similarly. "I was acquainted with the whole family; they were all anti secession including Newton Knight," Joel E. Welborn later said.

The most adamant anti-secessionists in the county were the Collinses, who gave stirring speeches in defense of the Union, with great effect. Family patriarch Stacy Collins had eight sons, all of whom would eventually fight the Confederacy. Neither Stacy nor his sons owned slaves or grew more than token amounts of cotton. Instead, they raised hogs, sheared sheep for their own wool, and grew crops for food. Their homes were made from immense pine logs, with timbers twenty-four feet long, and their sisters, Peggy and Sally, were just as tough as they were. Sally's second marriage to tavernkeeper James Parker had failed in 1857. When he sued her for divorce claiming adultery, she countercharged him with having sex with a mare.

If anyone wanted a fistfight, just let him argue politics with a Collins. On the stump, the Collinses echoed Lincoln's famous argument, paraphrasing the

Bible and Aesop's Fables, that if the South was to obtain a separation from the North, the country would be divided and "a house divided against itself cannot stand."

Plain folk of Jones County had little at stake in the slave and cotton economy and even less in the political affairs of planters. And Southern pride on its own was a thin reason to go to war. When it came time to vote, the men of Jones County cast their ballots overwhelmingly for the moderate "cooperationist" candidate John H. Powell, who also just happened to be Jasper Collins's father-in-law. The flame-spouting merchant-slaveholder John M. Baylis got just 24 votes, to 374 for Powell. Jones County was firmly Union. Powell was sent off to tell the convention so.

But when Powell arrived at Jackson in early January 1861, he found the city already celebrating as if secession were a foregone conclusion. Every hotel was "filled with excited visitors," and "crowds lined the streets to cheer a military parade" and to salute a new flag—with fifteen stars, one for each slave state. Amid the exultation, Unionists were once more shouted down as "cowards" and "submissionists" who would place the state under Northern tyranny.

A voice of dissent sounded like a whisper amid the din. Had secession been put strictly to a popular vote, it probably would not have passed. But the delegates in Jackson did not represent what was popular, only what was powerful: the "Bourbons" who were the wealthiest men of the state. The same men who controlled the state's religion, economy, and culture also controlled politics and the state convention.

Mississippi's Declaration of Secession was a document written by and for the planters. It announced their interests in the very first sentence: "Our position is thoroughly identified with the institution of slavery—the greatest material interest of the world. Its labor supplies the product which constitutes by far the largest and most important portions of the commerce of the earth."

The Declaration continued: "These products [of slave labor] are peculiar to the climate verging on the tropical regions, and by an imperious law of nature, none but the black race can bear exposure to the tropical sun. These products have become necessities of the world, and a blow at slavery is a blow at commerce and civilization." For Mississippians, the cause of the Civil War could not have been plainer: it was a war over slavery. The Bourbons equated slavery with civilization and universal freedom with barbarism.

In the state capital, Powell was one small rural delegate among powerful Mississippians such as James L. Alcorn, cavalier handsome with his trim bow of a mustache, rich gold watch chain, and an ivory-handled walking stick, his wife Amelia on his arm, lace at her throat and wrists. Or the orator Lucius Quintus Cincinnatus Lamar, an almost infernal-seeming figure, with his burning almond-shaped eyes, straight black hair whipped back from an eager face, whiskers plunging to a black necktie, his mouth a quick red slash.

As Powell walked among these impassioned men in the stately marble-columned capitol building and saw the galleries in the assembly hall overflowing with avid secessionists, he lost his nerve. He forsook the will of his constituents and voted **for** secession—along with the overwhelming majority of delegates. The vote was 84 to 15.

Many other anti-secession delegates betrayed their constituents and voted for the ordinance. Some of them did so because they were swayed by the moment, others were perhaps bribed with the promise of advancement, and still others had been told that a later referendum would enable the people to ratify or reject the ordinance. But there would be no referendum. On January 9, 1861, Mississippi became the second state to secede, after South Carolina.

At the public announcement of the vote in Natchez, fire bells tolled and twelve guns saluted. In Jackson, ladies presented to the convention a Bonnie Blue flag that bore a single white star on a field of blue.

Immediately the wheels of Southern independence started turning. The clause in the state constitution requiring elected officials to take an oath of allegiance to the United States was deleted. Congressmen and senators were summoned home from Washington. The state seized control of all federal property within its boundaries, including the regulation of the Mississippi River. The new flag was hoisted over the capitol building and became a symbol of Southern rights, inspiring the song "The Bonnie Blue Flag," which became one of the most popular of the Confederacy:

**We are a band of brothers, and native to the
soil,**
**Fighting for the property we gain'd by honest
toil;**
**And when our rights were threaten'd, the cry
rose near and far,**
**Hurrah for the Bonnie Blue Flag, that bears a
Single Star!**
Hurrah! Hurrah! for Southern Rights; hurrah!
**Hurrah! for the Bonnie Blue Flag, that bears a
Single Star!**

But back in Jones County, those who had voted for Powell were outraged. "Fact is, Jones County never seceded from the Union into the Confederacy," Newton insisted sixty years later, still arguing the matter. "Her delegate seceded." In Ellisville, an effigy of Powell was strung up and burned. An incensed Riley Collins called a meeting at the old Union Church in Jones County and gave a fiery speech, railing against the "injustice" of secession. Riley Collins urged the men of Jones "not to fight against the union, but if they had to fight to stay home and fight for a cause in which they believed."

Word reached Powell that it was literally unsafe for him to return home. "It woulda been kinder unhealthy for him, I reckon," Newton said. Powell remained in

Jackson for a full month, until the formation of the Confederate States of America. He would soon be rewarded for his secessionist vote: he was appointed the Confederate provost marshal of Jones County, responsible for arresting deserters, disloyalists, and traitors.

But in April 1861, the controversy over secession finally subsided, after rebels fired on the federal property at Fort Sumter. It was replaced by a wave of Confederate patriotism. Lincoln had called for 75,000 militiamen to suppress the Southern insurrection. His efforts at appeasement had failed; as he took office in March 1861, Congress had just sent to the states for ratification a proposed Thirteenth Amendment that protected slavery in the Southern states. Lincoln supported the proposed amendment and vowed not to fire the first shot: "The government will not assail **you,**" he told the insurgent states. "You can have no conflict, without being yourselves the aggressors." But Lincoln also made it clear that he would defend federal property.

There was a groundswell of support for the new nation, and formerly peaceable men became belligerently pro-Confederate. They were above all Southerners, whose home and honor were now being threatened by Northern aggressors. In Greenville, a plantation hub in the Mississippi Delta with planks for sidewalks and just five hundred white residents, a previously ambivalent twenty-nine-year-old lawyer named William L. Nugent suddenly caught the martial spirit. Nugent had the scholarly, contemplative temperament of an amateur poet and a limpid appearance: smooth haired, silky bearded, and gray eyed. He often packed a violin with his clean linens. He was recently wedded to one of the heiresses of the area, Eleanor "Nellie" Smith, daughter of a prominent judge and planter, and he had mixed feelings about secession. Not anymore. "I feel that I would like to shoot a Yankee," he wrote his bride in August of 1861.

Everyone was rushing to arms to protect their homeland, and there were more volunteers in the state than Governor Pettus or President Davis could handle. In each district, a man was chosen to gather local volunteers and issue uniforms and preliminary orders. In the Piney Woods, the officious Amos McLemore became one of the most enthusiastic enlistment officers, opening his recruiting station in an old log house on a local creek, where a line formed of battle-hungry men. "They thought it was big to get the big guns on," said Maddie Bush, a Jones Countian who became a corporal in the 7th Mississippi Battalion.

McLemore's company of 134 was just the second of eight companies that would come from the area. He dubbed it "The Rosinheels," a term for the rearing of an eager horse. The outfit became Company B of the 27th Mississippi Infantry, and it was full of McLemore's cronies. Another member of the company was Jesse Davis Knight, who no doubt joined at the encouragement of his Baylis in-laws. The company was stocked with wholehearted rebels; it would lose only two men to desertion.

When mustering time came, runners went out all over the Piney Woods region, with word for men to gather their belongings and for their families to prepare for a farewell feast and rally. It was a scene repeated across Mississippi: "Joyfully and with alacrity the young chivalric sons of the slave holding aristocracy responded to the call for volunteers," recalled the minister Aughey, who witnessed the rush to volunteer. "The young ladies presented company and regimental flags of costly material, deftly embroidered by their own fair fingers with rare and significant designs, to every regiment as it left for the theatre of war. Upon their departure to the seat of war, they were given an ovation, barbecues were held, grandiloquent orations were pronounced, in which the superiority of the South over the North in valor, military skill, and chivalric spirit was announced in terms that admitted no contrary opinion."

On the appointed day for muster, ox wagons approached from all directions at the appointed location at a local creek. The men who signed up were issued their uniforms, and officers formed them in a line. A drummer, fifer, and fiddler were appointed, and at an officer's command the drummer stepped forward and rat-tat-tatted. As the men swung into drill motion with a clanking of weapons, the crowd chanted,

We will keep our niggers all at home,
To raise our cotton and our corn
We will show them to the cannon's mouth
They cannot come it on the South

After the drill, the families sat down to a sumptuous banquet of chicken pies made with precious
hand-ground wheat flour, biscuits, cornbread, barbe-
cued beef and mutton, and boiled pork hams. The
soldiers were served first, then their wives and children. When all the whites had eaten, their slaves were
invited to take the leftovers.

At the finish of the dinner, officers commanded the
men to form in line again. Like so many other Southerners, the men of Jones kissed their wives, formed
companies, shouldered their gear, and marched away
over the hills, and to war. The women left behind
cleared the tables and loaded the ox wagons for the
long dispiriting drive home, back to their farm drudgery with no husbands to help.

Many of the men who marched away had opposed
secession. But they found that in the wake of Fort
Sumter, opposition to the Confederacy was virtually
impossible: dissenters were no longer merely glared at,
they were being arrested for treason and threatened
with hanging.

Across the state, reports circulated of coercion. The
St. Louis Democrat published a letter from a wealthy
Mississippi planter to a Southern gentleman in New
York warning that unless he speedily returned to demonstrate his loyalty, his land would be seized as that of a
"disaffected person" and that he himself was "a Union
man but dar not say so, for fear of mob violence." In
Tishomingo County, a twenty-two-year-old mechanic
named E. J. Sorrell recalled that all Union men were
"threatened in a general way." In Corinth, according

to Union activist M. A. Higginbottom, "it was a common expression that every man who would not take sides with the Confederacy 'ought to be hung.' " The editor of the local Republican newspaper, James M. Jones, was "surrounded by infuriated rebels, his paper was suppressed, his person threatened with violence, he was broken up and ruined forever, all for advocating the Union of our fathers." In Alcorn County, citizens threatened to put Mathew J. Babb in prison if he "did not cease talking against secession." In Tippah County, farmer Samuel Beaty had his property destroyed by a mob. In Columbus, when Presbyterian minister James Lyon continually preached that slavery was sinful and railed against "blood and thunder" politics, Confederates retaliated by arresting his son Theodoric, court-martialing him, and sending him to prison in Virginia.

Unionists in the Deep South were in positions of thankless isolation, as the definition of loyalty was turned on its head. Allegiance to country was inverted into treason, and supporters of the Stars and Stripes ironically labeled un-American, as Southerners jeeringly called them "tories," in reference to those who had supported Britain's George III during the American Revolution.

John Hill Aughey, who would be imprisoned for his loyalty, wrote a letter to Secretary of State William H. Seward describing what the Unionists in Mississippi faced. "Our property is confiscated and our families left destitute of the necessaries of life, all that they possessed . . . Heavy iron fetters are placed upon our limbs and daily some of us are led to the scaffold or to death by shooting. Many are forced into the army, instant death being the penalty in case of refusal, thus constraining us to bear arms against our country, to become the executioners of our friends and brethren, or to fall ourselves into their hands."

These loyalists received precious little congratulation then or later for their honorable stances, or for what they endured. An Alabama Unionist told a congressional committee in 1866, "You have no idea of the strength of principle and devotion these people exhibited towards the national government."

Aughey, who had dared to cast his vote publicly against secession, was hounded. Aughey was doubly suspect because he was originally a Yankee hailing from New York, only a Mississippian by marriage. Aughey was an almost prettily handsome thirty-two-year-old, over six feet tall with a sweep of rich black hair and pronounced cheekbones, but there was nothing delicate about his moral disposition: slavery was sin, secessionists were traitors, and the newly formed Confederacy was unconstitutional. He continued to preach this message on his evangelical circuit around Choctaw and Attala counties, at peril of his life.

"It was now dangerous to utter a word in favor of the Union," he wrote in a memoir of his experiences. "Many suspected of Union sentiments were lynched . . . Self constituted vigilance committees sprang up all over the country, and a reign of terror began."

A local slave was detailed to issue a frightening summons to him. On a piece of paper was sketched a coffin, a freshly dug open grave, and a figure with hands tied behind his back and a sack over his face, ready for execution. In bold letters was written, "Such be the doom of all traitors."

The atmosphere in the state became even more inflamed after July 21, 1861, when the Confederates won the first major battle of the war, at Manassas, Virginia. Rebel troops under Generals P. G. T. Beauregard and Joe Johnston forced the Northerners into an uncontrolled retreat back to Washington, D.C., along with panicked congressmen's wives who had come to picnic. News of the victory was greeted with delirium, and pressure on Southern men to enlist increased: only the traitorous or cowardly held back.

A sergeant in the 24th Mississippi wrote to his sister, "I much reather [sic] be numbered amongst the slain than those that stay at home for it will be a brand upon their name as long as a southren lives."

A week after Manassas, on July 29, 1861, Newton Knight responded to local pressures and enlisted. He joined Company E of the 8th Mississippi Infantry, an outfit raised in Jasper County by a local landowner named B. F. Moss. Although no one was formally impressing troops yet—it would be several months before Newton was forced into the 7th Mississippi Battalion and marched off to Corinth under the First Conscription Act—his reasons for this first enrollment can be guessed at.

Newton had any number of incentives to enlist. He did not want to be perceived as a coward or a submissionist, and it had become dangerous to oppose the war and to resist military service. Also, the enlistment came with the provision that he would be furloughed until September 18, 1861. There was a general assumption that the war would be over before the fall harvest. He might never have to report for actual duty. Finally, it was a regular paycheck, and being a soldier affirmed his sense of manhood.

Even so, he enlisted reluctantly, and perhaps even under coercion. B. F. Moss was no great friend of Newton's. The two quarreled when Moss's brother, also a Confederate officer, impressed a local woman's horse purportedly for the army's use. A horse was a farmwife's livelihood, as Newton well knew, and he came to the woman's aid and forced the return of the animal. The incident left lingering ill will between him and the Moss brothers. According to his own account years later, Newton only reported for mustering into Company E, 8th Mississippi, "under guard."

By coincidence during this period, Newton's Jasper County home burned to the ground, and everything he had in it was destroyed. It was Newton's belief that the local Confederates led by Moss retaliated against him for his Union sympathies, and for his interference in the matter of the horse, by torching his property. "His residence with all its contents together with all of his corn and out houses . . . around his plantation were burned by his enemies," his friend William Welch recalled.

The suspicion was shared by some of his friends

in Jones County, who after the war filed a deposition in his behalf. "Before and during the late rebellion we know that he was opposed to the war and refused to take up arms against the United States, and the rebels was determined to make him fight or kill him they destroyed all his effects horses and muls and his household and left his family destitute."

Whether or not Confederates burned his farm, Newton's stay in the 8th Mississippi was brief. The unit formally entered Confederate service in October of 1861 and was sent to Pensacola under Braxton Bragg. But Newton served just three months before he received a special discharge from Bragg on January 2, 1862. Discharges were rare; the Confederacy sought every able-bodied man, but under special circumstances soldiers were released from service if they were needed back home. Newton was probably discharged to attend to an urgent family matter.

Newton's family indeed needed him at home: his father, Albert, had fallen gravely ill and was on his deathbed, and there was no one to look after his mother or wife. Serena was living with his parents in their cabin near the Leaf River, in a household full of dependents. In addition to the fifty-five-year-old Mason, soon to be widowed, there were Serena's three baby boys and Newton's two youngest siblings, sixteen-year-old Martha, who was newly married, and twelve-year-old Taylor.

There may have been another reason Newton was needed at home: the teenaged Martha had married badly, to a local criminal. Her new husband was a mysterious man who went by the name of "Morgan," and he was uniformly described as a rough character, a killer and an outlaw who thieved cattle. In the absence of any other men, Morgan had taken over the household. Newton began receiving alarming reports from Serena that Morgan was abusing his children and frightening the women. Also, he was apparently a Confederate informant.

"He would keep the Confederates' cavalry posted about my father," T. J. Knight wrote. "He made himself mighty busy attending to other people's business."

Morgan's identity has been lost, but he may have been Morgan Lines, a twenty-one-year-old day laborer and convicted murderer. His father, Thomas Lines, was also a killer: on the 1860 federal census for Jones County, in a section reserved for criminal convictions, both men carried notations for murder. According to the Knights' neighbor, Ben Graves, who lived two farms over, Morgan was "a regular outlaw, a bad man. Everybody was afraid of him."

Tom Knight was too young to remember the events of 1862, but his mother told him the story later. Morgan had a vicious habit of hitting the small children in the house. "Mother said nearly every time I went to the table to eat that man would bounce on me and whip me just because he could and wanted to show off smart. So my mother got tired of it and told my father."

Newton demanded that Morgan leave the house

and said he did not want to hear of him laying a hand on another child. Morgan refused to leave. Newton did not react immediately, as he apparently viewed Morgan as highly dangerous. "He was one man Newt was afraid of," Ben Graves said. "He was afraid Morgan would slip up on him and kill him."

Graves and Tom Knight gave slightly differing accounts of what happened next, but they agreed on the outcome: someone shot Morgan to death in the house. Newton was the main suspect. According to Tom, Morgan was sitting by the fire one night after supper, rocking a baby, when someone aimed a gun through an open window "and shot his brains out." Martha grabbed the baby out of Morgan's arms as he fell out of the chair dead. "So we never were whipped any more by him," T. J. reported laconically.

Graves, who was fourteen years old at the time, raced over from his farm to see what had happened. He claimed to be the first person outside of the household to view the corpse. According to him, Morgan was sitting on the front porch in the morning, with his feet on the doorstep, when someone came through the back of the house and shot him. "He fell over backwards dead," with a child still in his lap, Graves said.

Morgan lay on the porch until enough men could be summoned to hold an inquest and tend to the body. By afternoon, a crowd had gathered, and all of them "claimed they knew who shot Morgan," Graves said. "Everybody said it was Newt Knight." But there was not enough evidence to accuse Newton: Martha,

Serena, and Mason, despite the fact that all had been in the room, insisted that they didn't see who fired the shot.

Graves and the older men watched over the body on the porch through the day. Various wagons passed by, a cavalcade of travelers that included refugees and free Negroes "running from Mississippi to Alabama. They were passing in droves." But one wagon paused and halted. A young lady passenger stared at Morgan's body. "I know something of that man," she said. "That is one of the worst men that ever hit this country."

An older man watching over the body said, "Sister, you talk mighty plain."

"But I know it is true," she said. "I know of his marrying seven women. He is a thief and a robber and anything in the world as bad. He was a desperado."

Morgan's murder was never solved, and it's possible Newton was innocent. Martha eventually married again, to a man named Dick Yawn who was a fellow deserter-compatriot of Newton's. When Martha had their first child, she named the baby after Newton. A woman was not likely to name a child after the man who killed her first husband—at least, not unless that husband was so feared and hated that he demanded killing.

For a few brief months after his discharge from the 8th Mississippi in January of 1862, Newton lived at home as a yeoman farmer again. Home was the great stated cause of the Confederacy, and it was Newton's great cause, too. We can only imagine the peace he experienced for those few months, when he was able to tend to his farm and care for those who relied on him: the overburdened wife, the widowed mother, and children and younger siblings. He may have hoped that he could avoid the war altogether if he lived quietly enough planting peas and corn. His desperation can be envisaged when, four months later, conscription pulled him away from home again and sent him marching into the awful terror of Corinth. Home: it was the place he would fight toward across two hundred miles of thicket and swamp, as that most dishonored and hunted of men, a deserter.

Recollections of Colonel Wickham Hoffman, aide to William T. Sherman, traveling with Admiral David Farragut on the Mississippi River in the campaign against Vicksburg

The plantations along the banks were in the highest state of cultivation, the young cane, a few inches above the ground, of a most lovely green ... our flag had not been seen in those parts for over a year, and the joy of the Negroes when they had an opportunity to exhibit it without fear of their overseers was quite touching. The river was very high, and as we floated along we were far above the level of the plantations, and looked down upon the Negroes at work, and into the open windows of the houses ... Natchez, a town beautifully situated on a high bluff, was gay with inhabitants who had turned out to see us, the ladies, with their silk dresses and bright parasols, and the Negro women, with their gaudy colors, orange especially, which they affect so much, and which, by the way, can be seen at a greater distance than any other color I know of.

... The Confederate authorities had issued orders to burn the cotton along the banks to prevent it falling into our hands ... These men preceded us as we ascended the river; and burned their neighbors' cotton with relentless patriotism. The burning material was thrown into the stream, and floated on the surface a long time before it was extinguished. At night it was very beautiful to see the apparently flaming water. We had to exercise some care to steer clear of the burning masses.

THREE

The Swamp and the Citadel

November 1862, Abbeville, Mississippi

There was too much water in the backwoods of Mississippi, and not enough, for a deserter on the run. Newton waded through dark undrinkable pools, slime-covered bayous filled with rotted logs and shin-deep mud that sucked at his boots. He was perpetually damp, either from brown swamp water or his own brackish sweat, yet always thirsty. He soothed his swollen lips in ditches full of old rainwater, scooping green scum away and burying his face in stagnant puddles full of tadpoles.

After deserting near Abbeville, Newton had a journey of two hundred miles ahead of him, a trek almost the length of the state, on foot, to get back to Jones County. It was too dangerous to take the main roads or to cut through open pastures. Instead, he skirted civilization, hacking through undergrowth of dogwood, buckthorn, and wild privet, heavy with jessamine vines and other creepers and infested with snakes, centipedes, and, sometimes, alligators cloaked as logs. He was a skilled woodsman, but he had to forage for food without firing his shotgun, for fear of giving himself away.

As Newton stole through the woods, he wasn't alone. The Mississippi countryside was alive with the movements of men on the run: scavengers, runaways, deserters, and destitute civilians. There was fighting along the Mississippi River, and men and supplies shuttled to the front lines. Rebels burned cotton so it wouldn't fall into federal hands, making the horizon glow red-yellow, flames sharp edged beneath the gauzy gray smoke, visible for miles.

Escaped slaves sifted through the woods toward the victorious Union lines at Corinth that Newton had just left behind, emboldened by Lincoln's issuance of the preliminary Emancipation Proclamation in September 1862. William Tecumseh Sherman, commanding the Union forces in Memphis, counted six thousand of them in camp, and in November, U. S. Grant wrote to Halleck, "Citizens south of us are leaving their homes and Negroes coming in wagonloads. What shall I do with them?"

Newton dodged Confederate units, which dueled with Yankee patrols for possession of the roads. Civilian Mississippians, livid at the occupation of their home soil, were ever watchful for stray Yanks and deserters. William Nugent wrote to his gentle young wife, Nellie, that if any passed near Greenville, "take double barrel shotguns & pepper them like smoke. Kill, slay & murder them."

Patrollers with packs of dogs ranged through counties looking for fugitives, forcing Newton to go five and six nights without sleep, for fear of being captured. He scouted the countryside from treetops and sat in a cradle of branches, frozen, as Confederate cavalrymen bounded past him. The woods resounded with the deep-chested baying of bloodhounds on the chase. According to the Unionist preacher John Hill Aughey, who himself became hunted, men on the run were "never for an hour out of the hearing of howling hounds or yelping dogs."

Newton was more afraid of the dogs than any reptile or swamp predator. Patrollers used two types of dogs in pursuit. The traditional bloodhounds had thick jowls, pendulous ears, and long snouts and could track the redolent emanations of a human fugitive with a twenty-four-hour head start. But they were mere guides compared to the man hunters that ran with them, crossbred mastiff-bulldogs trained to lunge reflexively at any prey. Tensile and snap jawed, they chewed their victims into red indistinguishable pulp. A treed fugitive had just two choices: to be torn bloody or wait for the patrollers to arrive and surrender, to be manacled and imprisoned.

For the first time, Newton understood what it was to be a runaway slave. He was sleepless, parched, skulking, blistered, cut, and footsore. As he listened to the sound of the dogs threshing through the woods after him, an old abolitionist song may have occurred to him: "The hounds are baying on my track, Christian will you send me back?" As Aughey wrote, "A fellow feeling makes us wondrous kind."

Understanding turned to gratitude when slaves came to his aid. The men and women toiling on plantations were reliable sources of succor for fugitives; numerous accounts of runaways and Unionists in Mississippi make clear the extent of the mercies they received from slave quarters as they sought to evade Confederate authorities. Slaves would have fed Newton, led him to safe havens and shortcuts, and taught him ruses for eluding the dogs.

The account of other fugitives in Mississippi in the fall of 1862 shed light on the extent to which slaves aided Unionists behind the lines, and sought their own liberation as well. At roughly the same time Newton fought his way toward Jones County, the preacher John Hill Aughey was desperately stealing across the same section of countryside after escaping from prison in Tupelo, not far from Corinth.

Aughey was arrested in July 1862, for resisting conscription and for spying. He was part of a ring of ninety-odd other Unionists, who signaled meetings by lighting fires on local hilltops, conducted operations against the local rebels in Tishomingo County, and passed information to federal officers. Their motto was "Liberty and union, now and forever, one and inseparable."

Aughey was on a reconnaissance ride when Confederate cavalry surrounded him, took him into custody, and escorted him to Tupelo, where he was interrogated by Sterling Price and clapped in irons in a vermin-infested blockhouse to await execution as a traitor. The prison was a converted old grocery store with a tar of molasses on the floor, over which swarmed "grayback" lice. Aughey was shackled to prisoners of an astonishing variety: runaway slaves, American Indians, resisters, deserters, and captured Yankees who had been rounded up from the local countryside. The population of the crowded blockhouse rose and fell from day to day, as prisoners were called out and marched away for execution.

"We were a motley assemblage," Aughey wrote. "All the southern states and every prominent religious denomination had representatives among us. The youth in his non-age, and the gray haired man and very aged man were there. The learned and the illiterate, the superior and the subordinate were with us. The descendants of Shem, Ham, and Japheth, were here on the same common level, for in our prison were Africa's dark browed sons, the descendants of Pocahontas, the pure Caucasion. Death is said to be the great leveler; the dungeon at Tupelo was a great leveler. A fellow feeling made us [a] wondrous kind; none ate his morsel alone, and a deep and abiding sympathy for each other's woes pervaded every bosom. . . . when our fellow prisoners were called to die, and were led through our midst with pallid brows and agony depicted upon their countenances, our heartfelt expressions of sorrow and commiserations were loud . . . and deep."

There was nothing to do but plot improbable jail-breaks. The men traded tales of escape and advice on how to survive in the swamp. It was well known among them that slaves would help a renegade of any race. One man related that he had been hidden and nursed for a week by a slave named Isam and his wife Tabitha. Another told of being led by a small slave boy to a hiding place in a swamp, where he found a large group of other Unionists who were clandestinely fed and cared for.

As the date of his execution approached, Aughey's fellow prisoners helped him pick the locks on his shackles with a tool fashioned from a spoon. Iron fetters still on his ankles, he staggered into the thickets and hid. His experiences probably reflect Newton's: he subsisted on sassafras leaves and pond water and at times was so thirsty he contemplated opening a vein and drinking his own blood. As he moved surreptitiously through the swamps, he fell into accidental company with other fugitives. In one busy day, he spotted another Unionist shimmying down a tree trunk and crossed trails with a runaway slave.

The runaway showed him a novel method of eluding the dogs: he walked on planks. He would place a plank on the ground, stride a few paces on it, then place another down, picking up the one he had just trod on. It was a laborious method and made for slow progress, but it left no scent or tracks. He sang as he traveled:

My ole missus she promise me
Dat when she die she'd set me free
But she dun dead this many year ago
An yer I'm a hoin the same old row
Run, nigger, run, de patter-roller ketch you
Run, nigger, run, it's almost day.

With the aid of the runaway, who knocked a Confederate patroller unconscious as both men were on the brink of rearrest, as well as help from some underground Northern sympathizers, Aughey finally reached the safety of Union lines. Aughey was conducted safely east, where he became an army chaplain and wrote a memoir called **The Iron Furnace,** in which he detailed his experiences and wrote of his indebtedness to the Mississippi slave community. "These kind friends," Aughey wrote, "bore the image of God carved in ebony."

Another traveler through northern Mississippi in November of 1862 was a chronic runaway slave from the Alabama-Mississippi border area named Wallace Turnage, who bolted from his plantation after suffering repeated beatings for not harvesting his allotted load. "Tired of being whipped" by overseers, including one who used a walking stick on him, Turnage made for the Union lines at Corinth. It was an especially perilous undertaking for a slave. According to a general order issued by Confederate brigadier general Dan Ruggles the previous July, any Negroes caught attempting to pass to Union lines were to be shot on the spot.

Turnage's flight was similar to that of Newton's and Aughey's. He ducked buckshot fired by a patroller in Lowndes County. He leaped a broad ditch to shake the hounds from his heels. He hid in church steeples, rode a log across the Tombigbee River, and stole a rowboat. Five male slaves hid him and fed him near Aberdeen and told him "they gloried in my spunk."

But Turnage was recaptured when he was betrayed by a frightened slave woman who reported him after he begged for food at her cabin, just half a day's walk from Corinth. He was set on by dogs and mauled for four or five minutes while a white man with a bull-whip around his neck pointed a pistol at him. A gang of slave catchers hauled him to a cabin where they beat his head against the fireplace bricks and thrust his hands into the flames. He was then chained to the floor until his owner could retrieve him. On the way home, a squad of rebel pickets offered to tie him to a tree and use him for target practice.

These were the sorts of scenes and stories the fugitive Newton encountered as he moved across the violent panoramic landscape of Mississippi. Everywhere, it seemed, cotton was burning and men were running, fighting, or hiding.

He would have been a limping, scarecrow-like figure when he finally got home, more rags than man, mud caked and direly in need of a bath, with lice even in his beard.

Jones County looked as though it had been through

a war, too. Barns listed from lack of repairs and weeds overgrew fields. The Confederate cavalry had impressed all of the good horses, and the few left to plow were emaciated hacks with their ribs visible. Conscription had stripped the county of men, and without enough hands to help with the harvest, crops rotted. Rebel officials seized much of what was reaped, as taxes in kind, leaving family storehouses nearly empty. A major crop failure in the first year of the war exacerbated the problems.

Nor could anyone afford to buy supplies; inflation was raging, and the purchasing power of Confederate money had dropped by a factor of three. A barrel of flour sold for fifty to seventy-five dollars in December of 1862 and would rise to ninety to one hundred dollars by the following year. There were shortages of everything: salt, essential for preserving meat, coffee, tea, candles, soda, dyes, and medicines. Everyone was hungry and threadbare. And there was no quick end in sight to the war.

Newton seethed at what he saw. According to his son, "He made it [home] all right and found the people had been treated awful bad here in Jones County." Serena and other farmwives described to him how Confederate officials invaded their homesteads at will, emptying corncribs in order to feed the horses they had impressed and rounding up cattle, hogs, and chickens for slaughter. They even stalked up the steps of cabins and into parlors, where they seized cloth that women had woven to clothe their families.

Serena stood by, near tears, as officials appropriated

all she harvested by day and labored over by night. "It was awful cruel to have to stand out and see the cavalry come into their homes," Tom Knight wrote, "and take their knives and cut the cloth out of the hand looms, where they had spun the thread out of cotton that they had carded with cards at night after a hard day's work in the field, and dyed and sized it and warped it and threaded the old hand loom and then wove the cloth to make clothes for their children to wear; then to see them come and cut it out and carry it off with them for their own use."

The local cavalry plagued Jasper Collins's sister Sally. The tough, witty divorcée who had accused her estranged husband of sleeping with a mare worked her own farmstead on Tallahala Creek, but she was unable to fend off the Confederates who habitually plundered her hogs, chickens, and corn. They pushed her beyond endurance when, one afternoon, they caught her best horse and took it, leaving behind an overworked old deadhead.

Newton listened to the exhausted, distraught women and the half-clothed children crying with hunger pangs. Tom Knight summed up his father's reaction: "Ask yourself if any red blooded man could stand for such conduct and not resent it."

Confederate officials seemed insensible to the central unfairness of the tax-in-kind system: planters could afford the high taxes and appropriations, but they pushed small farm families, who provided the rank-and-file foot soldiers, to the brink of destitution.

A vicious circle plagued the Confederacy: tax seizures that were supposed to feed troops left their wives and children famished.

Jefferson Davis and Governor Pettus urged planters to do their part to feed the army, by planting one acre of corn for every laborer. But Newton noticed that those who had so violently urged secession weren't nearly so devoted to the cause when it came to shifting from cotton production to less profitable food crops.

A Piney Woods farmer named R. C. Saffold, from neighboring Smith County, summed up the fury of Newton and other yeomen in a letter to Governor Pettus on November 3, 1862. "If something is not done by the legislature to open the corn cribs that are now closed against the widow and the orphan, and soldiers families, who are destitute, I know that we are undone. Men cannot be expected to fight for the Government that permits their wives and children to starve."

Yet that's exactly what the Confederacy expected of Newton Knight and men like him. While conscription and taxes drove whole counties into economic distress, rebel authorities adopted an increasingly hard line against deserters.

It soon became apparent to the local Confederates that Newton was living at home, and so were other absentees. In late 1862, Major Joel Welborn came back to Jones County on leave and discovered that many of the men missing from his outfit after Corinth were hiding out there. Moreover, their families were abetting them. But when Welborn confronted the men, he was met with grim insubordination.

On November 1, 1862, Welborn wrote to Confederate headquarters at Jackson, reporting the presence of large numbers of deserters in Jones County. The men "say they will never return to camp," he warned, adding that their numbers were significant. "One man has no business in trying to collect these men," he wrote. He added, "I am well acquainted with that section of the country & am satisfied that there is some of the citizens that is encouraging these things."

Newton shuddered to think of what might happen to him if he were captured. Desertion was a capital crime. Early in the war the death penalty was rarely if ever enforced, because it defeated its purpose and diminished the number of troops. But as the war wore on, the Confederacy's culture of leniency where desertion was concerned was hardening. Harsher measures were called for, and execution became a real possibility. According to Newton's descendants, he asked a fellow Confederate soldier, "Do you think they'd really shoot me?"

There were several dreaded punishments short of shooting or hanging to keep men in the ranks. There were public floggings; shaving of one side of the head; marching men through the countryside like slaves in a coffle; imprisonment with hard labor; and of course branding. It wasn't lost on Newton that these forms of punishment all had their origins in masters' efforts to discipline insubordinate slaves. The typical prescription for flogging was thirty-nine lashes—the same number recommended to punish chattel.

As Newton knew, the most feared punishment other than execution was the brand. Offenders who were branded with a "D" on their cheek had "the mark of desertion forever scar [their] face." The procedure typically took place at the field hospital, so Newton knew the details: an orderly heated coals in a metal bin, and when the branding iron—made specifically for deserters—was sufficiently hot, the orderly gave it to the doctor on duty, who pressed it into the man's cheek. There was a sizzling sound, followed by the acrid-sweet smell of burning flesh and blood, and then a long wail.

Another corrective was to be clapped in shackles and fetters while they were red-hot, which also caused scarring. A blacksmith was ordered to "iron him securely, sir," and the glowing metal was placed around wrists and ankles, burning through cloth and boots. The chain threaded through the prisoner's shackles was about ten inches long, forcing him to walk in an enfeebled shuffle.

Some measures were calculated merely to haze and humiliate. Stragglers were marched through the camps under guard with boards tied to their backs, on which were written slogans such as "I am a coward" or "I am a shirker from battle." Others were tied hand and foot astride the neck of cannon, where they were exposed and on view for as long as sixteen hours. As absences became more frequent, such measures became an accepted, routine part of camp life.

With the mass desertions and troop shortages after Corinth, officers cracked down. Early in 1863, shortly after the new year turned, General Dabney Maury answered Welborn's report by urging that "the most energetic measures" be taken to bring in the missing men from Jones County. The local provost marshal, John H. Powell, received an order: round up the deserters for return to their units.

Powell, the turncoat secession delegate who had been rewarded with the job of county provost, wasn't happy about the duty. He knew better than anyone how difficult it would be to bring in such men since his son-in-law, Jasper Collins, was one of their leaders, which put him in an extremely awkward position. On February 1, 1863, he wrote to Governor John J. Pettus questioning how he was supposed to accomplish the job and suggesting that he was entitled to extra compensation. "Give me some instructions what to do, whether I am in authority or no," he wrote, "and Tell me whether I am in titled to Any pay for my services or not."

Somehow, Powell got the job done. Over the next few weeks, the majority of men were taken into custody and sent back to duty. If they came peaceably, they were treated as mere stragglers, allowed to return to their companies without a court-martial or severe punishment. This was the case with most of the AWOL soldiers in Newton's unit.

But Newton wasn't taken without a fight. He was seized, roped like a kicking steer, thrown into a wagon, and carted off to military prison. In addition, Newton was court-martialed, and probably tortured. According to his neighbors, the rebels "got holt of him and they tyed him and drove him to prison" and "there they cruelly treated him for some length of time." Newton must have violently fought arrest, because this kind of treatment was reserved for the most defiant resisters.

Most likely, Newton was flogged. We don't know all the forms of punishment that he endured, but we do know that it was standard for resisters to be stripped publicly and whipped in front of the entire brigade, a ritual excruciating for all concerned.

One Confederate described such a scene. "We are all drawn up in line and the poor man is tied to a pole about fifty yards in front of us. His hands are stretched above his head and his shirt stripped to the waist . . . The word being given, the executioner began his disgusting work, the wretched man wincing and his flesh shrinking neath every blow which one after another were delivered in quick succession until 39 were rec'd by the culprit. In truth it is a horrid sight, and the executioner was so overcome by his feelings that as soon as his work was done his eyes filled with tears and he wept—he wept!"

Newton was given a choice: fight for the Confederacy or face a firing squad. It was no longer the empty threat it had been earlier in the war. In early 1863, as rebel authorities grappled with the mounting problem of men leaving the ranks, deserters were indeed being shot. General Robert E. Lee believed firmly in firing squads as a deterrent and thought they had a "beneficial effect" on discipline. As commanding general of the army he would urge President Jefferson Davis to employ discipline more "uniformly" as the war went on.

At the prison camp at Tupelo, a hole was dug, and the condemned deserter was ordered to sit with legs dangling over it. A line of soldiers took up positions in front of him and fired. The body fell into the already-excavated grave, which was then filled with earth.

Newton agreed to return to his unit rather than face an open grave. He was reduced in rank to private and escorted back to his company under guard, listed as "present" but "in arrest" on his company muster roll of February 28, 1863. But he was hardly chastened. He had every intention of deserting again at the first opportunity. His feeling for the Confederacy, previously moral suspicion and gut resentment, had now deepened to abiding enmity. His capture and humiliation had irretrievably torn him loose from the Southern cause.

On December 30, the 7th Mississippi Battalion was dispatched to reinforce a Confederate strong point at Snyder's Bluff, a ridge just above the confluence of the Mississippi and Yazoo rivers. The line of defenses had come under heavy assault from William T. Sherman. "I want all the troops I can get," Confederate commander John C. Pemberton had wired urgently. The position, with sixteen guns and a long seam of entrenchments, was a vital one, for its purpose was to protect the most strategically valuable of all Mississippi cities: Vicksburg. Sherman was attempting to reach Vicksburg by punching through the Chickasaw Bayou.

Newton was not sorry to arrive late on the dispiriting scene. The other men of the 7th Mississippi Battalion had celebrated New Year's Eve in a chill fog and had made their beds in wet leaves during the weeklong assault by Sherman. Surgeons worked by lantern as they amputated, while abandoned dead moldered in the field. Ill-tempered rebel soldiers in the trenches glared at the slaves who worked with shovels to shore up the works, cursing the "damned niggers" who expected to be freed when President Lincoln's Emancipation Proclamation took effect on New Year's Day.

Sherman had shelled and assaulted the entrenchments from Christmas Day to New Year's, when he finally decided the line was unbreakable. In a dense fog, he loaded his wounded onto hospital boats and departed, as a Union band played "Dixie." As they moved away, the Confederate musicians answered them sarcastically, playing "Get Out of the Wilderness." But the Yankees would be back.

Newton and the other men of 7th Mississippi Battalion remained at Snyder's Bluff through the winter of 1863 in a state of alert, as the Union forces under U. S. Grant conducted various operations aimed at breaching the defenses of Vicksburg; all of them were unsuccessful. The **New York Times** announced that Grant was "stuck in the mud of northern Mississippi, his army of no use to him or anybody else." Grant's lack of success became a standing Southern joke. "Why is a hundred-dollar Confederate note like Vicksburg to the Yankees? Because they pass it but can't take it." The repeated failures injured Grant's reputation, and some advisors urged the president that he be replaced for incompetence. Lincoln refused. "I think Grant has hardly a friend left, except myself," he said.

On April 30, Sherman returned and assaulted Snyder's Bluff again, backed by a federal squadron that hurled artillery and left men covered in dirt and bits of shale. This was just a feint, however, to distract from the real event: Grant now marched on Vicksburg from the hilly southeast rear and threatened the city's back door. On May 17, the 7th Mississippi Battalion was urgently ordered to evacuate Snyder's Bluff and move into Vicksburg itself. Pemberton was drawing in his forces; every man would be needed to help fend off Grant's troops, which had battered their way into the hills ringing the landward side of the city.

Soldiers hurriedly spiked the big guns and rushed to fill every available wagon with munitions and stores and round up all the livestock from the countryside. By 2:30 a.m. the 7th Mississippi Battalion was filing into Vicksburg. By 8:00 a.m. they tramped through the center of town—and went straight into the main entrenchments.

It's unclear how much of the ordeal of the next few weeks Newton underwent. Sometime in this period, he deserted the Confederacy again, and for the last time. We know he was with his unit and in arrest on February 28, 1863, but his record from then on is a void. What's certain is that the men of the 7th Mississippi Battalion went into the Vicksburg trenches on May 18 and emerged as skeletal prisoners of war on July 4. Newton's closest friends and family members suffered the full range of its horrors. It seems plausible that he did too, especially given that he was under arrest.

As the sky changed from black to gray in the dawn of May 18, Newton and the men of the 7th Mississippi Battalion, heavy legged and laden with gear, dropped into rifle pits. With that, they were thrust into the most harrowing siege of the war.

Once in the city, there was no getting out.

For a solid year, Grant had tried various approaches to Vicksburg like a man rattling angrily at a series of locked doors. The seemingly impregnable city sat on a ledge above the Mississippi, crowned with guns and protected by a series of natural barriers. On the riverfront, a fast current swept around a fishhook-shaped bend, banked in places by limestone bluffs. On the landward side behind the city, a series of deep gorges and foothills of yellow clay naturally lent themselves to entrenchments. An observer described the topography: "After all the big mountains and regular ranges of hills had been made by the Lord of Creation, there was left on hand a large lot of scraps, and these were dumped down on Vicksburg into a sort of waste heap."

The city itself was substantial, if seamy and slum ridden in sections. Rounding the broad bend in the river, boats came upon a metropolis that sprawled for a mile along the east bank and ascended the bluffs in steps. A heavy traffic of steam packets dropped goods and people onto wharves, including thousands of cotton bales to be shipped to textile mills, as well as a diverse array of fortune hunters, opportunists, planters and their puff-sleeved, broad-skirted wives, itinerant gamblers, piratical boatmen, and whores. It was the most mixed population in the South outside of New Orleans. Criminals prowled the tenements in the low hills, which the resident aristocracy, among them Jefferson Davis, tried to cleanse periodically with hangings or tar and featherings. The cardsharps were outnumbered only by the stray dogs, which scavenged in the streets and became such a nuisance that in 1860 the local populace drowned 129 of them in the river.

The better Vicksburgians lived on the heights. There the city took on a more imposing appearance, with wide sidewalks covered by the galleries of three-story buildings. Manor houses sat in the shadow of the domed, massive-pillared Warren County courthouse, with its four-faced clock, and the tower and steeple of St. Paul Catholic Church, which offered a kind of skyline. They also offered excellent targets for the sights of the Yankee gunboats. One of Grant's gunboat shells struck the courthouse dome like a bull's-eye and dropped through to the floor.

By the spring of 1863, Vicksburg was still a fortress, but an isolated one. Union forces had seized every other Confederate asset along the Mississippi River: Forts Donelson and Henry, Island Number Ten, New Orleans, Baton Rouge, and Natchez had all fallen. Vicksburg, 225 miles above New Orleans, was the last citadel and stronghold; take Vicksburg and the entire Mississippi River would be in Union control, and the Confederacy literally would be split in two.

Vicksburg was the key, Abraham Lincoln said. "The war can never be brought to a close until the key is in our pocket." The president of the Confederacy agreed, though in slightly different terms. "Vicksburg is the nail head that holds the South's two halves together," Jefferson Davis said.

This was why Grant had maneuvered so incessantly against the town, at one point even attempting to dig his way past it by canal. Grant's most trusted officers, like Sherman, had questioned the wisdom of his latest campaign: had any part of it failed, the Union army would have been cut off in enemy territory. "I tremble for the result," Sherman said. "I look upon the whole thing as one of the most hazardous and desperate moves of this or any other war." But Grant had presided over a series of successful maneuvers. Federal gunboats had made a daring river run past the Vicksburg guns to ferry troops, and his men had marched and fought their way two hundred miles through the Mississippi marshes, winning five pitched battles in seventeen days at Port Gibson, Raymond, Jackson, Champion Hill, and the Big Black River. By the afternoon of May 18, Sherman gazed across the heights at the so-called Gibraltar of the South, straight at the point where the men of Jones County were entrenched. He turned to Grant. "Until this moment I never thought your expedition a success," he said. "I never could see the end clearly until now."

The Confederate troops in Vicksburg had been dealt a series of backward-reeling blows, inexorably driven into the trenches. The state capitol at Jackson had been sacked, and Grant's young thirteen-year-old son Fred had rushed up the building steps hoping to grab a Confederate flag as a souvenir. Now a cordon of Union bluecoats seventy thousand strong was fatally encircling Vicksburg, inside of which Pemberton's troops were penned up, many of them disheartened after the series of defeats. They had streamed into town, "wan, hallow eyed, ragged, footsore, bloody . . . humanity in the last throes of endurance," one Vicksburg woman wrote. Trailing them were siege guns, ambulances, and wagons "in aimless confusion." A band played "Dixie" and "The Bonnie Blue Flag," but it sounded disconsolate.

For the next forty-five days the fate of Vicksburg obsessed all Southerners. The Confederates tended to blame their predicament on their commander, Pemberton, who, despite a beard of heroic length and curliness, had a reputation for placidity. One rebel officer said of him, "General Pemberton tried to do his best, but he was always doing nothing." But this was at least partly Southern bias: Pemberton's critics alternately suspected him of disloyalty and incompetence because he was by birth a Philadelphian. A West Pointer, he had betrayed his family when he acquiesced to his Virginia wife in joining the South, and he had two younger brothers in uniform for the Union. Perhaps the worst that could be said of Pemberton was that he tended to be paralyzed by intolerable conflicts. His vacillations were a result of contradicting orders and advice: his colleague General Joe Johnston suggested he abandon Vicksburg, while President Jeff Davis insisted he stay and fight. He had done all he could to fortify Vicksburg, and his biggest mistake was probably to invest too much hope in aid from Johnston, who had a force of about thirty thousand in northeast Mississippi but no feasible way of cutting through. Everyone in Vicksburg, led by Pemberton, continued to believe he would come to the rescue.

It was Pemberton's misfortune to face the most implacable, plainspoken, clear-minded, authoritative, bloodily businesslike commander of the entire war in Grant. This poorly groomed, stubble-jawed man, in his wrinkled, slump-shouldered uniform, had no discernible vanity or flamboyant feature of generalship. What he did possess was field vision, the ability to sense a weak point and go at it, and an unyielding willingness to fight for just as long as it took to win. After the first day's defeat at Shiloh, he had simply said through teeth gritted around a cigar, "We'll lick 'em tomorrow."

He was a myriad-natured man, a warrior who hated blood. He had shuddered as a boy at his father's tanning business and would only eat his meat well done. He could be cruel to opposing soldiers but couldn't stand to see beasts mistreated. He was a virtuoso horseman. His mount during the Vicksburg campaign was a creature named "Kangaroo," which he had rescued from the Shiloh battlefield when no one else had any use for the scarred, neglected animal. Grant recognized that under the mud and gore was a high-bred horse and nursed the animal back to form. He said of himself, "The truth is I am more of a farmer than a soldier." He was wrong. Grant would use bombardment, assaults, and finally famine-inducing siege over the next forty-five days in winning one of the most backbreaking victories of the war at Vicksburg.

Newton and the men of the 7th Mississippi Battalion were fully invested in their part of the trenchworks by 8:00 a.m. on May 18—just in time to receive one of Grant's crueler assaults. The Mississippians covered their heads from a series of artillery salvos, the opening of an attack straight at their position. They were smack in the center of Vicksburg's labyrinthine inner defenses, an interlacing series of fortified trenches, batteries, lunettes, redoubts, and redans that twisted through the gorges around the perimeter of town.

Newton and his mates hunkered down facing eastward, between the Jackson and Graveyard roads, and looked at Grant's headquarters across the ravines. Their entrenchments were fortified with sandbags, cotton bales, and logs. They stretched blankets overhead, not just for shade, but to screen the dirt that rained on their heads from the continual artillery blasts.

A Union soldier from Iowa climbed a hill and trained a spyglass on the Confederate entrenchments and described what he saw in his diary: "The rebels works seem to consist of a line of large hills which extend in a half circle around the city, they present a powerful view, hard to take by assault, on account of their abrupt ascent, and the felled timber in the ravine before them, at one place a large stockade is seen on the works built of timber 7 feet high and 3 feet in diameter."

Despite this perfectly lucid view of the elaborate fortifications that zigzagged along the hills, Grant decided to try an all-out assault, seeking a quick victory to end the long campaign. His hope was to dislodge the rebels before they got too comfortable, and he sensed that his men wouldn't be content until they had at least made an attempt to take the town, or so he later claimed. But he also may have been overconfident after two weeks of consecutive victories, "a little giddy with pride," as Sherman described the mood of the blue troops.

On May 19, Sherman sent a column of men massed six deep charging up the embankments at the dirt and log walls of the rebels. Yankee infantrymen scrambled through the gullies, heads low under steam-whistling projectiles of grape and canister. Somehow they maintained order, until they came within seventy yards of the trenches. Then the rebels on the front line, who had patiently held their fire, rose up and shouldered their rifles and fired a volley that flashed like lightning. The curtain of lead was so thick that one Union outfit reported fifty-five holes in its regimental flag. To Sherman, it looked as if men disappeared "as chaff thrown from the hand on a windy day." Bluecoats could only lie in ditches and ravines and hope not to catch bullets in the back. One group of Yankees was trapped in a no-man's-land gully full of cane, which was gradually cut down by bullets, the stalks "lopped gently upon us."

The fragmented companies of Yankees continued to try to scale the hills, as rebels unleashed more sheet-lightning musketry—as well as flaming bales of cotton and ignited balls of twelve-pound shot, which they rolled down the hills with fuses sizzling. Some of the Yankees fielded the cannon balls like sparking baseballs and tried to hurl them back into the ditches. The rebels won the homicidal game of catch. The makeshift grenades finally discouraged the Union side. Grant halted for the day with 934 casualties, while administering just 200 or so.

Grant, however, was undiscouraged; he seemed to think the attack failed merely because it wasn't large enough. Still convinced the Vicksburg defenses could be overwhelmed, he ordered a second assault for May 22, this one grander. It seemed to him the city might fall in a day; at most, "I would say one week."

The Yankees dreaded the prospect of another rush at the rebel barricades. On the evening before the engagement, an idealistic eighteen-year-old soldier in the 72nd Illinois named Anson Hemingway scribbled in his diary. Hemingway was a neatly combed, abstemious sort who devoted his free time to prayer meetings rather than drinking. Anson and his brother Rodney had enlisted in Company D of the 72nd Illinois Infantry when he was still a month short of his eighteenth birthday, and their older brother George was with the 18th Illinois Infantry. Both Rodney and George would die of disease before the war was over, and Anson, up to this point, had spent more time battling filth and chronic dysentery than rebels.

But now there seemed to Anson a pretty good chance he could die. "How I do wish this war would end," Anson wrote. "This place is very strongly fortified and it will cost a man a life to take it—but it must fall. We must take it." Anson would survive, to imbue his grandson Ernest with an obsession with physical courage and a penchant for war reporting.

At daybreak artillery barrages from two hundred Yankee guns began to blow cascades of dirt and flesh in the air. At 10:00 a.m. a Union detachment came down the graveyard road carrying ladders and planks to be used in the onslaught. This presaged a coordinated wave of forty thousand troops. Another Illinoisan, Charles E. Wilcox, waited taut with nerves under a rain of shell fragments for the order to advance. "Oh how my heart palpitated!" Wilcox wrote in his diary. "The sweat from off my face run in a stream from the tip ends of my whiskers. God only knows all that passed through my mind. Twice I exclaimed aloud, 'My God why don't they order us to charge.' "

Again the 7th Mississippi Battalion was in the way of the Yankee advance. For the next eight hours there was no letup in the fighting that roiled all around the hills. Flags were shredded into rags, and the corpses of men walled up. Yankees were forced to simply lie down in "a hail storm of bullets, shot and shell" and wait for a chance to crawl backward, while more cannonballs with burning fuses rolled down upon them.

Some Yankees survived the uphill rushes only to keel over dead of sunstroke. After three failed dashes, Sherman said, "This is murder; order those troops back." This time Grant's casualties were 3,199, to just 500 or so for the Confederates—he had lost almost as many men in three days as he had in the previous three weeks. "This last attack only served to increase our casualties without giving any benefit whatever," he admitted. There would be no more assaults.

For the next three days, Newton and the men of Jones County sat in their stifling trenches, kerchiefs over their faces, trying not to retch or faint from the stench of the putrefying dead, visible just yards away, bloated and sun blackened and crawling with white maggots. At last Grant and Pemberton agreed to a truce to collect the dead. At 6:00 p.m. on May 25 men of both sides came out from their trenches, and for the next two hours they did the gruesome job of burying the dead, also pausing to trade news, greet old friends, swap coffee and tobacco, or search for kin fighting for the other side. Some men even played cards. "I saw my old chum, the friend of my boyhood, the best friend I ever had coming from the rebel works," one man wrote. ". . . I had a long talk with him. He seems to be a staunch rebel. God save him."

With the field cleared, the rebel soldiers returned to their rifle pits and settled down to a steady routine of digging, ducking fire, and suffering. Soldiers and civilians alike burrowed into the hills like moles, trying to escape the continual gusts of jagged metal from hundreds of pieces of artillery and gunboats offshore. Since Grant could not storm the town by force, he resolved to bombard and shovel his way there. The Yankees stabbed at the earth with picks and spades, tunneling toward the Confederate lines and laying charges that blew through the sand and clay hills. As they dug and detonated ever closer to the rebel fortifications, the Southerners had to toil around the clock to raise their own works. Vicksburg began to resemble a gigantic swarming anthill.

When men weren't moving earth, they encamped in shebangs, hollowed-out holes in the steep embankments covered with planked roofs and blankets. It was oven hot in the trenches, but a man who stood up to get a breath of air risked being riddled by Minié balls from sharpshooters; Union snipers fired as many as 150 rounds daily. There was nothing to do but dig and then lay still as the sweat rolled off their bodies. "Have nothing to do but eat, sleep, read, walk about, talk and dodge rebel bullets," one Yankee wrote in his diary. "I feel dirty and lazy."

Night was hardly any cooler, and artillery continued to boom and shriek through the dark. There was no safe rear area in which to hide from the fire. One Illinois unit sought shelter behind a stately manor on a hill outside of town and had just put a pot of beans on for their dinner when a stray fragment flew shrilly into the campsite—and landed in the kettle, blowing it into the ground. "Boys, your beans have gone to hell," a cook said.

Civilians took refuge in black-mouthed siege caves that honeycombed the bluffs. The hills were so pockmarked with holes "that the streets look like avenues in a cemetery," a Vicksburger observed. The caves were stifling and plagued by mosquitoes and snakes. Those who tried to stay in their homes risked being atomized or buried under collapsed walls, as formerly fine residences were battered into slack-roofed ruins. Sidewalks buckled and the sky continually rained a fine mist of stone, plaster, splintered glass, and wood. "We are utterly cut off from the world, surrounded by a circle of fire," one Vicksburg woman wrote in her diary. ". . . People do nothing but eat what they can get, sleep when they can, and dodge the shells."

On Sundays, chaplains conducted religious services and tried to preach over the screaming of shot and shell. There were just three intervals when the murderous bedlam stopped, to cool the guns and feed the artillerymen, at 8:00 a.m., noon, and 8:00 p.m.

The soldiers passed the time by trying to identify the caliber of shells that passed over them from the pitch of their whistling. "That's a mortar shell," someone would say. "There goes a Parrott. No, that's a rifle shell." They played varieties of card games, mostly poker, and began wagering hugely out of pent-up boredom. "Whether we lost or won was of little consequence," one soldier wrote. "This sport soon grew stale and one could pick up $20 and $50 bills anywhere in camp."

There were times during the daily bombardments when the hot air, mixed with smoke, made it difficult to breathe, and men passed out. The Union forces tunneled so close to the 7th Mississippi Battalion lines that men in opposite trenches could hear one another conversing. On June 25, Union mines packed with 2,200 pounds of explosives blew up the Louisiana Redan, a giant fortification near the 7th Mississippi Battalion. It ripped a hole forty feet wide and thirteen feet deep.

Corpses floated by in the Mississippi, fish gnawing at them. Malaria and dysentery set in, and so did inflation. A barrel of flour sold for six hundred dollars. A Vicksburg wife noted in her diary, "I think all the dogs and cats must be killed or starved, we don't see any more of the pitiful animals prowling around." The **Daily Citizen,** the town newspaper, published under increasing difficulty as supplies dwindled. On May 28 it was printed on a strip of paper a foot and a half long and six inches wide. By June 18 it was printed on strips of wallpaper.

Mule meat became a staple. In one Confederate encampment, men amused themselves by drawing up a faux restaurant menu on a scrap of paper. They labeled it "Hotel De Vicksburg, Bill of Fare for July, 1863" and accompanied it with a sketch of a mule's head, with a knife poised above it:

Soup
Mule Tail

Boiled
Mule bacon with poke greens
Mule ham canvassed

Roast
Mule sirloin
Mule rump stuffed with rice

Vegetables
Peas and rice

Entrees
Mule Head stuffed a-la-Mode
Mule Beef jerked a-la-Mexicana
Mule ears fricassed a-la-gotch
Mule side stewed, new style, hair on

Mule spare ribs plain
Mule liver, hashed

Side dishes
Mule salad
Mule hoof soused
Mule brains a-la-omelette
Mule kidney stuffed with peas
Mule tripe fried in pea meal batter
Mule tongue cold a-la-Bray.

Jellies
Mule foot.

Pastry
Pea meal pudding, blackberry sauce
Cotton-wood berry pies
China berry tart.

Dessert.
White-oak acorns
Beech nuts.
Blackberry leaf tea
Genuine Confederate Coffee.

Liquors
Mississippi Water, vitage of 1498, superior, $3.00
Limestone Water, Late Importation, very fine, $2.75
Spring Water, Vicksburg Brand, $1.50

Meals at all hours. Gentlemen to wait upon themselves. Any inattention on the part of the servants will be promptly reported at the office. Jeff. Davis & Co., Proprietors.

Union soldiers discovered the menu after the surrender while wandering through the town. It was published in the **Chicago Tribune** and also picked up for Confederate audiences by **Southern Punch** magazine, which added the feeling comment, "The most melancholy thing about it is the reflection which must suggest to a thoughtful Yankee—if there be such an animal—on the prospect of conquering men who can live and jest on such fare."

But by the end of June, even mule steak became scarce. The rebels' daily food issue fell to a quarter pound of bacon, a bit of rice flour, and a twelfth of a quart of peas. Some men saved their rations and fasted for a day, so as to have a larger portion when they did eat. With no cornmeal, cooks ground the peas into a powder and tried baking it into bread. Men choked on the peabread, which tasted like green dust.

Soon there was no longer anything recognizable as food to be had. Rats appeared in the stalls of the town market dressed as meat. John Ellzey, who served with Newton in the 7th Mississippi Battalion, recalled that the men were so desperate they ate the rats and even tried to make soup from boiled shoestrings. Men were so emaciated that "one would believe them dead lying down," wrote an observer.

The soldiers neared a state of mass insubordination and issued an **"appeal for help"** to Pemberton on June 28. "Our rations have been cut down to one biscuit and a small bit of bacon per day, not enough scarcely to keep soul and body together, much less to stand the hardships we are called upon to stand . . . Self-preservation is the first law of nature, and hunger will compel a man to do almost anything. You had better heed a warning voice, though it is the voice of private soldiers: This army is now ripe for mutiny, unless it can be fed."

Pemberton briefly considered trying to cut his way out of Vicksburg. But when he surveyed his officers as to the condition of the men, he received a series of angry replies: the troops were no longer capable of walking, much less fighting. "This inability on the part of the soldiers does not arise from want of spirit, or courage, or willingness to fight," wrote Newton's brigade commander, Louis Hébert, "but from real physical disability, occasioned by the men having been so long shut up and cramped up in pits, ditches, &c., in the trenches; many are also in ill-health, who still are able to remain in the works. The unanimous opinion of my officers I fully concur in, and I unhesitatingly declare that it is my sincere conviction that, so far as my brigade is concerned, it cannot undergo the marches and fatigues of an evacuation. The spirit of my men to fight is unbroken, but their bodies are worn out."

After forty-eight days, Pemberton was out of options. Pemberton officially contacted Grant, offering to discuss terms of surrender. "Gentlemen, I have done what I could," he told his officers. An Iowa private observed that there were two good generals at Vicksburg, "General Grant and General Starvation." On July 3, the shelling stopped. The battle was over.

On the morning of July 4, Vicksburg was strangely quiet save for the crying of a baby that had been born in the caves. A handful of soldiers in blue came up a street. Then a whole group of them gathered on the courthouse hill, "and the flag began to slowly rise to the top of the staff." As the Stars and Stripes unfurled over the city, larger columns from the blue army began to file through the streets. "What a contrast to the suffering creatures we had seen so long were these stalwart, well-fed men, so splendidly set up and accoutered," wrote a female resident. "Sleek horses, polished arms, bright plumes."

As more Union troops entered Vicksburg, the eerie silence continued. It was the first time in almost two months that the Union guns were quiet. Despite the victory and Independence Day, Grant's men were not celebrating. They were too shocked at the conditions of soldiers and citizens in Vicksburg, and relieved that the long siege was over.

The Yankee troops had spent more than a year conquering "a country where nearly all the people, except the negroes, were hostile to us and friendly to the cause we were trying to suppress," as Grant noted. But instead of victorious gloating, there was only "a feeling of sadness among the Union soldiers at seeing the dejection of their late antagonists," Grant wrote. Union boats arrived with supplies at the wharves, and starved Southerners rushed down and carried away goods in both arms.

Grant allowed the malnourished rebs to draw federal rations. "Very few of them could walk without aid twenty rods," observed a Yankee soldier. ". . . The hip bones of some of them had worn through the skin, and their bodies were a mass of sores caused by the vermin." They were so lice and scurvy ridden that every article of their clothes would have to be burned.

In Washington, Lincoln greeted the news of Vicksburg's surrender with such intense relief that he rose and threw an arm around his secretary of the navy, Gideon Welles. "I cannot in words tell you my joy over this result," he said. "It is great, Mr. Welles; it is great." There would be two more years of war ahead, but the key was in his pocket. As he later wrote, "The Father of Waters flows unvexed to the sea again." Grant's victory had secured the Mississippi River and cut the South in two. "Grant is my man, and I am his the rest of the war," Lincoln declared.

Those Southern soldiers who still had the energy to feel something other than hunger were furious with Pemberton. Confederate casualties for the entire campaign were 9,091 killed and wounded, and there were nearly 30,000 prisoners garrisoned in the town. The brigade in which Newton and the 7th Mississippi Battalion served had lost 203 killed and 480 wounded. One Confederate soldier said to a Vicksburg woman who had endured the siege, "A child would have known better than to shut up men in this cursed trap to starve to death like useless vermin. Haven't I seen my friends carted out three or four in a box, that had died of starvation! Nothing else madam! Starved to death because we had a fool for a general."

The scarecrow Confederates of Vicksburg stacked arms—among the booty Grant captured were 172 cannon and sixty thousand muskets and rifles—and sat wearily down to wait for parole. There were simply too many prisoners for Grant to guard and feed them all. The job of transporting thirty thousand captured Confederates north to prison camps would tie up every transportation route and his whole army. Instead, Grant and Pemberton negotiated terms: the prisoners would take oaths pledging not to bear arms against the Union and report to a parole camp at Enterprise, Mississippi, to await exchange. The parolees could only return to fighting if the Confederacy released an equal number of Union prisoners.

Grant doubted many of the parolees would ever fight again, for they were too starved and disenchanted. "I knew many of them were tired of the war and would get home just as soon as they could," Grant wrote. He suspected that turning thirty thousand disaffected men loose on the Mississippi countryside might sow dissension and be a larger problem for the Confederacy than if he transported them to prison camps.

Parole was a risky policy and so controversial that a delegation of Washington officials called on Lincoln to demand Grant's dismissal for dereliction of duty. They believed the terms were too generous and the

South would violate the parole terms by reconstituting Pemberton's army and putting it back in the field. (In fact, the Confederacy would soon issue a call to the paroled men to return to their units, in violation of the agreement.)

But Lincoln defended his general and offered as a counterargument a country story about a dog. His audience listened, baffled, as Lincoln meandered through the tale of a man he once knew named Sykes, who had a yellow dog. Sykes set great store by the dog, but it was intensely disliked by the other local boys. They despised the beast so much, in fact, that they connived a way to kill it: they wrapped an explosive cartridge in a piece of meat and attached a long fuse to it. They whistled for the dog, and it dutifully wolfed down the meat and cartridge, at which point they touched off the fuse, blowing the dog up. When Sykes saw the remains of the animal, he picked up the tail and said, "Well, I guess he'll never be much account again—as a dog." At that point Lincoln paused in his telling of the story and then delivered his own punch line. "I guess Pemberton's forces will never be much account again, as an army," he said.

The parolees of Vicksburg would act as explosive cartridges in the stomach of the Confederacy. As Grant predicted, scores of men simply walked away. They tired of sitting in the hot sun or standing in long lines for the tedious paperwork of parole, which was slowed by the fact that many men couldn't read or write. Newton's cousin Ben Knight, who served in Company B of the 7th Mississippi Battalion, received his official parole on July 10, as did Jesse Davis Knight's son John Melton Knight, a corporal who was wounded and in a field hospital. Others didn't wait for papers.

Several hundred Southerners refused to sign their paroles at all, saying they preferred to go north as prisoners rather than be sent back to fight again. Others hid or "kept out of the way," according to Grant, to avoid being counted. Pemberton twice asked Grant for arms, to guard his own men to prevent them from deserting. Grant refused. Deserting, he wrote, "was precisely what I expected and hoped that they would do."

Newton and the other men began breaking ranks, even though Pemberton ordered them to remain with their companies. Almost to a man, the rank and file blamed Pemberton for starving them, and many of them vowed never again to serve under him. Men in tattered dun uniforms melted into the ravines and headed home, never to return to the ranks, despite repeated Confederate orders.

Among them was Newton. On his next muster roll, for the period of June 30 to October 31, 1863, he was listed as "absent without leave." He was just one among thousands. A total of thirty-nine men from Company F alone—more than half—would go AWOL. Not all of them were disloyal; just because a man walked away didn't mean he was sympathetic to Grant's army. Desertion did not necessarily make a man Unionist or mean that he identified with the United States of America and its new slave emancipation policies. Even some of the most loyal men went AWOL in the post-Vicksburg chaos: the secessionist John M. Baylis, for instance, temporarily lost his will to fight after his brother Wyatt, an officer with Company B of the 7th Battalion, died of wounds at Vicksburg. Baylis was absent from July until the following November, when he finally returned to uniform.

But the woods also swarmed with men like Newton, who had turned their backs once and for all on the Cause. Newton would not fight for the Confederacy again; instead, he would only fight against it. A measure of his Unionism was a ballad of the Civil War (not a very good one) he composed that ended with Grant as the hero and victor: "General Van Dorn was a warrior too. / He was superiored by General Lee. / Gen. Van Dorn and Gen. Price too / Both lost their ranks when they met of Gen. Grant."

From Vicksburg onward, Newton clearly considered himself an ally of Grant and the Union army. It was as if he had decided, like Lincoln, "Grant is my man, and I am his the rest of the war."

Letter from Captain Walter Rorer, 20th Mississippi Infantry, CSA, to His Cousin

We are almost entirely without tents. I do not think the history of the world can show as many lives sacrificed in any war, as have already been sacrificed in this, and so little accomplished, and all of this terrible sacrifice has been made, not so much by ignorance and incompetence on the battlefield, and we all know it has been terrible enough there, but by carelessness and indifference and a most criminal incompetence of our officers.

FOUR

The Hounds

September 1863, Countryside
Surrounding Vicksburg

War destroyed all that was familiar
to Mississippians; it collapsed the old cer-
tainties like bricks and boards and altered the physical
profiles of things into narcotic-seeming visions. In a
clearing outside of Vicksburg, an elegant bedstead sat
on a fine carpet on the grass, accompanied by a table
and chairs. The eerie outdoor room was the work of
a Yankee officer, who dragged the furnishings from a
deserted plantation. "I have a magnificent parlor here
in the woods," he wrote in his diary, as if it were an
everyday occurrence to sleep on a feather mattress in
a swamp.

The capital of Jackson was a barely recognizable
heap of ruins nicknamed "Chimneyville" by its resi-

dents for the rows of burned-out lots where nothing was left standing but chimneys. Newly elected governor Charles Clark, a planter who had lost the use of a leg at Shiloh, advocated mass suicide over defeat as if it were a reasonable proposition. Better to drown in the cobalt waters of the Gulf than surrender to Yankees and let Negroes invert society, suggested Clark, eminent in his gray broadcloth.

"Humbly submit yourselves to our hated foes, and they will offer you a reconstructed Constitution providing for the confiscation of your property, the immediate emancipation of your slaves and the elevation of the black race to a position of equality, aye, of superiority, that will make them your masters and rulers," Clark threatened. "Rather than such base submission, such ruin and dishonor, let the last of our young men die upon the field of battle, and when none are left to wield a blade or uphold our banner, then let our old men, our women and children, like the remnant of the heroic Pascagoulas, when their braves were slain, join hands together, march into the sea and perish beneath its waters"

But such suicidal grandiosity hardly helped those Mississippians such as Newton who wished to survive, nor did it help Clark cope with the more tedious and inglorious emergencies he faced as governor in the fall of 1863. Federal flags now flew over Corinth, Natchez, and Vicksburg, from which the Yankees could ravage the state's interior. Clark and the legislature were continually forced to flee for safety, from Meridian, to Columbus, to Enterprise, to Macon.

The cotton speculator and future governor James Lusk Alcorn described what one raid did to his region. The Yankees "made sad havoc on their march; burnt old man Shelby's gun house also Hulls—and Hatchez—burnt all Hull's fence, killed most of his stock, took all that they had left, clothes, bedding, burnt all his doors, broke out his window sash, and burnt two of his cabins . . . they broke all that fine furniture and threw it in the yard, searched the house and robbed it of ten thousand dollars in money . . . They took off about twenty of Hill's negros, and killed a great amount of the stock."

As the Vicksburg survivors made their way through the region, they came across odd drifting scraps of paper. These were the bits and pieces of Jefferson Davis's collection of books and papers, shredded by the Yankee victors. A slave named Alfred led hundreds of Northern soldiers to the plantation where "Old Jeff's" furniture, books, and wine were cached. For two consecutive days they took special pleasure in ransacking and wrecking the property of the Confederate president, until the flotsam floated through the woods for miles. Troopers stabbed at the volumes with the points of their bayonets "as often as they could find a piece of paper large enough to receive the point of a knife," a caretaker wrote to Davis. When the frenzy was finally over, the Yankees rode away with hacked-up pieces of Davis's carpets as saddle blankets and pieces of his curtains for tents.

To Major Walter Rorer of the 20th Mississippi Regiment, surreptitiously patrolling the area on horseback, it was as if all of society had been flipped upside down. Rorer was a fine example of an antebellum Mississippian, literate and valorous, a successful sawmill owner from Aberdeen who entered the army as a captain and rose in rank to lieutenant colonel, second officer of the regiment. He'd fought like a lion at the battle of Raymond, trying to halt Grant's progress toward Vicksburg, for which he was cited for gallantry. "He was continually going up and down the line encouraging and directing the men as though no death messengers were nigh, exhibiting that noble daring and eminent tact which has rendered him so dear to every man in the regiment," according to a report.

Rorer thought he was beyond shock, but what he saw when he rode out to survey the countryside under Yankee dominion gave him pause. He described his observations in a series of letters to a Virginia cousin. "I think any man would prefer death to such a life as many of those live who are left within enemy lines," he wrote. "Every thing is taken from them before their eyes and given to their Negroes or taken by the soldiers, ladies dresses are given to Negro women, Negro men are dressed in Yankee uniform and formally mustered into the Service of the United States in the presence of their masters, and those families who are stripped of everything are limited to one suit of clothes and a daily ration that is issued to them by the federal commissary. It is a very wealthy country between the two rivers (Big Black and Yazoo) and some who were once worth a million are now worth nothing."

Rorer's sense of disorientation grew when he visited his home in Aberdeen on furlough in August, in the wake of the Vicksburg defeat. The passenger trains were so crowded with fleeing civilians that Rorer couldn't get a seat, so he hopped a freight train instead. He arrived eight miles from Aberdeen at dark, borrowed a mule from an acquaintance, and made his sad, plodding way toward town.

> I arrived before ordinary bedtime, but I could not hear a sound or see a light, the town seemed almost a city of the dead, I rode along the deserted streets to the principal hotel, the streets are brown and beautifully shaded; but their appearance made me sad indeed; arrived at the hotel, I found nothing but a Negro asleep on a bench, I roused him up, but he was a strange Negro and did not know me. The old hotel, that had been a home to so many of us, had changed owners and was almost deserted, the joyous crowd that once thronged its halls, will be seen there no more, they lie dead on a thousand battlefields. I do not know when I ever felt more depressed . . . the absence of all the familiar sounds, and being in the midst of an almost deserted city at night, is enough to inspire sad thoughts at any time, and more particularly when our beloved country is bleeding, as it were, at every pore.

But Newton had little sympathy for planters who bemoaned their lost world or were plundered by Yankees. Rebel forces were perpetrating equally savage violence on the countryside, if not worse. Union troops patrolling the Louisiana side of the Mississippi River were aghast to find that rebel raiders had slain or set fire to everything in their path that might be put to use—including the slaves, who were shot or burned alive to prevent them from defecting. A Yankee cavalry commander reported,

> The rebel atrocities committed the day before were such as the pen fails to record in proper language. They spared neither age, sex, nor condition. In some instances the negroes were shut up in their quarters, and literally roasted alive. The charred remains found in numerous instances testified to a degree of fiendish atrocity . . . Young children, only five or six years of age, were found skulking in the canebrake pierced with wounds, while helpless women were found shot down in the most inhuman manner. The whole country was destroyed, and every sign of civilization was given to the flames.

With both sides determined to starve and burn the other out, swaths of the state were destitute, and yeoman families like Newton's were caught squarely in the middle. Corn was up to four dollars a bushel and far beyond the means of soldiers' families.

Newton's wife, Serena, was on the brink of starvation and struggling to feed her children. She moved through an endless ring of chores on the Knight farm, a circuit of heavy manual labor from field to storehouse to smokehouse to corncrib. When a fence rail broke, there was no one to mend it for her. When the livestock strayed, there was no one to help her search it out. She wielded the heavy ax herself, yoked the animals, and drove the heavy plow. Night brought no relief from work, for once the children were asleep she sat up late at the spinning wheel, or shelled corn, or darned and laundered their fraying clothes.

Her continual physical exhaustion was compounded by anxieties—over what weather might do to her meager crops, whether she would be able to feed and clothe the children for another month, whether Newton would come home safely. Things began to wear out, with no way to replace them. Without Newton to tan, there were no new shoes. Pieces of farm equipment broke, with no way for her to fix them.

Serena wasn't just tired; she was beset by loneliness. Her spirituality gave her some solace, but it became impractical to go to church. The farm animals needed a rest from farm work, so travel was just too difficult. Church attendance had dropped all over the state, as families lost their mules and horses to the Confederacy. "The ways of Zion languish and mourn," wrote the Mississippi Synod. "Pastors are parted from their flocks, God's worship interrupted or forbidden, while from many churches God's people are exiled sheep scattered without their shepherd."

All in all, Serena probably endured as many hardships as Newton himself. At least as a Confederate conscript he'd had fellowship, something to eat, clothes to wear. His wife did not even have that much. Serena's only company was a household full of needy children, none of whom were old enough to help her.

Nor could she expect any sympathy or support from the Confederate government. The bureaucracy was oblivious if not outright hostile to her deprivations; it expected her to sew flags and garments for the army and turn over her foodstuff and cloth without complaint, at risk of being labeled treasonous herself. Another yeoman wife, this one in North Carolina, summed up the state of women like Serena in a letter to her governor beseeching him for relief.

> I set down to rite you afew lins and pray to god that you will oblige me i ame apore woman with a posel of little children and i wil hav to starv or go neked me and my little children if my husban is kep a way from home much longer . . . i beg you to let him come . . . i have knit 40 pare of socks fo the sogers and it take all i can earn to get bread . . . if you cud hear the crys of my little children i think you wod fell for us i am pore in this world but i trust rich in heven i trust in god . . . and hope he will Cos you to have compashion on the pore.

Instead of aid from the government, Serena received only harassment, or worse. The rebel officers who came hunting Newton may have physically abused her—it was not uncommon—when they didn't ransack her storehouse or ruin her crops. Women who refused to tell the whereabouts of their men sometimes found themselves knocked to the ground with rifle butts. Her Confederate neighbors also deliberately set out to ruin her, as revenge for being married into a Unionist family. Even when Serena did have corn, she often could not find anyone to mill it for her, because Confederates ran the gins.

The brutally punishing attitude of rebels toward a Unionist spouse was reflected by the experience of one Alabama yeoman's wife, who was left to cope with persecution in her local community after her husband escaped to the federal lines. She was set upon by Confederate soldiers, who tossed her spinning wheel, dresser, and dishes in the yard "as far as they could throw them." They yelled at her "that her god dam'd Yankee husband had escaped from their prison and had gone to the Yanks."

With the river ports and market towns in the hands of the Yankees, lines of wagons moved toward them, full of hungry yeoman wives, so desperate they were willing to defy Confederate law to trade goods. William L. Nugent's cavalry unit caught a half dozen weathered farm women attempting to reach Union lines in hopes of bartering for needed supplies. They had traveled one hundred miles with a single bale of cotton in each wagon. The Confederates confiscated their meager goods and imprisoned two of them. To Nugent, who wrote about the incident to his own refined young wife, they seemed unwashed slatterns.

Think of a female with the dirty colored tobacco streak around her mouth & on her lips, squirting discolored spittle all around her . . . you must, though, add to the pitiable picture a tousled head, unwashed face, drabbled dress, (no corsets) heavy shoes, a guffaw laugh, and sidelong leer. A dirty baby, too, is no infrequent addition to the scene . . . We have two of these women in the Guard House for practicing their tory principles and keeping our people in dread. The Yankees have unhinged things terribly here.

But nothing unhinged Mississippi like desertion. Against this mural of ruin, Newton and his fellow Johnnies, bedraggled in clothing stained the color of dirt, staggered home from Vicksburg. Deserters swarmed over the state, until in some counties, blacks found that the woods were "so full of runaway white men that there was no room for them."

Grant had made a shrewd decision to accept surrender with parole. As he predicted, the released and disillusioned soldiers became a crisis for the rebel army: a month after Vicksburg fewer than fifteen hundred of thirty thousand had reported for duty. All across the South, in Alabama, Florida, and Louisiana, men were missing from their units. In Mississippi, there were at least five thousand deserters, stragglers, and absentees, according to an inspecting officer for the Conscription Bureau. Men were leaving the rebel army faster than they were being rounded up, the officer noted with alarm.

The Confederate high command did its part to transform these parolees into disloyals. Amazingly and perhaps intentionally, the Confederate staff lost the official parole rolls. The high command used this as an excuse to violate the parole agreement and began attempts to force men back into the ranks whether or not they had been exchanged. For many soldiers, despair turned into open rebellion. Thousands of poor whites followed Newton Knight and became self-described Unionists.

Many of them went home to rural counties to find disaffection had already set in there. Reports of armed bands of deserters resisting Confederate authority had been pouring into the Mississippi governor's office since the spring of 1863: Scott, Lawrence, Leake, and Marion counties all requested military aid to deal with the festering issue. In Simpson County, a band of twenty-five deserters busted out of the local jail and attacked citizens who had aided in capturing them. A similar account came from Gainesville, a town on the banks of the Pearl River in Hancock County, where deserters were so resistant that local authorities couldn't confront them "without endangering their lives." One man who lent his horse for an action against the deserters was "severely beaten and brused," a Confederate official complained, adding, "It is not safe for any officer to ride through the country alone not knowing what minute that he may be waylaid and shot down from the wayside."

Newton was not the only man in Jones who swore

he would rather die than rejoin the Confederate army again. A large band of seventy-five to one hundred or so deserters already prowled through the thickets of the county, with hundreds more lurking deeper in the swamps, led by Jasper Collins and his brothers. The men loosely cooperated in evading Confederate authorities and filched supplies from the homes of loyal rebels. Their presence provoked a typical letter to the governor, this one sent on June 1, 1863, from Company K of the 8th Mississippi Infantry. The men of Company K, known as the "Ellisville Invincibles," were the most zealous Confederates in Jones, battle-tested veterans who had fought at Perryville. They were incensed at the reports of shirking and thieving they received from home and requested special duty to go back and round up the absentees. Second Lieutenant Harmon Mathis informed the governor that he and his men "all are desirous of being detached to Jones County, Miss. for the purpose of apprehending [and] arresting a body of deserters now lurking in said county . . . there is between seventy-five and one hundred deserters who are lying out in the swamps and prowling from house to house stealing everything they can get their hands on."

The desertion problem had begun even before Vicksburg, but it bloomed into a perpetual crisis after. Why did deserters risk dishonor, imprisonment, and even execution rather than go back? The plain fact is that without conviction to carry a man, service in the Southern army was insufferable. Living in a swamp was in some ways preferable. It wasn't just the ordeal of combat, it was the Southern soldier's everyday existence, of comfortless exhaustion, chronic exposure, pauper's pay, and rancid diet, and all of it enforced by tyranny from above.

There was no soap, and clothing rotted on their bodies from living outdoors; men didn't change shirts for weeks at a time. Uniforms were worn so threadbare it became a source of joking. "In this army, one hole in the seat of the breeches indicates a captain, two holes is a lieutenant, and the seat of the pants all out indicates that the individual is a private," a Confederate wrote. Overcoats and blankets were so hard to find after the first year of the war that men cut holes in pieces of scavenged carpet and slipped them over their heads for warmth. It was an army that went everywhere on foot, and yet by the winter of 1863 reports of shoeless men leaving smears of blood on the ground came from all over the service.

What clothes they did have swarmed with lice— one soldier described standing over a fire and hearing them pop like corn. Men tried turning their shirts inside out, which they called "executing a flank movement," but they were never free of pests, which in turn made them sick. Measles disabled men as often as bullets.

Camp life was spiritually desolate as well as physically debilitating. Regiments flattened everything in their path; each stopping place became an indistinct landscape with trees hacked down for miles, the ground deadened, the grass browned and gouged by boots and hooves into a sepia expanse, atop which shabby tented villages sprouted. Men turned foul tempered and hard-hearted, their only diversions gambling, drinking, and fighting. "You have no idea how demoralizing camp life is and how difficult it is for one to preserve his consistency of life and his inward purity of heart," the cavalryman Nugent wrote home. "Oaths, blasphemies, imprecations, obscenity are hourly ringing in your ears until your mind is almost filled with them."

Every soldier in the Confederacy understood the impulse to go AWOL, just for relief from the physical discomfort. Certainly the thought of desertion occurred to Nugent, whose wife and baby were now behind Grant's enemy lines in the town of Greenville on the banks of the Mississippi River. Nugent's once-fanciful feeling that he would "like to shoot a Yankee" had curdled into a hard realism and conviction that war was sacrilege. "God grant I may never see another war and never participate in one! Blood, butchery, death, desolation, robbery, rapine, selfishness, violence, wrong: a disregard for everything holy or divine, and a disposition to destroy," he wrote to his wife. All that prevented Nugent from bolting was what bound all men to their units, in all wars: responsibility to the soldier next to him and fear of disgrace. Nugent may have been tempted and even entreated to come home, but he wrote to his wife that he couldn't leave the army "without being everlastingly dishon-

ored and disgraced, thus involving you & my innocent little babe in my own personal ruin."

As a wealthier member of the officer class, Nugent
could at least purchase comforts. For the yeoman and
foot soldier, there was no such relief. Their pay of just
eleven dollars a month in near-worthless Confederate scrip was six months in arrears, and the disparity
between their circumstances and the perceived advantages of the officers was yet another factor that bred
thoughts of disloyalty, especially when the high command seemed insensible to the hardships of soldiers
on the ground. Some senior officers had a shameless
habit of dining luxuriously and staging gaieties while
their men suffered. "The General officers are all the
time giving their attention to parties, balls &c and
neglect their troops," Nugent wrote. Rorer of the 20th
Mississippi made the same observation from his camp
in Canton, Mississippi, in November of 1863. "Parties
and balls are quite the rage here at present. I am rather
at a loss to know how people can reconcile it to themselves to spend their time in gayety and dissipation as
many of them are doing . . . Our Army here is cursed
with incompetent and drunken officers, yet there is
no way to get rid of them."

The men in the ranks clearly resented their condition, and they made their complaints plainly au-
dible to Rorer during a parade drill that was viewed
by the ladies of Canton. As they marched, Rorer
heard a number of them ill-temperedly snarl that the
organdy-clad belles "had better be at home knitting

socks for the army." From that he inferred that many of them needed socks.

Officer incompetence manifested itself in senseless marching, a source of the bitterest complaints. One cavalry unit from Jones County was marched and countermarched so brutally in the fall of 1863 that a man died. The outfit was sent in pursuit of Union raiders who had torn up the Mobile and Ohio Railroad and spent three days and nights tramping in sleet and rain, with no cover, from Okolona to Oxford to northern Tennessee. "We had no shelter at all: just stayed outside the town by open fires," the cavalryman recalled. "Newt Bryant, from Old Sharon Church in Jones County, froze to death . . . We had marched all day in the sleet. When we stopped for the night he was so tired that he went off and went to sleep on some cotton seed and froze."

Next they were shipped to Selma, Alabama, packed so densely in boxcars that the men who couldn't fit inside were ordered to ride on the tops of the trains. They had to lie down flat and hold tight to keep from slipping off the edges, while sleet mixed with cinders flew into their faces and burned their eyes. At Selma, they were loaded onto a passenger steamship en route to Montgomery. One night a man slipped overboard in his sleep and had to be abandoned because it was too dark for a rescue effort. They assumed he had drowned, but he turned up a day later wet and barefoot. His messmates told him he'd let a perfect opportunity to desert go by. "Why in hell didn't you go home?" they asked him. "Everybody thought you were dead!"

Home beckoned to every man in the ranks, often via a letter from a destitute wife pleading for help, yet furloughs were granted so sparingly they were almost nonexistent. Men longed for home to the point that they actually wished to be struck by a Minié ball. A foot soldier wanted to be wounded "just severely enough to send me home for 60 or 90 days, I would kindly welcome such a bullet and consider the Yankee who fired it as a good fellow." A story circulated of a soldier who stood behind a tree during a pitched battle and waved his arms up and down, hoping to catch a bullet. When an officer asked him what he was doing, he supposedly replied, "I'm feeling for a furlough."

Desertion was the ultimate furlough. Among the hundreds of men lurking with Newton in the Jones County swamps was one deserter who feigned his own death to get out of the army. He cut his fingers with a knife, rubbed blood on his saddle, shot a hole through his hat, and left his horse with the saddle on. He would stay with Knight and the other men until the war ended.

Confederate authorities were not insensible to the reasons for desertion; they understood it was a problem with myriad causes and no easy solution. But by August, a month after Vicksburg, as it was apparent that large numbers of AWOL men had no intention of coming back, the high command also realized the scale of the problem. It would clearly weaken the war effort if it wasn't resolved—in addition to Vicksburg, awful casualties at Gettysburg and Port Hudson that summer had left a critical shortage of Southern troops.

They responded with a dual approach. First, they invited the missing men with pardons. Next, they started shooting them. On August 5, 1863, Jefferson Davis announced a twenty-day amnesty period: all men who reported back for duty could do so with no penalty. But those who failed to report within that window would do so at peril of execution. By the fall, firing squads were causing comment in rebel units.

In September, a Confederate surgeon witnessed nine executions in a single day in Virginia. The surgeon noted that among those sentenced to death was a soldier who had lost his willingness to fight after reading anti-Confederate newspaper articles. "He was a very intelligent man and gave as his reason for deserting that the editorials in the Raleigh 'Standard' had convinced him that Jeff Davis was a tyrant and that the Confederat cause was wrong. I am surprised that the editor of that miserable little journal is allowed to go at large. It is most unfortunate that this thing of shooting men for desertion was not begun sooner. Many lives would have been saved by it, because a great many men will now have to be shot before the trouble can be stopped."

But executions hardly were a solution to the manpower crisis, and Confederate authorities sought a middle way. The Volunteer and Conscript Bureau under Brigadier General Gideon Pillow was empowered to hunt absentees and march them back to duty at gunpoint. If nothing else, this would give Pillow something to do. Owner of one of the wealthiest estates in Tennessee, called "Clifton Place," Pillow was a near cartoon of arrogance and ineptitude. As a major general in Mexico he'd fought with gusto but took credit for battles he did not win and was rumored to be so unwitting that he dug a trench on the wrong side of a parapet. Grant considered him a buffoon, and in fact it was Pillow's presence at Fort Donelson that convinced Grant to storm it and win his first great victory of the war. Grant had known Pillow in Mexico and "judged that with any force, no matter how small, I could march up to within gunshot of any intrenchments he was given to hold." As Grant menaced the fort, Pillow abandoned his men, among them Walter Rorer and the men of the 20th Mississippi, and made an ignominious escape by boat at night. Grant joked to his prisoners, "If I had captured him, I would have turned him loose. I would rather have him in command of you fellows than as a prisoner."

But Pillow attacked his new job with zeal and recognition of the complexity of desertion. He detached a fleet of respected front line officers from their units and sent them to their home counties to round up missing men. His hope was that these officers would sway the disaffecteds and appeal to their latent loyalties, in a way that the local bureaucrats in charge of policing conscription couldn't. If the deserters still resisted, the officers were to bring the men in by force.

Pillow was especially concerned with the Piney Woods swamps and their environs. Men from across the lower South sought refuge there, because of the infinite number of hiding places offered by quagmires, marshes, and boggy islands unapproachable by horseback. It would require a man with intimate knowledge of the terrain to deal effectively with the deserters there. Pillow was determined to clear out the Piney Woods, and the man he selected for the job was Amos McLemore, a rising officer of the 27th Mississippi and the former Masonic leader and social arbiter of Ellisville.

August 1863, Ellisville

McLemore was coming home to Jones County, and he was coming plumed and tasseled, with a major's starred insignia on his collar tabs, double rows of gold buttons winking on his broad-breasted coat, a swirl of braid at his cuffs, and a walnut-gripped service pistol and curved, brass-hilted saber at his belt. It embarrassed McLemore that the Confederate high command had identified Jones as a hotbed of deserter resistance, and he intended to carry out his special assignment to round up Newton Knight and his fellow deserters by blade and pistol if necessary.

McLemore was handpicked for the job both for his knowledge of the area and the obvious toughness of his skin. He had charged into a sleet of bullets in the battle of Perryville, where 7,600 men were wounded in just six hours, among them himself and half his company. He recovered to fight at Murfreesboro, where he and the men of the 27th Mississippi lay in a shallow ditch for three days, pelted by icy rain and under bombardment, unable to make a fire for food or warmth. Though weak from exposure, they captured a Yankee battery and a company of sharpshooters. McLemore was rewarded with a promotion in the spring of 1863, making him the third-ranking officer in the 27th Mississippi, which went on to fight at Chickamauga without him.

McLemore arrived back in Piney Woods in mid-August and made his headquarters in the tumbledown little market square of New Augusta on the banks of the Leaf River. He was confident of success; he knew the lay of the land, and he knew many of the missing men personally.

He mustered a force of regular troops, local militia, and conscript officers and established a series of collection stations in surrounding counties for holding deserters. He also acquired a pack of bloodhounds. Then he rode out into the countryside and began hunting down men. In the space of just five weeks, McLemore was able to report that he had hauled in 119 men for return to their regiments.

A violent confrontation between McLemore and Newton was inevitable. They were diametrically opposed in purpose, and in personal attributes, and represented all that the other was fighting against.

Newton must have viewed McLemore as the embodi-
ment of the swaggering, slaveholding rebel elite. To
McLemore, Newton was a dirt-farming slacker, if not
a traitor. They shared only the conviction that the
other's presence in Jones County was intolerable.

Newton also viewed McLemore as corrupt. Mc-
Lemore's merchant set in Ellisville had become local
agents for the Confederate government's impressments,
and they were suspected of abusing their powers. Mc-
Lemore's uncle by marriage, a local Baptist minister
named William Fairchild, held the despised position
of taxes-in-kind collector. He was an object of local
hatred for his seizures from farming families purportedly for the rebel army. High-handed procurement
methods employed by tax collectors were a source of
continual resentment across the South, even among
loyalists, and men who held the position were continually suspected of profiteering. A Jackson newspaper
protested: "The Government has employed an army
of Barnacles to go out in swarms like the locusts of
Egypt, into every section and neighborhood." It was a
common belief among soldiers and their families that
tax officers were enriching themselves on the job. One
Mississippian wrote of swindlers "speculateing and
extortioning on those who try to live honest . . . impressing officers have pressed that to which they have
no right for the intention of speculation."

Newton suspected that part of McLemore's purpose
in scouting the countryside was not just to scout deserters but to size up the holdings of local citizenry, in

order to pass the information for seizure to Fairchild and his fellow collector, Sheriff Kilgore. "He would ride around in the county looking up the people's fat cattle and hogs and would let one man by the name of Fairchild and another by the name of Kilgore know about them," Newton's son Tom recounted. Newton sent a message to McLemore warning him to stop informing. Newton and his men "got tired of him making himself a news toter, and they ordered him to stop," Tom wrote. "But he kept on carrying news."

Newton and McLemore played a dangerous game of hide and seek in the woods, each trying to waylay the other. As the rebel officer scouted the county, his rides took him uncomfortably close to Newton's property on the border of Jones and Jasper counties, and the two men exchanged menacing messages. Newton sent McLemore word "to leave their business alone."

McLemore replied just as threateningly. "I know my business," he said, "and I expect to attend to it."

On the night October 5, Newton settled the business for both of them. One of the stations McLemore established for collecting stragglers was in northwest Jones County near a church named Big Creek, in the heart of the Knight family territory. Local oral tradition holds that McLemore and his men rode through Newton's province that day, looking for his hideout, intending to arrest him. This provoked Newton, who allegedly scrawled a note to McLemore threatening to fill him "full of lead." Newton supposedly told others, "His is the first name I've got carved on my gun barrel. I have sent him word that I will tolerate no meddlin', but if meddlin' is what he wants to do then I can stop that."

Newton knew that McLemore made it a habit to stay at the Ellisville home of his friend Amos Deason when he was in Jones County. Deason, the merchant turned state legislator, made his parlor a social center for high-ranking Confederate officers. Uniformed men came and went regularly from the home, which, with its beautiful portico and façade, stained pine panels shipped from Mobile, and painted weatherboarding that resembled marble, looked like a mansion next to the rude farmhouses.

The night of October 5 was a stormy one, and McLemore and six or eight officers tied up their horses and trooped up Deason's front steps for a hot dinner and a night's rest. McLemore and his men were soaked from patrolling in the rain and too muddy for the parlor. They moved into a bedroom, where the fire was built up as they shed their sodden broadcloth coats and forage caps and damp boots. The men then arranged themselves around the hearth.

Outside, Newton and two of his fellow deserters crept toward the well-lit house. Newton climbed the fence, rather than use the gate, so that it wouldn't creak. He could hear McLemore in conversation from deep inside the house. Behind the imposing façade, the residence meandered in typical Southern clapboard style, a warren of rooms connected by breezeways, built for coolness. Newton and his men slid along the outer walls, toward the sound of McLemore's voice.

Only Newton Knight and his two accomplices knew the truth of the next few minutes and the dark event that took place. According to Knight family tradition, one of the two men who accompanied Newton was his young cousin and close friend Alpheus. The three men drew broomstraws, to see who would accost McLemore. "They intended to stop him from spying out what little liberty they had, and did," Newton's son Tom wrote.

Alpheus pulled the short straw. But as the young man started to move toward the bedroom, Newton whispered and pulled him back—he didn't trust his aim. Instead, it was Newton who eased around the house, toward the firelight glowing and the drifting sound of the Confederates conversing.

Inside, the rebel officers sat and stood around the fire. McLemore sat in a rocking chair facing the fire. Suddenly the bedroom door slammed open, as if from a gust, and a figure loomed in the frame. A blast rang out. McLemore was lifted by the force of the gunshot and dropped to the floor like a heavy lifeless sack, a hole in his chest. As his blood began to seep into the floorboards, the other officers scattered in panic. Some grabbed for their firearms and rushed from the room after the assailant, not waiting to pull their boots on. But the shooter escaped into the squalling night.

No one in the room could identify the attacker. Their senses were concussed, their ears ringing, and their eyes filled with the bitter cordite smoke. According to a local newspaper report, "Some six or eight persons were in the house at the time of the shooting, but at last accounts no clue to the murderer. It was supposed to be the act of a deserter." The **Louisville Daily Journal** only suggested that the killing was a result of the fact that McLemore "was on duty at Ellisville, Miss., gathering up conscripts and deserters."

No one was ever charged with McLemore's murder, but it was accepted in Jones County that Newton was the man who had gunned him down. Newton apparently didn't deny his involvement to his son T. J., who claimed to have a firsthand account from his father, albeit a vague one on the subject of who pulled the trigger. "One of the three shot him and he died," Tom related.

The details of McLemore's murder generated debate, argument, and ghost stories. The specific details of that night became confused by the agendas of those doing the telling. To Confederate loyalists, the killing of McLemore was an act of cowardice. In their version, McLemore was sitting in a rocking chair when Newton crept up to a window, poked his gun barrel into the room, and shot him in the back of the head. It's an unlikely account: in the first place the window was undoubtedly closed, since it was a stormy October night and the officers were drying themselves by the fire. In the second place, McLemore fell to the floor across the room from the window.

A more likely scenario was published in the **Clarion-Ledger** on the anniversary of McLemore's death on October 5, 1967: Newton must have kicked open the bedroom door and fired almost point-blank at McLemore, who was either standing before the fireplace or just rising from a rocking chair. Bloodstains discovered on the underside of the floorboards during a modern restoration of the house indicate that McLemore bled on a spot between the door and the fireplace. All that can be said for sure is that a deserter, probably Newton Knight, shot McLemore by the fireside in the Deason home while he was visiting with fellow officers.

The Deason house, which still stands in Ellisville and is held by a historical trust and is under renovation, is said to be haunted, and local children and construction workers alike insist they've witnessed odd occurrences. Bloodstains are said to be visible in the floorboards when it rains (not true), the door through which Newton fired supposedly flies open and closes on its own at eleven o'clock, the hour at which McLemore was shot (sort of true), and laborers on the restoration project say some of their work mysteriously comes undone (true). Until 1967, the house was inhabited by Deason's descendants, Welton and Frances Smith, who did their best to dispel the more lurid stories—the tale of the reappearing bloodstains was impossible, since the original flooring had long ago been covered over with new planks and carpet, they pointed out. However, they acknowledged that the door occasionally **did** open of its own accord. "I think it's the hinge," Welton Smith said.

In October of 1863 McLemore wasn't a ghost but a vividly bloody corpse, and a highly political one, a senior Confederate officer who had been murdered while on duty. It was a breathtakingly militant act and a declaration of open hostilities against the Confederacy. There can have been no question in Newton's mind of the consequences: he'd crossed over, he was no longer a mere deserter but an enemy combatant. If caught he'd be hanged, shot, or worse.

It was also a declaration of independence of sorts, a statement by Newton that the Confederacy had no authority in Jones County. Previously, the deserters in Jones were shirkers and thieves, unpatriotic nuisances whose worst offense was that they peripherally hurt the war effort. But "the killing of a senior Confederate officer engaged in an activity that was vital to the ability of the Confederate government to wage war was a distinct departure," as neo-Confederate historian and McLemore's descendant Rudy H. Leverett observed.

What changed in Jones County? One answer is, Newton Knight came home. What seems clear is that with Newton's reappearance in the county, deserter activities took on a more belligerent aspect: men weren't merely evading service, they had begun defying tax seizures, actively resisting capture with force of arms, and now they had murdered an officer. Newton and his fellow deserters had become "a quasi-political force."

Something in Newton himself had surely changed, too. Prior to the summer of 1863, he was an independent farmer who wished to be let alone and a reluctant conscript who tried to refrain from fighting by tending to fellow soldiers as a medic. But the Newton Knight who returned to Jones County after Vicksburg was a strike-first killer and a dedicated enemy of the Confederacy who turned his gun on other men. His transformation was surely the result of a concentrated gathering of his various thoughts and emotions over the thirty-three months since the war broke out: the awfulness of battle, arrest, punishment; his urgency as a fugitive; and the realization that he had more in common with the slaves he had met in the swamps, who treated him better and showed him more basic humanity, than the Confederate authorities who claimed to be his countrymen. Whom, by rights, should Newton Knight have felt more loyalty to?

October 13, 1863, Jones County, Mississippi

A week after the killing of McLemore, men came out of the woods as if through a sieve. A throng of deserters, Unionists, and disillusioned yeomen gathered in a plank-floored trading post a few miles north of Ellisville, called Smith's Store, for a clandestine meeting. Fifty to sixty men crowded inside the store, cradling their guns, mostly double-barrels, though some had the four-and-a-half-foot-long Enfield rifles they had borne for the rebel army. They had come to declare their independence from the Confederacy and to pledge their armed service to the Union.

What, after all, was an army but a self-organized body of armed men? The Confederacy had created a vast army out of thin air in two years, but what made it more legitimate than an army of Southern Unionists? Nothing, as far as these men were concerned. They had neither voted for nor supported the new Southern nation. They did not view themselves as criminals or outlaws, but rather they were men who believed they represented the will of the majority in their region.

The men came from four surrounding counties—Jones, Jasper, Covington, and Smith—but their concerns were the same: they were tired of undemocratic seizures, of having their crops, food, mules, homes, and family members impressed by Confederate officials. And they had become convinced of the need to organize. With McLemore dead, the area would soon be infested with more rebel overlords looking for revenge, and the men at Smith's Store were determined to oppose them.

Many of them were friends and kin: five Collins brothers were in the room, and so were five Knights. There was Newton and also his favorite cousins, Alpheus, Ben, and Dickie. At the front of the room, one of the elder Collins brothers, Vinson, acted as a justice of the peace. He led the men in swearing an oath: they vowed to aid "the United States government in putting down the rebellion."

As an emblem of their official pledge to the Union, the men chose a name for their unit: they would be the "Jones County Scouts." They specifically chose the name to describe the nature of their outfit: "scout" was the term the Union used to describe Southern spies and Unionists offering assistance.

Their first order of business was to elect officers. For their leader, they chose the man they regarded as the most fearless Unionist among them: Newton Knight. He was unanimously elected captain.

Years later, in applying for a Union pension, Newton was asked on whose authority he had formed the company. "The people of Jones County," he answered. The unit was raised because "it was thought necessary for the protection of the loyal people for their safety," he said. The men pledged "to stay together and obey all orders from the Government of the United States."

Other men in Smith's Store recalled making their pledge in similar terms. To Jasper Collins, the object of raising the company "was for protection and to be loyal to the U.S. government." Jasper, always the most vociferous and politically involved of Jones Countians, had long been urging his fellow citizens to organize. He spoke of "the injustice that had been done to them and stated that they would not fight against the Union but if they had to fight they would stay at home and fight for a cause in which they believed."

Another company member, R. M. Blackwell, recalled that "we were sworn to support the constitution of the union." J. M. Valentine remembered that they agreed to serve "for the defense of the union."

Thirty years later, several citizens from Jones, Jasper, Covington, and Smith counties filed an affidavit

in the pension case of Newton and his men, supporting their accounts and describing the forming of the
company as a popular uprising of sorts, to fight back
against Confederates plundering their communities.
"Said company was raised at the instance of a <u>mam-
moth</u> mass meeting of the Union men of the afore-
named Counties. (of which there was a large majority
at that <u>time</u>.) That thefts, robberies, rapes and murders
were so common amongst us that it became an actual
necessity for Union men to form an organization for
their defense, and the Country at large. That Newton
Knight were known to us at that time as a faithful
and fearless Union man was unanimously chosen to
command the said 'Jones County Scouts,' which was
comprised of the best men in our Country."

The nature of the swearing in and the motivations
of those who joined the band would be argued for
the rest of Newton's life and beyond. To Newton's
Confederate enemies and critics, as well as skeptical historians, Knight and his men were desperados,
less concerned with the fate of the country than with
evading Confederate service and feeding themselves.
Mississippi's postwar neo-Confederate governor J. M.
Stone, for one, refused to believe that the insurrection in Jones County was politically motivated, insisting the men were too ignorant. "A large portion
of the population of the county was composed of illiterate persons who had been reared in the interior
far from railroads and other means of transportation,
and mainly without schools. Many of them declined

to go into the army in the beginning, but so far as any formal withdrawal . . . no such thing ever occurred in Jones County . . . (they), with others who had refused to go into the service, did join together in little bands to protect themselves against the conscript officers, and resisted the authority of the Confederate Government; but there was no general organization of such character."

But the Unionist nature of the Jones County Scouts was perfectly obvious to the local Confederates who had to deal with them. To the avowed rebel Joel E. Welborn, former major in the 7th Mississippi Battalion, who was home on a medical discharge, it was common and unsettling knowledge that Newton Knight and the deserters were organizing "a company to resist the confederate forces." Welborn demonstrated an odd combatant's respect for Newton and his men. "My understanding was that they were Union soldiers from principle," Welborn recalled. ". . . It was currently reported and generally believed that they were making an effort to be mustered into the U.S. Service. I was inclined to believe and think this from my acquaintance with several of his men, from intimate neighborship, from men who were regarded as men of honest conviction, and Gentlemen."

That the Jones County Scouts considered themselves a military unit was evident from the way they organized themselves. They adopted the structure of any standard infantry company in 1863. After Newton was elected captain, the next order of business was to elect and assign rank to a half dozen other men who would help command the company. Newton started a muster roll, and atop it he wrote the names of his officers: J. M. Valentine was his first lieutenant, Simeon Collins second lieutenant, Jasper Collins was first sergeant, W. P. Turnbow was second sergeant, young Alpheus Knight was first corporal, and S. G. "Sam" Owens was second corporal.

According to Ben Sumrall, a relative of the band member Will Sumrall, Newton instructed the men not to destroy the property of anyone, not even their enemies, and not to kill anyone except in the defense of their lives or the lives of their company and families. They were given a password, which was "I am of the Red, White and Blue." The response of the sentry guard was "I am a friend to you, come up to the camp and be recognized."

Each of the men had horns, commonly used on their farms for calling cattle or men to suppertime. The horns would be their signal callers: they would blow notes to summon one another or to warn of the approach of Confederates. They selected a nearby field, nicknamed Salsbattery, as their camp of instruction for drilling and military training. They also agreed to toil cooperatively in working and repairing one another's farms. "They selected several camping places and would go from one field to another and work in a body," according to Sumrall.

After taking the oath and receiving instructions, the men sang Union songs. According to one account, the men of the Knight band often sang anthems of the federal cause, including the famous "John Brown's Body":

John Brown's body lies a-mouldering in the grave,
John Brown's body lies a-mouldering in the grave,
John Brown's body lies a-mouldering in the grave,
His soul is marching on.
Glory, glory, hallelujah! Glory, glory, hallelujah! Glory, glory, hallelujah!
His soul is marching on
He's gone to be a soldier in the army of the Lord.

Their meeting concluded, the men filed out of Smith's Store and moved back into the woods to brace for the crackdown that was sure to come from Confederates in response to the killing of McLemore. As they slipped noiselessly into the thickets, they could perhaps already hear the baying of the dogs.

In Ellisville, there was a frenzy of activity as rebel officials organized a hunt for McLemore's killers. Uniformed members of Company F of the 26th Mississippi Infantry, who had been stationed in the area since August, streamed into town, along with mounted vigilantes with mule-drawn wagons loaded with crates full of dogs, wailing at their confinement.

Again, Newton was more afraid of bloodhounds than he was of rebels. He had heard stories, while under arrest, of what happened to deserters who were chased down by hounds. In one account that circulated, a deserter came home to Covington County, just west of Jones, and when conscript officers came looking for him, he fled to the swamps. The officers sent in the dogs, which finally cornered him in an old abandoned log cabin. The deserter had six bullets in his repeating revolver, but there were eight hounds. The fight lasted two hours. At the end of it, two hounds were still alive, and the man was so torn up and disfigured that his wife did not recognize his lifeless body when the conscript officers brought it back to her. Newton instructed his men that if they became trapped to shoot at the dogs first.

Slowly but surely, Newton's company organized the county against the Confederacy. The blowing of horns from hilltops was a time-honored way for yeomanry to call one another to action. A horn hung on the wall in the home of every pioneer family in Jones, for signaling distress. The Knight company worked out a series of signals with the horn blasts, "which each and every member of the Company understood," according to Tom Knight. Horn blasts told the men when a relative needed help, when it was safe to visit their homes, and when to gather for an ambush.

Newton's horn was distinct from all the others, solid

black, with a unique sound recognizably his, "so that when he received any news about the cavalry coming in, he would go to a certain place with which all were familiar and blow his horn, and soon the other members of the company would gather around him for orders." The sound of horns resounded through the Piney Woods: three short blasts called the men together for attack orders. The horns would echo down the line through the hill country.

The men traveled in parties of six to eight to avoid capture. At night, scouts and pickets hid in the crotches of trees or crouched in the brush, disguising themselves as black tree stumps. Their hideouts were seemingly inaccessible islands in the swamp, with crossings only a backwoodsman like Newton, who knew every trail of the county, could find. They chose lairs with deep cover and narrow access. Devil's Den was one of these, a cave set in a deep hollow below some high chalk bluffs of the Leaf River, concealed by briars and vines and reachable only through a passage in a ravine. Another sanctuary was a patch of high ground in the midst of a horseshoe-shaped lake, surrounded by thirty acres of mire and quicksand, accessible only by a narrow spit opposite the Leaf River. It became known as Deserter's Lake.

The Confederates were frustrated by these guerrillas who were ever-moving targets, unwilling to show themselves and engage in a traditional gunfight. Only occasionally could they pin them down. On November 1, 1863, Newton and some of his men were caught in a running skirmish through the fields of a farmer named Levi Valentine, an old neighbor of the Knights. A detachment from the 26th Mississippi managed to inflict some casualties, and John H. Harper, who had been maimed at Corinth, was killed in a shootout before the band drove the rebels back into Ellisville. There, the soldiers enlisted the aid of Joel E. Welborn as a guide. But when the rebels returned in hopes of mounting a counterattack, Newton and his men had evaporated back into the swamps, untraceable.

The men hid out in the swamps night and day, living off wild hogs, trout, and roasted possum, a delicacy. Sometimes they snuck into barns to sleep on some hay or a pine floor, but such surreptitious visits were dangerous. The Confederates staked out their farms, and on January 10, 1864, caught a young member of the Jones Scouts named Tapley Bynum, who gave in to temptation and slipped home to see his wife and newborn baby daughter. Bynum had just a few minutes with his family before he heard a noise at the gate and peered out the door. He bolted from the porch as a posse of cavalrymen rode through his fence. They shot him down in the yard.

Newton made the Confederates pay. A company from the 26th Mississippi was encamped near the property of Sally Parker, the sister of Jasper Collins and a staunch ally who often cooked hot meals for the Scouts. Newton and thirty of his men stole through the woods and encircled the rebel camp. Shotguns thundered and smoke billowed from the tree line as they ambushed the Confederates. The official Confederate report read, "In a skirmish with Torys, camped on Tallahala Creek near Ellisville, we lost one man killed and two severely wounded."

But mostly Newton, now wanted for murder and treason as well as desertion, kept completely out of sight. He quit seeking shelter in barns and made his home deeper in the woods and in the swamps. He didn't go home; there was no home to go to. Newton's wife Serena and the children were still living with family while Newton moved around for protection. He never knew who might be a Confederate informant, and the government was now offering rewards for rounding up deserters.

Newton was used to the swamp by day, but at night, alone, it was a surreal new world. Cypress hung heavy over shallow pools, and the moon cast long shadows over strange life-forms. Will-o'-the wisps and glowworms shined with an eerie incandescent light, their contours crisscrossing and blurring into one another. The bulrushes looked like animals, and the birds overhead sounded like war. The moss dangling down into the swamp seemed twined and ropelike. Tangled limbs of oak and tupelo crowded the sky and made it blacker. The ground, softly carpeted by lichen, moss, and fern, felt alive and crawling—in fact, the entire swamp seemed to be in motion. Even the vegetation appeared to be dangerously moving, writhing. Moss waved, vines curled like the poisonous snakes in the water, and the huge frogs dipping up and down in the water could easily, to a man in the grip of fear, look like the noses of alligators.

Yet it was a sublime place, not without its beauty. Newton discovered that within the swamp was a civilization that came alive at night. The more he penetrated its depths, the more of its life awakened; the birds and ducks seemed to "throng the morass in the hundreds of thousands," their garrulous throats pouring forth with "multitudinous sounds," wings fluttering and beaks plunging. Late at night the illusory quality of the swamp only deepened; it seemed "all the fowls of the air, and all the creeping things of the earth, appeared to have assembled together," filling the swamp with "clamor and confusion." Another refugee of the Piney Woods marshes and bogs, a fugitive slave named Solomon Northup, himself an expert on survival, observed: "Even in the heart of that dismal swamp, God had provided a refuge and a dwelling place for millions of living things."

Including other humans. During those long swamp-bound nights, Newton heard strange voices, familiar yet unfamiliar. They were the voices of black fugitives, also in hiding. At first, Newton would have been alarmed at these human whispers when he sought refuge in the swamp: they might mean the enemy. Another onetime fugitive, Frederick Douglass, described how a runaway responded to the sound of human voices in the swamp while being pursued: "I dreaded more these human voices than I should have done those of wild beasts."

But the voices of fugitives became the voices of allies for Newton. They were men and women who like him were evading the Confederate army, which was aggressively impressing slaves to do the backbreaking labor involved in war, building fortifications, hauling goods, and burying rotting corpses. Many of them were lying out in the Piney Woods burrows until they could find a way to reach the Union lines in Vicksburg or Corinth.

The swamps had become a kind of highway for refugees. A Yankee soldier with the 6th Iowa watched bedraggled fugitives, both black and white, file into Corinth after fleeing the Confederate service and traveling through the swamps and counted six companies' worth. "The rebels are pressing all able bodied men into the army, without regard to age, in Miss. and Alabama," he wrote home. "All 'Niggers' with any white blood are declared liable to conscription . . . The men have been hunted by the rebels with bloodhounds for weeks, and are men that will fight till death in support of laws they so much need."

We don't know exactly whom Newton encountered during his stay in the swamp, but we know that he was aided and protected by at least two members of the slave community—Rachel and a man owned by a branch of his family, Joe Hatton—and we can try to reconstruct his experiences based on the available evidence from other fugitive memoirs.

It was a fugitive slave who might well have stopped Newton as he groped his way toward the trunk of a fallen tree, thinking to sit or lie down. As he began to recline into it, a shadow—for it must have looked like a shadow—pushed him to the ground. The fugitive took a step backward, picked up a stick, and then poked the stump as if stoking a fire. There was a rustle, and the stump sprouted vines of water moccasins. This was how fugitives learned that water moccasins nested in the stumps of fallen trees, and whoever taught Newton this probably saved his life, for the moccasin's bite was "more fatal than that of the rattlesnake," as Solomon Northup noted.

Alligators were a nightmarish problem, but loud noises startled them and drove them into the deeper places, as Northup could have told Newton. But no matter how careful you were, there were times when you came face to face with these monsters before you knew they were there. If a man ran backward a few yards and then cut to the side, he could "in that manner shun them." Straight forward, alligators could cover a short distance rapidly, but since they could not move side to side quickly, "in a crooked race there [was] no difficulty in evading them," as Northup explained.

Newton would have come across men like Octave Johnson, a cooper by trade who ran away from a whip-handed overseer and lived for a year and a half in the bayou with a group of thirty other runaway slaves, ten of whom were women. Octave and his fellow fugitive stole food from a plantation four miles away, pilfered turkeys, chickens, and pigs, and sometimes even roped cattle and dragged them to their hiding places. They surreptitiously bartered for cornmeal with friends on the plantations and obtained matches from them. They slept on logs and burned cypress leaves at night to keep the mosquitoes away. They could have taught Newton how to make a dry bed on the damp grass with pine needles; how to hide in the hollow of a cypress; how to kill the scent tracked by hounds by diving into the water.

Johnson could have shown Newton how to lure the dogs into the marshes, where they were bait for the alligators. This was a trick Johnson learned out of desperation, when he was hunted to the water's edge by a pack of twenty dogs. He managed to kill a few of the hounds with his bare hands before he jumped into the fen in terror. The dogs followed him in— only to be set upon by the pale yawning maws of the alligators. It was in this death-defying way that Johnson learned alligators "preferred dog flesh to personal flesh," he said.

Newton would have learned how to hunt in the swamp for coon and opossum at night in the heat of the summer, when they were hidden and sleeping. Swamp possums were round, long-bodied little animals, of a whitish color, with noses like pigs, and they burrowed among the roots and in the hollows of the gum tree. They were clumsy but deceitful and cunning creatures that would feign their own deaths at the tap of a stick, only to scamper away. Newton also would have learned how to make a fish trap, a box made of notched boards and sticks, between two and three feet square, baited with a handful of wet meal and cotton wadded together. A fish swimming through the upraised door toward the bait would strike one of the small sticks and turn a handle, and the door would fall shut.

But Newton's most reliable ally and source of sustenance was Rachel. It was during this time, when he was a fugitive and she remained in bondage to his family, that their partnership began. According to Knight family tradition, it was Rachel who helped hide Newton when it became too dangerous for him to go back to Serena and his children. They had an agreement: she would provide him with food, and he would work to secure her freedom.

The young woman knew both the ways of the swamp and the kitchens of Confederates. Rachel ferried food, clothing, and information to Newton. She regularly crossed the boundaries between Confederate households, the slave cabins, and the hidden civilization in the swamp, carrying news to Newton and keeping him apprised of rebel movements, information she may well have overheard in the loyal kitchen of Jesse Davis Knight. For the rest of the war, Rachel would operate as Newton's "intelligence," according to a family member. She became Newton's spy, his eyes and ears.

Rachel showed Newton and his men methods of poisoning or killing the dogs that pursued them. She ground up red pepper into a fine powder and scattered it to foul the noses of the hounds and taught Newton to dig up wild onions or garlic and rub them on the soles of his shoes and then cross a road backward, to baffle the dogs. She supposedly told Newton, "There's lots a' ways to choke a dog 'sides on butter."

The deserters' wives also conspired to wound or kill dogs. The hounds were kept ravenous, so that they would hunt, since a dog with a full stomach would only sleep. According to one account it was Rachel who taught the local women how to hide glass splinters, strychnine, and other poisons in the dog food.

But sometimes the men were cornered and alone in the swamps and had to hope their trigger fingers were faster than the jaws of the mastiffs. "Some of them died of lead poisoning," Newton said, laconically.

Outwardly, Rachel and the other slaves of Jones County went about their business, doing their chores and obeying Confederate laws. But these were phantom gestures, veneers, as they awaited their liberation. The men and women in the slave quarters surely felt a personal stake in the survival of Newton and his band and guarded against their recapture. There was not a black in the Piney Woods unaware that Newton had run away from the army and was willing to fight to free slaves from bondage.

According to the Union government they were already free. Word of the Emancipation Proclamation had reached Jones County, and possibly so did word that in January of 1863 the Union forces occupying Corinth had held emancipation ceremonies, led by chaplains. Thousands of freedmen and women who had made their way to federal encampments were declared liberated—and then armed with pistols.

Mississippi slaves in the path of Yankee troops rejoiced at their arrival, demonstrating that they were acutely aware of their personal status. A twenty-four-year-old Yankee captain from Iowa who marched through the Jackson area in the late spring of 1863 was practically mobbed by overjoyed freedmen. "Passed by many a fine deserted place," he wrote in his diary. "The colored people manifested great joy at our approach, and told us they prayed constantly for our success and had been praying for this time for many years. Many a god bless you was sent after us as we passed them."

Men and women who had previously seemed subservient were no longer. In Vicksburg, no sooner had the Confederates under Pemberton surrendered than slaves in the town declared themselves no longer bound. One woman announced "her intention of going to search for her sons, as she was free now . . . she would not wait a day." Another woman demanded wages from her mistress—and was turned out of the house for it.

Even small children were aware of what was at stake in the war. In Lauderdale County, Mississippi, a young girl named Susan Snow became infuriated when she heard white children singing a song in praise of Confederate president Jefferson Davis:

**Ol' Jeff Davis, long an' slim,
Whupped ol' Abe wid a hick'ry limb.**

Jeff Davis is a wise man an' Lincoln is a fool,
Ol' Jeff Davis rides a gray an' Lincoln rides a
mule.

As soon as the children had finished singing, Snow hopped up and chanted in reply:

Ol' Gen'l Pope, he had a short gun,
Fill it full of gum,
Kill 'em as dey come.
Call a Union band,
Make de rebels understand
To leave our land,
Submit to Abraham.

Unbeknownst to Snow her mistress had come out to the porch and heard her song. "Ol' mistis was standin' right behin' me! She grabbed up de bresh broom an' she laid it on me. Ol' mistis made **me** submit. I caught de feathers, don't you forgit it."

As the Yankee occupation of Mississippi broadened, thousands upon thousands of freed slaves made an army in their own right as they moved toward Union lines. Once there they took an increasingly vital role in the Union war effort: according to one estimate there were twenty thousand black refugees in the Vicksburg area alone, doing hard labor for the North instead of the South. John Eaton, the chaplain of the 27th Ohio appointed superintendent of the freedmen by Grant, organized work programs for which they could earn wages, plowing on abandoned plantations leased to Northern speculators or wielding axes in woodyards.

Eaton described the waves of humanity that flowed toward the Union positions in Mississippi: they came "in rags or silks, feet shod or bleeding; individually or in families; and pressing towards the armies characterized as Vandal Hordes. Their comings were like the arrivals of cities. Often they met prejudices against their color, more bitter than they had left behind. There was no Moses to lead, nor plan in their exodus. The decision of their instinct or unlettered reason brought them to us. They felt that their interests were identical with objects of our armies. This identity of interest, slowly but surely, comes to be perceived by our officers and soldiers, and by the loyal public."

Some of the freedmen were determined to do more than work—they wanted to fight. In the spring of 1863, freedmen began to volunteer in the first black regiments, mustered by General Lorenzo Thomas and led by volunteer white officers. By the end of the year about fifty thousand freedmen would be serving in the Union army, most of them in the Mississippi Valley. Southerners reacted to the arming of freed slaves as if it were an act of barbarism. The poetical Lieutenant William Nugent of the 28th Mississippi Cavalry saw it as "flagrant, unwarranted and demoniac violations of the usage of a civilized warfare," as he wrote to his wife.

As the Union soldiers became increasingly accustomed to working with liberated slaves, their views continued to evolve. "I don't care a damn for the darkies," wrote an Illinois lieutenant, "but I couldn't help to send a runaway nigger back. I'm blamed if I could. I honestly believe that this army has taken 500 niggers away with them . . . I have 11 negroes in my company now. They do every particle of the dirty work. Two women among them do the washing for the company."

Even William T. Sherman, who "was no professed friend of the Negro," viewed the freedmen as valuable additions to the service, though menial ones. "Every Negro who came within our lines—and there were hundreds of them—was enrolled on the quartermasters books, clothed, fed, and paid wages, the price of his clothing being deducted," recalled aide Wickham Hoffman. "They were proud of being paid like white men." Hoffman was struck by the energy with which they trundled wheelbarrows filled with earth, at the double-quick.

Rachel and the unliberated slaves in the Piney Woods interior would also have received word through the grapevine of the battle in June of 1863 at Milliken's Bend, where black troops proved that they were good for more than shoveling or laundering. The arming of freedmen had been a controversial exercise, primarily because white officers did not believe they could fight. Nevertheless, Grant saw that with black troops to guard garrisons, he could free up white units to campaign.

But at Milliken's Bend, a Union position on the

Mississippi just a few miles above Vicksburg, black troops proved their mettle, as they fought and died equal to the bravest men of either side. Initially part of Grant's supply line during his drive on Vicksburg, the garrison at Milliken's Bend had become largely irrelevant, and Grant left it in the hands of five regiments of black troops, mostly raw recruits, as he went on about the business of besieging the city.

On June 5, a Confederate brigade under H. E. Mc-Culloch attacked, aiming to take the bend in order to drive cattle across the river to the rescue of the starving troops there. The rebels charged at dawn, crying, "No quarter!" The fighting was hand-to-hand, from trench to trench, men savagely raking at one another with bayonets. The inexperienced black troops were pushed to the river, where they stood their ground and finally repulsed the Confederates with the help of fire from two federal gunboats. The casualties were staggering: of the 1,061 black soldiers who fought, 652 were killed, wounded, or missing, along with 160 white officers. Rear Admiral David Porter surveyed the battlefield and reported to Grant that it was "quite an ugly sight. The dead Negroes lined the ditch inside the parapet or levee, and were mostly shot on top of the head. In front of them, close to the levee, lay an equal number of rebels stinking in the sun."

One white officer leading a regiment of black troops, Captain M. M. Miller, formerly of Yale University and Galena, Illinois, wrote an account of the engagement for his local paper in which he passionately praised his soldiers. "We had about 80 men killed in the regiment and 80 wounded so you can judge what part of the fight my company sustained! I never felt more grieved and sick at heart than when I saw my brave soldiers slaughtered—one with six wounds, all the rest with two or three, none less than two wounds. Two of my colored sergeants were killed, both brave, noble men; always prompt, vigilant and ready for the fray. I never more wish to hear the expression 'the nigger won't fight.' Come with me a 100 yards from where I sit and I can show you the wounds that cover the bodies of 16 as brave, loyal and patriotic soldiers as ever drew bead on a rebel. The enemy charged us so close that we fought with our bayonets hand to hand. I have six broken bayonets to show how bravely my men fought."

Milliken's Bend was a negligible fight strategically; soon after it was over, the garrison was abandoned. But the troops who fought there won the first significant victory over bigotry in the Union service—and they did so a full six weeks before the 54th Massachusetts would make their legendary assault at Fort Wagner. Charles A. Dana, the assistant secretary of war, later remarked, "The bravery of the blacks at Milliken's Bend completely revolutionized the sentiment of the Army with regard to the employment of Negro troops."

It was under these conditions, then, of emancipation, mass slave defections, inductions into Union uniform, heroism, terror, vengefulness, and atroc-

ity, that the slaves of the Piney Woods aided Newton Knight and his band. They undoubtedly saw it as
their contribution to the war effort, their way to get
into the fight. According to numerous accounts, Joe
Hatton, who lived in the household of Newton's uncle
William Knight, believed that as "a useful messenger"
for the Jones County Scouts, he was working "in the
service of his peoples" and may have even considered
himself a fellow soldier of Newton's.

It was a fearful risk, as accounts from other slaves in
nearby counties who aided deserters reflect. "I remember how the men would hide out to keep from going
to war," remembered a slave named Jeff Rayford. "I
cooked and carried many a pan of food to these men
in Pearl River swamp. This I did for one man regularly. All I had to do was carry the food down after
dark, and I was so scared I was trembling, and while
walking along the path in the swamp, pretty soon he
would step out from behind a tree and say: 'Here, Jeff.'
And then I would hand it to him and run back to the
house."

Julia Stubbs, a slave in Simpson County, recalled
how she collaborated with the local farmwives to aid
deserters hiding from the Confederate cavalry hunting them. "During de war deir wuz a heap o' deserters
hid out. De Calvarymen would ride through a hunting 'em. We could might nigh alwas' hear 'em a coming long fo' dey got in sight, de womens would blow a
horn sos dey could hide from 'em. I'se carried food to
de woods to de deserters. Sometimes we would have
to take it a long ways an' agin dey would be near by."

No one risked more than Rachel. As a fugitive, Newton was both vulnerable and reliant on Rachel, and according to their descendants he would not have survived the war without her. It was a constant temptation for the fugitive to return to the known and comfortable, and Rachel's cabin in the half-abandoned slave quarters must have offered a rare refuge. In turn, Rachel may have seen the angular, black-haired, buccaneering Newton as a champion who emboldened her to act.

Frederick Douglass described an escapee's poignant glimpses of "civilization" and the mixed feelings they provoked. "Peeping through the rents of the quarters, I saw my fellow-slaves seated by a warm fire, merrily passing away the time, as though their hearts knew no sorrow. Although I envied their seeming contentment, all wretched as I was [in the swamp], I despised the cowardly acquiescence in their own degradation which it implied, and felt a kind of pride and glory in my own desperate lot. I dared not enter the quarters—for where there is seeming contentment with slavery, there is certain treachery to freedom."

It's entirely possible that Rachel and Newton gave each other a sense of bravery, and cause. The affair between them apparently began in this netherworld of wartime resistance and hiding. Love was surely an accident; they were constrained and facing several dangers, and the Civil War was not an event that gentled the emotions. What began as an alliance at some point deepened, and the experience must have been unsettling for two people who needed every ounce of calculation and self-possession for survival. But war was also distilling. Among the effects of what W. H. Auden called "the nearly religious mystery" of romantic love is a sharpening of self-definition. "You find out who you are when you are in love," Auden observed. And when you are at war.

At almost every turn, every day, the events of the Civil War demanded that Newton and Rachel decide who they were: was Newton a coward or traitor, Unionist or rebel? Was Rachel a bondswoman or free soul, a passive victim or an active fighter? Attraction must have been one more desperate factor in an existence already reduced to daily urgency. With the old society smashed to pieces around them and death a Minié ball or a rope end away, what did vows mean? To whom did they truly belong?

There is precious little direct evidence of their relationship, no love letters or locks of hair. All that's left are legions of great-great-grandchildren, who received whispers and faint impressions of the original relationship: Newton loved Rachel "deeply" and felt "responsible" for her. She felt "protective" of him and "sheltered" him. Their descendants are not always in agreement in the details passed down to them, but they are unanimous on one fact: at some point, Newton came to belong more to Rachel than to his own wife, Serena.

The relationship may also have begun to blossom in the absence of others. In midwar, Serena finally found it impossible to subsist in Jones County and left Mississippi for a period to live with relatives in Georgia, although it's not clear when or for how long. She must have done so because she was no longer able to support the family, once the rebels had burned them out. On an undated Confederate document, she was listed as "destitute." She may have also fled because of the danger of Newton's activities, or because she didn't understand his transformation into an anti-Confederate Unionist leader and a comrade of blacks.

More significantly, Jesse Davis Knight was dead. He was slain not by a bullet in battle, but by one of the most commonplace killers in the army: measles. He fell ill in the fall-winter of 1863 while in Georgia with the 27th Mississippi Regiment, and it worsened into pneumonia. He expired December 17, 1863, in the Institute Hospital in Atlanta and was buried in a soldiers' graveyard in Marietta, Georgia. However, he must have visited home shortly before his death: Rachel became pregnant again and would bear Jesse Davis's daughter, a mulatto infant named Fannie, in the spring of 1864. It was Rachel's first child since shortly before the war began. With most of the able-bodied white men away in uniform, she apparently had been spared their sexual attentions.

Rachel had been raped, seduced, or sexually exploited by a white man but perhaps never before loved by one. What few cases of interracial romance she and Newton might have heard of had ended tragically: if a white man acted on romantic feelings for a black woman, he found himself an outcast in white society.

Most of Newton's comrades viewed such a romance as "illicit and immoral"; while they could comprehend the sexual urge, they couldn't comprehend how a white man and black woman could be "faithful, loyal, and true" to each other.

Institutionally structured concubinage with white men was common in Rachel's world, but love was not. Black women were reputed to be promiscuous, as opposed to the prudish white women who were symbols of purity, and consequently they were targets of force and also of "seduction under the implicit threat of force." In fact, many masters believed that it was this system of sexual force that protected the purity of white Southern women. According to the Yazoo planter James J. B. White, "everybody who has resided in the South long enough to get acquainted with ou' people and thar ways must know that the nigro women have always stood between ouah daughters and the superabundant sexual energy of ouah hot-blooded youth. End white mens' right to do as they pleased with black women," he said, "and ouah young men'll be driven back upon the white ladies, and we'll have prostitution like you all have it in the North, and as it is known in other countries."

For a slave woman like Rachel to fall in love with a white man, even an antislavery yeoman like Newton, was anything but the norm. Still, such relationships existed. Defining these relations as love rather than as exploitation can all too easily ignore the power that white men could wield over black women. Yet to deny that love existed ignores the reality of human feelings. The Virginia slave Harriet Jacobs took a white lover to ward off the violent advances of her master, justifying it by saying: "There is something akin to freedom in having a lover who has no control over you, except that which he gains by kindness and attachment. A master may treat you as rudely as he pleases, and you dare not speak. . . . It seems less degrading to give one's self, than to submit to compulsion."

Given the social taboo against interracial romance, Newton and Rachel's relationship must have involved deep emotional confusion and perhaps even been "marked by a self-contempt projected onto the other." As the scholar Eugene Genovese notes, "the tragedy of miscegenation" lay in the "terrible pressure to deny the delight, affection, and love that so often grew from tawdry beginnings. Whites as well as blacks found themselves tortured as well as degraded."

Only a planter with enough wealth and social standing could thwart custom and didn't have to hide his slave mistress. David Dickson of Georgia, one of the most celebrated leaders in the movement to reform Southern agriculture, lost his wife, took up with a mistress, and accepted outcast status to live openly with her and their children. The first mayor of Memphis, Marcus Winchester, had a beautiful free quadroon mistress whom he married and took to Louisiana, and his successor, Ike Rawlins, also lived with a slave mistress. Richard Mentor Johnson, the vice president of the United States during the Martin Van Buren administration, never married and had a long-term relationship with Julia Chinn, a mulatto he inherited from his father's estate. A wealthy planter from Kentucky, Johnson made no attempt to conceal the relationship: their two daughters were raised and educated as his children, and on several occasions he insisted on their being recognized in society. After Chinn died, he had other mulatto mistresses, thus providing his political enemies with a steady supply of ammunition to use against him.

But such conduct invited backlash, even explosions of rage. Henry Hughes of Mississippi, for instance, condemned these unions by saying, "Hybridism is heinous. Impurity of races is against the law of nature. Mulattoes are monsters. The law of nature is the law of God. The same law which forbids consanguinous amalgamation forbids ethnical amalgamation. Both are incestuous. Amalgamation is incest."

Relationships such as Newton's with Rachel were the very things many white Southerners believed they were fighting the war to prevent. Later in the conflict, when large numbers of Confederate prisoners were taken in Sherman's Atlanta campaign, Yankee troops questioned the rebels as to their motives for fighting so bitterly. They answered, "You Yanks want us to marry our daughters to the niggers."

To the Mississippi cavalryman William Nugent, the war had become a sacred crusade to rescue civilization from the "unholy alliance" between crude Northern tartars and the bestial Negroes. As Yankees poured into the interior of the state after Vicksburg,

Nugent wrote to his wife lamenting the tactics employed by Grant and the grave consequences of a defeated South.

If the Yankees should force surrender, "Our land will be a howling waste, wherever it has been invaded & we will be forced to abandon it to the **freed Negroes** & the wild beasts," he warned. ". . . The commerce of the South will be nothing and certainly no one, unless his pretensions be very humble, will be content to live in a land where the intermixture of races will breed a long train of evils."

The alliance between Newton and Rachel could not have been more perilous. What enabled two people to cross every permissible emotional line, even under the threat of mortal danger? The answer can only be conjectured, but a variety of forces surely had something to do with it: The cataclysmic nature of the war, the dissolution of old Mississippi around them, the unfamiliarity of the shattered countryside. The blank lack of a tomorrow.

None of the old rules applied—except perhaps those they clung to from the Bible. The first book of Samuel, 16:7, told them: "For the Lord sees not as man sees; man looks on the outward appearance, but the Lord looks on the heart." Acts 17:26 said: "And God hath made of one blood all nations of men for to dwell on all the face of the earth."

Or perhaps it simply had to do with their fearless natures. "Do you know," Newton liked to say, with a slow smile, "there's lots of ways I'd ruther die than be scared to death."

Deposition of Confederate major Joel E. Welborn in the case of *Newton Knight, et al. v. The United States,* March 6, 1895

Q: How long did Newton Knight serve in the 7th Mississippi Battalion of Infantry. And what was he doing in the latter years of the war.

A: He served but a short time ... I could hear of him and others raising a company to resist the confederate forces. In August of 1863 there was a company of Confederate cavalry sent here to arrest all the deserters and carry them back to their Commands. At that time Newton Knight and his band, or company, or whatever it was, was becoming a terror to the country; in November following Newton Knight and his crowd had a little fight with this cavalry up here about four miles above Ellisville in the Tallahola [*sic*] swamp. The Confederates retreated and came back to town, pressed me to go with them and a team to the battleground to bring in one of their number that they knew was killed and I subsequently learned that one or two of Knights party was wounded. The night after the battle they pressed me and the sheriff here, Divall, to go with them up the Paulding road which runs up the east side of the Tallahola creek to see if they could not be approached from the east side of the creek but whenever we reached the point opposite where the battle was, we discovered that they had left there and took up their camp somewhere else. After that they had various skirmishes. About Christmas 1863 Knight and some of his crowd, supposed to be them of course, approached the confederate camp at Ellisville and fired on them and wounded one or two, and they had these skirmishes all until the end of the war.

Q: Did it ever come to your knowledge or understanding in any way that Knight and his men were banded together for the purpose of entering into the service of the U.S. government, or was it their object simply to protect themselves from being arrested and taken back into the Confederate Army at the front.

A: My understanding was that they were Union soldiers from principle. I was inclined to believe and think this from my acquaintance with several of his men, from intimate neighborship, from men who were regarded as men of honest conviction; and Gentlemen. It was currently reported and generally believed that they were making an effort to be mustered into the U.S. service.

FIVE

The Third Front

January 1864, Chickasawhay Swamp,
Mississippi-Alabama Border

The Jones County Scouts stole through the murk toward the Confederate wagon train, moving like shadows among the shadows until they had it surrounded. With a silent gesture, one of Newton's men lifted a horn to his lips, and a blast cleaved the night air. It jarred men and animals alike in the rebel camp. Panicked livestock jerked at their tethers, and alarmed men snatched up their weapons and pointed them in the direction of the noise. Just then, from the opposite side of the woods, came another ear-rending blast. As this noise faded, a third, jeering call came from in front—and then another from behind. The rebels whirled in confusion.

"Those drivers must have thought we had an army in the woods," Newton said later.

To Newton and the gaunt-faced, squint-eyed men who peered through the Chickasawhay Swamp, the Confederate wagon train, fat with corn, looked like a sumptuous and lazily offered banquet. An even more inviting target was the leader of the train, William Fairchild, the unloved Confederate tax-in-kind collector for Jones County.

The train was encamped along the old trace road to Mobile, four wagons heaped high with shelled corn, bales of cotton, and velvety wool and surrounded by burly oxen and cattle swaying under the prods of drovers. Fairchild's guard was down; they were fifty miles south of Jones County, about halfway to the Alabama coast, and it had been a trouble-free trip in the fine late-autumn weather. Fairchild was placid and pleased with himself; he had already been paid in gold for half the load, contracted for shipment to Robert E. Lee's army in Virginia. As twilight came on, the train had drawn to a halt still well inside the gloom of the swamp. Threats had seemed far away—until the horns sounded.

As the last note died, Knight's men opened fire. Shotgun explosions bleached the night and a squall of shotgun pellets blew into the camp. Amid the iterating thunder, men screamed. Some of the teamsters fired back aimlessly at the vague enemies in the stygian dark. Musket fire and buckshot guttered, and cattle and oxen broke loose and bolted into the woods. After a brief firefight, Fairchild's men scattered with them, fleeing through the trees and leaving the stores for the Jones County Scouts.

"We came a-shootin' and they cut and run," Newton recalled.

With the teamsters fled, the Jones Countians rode out of the timber and began to sack the train. They efficiently stripped it, packing away all of the corn and as much of the other stores as they could carry, including a fresh supply of powder and lead for their guns. They quit the clearing and disappeared back into the swamps with their haul, as quickly as they came.

The escaped Fairchild reemerged from the brush to find several of his men wounded or killed, the rest dispersed up and down the swamp. The tax collector spent the next several days gathering survivors and recovering what oxen and cattle he could find. With this vestige of his train he finally made it to Mobile, where he reported the raid to Confederate authorities. He then headed home, no doubt livid at the brazenness of the attackers.

Once back in Jones, Fairchild's losses only made him more heavy-handed. He immediately went on a hunt for fresh livestock among the yeomanry, and this time he brought with him the strong arm of Sheriff Nat Kilgore. Together, Fairchild and Kilgore stalked a swamp known as the Bogahoma Creek, popular among farmers for hiding livestock from the prying eyes of tax agents. They found it filled with fleshy, free-grazing hogs.

Fairchild and Kilgore went to the nearest homestead and angrily threatened the wary wife who came to the door. Her husband would have to gather the hogs for tax seizure by the time they returned, or he'd be shot. They did not want to have to round up the hogs themselves.

"But if we do have to gather them up, and happen to find him while hunting the hogs we will shoot him quick as we would an old buck," they warned.

The bullying, however, had the opposite effect from that intended. As soon as Fairchild and Kilgore departed for the ride back to Ellisville, the wife sent out a distress call. Word of the threat spread among the yeomanry, and men gathered. After some discussion, they were roused to do murder. Two young members of the Jones County Scouts were chosen for the job of intercepting the government men and killing them. They cradled their guns and moved off toward the Ellisville road.

But Newton may have followed to be sure they did the job right. As Tom Knight tells the story, the two young men found an ambush spot behind an old rotting half-unearthed tree stump. They cut holes in the wood for their gun barrels, and once situated, settled down to wait. "But there was one man in the crowd that did not have any faith in these boys for the job," Tom Knight recounted, "so he took a stand by the road in another place." When Fairchild and Kilgore came riding down the road, both boys shot, but both missed. The second man, however, "gave them both barrels and killed them both."

Tom's implication is that his father was the third shooter. Once again, Newton Knight was never positively identified as the shooter, but it was commonly accepted by Fairchild's descendants that he pulled the trigger. The Fairchilds, like most of Newton's enemies, accused him of cowardice. According to a Fairchild family memoir, William was "on a buying trip through the county when Newt pluged him, in the back."

Whether Newton was the guilty party or not, it had plainly become dangerous to conduct official Confederate business in Jones County. The rebels were no longer in charge. The Jones County Scouts were.

Military authorities responded by once again unleashing the hounds and scouring the woods. But Newton and his men only responded by gunning down yet another prominent Confederate.

The pack of dogs hunting the guerrillas now numbered nearly one hundred, and most of them were owned by a local merchant and landowner named William McGilvery, a forty-two-year-old slaveholder, who joined the search parties as a vigilante and rode out behind his animals.

McGilvery chased the renegades so aggressively that he followed his dogs straight into one of the company's hideout camps, near a fork known as Horse Creek. Newton was cooking some provisions at a nearby farmstead belonging to a woman named Sallie Dulancy when he heard the baying, followed by horsemen. He dashed into an open field and cut across it toward the woods to warn his fellow guerrillas. Rebel bullets strafed him as he ran, cutting his shot-bag strap in two and putting two holes in his hat, and three more through the flying tails of his coat, before he reached the cover of the woods, where he threw himself over an embankment and rolled down into the swamp.

The pursuing rebels, fearful of penetrating too deep into the thickets, pulled up at the edge of the woods—all but one, McGilvery, who charged into the brush behind his prowling, pattering dogs. The hounds loped into the hidden encampment, where the guerrillas awaited them with hammers cocked. A roar of shotguns met the dogs, which fell with giant bloody holes in them. As the fire died down, McGilvery, who had finally reined in his horse, hollered out, "You quit killing my dogs!" In response, one of the Knight men stepped behind an oak tree, laid his rifle across a branch, sighted, and shot McGilvery out of his saddle. He fell heavily to the marshy ground, bleeding from a head wound, and as Knight's men surrounded him, he begged them not to shoot anymore and asked for water. One of Newton's army raised him up and gave him a draft. They then carried him to Sallie Dulancy's house, where he died that night.

The slayings of Fairchild, Kilgore, and McGilvery in early 1864 marked another escalation in the war in the Piney Woods. Over the next several weeks the emboldened guerrillas conducted a campaign to cleanse the countryside of Confederate loyalists. Two more men caught bullets; a well-known potter and landowner named B. J. Rushton and an affluent fifty-six-year-old Baptist preacher in Jasper County named John Carlyle. Other prominent rebels were assaulted and intimidated and run out of the county with nothing left. Their houses began to burn.

"These deserters brought terror into the hearts of people who sympathized with the Confederacy," recalled J. C. Andrews, a teenaged conscript who worked a gin mill in Jasper County. "They robbed George Harbor and beat him and left a notice for him to leave the country at once, which he did. Neal McGill, a Mr. Patterson, and S. A. Allen were also robbed and beaten and their lives threatened. They left the country to save their lives." Another teenaged Jones County rebel conscript, Maddie Bush, recalled that virtually every local Confederate bureaucrat fled, until there was no civil authority left. "There was nothing to support the officers, and there was nothing to assess," he said. "There was no sheriff, assessor, or tax collector."

The theme of the attacks was clear: Newton and the Jones County Scouts were making war on anyone aiding the rebel cause, hounding them just as Unionists like Newton and John Hill Aughey had been hounded after secession.

Pleas for help flooded the offices of Confederate authorities. On February 8, 1864, a Captain William H. Hardy in Raleigh, the seat of Smith County, warned Governor Charles Clark that between two hundred and three hundred deserters in Jones were "confederated" in driving respectable citizens out and that they had murdered a Baptist minister in the southwestern part of Jasper. Hardy asserted that local troops were incapable of dealing with the guerrillas and that citizens refused to act against them "for fear of some private injury." On the very same day, Clark received another equally dismaying account from the sheriff of nearby Perry County, G. W. Bradley, who declared that he was so threatened by guerrillas that he could not collect taxes except "at the risk of my life."

It had become obvious to the Confederate high command that something disquieting was happening in the Piney Woods. There was a sharp difference between deserter bushwhacking and this new more concerted militancy, which seemed to be spreading. The reports suggested that the guerrillas in Jones were highly organized, and growing in size and control, and they seemed to be forming fluid partnerships with other bands of disaffected insurrectionists in surrounding counties. In fact, Newton would later claim to have collaborated with men across five counties.

But what alarmed military authorities the most was evidence that Newton had established contact with the Yankees. On January 28, 1864, citizens of Jasper and Smith counties wrote to Governor Clark pleading for protection from at least three hundred Union-friendly deserters in Jones who, in addition to driving rebel loyalists out of the area, were rumored to be getting ammunition from Yankee sources on the Gulf coast. The loyalists implored the governor to send a "strong force" to their aid.

Newton and the Scouts had illustrated their range

with the attack on Fairchild's Confederate wagon train in the Chickasawhay Swamp. The place where they had struck was fifty miles southeast of Jones, virtually on the Alabama border. Clearly, Newton's influence was broad and he was well traveled, and Confederate authorities therefore had plenty of reason to believe he was in contact with Union officers from Grant's occupying army.

The Confederate commander of the Department of Alabama, Mississippi, and East Louisiana, Lieutenant General Leonidas Polk, was especially disconcerted by word that the Jones County Scouts were threatening to destroy the rail bridges in their vicinity. These were no mere bushwhackers simply out to heist some corn. They were political militants. "Southern Yankees" Polk labeled them.

On February 7, 1864, Polk ordered General Dabney Maury, the commander in Mobile, to dispatch a cavalry unit of no less than five hundred troops, who were to descend on Jones County and clear out the guerrillas. Polk warned that the terrain would be difficult and they would need local guides. The cavalrymen were to be led by Maury's cousin, Colonel Henry Maury.

"I find the officer in charge of the guards at Red Bluff bridge, on the Mobile and Ohio Railroad, has been made uneasy by the messages he has received from those deserters, & c., in Jones County, that they propose to burn the bridges on that road," Polk wrote to Maury.

I advise that Colonel Maury proceed without delay on his expedition against them. He will find 500 men ample for his work; but he cannot do it on horseback; he must dismount his men, and artillery will be of no service. His best place to proceed to is Winchester, on the Mobile and Ohio Railroad, where I have ordered a half a dozen guides to be sent to meet him and report to him. These are men whose houses have been burned by them, and whose families have been insulted. They are soldiers from Enterprise and are anxious to join the expedition and make thorough work of it. If the colonel cannot get forage in that country (as he cannot) for his horses he had better order it down to Winchester and press wagons to haul it out to where he will leave his horses. My orders are that as these men have become a lawless banditti, having murdered a conscripting officer [McLemore] and several of the peaceable citizens and plundered them, as well as burned their houses, they be dealt with in the most summary manner, and I entrust this duty to the colonel because I believe he will accomplish it satisfactorily. No time should be lost.

But it would be nearly a month before Maury and his cavalrymen finally responded and made it into Jones County. The Confederates were too busy dealing with a real Yankee: one named Sherman.

At the same time urgent reports of disaffection in Jones and the surrounding counties were reaching the desk of the governor, the rebel military commander

Polk was becoming aware of a large movement of Union troops. On February 3, Sherman had launched an arrowing campaign from Vicksburg into the heart of the Mississippi interior. His goal, 150 miles across the state, was a large depot town, Meridian.

His red hair bristled like a currycomb, and he issued a glare from a face as creased as the folds in an old dog. When he talked he was so manic and stunningly fluent that the conversation left listeners exhausted. But in fact, William Tecumseh Sherman, "Cump" to his friends and "Uncle Billy" to his troops, was a clearheaded man, especially about the nature of war, a subject on which he was incorruptible. He couldn't stand high-flown rhetoric about it. "Its glory is all moonshine; even success the most brilliant is over dead and mangled bodies, with the anguish and lamentation of distant families," he said.

Sherman's insight into the anguish and lamentation of families was based on experience: his nine-year-old son Willie had died of typhoid on a visit with his father to Mississippi in 1863, an event that bored a hole in the soldier's heart. The loss both heightened his sensitivities and hardened his judgment that the only relief to such a brutal conflict was a quick end. Later, when the mayor of Atlanta asked Sherman to spare civilian homes, he replied grimly, "You might as well appeal against the thunderstorm as against these terrible hardships of war."

For Sherman the fight against the South was personal as well as professional; it did not just involve hostile armies "but a hostile people," whose excessive pride was to blame. He believed he possessed an understanding of Southern manhood and therefore the stubbornness of the conflict. He had spent 1859 to 1861 as the superintendent of a military academy in Baton Rouge and knew well "the young bloods of the South," as he called them,

> sons of planters, lawyers about towns, good billiard players and sportsmen, men who never did any work and never will. War suits them, and the rascals are brave, fine riders, bold to rashness, and dangerous subjects in every sense. They care not a sou for niggers, land or any thing. They hate Yankees per se, and don't bother their brains about the past, present or future. As long as they have good horses, plenty of forage, and an open country, they are happy . . . and they are the most dangerous set of men that this war has turned loose upon the world. They are splendid riders, first-rate shots and utterly reckless. These men must all be killed or employed by us before we can hope for peace . . . At present horses cost them nothing; for they take where they find, and don't bother their brains as to who is to pay for them; the same may be said of the cornfields, which have, as they believe, been cultivated by a good-natured people for their special benefit.

Nothing short of total devastation would cure them of fighting, Sherman believed. The Union should "make them so sick of war that generations would pass away before they would again appeal to it." Together with Grant, Sherman settled on a "strategy of exhaustion" calculated to demolish the home front that supported the Confederate war effort. The sooner he broke the Confederate will, the sooner the war would be over. "I would make this war as severe as possible, and show no symptoms of tiring until the South begs for mercy," he said. "Indeed I know . . . the end would be reached quicker by such a course."

Sherman's purpose in marching to Meridian, a hub of storehouses and railroads just fifteen miles from the Alabama border, was as simple as it was savage: to gut the state. He proposed to burn rails, gins, houses, barns, fences, and fields. He would cut an inland swathe of 150 miles, straight eastward across the length of Mississippi. He left Vicksburg on February 3 with a column of twenty thousand troops carrying light rations and armed with pickaxes and other tools of destruction. At the same time, he ordered seven thousand cavalry under General Sooy Smith to drive south from Memphis.

These movements froze the Confederate commander, Polk, who lapsed into confusion. Polk was the six-foot-tall former Episcopal bishop of Louisiana, and though his men called him "The Bishop," they quickly lost faith in him. Portly, with bad teeth and muttonchops, he struck Walter Rorer of the 20th Mississippi as "a man who loved good living before the war and would have no objection to it now if he could get it . . . I think him a good man and a true one, but can not by any means think him a preeminent man."

Polk fretted over Sherman's destination, concerned that his real aim was the crucial port of Mobile. He shifted his men around uncertainly—Rorer's unit was ordered to advance to Jackson, only to be ordered to fall back without firing a shot, despite the fact that they could see the enemy campfires. Finally, Polk ordered a complete withdrawal from Mississippi. It was an order issued out of caution: Polk believed he could better protect the factories of Alabama, and block an advance on Mobile, by evacuating to Demopolis, Alabama. Columns of men filed out of Meridian carrying stores and marched toward the state border.

They made a slow, bitter night march through dense pine barrens and across the Tombigbee River. Artillery and baggage trains constantly stuck in the mud, behind which columns of men came to a halt and were forced to wait for long hours in mud and standing water. Frigid men built fires while they waited and stamped their feet beside the flames, and soon others fell out of ranks to warm themselves and refused to move when their companies did, dissolving the columns into chaos. The lines of stragglers stretched for miles.

Men gathered pine knots and built bonfires at the bases of trees. Some of the pines were dead, and as the flames leaped upward they caught at the bark and spiraled, turning the trees into huge columns of fire. The road was illuminated for miles with these towers of flame, as well as smaller lights of campfires, making an eerie and "grand sight," Rorer observed.

By daybreak, Rorer's 20th Mississippi had moved just two miles, and it would take them fourteen more days to complete their journey. Some of the men were without shoes, and Rorer could not fathom how they continued to stand, much less walk. "The men suffered a great deal, many making the latter half of the trip barefooted, those who were barefooted were mostly boys, they would make the marches on dark nights when it was so cold I could scarcely ride," he wrote.

Mississippi troops were furious on the retreat, shamed and reluctant to leave their home state undefended, with its regnant old oaks hanging heavy over the dark green river bends and sandbars, the gorgeous riverside cities, and the purple- and black-tinged bayous. Officers watched the columns thinning before their eyes as men dropped out of ranks, many of them never to return. "Now the whole State was to be abandoned without a single blow," wrote Captain John B. Love of the 15th Mississippi Infantry. "No wonder the hearts of her sons burned within them; and no wonder if they learned to distrust the policy that gave their homes to the torch and their families to the tender mercies of the foe . . . So many had left the regiment that some companies were slimly represented . . . I doubt if I ever see one of them again but these men are neither traitors nor deserters."

Meanwhile, the advancing Yankees laid waste to

everything they came across. Each day, large parties were sent out to destroy dwellings, tracks, roads, bridges, and fields, until the entire horizon was left flattened and smoking. Soldiers burst into homes and seized every article and morsel, sometimes even sweeping food off of plates. Sherman tried to control pillaging and ordered that occupied homes weren't to be burned and civilians weren't to be molested, but some of his soldiers were intent on punishing Southerners for their treason. A soldier named Lucius Barber of the 15th Illinois observed, "The country was one lurid blaze of fire; burning cotton gins and deserted dwellings were seen on every hand. I regret to say it, but oft-times habitations were burned down over the heads of occupants . . . I have seen the cabin of the poor entered and the last mouthful taken from almost starving children."

Sherman's columns marched the 150 miles to Meridian in under two weeks, reaching the outskirts of town on the afternoon of February 14. There was nothing left to hinder the Yankees but some Confederate cavalry, who harassed them with a brief skirmish, and some trees that had been felled by retreating rebels. The residents of Meridian hid behind locked doors and peered through their windows as the Yankees walked through their front yards and occupied the town.

A well-to-do Meridian woman, Mrs. Ball, described the wrecking and ransacking that ensued in a letter to her mother in Mobile, which found its way into a newspaper. "After the skirmishing stopped, the mob ran around going into houses, breaking open doors, trunks, locks &c. tearing up and destroying everything they could," she wrote. "Caught all the chickens in the place in half an hour." Five men entered her home and demanded her keys, as well as any arms, gold, and silver she had. Men carried off blankets and the sacks of flour in her pantry. A Yankee captain paused to admire a small child named Mary and told her that if she would only go home with him, she would not be in any more war. She replied, "No: I am a rebel, and I do not want to be with the Yankees."

The Confederate arsenal and warehouses were burned to the ground, as were all of the public buildings. Every store, as well as the printing office and the town's three hotels, Ragsdale's, Terrill's, and the Burton House, were in cinders. There was not a milk cow or horse left in the town, or for ten miles around for that matter. "Oh, such destruction! I do not believe you or anyone else would know the place. There's not a fence in Meridian. I have not one rail left."

The Yankees occupied Meridian for six days—"They stayed here from Sunday until Saturday morning, and it appeared like a month," Mrs. Ball wrote—and by the time they were done with the residences, some women were left with only the dresses on their backs.

Meridian was merely the orbit point for Sherman's troops. They reached out into the countryside and systematically tore up the Mobile and Ohio Railroad for fifty miles. Their destruction extended on each point of the compass, north to Lauderdale Springs, east to Alabama, west all the way back to Jackson, and as far south as Quitman, only thirty miles from Jones County, which they "devastated." Every unit was assigned a portion of track to destroy. The men pulled up ties and rails, heaped them into piles, and made bonfires of them. When the rails were red hot, they bent them around trees to render them unsalvageable. The twisted metal shapes were dubbed "Sherman's neckties."

"For five days 10,000 men worked hard and with a will in that work of destruction with axes, crowbars, sledges, clawbards, and with fire, and I have no hesitation in pronouncing the work as well done," Sherman wrote remorselessly in his official report. "Meridian, with its depots, store houses, arsenal, hospitals, offices, hotels, and cantonments no longer exists."

There was some malice in the destruction wrought by the Yankees, who like their commander were war-sick and bent on punishing Southern arrogance for perpetuating the conflict. The days when Union soldiers were curious or charmed by the graciousness of the region were long gone, replaced by boiling resentment. A Northern soldier summed up their mood when he wished for the "chance to try our Enfields on some of their villainous hides and let a little of that high Blood out of them, which I think will increase their respect for the northern mud sills."

One of Sherman's men torched a home over the head of a Southern woman who had spat in his face.

When she fled to the home next door, he touched his torch to that home, too. The Yankees, bone chilled and stiff after two weeks of living outdoors in temperatures that left an inch of ice in their water buckets, stripped every home of featherbeds, blankets, quilts, and clothes and wielded their axes on buildings indiscriminately for firewood.

The destruction was fearsome, and Sherman in his official report seemed to take pleasure in the numbers that described the scale of it: fifty-three bridges and culverts burned, nineteen locomotives and twenty-eight rail cars torched, 6,075 feet of trestlework and fifty-five miles of road destroyed. He bragged that his campaign had "stampeded" Polk into Alabama, leaving him to "smash things at pleasure, and I think it is well done . . . Our loss was trifling, and we broke absolutely and effectually a full hundred miles of railroad at and around Meridian. No car can pass through that place this campaign. We lived off the country and made a swath of desolation 50 miles broad across the State of Mississippi, which the present generation will not forget. We bring in some 500 prisoners, a good many refugee families, and about 10 miles of negroes."

Sherman was not exaggerating about the legion of humanity that followed his army. Along the way his men had liberated some ten thousand enslaved souls from plantations. About half of these disappeared into the swamps and forests, to fight a more invisible war, or stayed in the area. The rest, mostly women and children, followed him back to Vicksburg, doubling the length of his columns. "I am afraid to guess at the number, but it was a string of ox wagons, Negro women, and children behind each brigade that equaled in length the brigade itself, and I had 12 brigades," Sherman said. Along with them came about one thousand white refugees, as well as three thousand horses, mules, and oxen pulling an enormous quantity of seized wagons and vehicles.

Sherman brought back something else too: evidence of underground anti-Confederate resistance taking place in the swamps. In a letter to Major General Henry Halleck in which he described his campaign, Sherman included a curious item. He had received "a declaration of independence" from "certain people who are trying to avoid the southern conscription and lie out in the swamps," he wrote. "I promised them countenance, and encouraged them to organization for mutual defense." He was forwarding this document to Halleck, "for such action as you please."

The fact that Sherman bothered to send the declaration to Halleck, the commander of the entire army, suggests how seriously he took it. Ordinarily, Sherman sneered at professed Southern Unionists, whom he considered useless half cowards. Only six months earlier, after conquering Vicksburg, he had written to Halleck of his contempt for them. "The Union men of the South," he wrote, "I must confess, I have little respect for this class. They allowed a clamorous set of demagogues to muzzle and drive them as a pack of curs. Afraid of shadows, they submit tamely to squads of dragoons, and permit them, without a murmur, to burn their cotton, take their horses, corn, and everything; and, when we reach them, are full of complaints . . . They give us no assistance or information . . . I account them as nothing in this great game of war."

Evidently in Meridian, Sherman encountered a group that he believed **could** aid the Union war effort. It's impossible to know whether the "declaration of independence" was from Newton and his men, because the document has been lost. But the Jones County Scouts' campaign of violent opposition was surely what Sherman was looking for from Southern allies and would have won his support. Whoever the swamp deserters were, Sherman respected them enough to promise them "countenance" and forwarded their document up the chain of command.

It is quite possible that a member of Newton Knight's company could have reached Sherman's army to declare independence and request aid, such as arms and rations. Some of Sherman's men came within twenty miles of Jones. The Yankees destroyed a railroad bridge over the Chickasawhay River below the town of Quitman, very close to Newton's old territory in Jasper County.

Also, large parties of Sherman's men were continually in the countryside scavenging for provisions. Sherman sent as many as one thousand troopers a day out to forage, and a number of these men became isolated from the main columns and were cut off. The foragers, who moved in parties of fifty to one hundred men, were the most exposed part of the army, preyed upon so constantly by Confederate cavalry that more Union soldiers were lost this way than in combat in the campaign. Yankees who were cut off undoubtedly found succor with deserters and Southern Unionist guerrillas in the remote swamps that by now had become home to transients of every stripe, including Unionist followers of John Hill Aughey's from up in Lauderdale County.

Somehow, Newton established enough of a reputation with Sherman's men that just after the war, in July 1865, he would have a personal interview in Meridian with General William Linn McMillen, one of Sherman's favorite subordinates. McMillen was a fast-rising infantry officer from Ohio who would fight ably from Bull Run through the capture of Mobile and earned special praise from Sherman. Though he was not with Sherman in Meridian, he had led a brigade in the siege of Vicksburg and would range through much of interior Mississippi between 1863 and his mustering out in August of 1865. After the war, Newton named McMillen as someone who could vouch for his company's loyalty to the Union. McMillen thought well enough of Newton to give him his post office address in Columbus, Ohio.

Whether or not Newton was in direct communication with the Yankees at Meridian, he seems to have gotten something out of the campaign: ideas. The success of the Yankee raid was clearly inspiring. Over the next month, he and his followers would launch yet another series of effective partisan raids.

Every detail of the twelve-gauge, muzzle-loading shotgun that Newton aimed at the Confederate guard shone with menace. It was so highly polished it seemed to have just come from the maker, the wooden stock well oiled and without a crack, the double barrels glaring like a pair of black eyes, the twin hammers cocked and ready to strike the nipple-shaped percussion caps, and the thin wooden ramrod clipped beneath the barrels to prime for reloading.

Had the Confederate guard known what was in the gun, he'd have been more cooperative. Newton packed each of his barrels with double loads of lead balls, heavy charged with powder behind them. There were thirty-six pieces of shot in Newton's gun—it was his way of evening the odds against the entire Confederate army. All of his men had learned to pack their guns the same way, using any kind of lead they could find; Minié balls, rifle bullets, or homemade scraps they melted down. Once, they hauled one of their victims to a doctor with eleven wounds. The surgeon said to them, "You must be right smart shooters to hit one man 11 times with rifle bullets."

The recalcitrant rebel guard stood before the locked door of the Confederate commissary and tax-in-kind depot in Paulding, Mississippi. Newton had learned via the grapevine that the storehouse contained a huge mound of cornmeal intended for shipment to troops. Newton had ridden into Paulding with two hundred men and half a dozen ox-drawn wagons he commandeered from local farmers. But now the raid was faltering, because the guard refused to open the door, despite the shotgun.

"Open the door," Newton said.

"I've got no orders to open the door," the guard said.

"Bring me an ax," Newton called to one of his men.

A Jones Scout hefted an ax out of a wagon and handed it to him. Newton stalked around to the side of the warehouse, lifted the blade, and stroked it into the side of the pine-timbered building with a **crack.** He pried it loose, then sank it once again into the pine, dislodging a chunk of wood.

The doorkeeper hollered out, "Don't do that, Captain Knight! I will open the door for you."

Newton replied, "I asked you to open the door but you said you had no order to open up, so you need not bother yourself. I will soon have a door open around here."

Newton hacked at the wall until he had cut a hole in the building large enough to walk through standing up. His men drew the wagons around and began shifting loads of corn from the warehouse into the wagon beds. While they worked, Newton strode over to the local saloon and summoned the bartender. "Don't let my men have any whiskey," he said. "If you do, I'll shoot you." A raid on the Confederate warehouse in broad daylight was hazardous enough without his men getting drunk for the return trip.

As the men continued shuttling corn out of the warehouse, a group of empty-eyed, ragged, beggar-like men and women approached Newton. They were Irish indigents, despised by the local Confederates because their men refused to serve in the army. They were out of bread and their families were starving. Could Newton and his men give them some supplies from the warehouse? "They were pretty hard off," Newton remembered. "They didn't want to fight, and the Confederates wouldn't give 'em or sell 'em anything."

The wagons were brimming and heavy on their axles with sacks of corn. As the Jones County men were mounting their horses and climbing onto the buckboards to depart, Newton halted them. He turned to the Irish. "Take all you want," he said. The families eagerly helped themselves to all of the corn they could carry. When their arms were full, Newton said the Lord's Prayer.

The wagon train then resumed its slow procession out of Paulding and back toward Jones County, where the men "distributed corn out to all who needed it," Newton recalled. They stashed the rest at their various headquarters in the woods, to which they retreated as rebel troops descended on the county in response to a call from the Paulding sheriff. The rebels recovered most of the wagons, but men and corn had vanished into the dense underbrush and reed brakes.

The Paulding raid established Newton's legend as

a swamp pirate, though Newton didn't regard it as his greatest feat. "Shucks, that warn't much of a job," he said later. But it stirred indignation among Confederates, for though it was a small raid it was a humiliating one that came immediately on the heels of the larger humiliation of Sherman's incursion. Meridian was still smoking when Confederate officials received the official report of Newton's caper on March 3, 1864. Whether or not Newton was in literal touch with Union commanders, he seemed to be speaking to them—and perhaps imitating them.

Word of the events at Paulding came from a Confederate lieutenant named A. H. Polk, who was sent to survey the damage wrought by Sherman. During his reconnaissance, Polk discovered that the entire area from Meridian to Jones County had become hazardous ground because of Unionists. He described what he found:

> At Meridian, I found that the enemy had burned and destroyed all of the Government houses except one house, in which a family was living. They also burned a good deal of private property, consisting of two hotels and all the stores in the place, as well as the Clarion office. In Enterprise all of the Government houses were burned, as well as a good deal of private property. The bridge across the river was also burned. All the cotton along the road was burned.
>
> I beg leave also to say something in regard to

tories and deserters, who infest Jones County and a portion of Lauderdale [where Meridian is located]. The tories in Jones County made a raid on Paulding not many days ago, about 200 strong, and carried off a good deal of corn as well as other property. They are becoming very troublesome, as well as dangerous, to the country around.

Within the week, the Piney Woods Unionists launched a far more serious attack on a Confederate installation in New Augusta that demonstrated just how brazen they had become. Fifty Jones guerrillas collaborating with allies from neighboring Perry County assaulted the old conscription station where Amos McLemore had headquartered. Two men calling themselves "captains," including one named Landrum from Jones, led the party. This may have been Thomas Landrum, a yeoman farmer and neighbor of the Knights and a Unionist who would join the Yankee forces in New Orleans later that spring.

The men had marked on their hats "U.S. Victory or Death." They surrounded the home in which the local conscription officer, Captain John J. Bradford, of the 3rd Mississippi Regiment, was staying. In broad daylight they called him outside and took a vote on whether to hang him. He was "paroled" after he promised to quit the conscription service and swore never again to enter the county or to in any way aid in attacks against them.

They took three more prisoners at gunpoint, liberated the local slaves, and seized a dozen horses, government stores, ammunition, and cooking utensils. They issued provisions to destitute families in the neighborhood. And before they left, they made a triumphal brag, according to the official Confederate report: "They stated they were in regular communication with the Yankees, were fighting for the Union, and would have peace or hell by August. They told the negros they were free."

The rebel high command was finally driven to act. General Dabney H. Maury in Mobile ordered his younger cousin, Colonel Henry Maury, to carry out his previously suspended assignment: he was to go into Jones County and smash up a "body of armed traitors," now rumored to be five hundred strong. "They have been seizing Government stores, have been killing our people, and have actually made prisoners of and paroled officers of the Confederate army," General Maury wrote incredulously. They had even threatened to cut the M&O rail line, which was so continually besieged by guerrillas that it couldn't operate without an armed guard—the railroad had requested seventy-five men from the Confederate army to help protect it.

The cavalrymen went by rail to Shubuta and from there they moved into Jones, which they found to be in "open rebellion." The adjoining counties, Perry, Greene, and Covington, were "in just as bad a condition," they discovered. Colonel Henry Maury decided to make an impression on the local populace: he burned the house of an unnamed "leader of the Tory gang" and announced to the families of the guerrillas that all who would come in voluntarily would be pardoned; but those he caught, he would hang on the spot.

Over the next several days, Maury and his men drove through the swamps on horseback. The cavalrymen rose at dawn each morning to "Boots and Saddles" and scoured the swamps and pine barrens in formation; infantry took the middle of the woods on foot, combing the underbrush, while the cavalry rode at the edges so as to cut off any routes of escape. But their efforts yielded few returns.

It was dangerous work—more dangerous than perhaps Maury had expected. Knight and his men baited the cavalry, hoping to lure parties of them deeper into the swamp and cut them off. One night, a company of cavalrymen on picket in the Bogue Homa Swamp glimpsed firelight in the distance, about half a mile away. Four men were sent to reconnoiter and edged cautiously toward the firelight with their guns cocked. They came within a few paces of the fire when they saw that it was abandoned. Just then, they sighted another fire, still another half mile off. "It was very evident that the tories were trying to decoy us into the swamp and away from our camp," a trooper reported. "Our force being so small, the Lieutenant thought we had better return to camp, which we did."

Another, better-laid trap succeeded. Some of the area farmwives invited the troopers to a dance party at Levi Valentine's. The cavalrymen arrived to find a Ne-

gro fiddler sawing on his instrument and friendly local girls eager to waltz. But as they cavorted, the Jones
County men crept up on the guards for an ambush.
As the cavalrymen realized the trap, chaos erupted.
The women fled out the back door, while the rebels
bolted toward the front porch, where Newton's men
met them with a brace of gunfire. Two cavalrymen
and one guerrilla were killed in the exchange.

Yeoman wives continued to aid the Unionists
clandestinely, as did their children. They hid them,
fed them, armed them, and helped them melt into
the woods. One widow provided them with fifty
pounds of lead with which to make buckshot for their
shotguns.

Seventeen-year-old Sil Coleman and his younger
brother Noble, the sons of Tom Coleman, slain by
Sheriff Kilgore before the war, were firm allies of the
Knight band, idolizing the men and often riding with
them. Their teenaged sister Cornelia carried food to
their swamp encampments, swimming the Leaf River
on horseback holding baskets of provisions above her
head. Young Martha Knight was another reliable
supporter of the band, often carrying baskets to her
brother disguised under piles of corn shucks. One afternoon she crossed paths with a Confederate patrol
but managed to fool them by scattering the shucks
and calling for hogs.

The yeoman loyalty to the Knight band was based
on kinship, hunger, and resentment of the Confederate cavalry. Maury, who had grown wealthy as a

Mobile trader before the war, was an uneven officer who was twice accused of drunkenness, and he allowed his men to carouse and purloin goods from the local populace, enraging them. Another Confederate officer who visited the county a month later observed that the disaffection in Jones was at least in part exacerbated by "the many outrages that have been committed by many small commands of cavalry sent into this country," which had improperly robbed and stolen from those who could ill afford it.

The stealing sat bitterly with people who were already on the brink of destitution and had nothing left to give. Colonel William Nugent of the 28th Mississippi had vividly observed the poverty of the Piney Woods when he rode through the area that January while returning from a furlough.

"As I have often said a large portion of Mississippi territory is almost worthless," he wrote to his wife, Nellie.

> Rugged clay hills and boggy unproductive bottoms are quite a dreary prospect . . . A great many of them are in such a deplorable state of destitution that it is utterly impossible for them to supply even a single person with a meal, without stinting themselves almost to the point of starvation . . . For an instance of this destitution I called at a little log cabin by the road side and counted thirteen children besides four or five grown persons. The house was rudely constructed at the base of a

long and dreary looking hill, whose sides were covered with the withered sledge so common to old
fields in this country and a few scattered pines. At
a point where the hill flattened into a miry bottom
there was a corn field of about ten acres, the stalks
of maize resembling . . . pipe stems. This was, as
far as I could discern, the only source of supply for
bread they had. A few peaked nose specimens of
the swine tribe lazily grunted around the door and
about a dozen chickens were busily picking up the
few crumbs that fell in their way. How these and
other people in their circumstances manage to exist is an enigma to my mind. And yet they do live
and multiply almost ad infinitum. It is, however,
from such retreats as I have been describing that
our soldiers have, to a great extent, been drawn.

It was small wonder that the yeomanry was more
loyal to Newton's men, who shared their lucre from
raids such as the ones on Paulding and New Augusta
with penniless local families. Many of those families
contended that Newton Knight was all that saved
them from starvation, and their gratitude lasted for
generations afterward.

Newton was credited with a grim joke about the
privations of the county after one skirmish with Confederates left men dead on a field. "They'll never come
up with the Resurrection," he supposedly said of the
corpses. "The ground's too poor to sprout them."

Under the circumstances, Maury was bound to fail.

He rounded up only a small handful of twelve to fifteen deserters, three of whom resisted arrest. These
men received the full wrath and frustration of the
Confederate troopers. Maury ordered them hanged.

On a Saturday morning the three men, Morgan
Mitchell, Jack Smith, and Jesse Smith, were placed
into a wagon under a party of guards and driven along
an old trade road to an oak grove near Errata, Mississippi. As word circulated that the deserters were to
be executed, rebel soldiers gathered for the event as if
for a political rally. Young J. C. Andrews, the teenaged Confederate conscript who worked at the mill,
witnessed the event. A pole was set between two trees,
and the wagon with the condemned men was driven
beneath it. Nooses were placed around the necks of
the prisoners, the ropes thrown over the pole. A blast
from a bugle sounded. The wagon lurched, the men
writhed, "and three miserable wretches were launched
into eternity," one of Maury's troopers reported.

Instead of cutting the bodies down, the troopers
left them dangling in the air, as a gruesome reminder
of rebel authority. They remained suspended until
Monday, when their wives were finally permitted to
come and retrieve them for burial.

On March 12, Colonel Maury decided his assignment was concluded, and he and his men moved to the
Leaf River for the trip back to Mobile. First, he paused
in Ellisville to pen a self-congratulatory account of his
actions to General Dabney Maury. "I am satisfied that
there no longer remains any organization of deserters

in this county, although some few have to be hunted out with dogs," he wrote. It was his opinion that Jones had been home to about 150 "resident" deserters, and he had cleared out all but 20 or so.

But Confederate commanders who read Maury's letter had reason to be worried, for it was clear that Maury's cavalry hadn't destroyed the Jones County Scouts, only temporarily dispersed them, and that they retained their insolence. "They brag that they will get Yankee aid and return," Maury confessed.

In actuality, Maury was probably lucky not to have been killed. The guerrillas were so guileful and skilled at maneuvering in the swamp, Maury admitted, "their leaders twice got them in position to ambush me" before he managed to escape. And just as Maury prepared to depart, he received a dispatch from a local officer. "Don't leave a company in Jones County," it warned him. The implication was clear: an undefended company would be wiped out.

Maury had merely driven the deserters southward, to a refuge called Honey Island, a grassy atoll in Hancock County almost on the coast between two branches of the Pearl River, where its bayou waters eddied into the Gulf. In this hidden stronghold, Newton and his fellow guerrillas rested and replenished themselves on two thousand stolen beef cattle that grazed there. It was a haven for other fugitives, too, particularly runaway slaves who milled about the bayous in large numbers.

At the end of March, a rebel informant named Daniel Logan tracked the Jones County men to Honey Island. Logan reported to the Confederate provost marshal for the district that the deserters had recongregated there and were as active as ever, terrorizing the entire region from Jones to Marion County on the Louisiana border.

> Major: In accordance with your orders I have to report that a band of deserters still continue prowling about the country, doing considerable damage to the farmers and molesting travelers. Though dispersed from Perry and Jones Counties, they appear in other parts. Large numbers of these from Jones County have gone down Pearl River to and near Honey Island where they exist in some force and hold the country in awe, openly boasting of their being in communication with the Yankees.
>
> In fact, it is dangerous to travel in that part of Louisiana. In Marion County, Miss., and the upper part of Washington Parish, La., they are banded together in large numbers, bid defiance to the authorities, and claim to have a government of their own in opposition to the Confederate Government.

Honey Island may have also been a contact point for the Yankees. According to a Knight family account, it was at Honey Island that Newton and his men received arms and provisions from federal sources. The Jones Countians then floated the gear upstream on the Pearl by flatboat, then on to Jones, where they cached it in Devil's Den.

Federal steamboats occasionally plied the bayous around Honey Island, and that same week, on April 4, one named the **Lizzie Davis** hazarded the shallow waters. A major named Martin Pulver of the 20th Infantry, Corps d'Afrique, landed three companies of his black troops, and the men traversed the island and marched up the Pearl to salvage another Union steamer, the **J. D. Swaim,** which had been mudbound there for two years. There is no mention in Pulver's report of contact with Southern Unionists on the expedition, but Pulver did return with sixty-four escaped slaves who had been hiding out there.

But contact with the Yankees was extremely hazardous and intermittent. At around this time, Newton launched efforts to have his men sworn in officially as federal troops by dispatching Jasper Collins on a marathon journey to Memphis. Collins's errand was an arduous one; he traipsed miles across the war-torn countryside, only to be greeted at Memphis by a Union officer who referred him to higher authorities in Vicksburg. Collins then made his way to Vicksburg, where he met with a staff officer (possibly General Stephen Hurlbut), who gave him some "orders and instructions" to carry back to the Knight company "of a military character." These presumably involved ways in which the Jones resisters could best aid the Union cause.

Newton also sent a separate courier to New Orleans, where, he later claimed, a Union officer arranged to ship them four hundred rifles. Members of the Scouts also believed that a company of Yankees was dispatched to Jones County to swear them in but was unable to break through. There is no evidence that such a mission actually took place, and this belief may have been wishful thinking. The Union army had larger battles to fight than the one in Jones, and the Scouts largely had to fend for themselves.

Newton and his men were soon back in Jones and in control of the region again. No Confederate could operate there without feeling menaced. Sheriff William H. Quarles of Smith County reported that he had been "ambushed and shot" near his plantation by guerrillas; "no man's life is safe who dares speak out against them." On March 21, 1864, Jones County's Confederate clerk, E. M. Devall, wrote to Governor Clark in a similar state of anxiety. The Knight men had so intimidated the local Confederate bureaucrats, he said, that it was impossible to do any state business at all.

"They have gone so far as to press wagons and teams and have halled [sic] away a good deal of the tax in kind from the different places in the adjoining counties, not only the deserters in this county, but others," he wrote. "Deserters have joined them from different counties and have stopped the government agents from driving stock out of the country." The guerrillas, he reported, had "resolved not to pay any tax neither state, county, nor confederate."

The rebel quartermaster for Mississippi and east Louisiana reported that as far as he could tell, the Confederacy had lost complete control of the area. The deserters had "overrun and taken possession of the country, in many cases exiling the good and loyal citizens or shooting them in cold blood on their own door-sills." The rebel tax agent in Jones was ordered to leave, at peril of his life. He was not heard from again. The tax agent in neighboring Covington County was not only warned to cease collecting tithes but to distribute what he had seized to the local families. He continued his duties only "at risk of his life and property."

A rebel lieutenant named W. C. Parsons of the 12th Louisiana wrote his own observations of the subversives operating in Jones in a report to the regional provost marshal: "They are committing every kind of outrage—driving all the loyal citizens out of the county, and killing all those who have acted as guides to our forces. They have killed several citizens, and eight men belonging to our forces sent there to arrest them."

Newton and his allies had reached the high watermark of their war. The Confederacy had virtually lost southeast Mississippi: the entire lower third of the state was in the hands of Unionists and renegades. They controlled Jones, Jasper, Covington, Perry, and Smith counties and exhibited such far-flung mobility that they apparently came and went from Hancock and Marion counties freely. Their loose alliances with other bands extended over a wide swath of territory to the north; there is evidence that they even collaborated with men in Greene and Lauderdale counties, where disaffection seemed to be spreading rapidly.

Robert S. Hudson, a fire-breathing circuit court judge who traveled through several counties from Leake to Yazoo in March 1864, was aghast to observe a mobile community of guerrillas and disloyal men who seemed to filter from county to county with impunity. Hudson wrote several letters to President Jefferson Davis of almost hysterical agitation, warning that the deserter problem was liable to cost him the entire state, if not the war. He urged Davis and his aides to deal with the deserter problem "with an iron hand and hearts of stone."

Hudson described Unionists who "gave parties for deserters & danced over the fall of Vicksburg & all our defeats. They are all rotten as hell . . . There are hundreds of others, settled in the hills and swamp, and unless you get them out they will destroy you. They are abolitionist, spies, deserters, liars, murderers, and every thing foul & damnable."

They were also elusive, and cunning. "They are sly & shy and skilled in hiding and woodsing," Hudson said. "Let me again urge you by all that is sacred & manly, noble and generous to put every element at work that can arrest them and this hellish tide."

"The state," Hudson advised Governor Charles Clark, "is now under the tacit rule of deserters, thieves, and disloyal men and women."

A rebel officer named Wirt Thompson, a captain in the 24th Mississippi, returned home to Greene County on a furlough in late March to discover he had to fear for his life. Saboteurs had wrecked and looted the region's entire infrastructure. It was apparent to Thompson that they had a clearly organized command structure and good weaponry, and he even heard a rumor that an American flag had been raised over the courthouse in Jones.

Thompson was so moved that he wrote a long missive to James A. Seddon, the Confederate secretary of war.

"The whole southern and southeastern section of Mississippi is in a most deplorable condition, and unless succor is sent speedily the country is utterly ruined, and every loyal citizen will be driven from it or meet a tragic and untimely fate at the hands of those who are aiding and abetting our enemies," Thompson wrote.

> Several of the most prominent citizens have already been driven from their homes, and some have been slaughtered in their own homes because they refused to obey the mandates of the outlaws and abandon the country. Numbers have been ordered away and are now living under threats and in fear of their lives. It is a matter of great personal danger and risk for an officer or soldier of the Confederate army to make his appearance in the country, and so perfect are these organizations and systems

of dispatching that in a few hours large bodies of them can be collected at any given point prepared to attempt almost anything.

Government depots filled with supplies have been either robbed or burned. Gin-houses, dwelling-houses, and barns, and the court-house of Greene County, have been destroyed by fire. Bridges have been burned and ferry-boats sunk on almost every stream and at almost every ferry to obstruct the passage of troops; their pickets and vendettas lie concealed in swamps and thickets on the roadside; spies watch the citizens and eavesdrop their houses at night, and a Tory despotism of the most op-pressive description governs the country; citizens' horses, wagons, guns, & c., are pressed at the op-tion of any outlaw who may desire them, and if the citizen makes any remonstrance he is treated to a caning, a rope, or is driven from the country. Deserters from every army and from every State are among them. They have colonels, majors, cap-tains, and lieutenants; boast themselves to be not less than a thousand strong in organized bod-ies, besides what others are outsiders and disloyal citizens (of whom I regret to say there are many). They have frequent and uninterrupted communi-cation with the enemy on Ship Island and other points; have a sufficiency of arms and ammunition of the latest Northern and European manufacture in abundance, and I was told that they boast of fighting for the Union.

Gentlemen of undoubted veracity informed me that the Federal flag had been raised by them over the court-house in Jones County, and in the same county they are said to have fortified rendezvous, and that Yankees are frequently among them. Companies of 40 or 50 men go together to each other's fields, stack arms, place out a picket guard, and then cut and roll logs, repair fences, & c., and in this way they swear they intend to raise crops and defend themselves from cavalry this season. The country is entirely at their mercy.

It was Thompson's advice that the Confederacy would need a full-scale military operation to reclaim the region; nothing less than a brigade of "well-drilled infantry troops" could wipe the Unionists out.

Lieutenant General Leonidas Polk had already reached the same conclusion. He wrote to Jefferson Davis describing the intolerable state of affairs. The Jones Countians were "in open rebellion, defiant at the outset, proclaiming themselves 'Southern Yankees,' and resolved to resist by force of arms all efforts to capture them."

Polk decided to settle the problem once and for all: he ordered elements from two of the most battle-hardened regiments in the whole of the Confederate army, the "Bloody" 6th Mississippi and the intensely loyal 20th Mississippi, to conduct an expansive sweep of lower Mississippi, combing the several counties between the Pearl and Tombigbee rivers for deserters.

To command the special operation, Polk selected a stony-eyed colonel from the 6th Mississippi, and a native of the Piney Woods who had risen above his country roots, Robert Lowry. There was hardly a more aspiring or devoted officer in the Confederate army. The peacetime lawyer and legislator had begun the war as a private. He still bore the scars of Shiloh on his arm and on his chest: his unit had gone into the battle with 425 men and emerged with just 115. Lowry experienced a metamorphosis after Shiloh; promoted to the rank of major, he had ascended steadily until he commanded the entire regiment. He was one of the South's fightingest officers, campaigning at Corinth, Port Hudson, Port Gibson, Bayou Pierre, Champion Hill, and Vicksburg, and he would be promoted to general in 1865.

In Lowry, the Confederacy had called a response down on the heads of Newton and his men that would make their previous conflicts seem like skirmishes. Lowry was bringing with him crack infantry, cavalry, and ropes for more hanging. "The most rigid and summary punishment is necessary to correct these evils," Lowry announced.

Recollections of Newton Knight, interview with Meigs O. Frost, 1921

We knew we were completely surrounded by the rebels. But we knew every trail in the woods. So we stayed out in the woods minding our own business, until the Confederate Army began sending raiders after us, with bloodhounds. Then we saw we had to fight. So we organized this company and the boys elected me captain . . .

Yes, sir, there was right smart trouble then. We were pretty quiet for a while. We figured out that the rebels were too strong for us just then to fight our way through to jine up with the Union forces. And we thought that we'd wait until the federals fought their way down closer to us or we got stronger.

But the rebels started to build a fire under us.

SIX

Banners Raised and Lowered

March 1864, Smith County, Mississippi

The flag was a hopelessly makeshift rag, "a rather ludicrous representation," sneered one of Lowry's men, who confiscated it from a Unionist in the Piney Woods. It was roughly made, with hand-drawn stars, the sketched outline of an eagle, and stamped with the letters "U.S.A."

There was nothing ludicrous about the sentiment behind it, however. To soldiers and citizens alike flags signified possession. They were the ensigns of cause and the colors of armies; they told which side a man was on, to what corps, division, and brigade he belonged, and the bloodstains on them were emblems of reputations. A raised standard meant triumph, a lowered one meant grief. The poet Walt Whitman, who was working as a hospital orderly that April, marveled at the blood spent to save a single regimental square of cloth.

"It was taken by the secesh in a cavalry fight, and rescued by our men in a bloody little skirmish. It cost three men's lives, just to get one little flag, four by three," he wrote. "Our men rescued it, and tore it from the breast of a dead rebel—all that, just for the name of getting their little banner back again . . . There isn't a reg't . . . that wouldn't do the same."

The flag seized by Lowry's men belonged to a local Smith County mill owner named Hawkins, who flew the "ludicrous" symbol from his establishment as a signal for convening assemblies of Unionists and fugitive deserters. Hawkins, encouraged by Sherman's Meridian campaign, had believed that the Union presence in southeastern Mississippi was a permanent one and that the Confederates had been driven from the state for good. As Lowry's men occupied the county, the flag was hastily lowered and hidden. "It was concealed on the person of Mrs. Hawkins, who would not deliver it until after much persuasion and few threats," a rebel reported. We can only imagine the terrified stubbornness of the woman, surrounded by combat-hardened infantrymen, her husband taken into custody as a traitor.

To Lowry's men, the flag signaled the depth of local disloyalty. The mere existence of such a scrawled and tattered rag angered them; it suggested the resisters had "hung out the banners on the outer walls," as one of Lowry's men said. It also demonstrated that they were dealing with "bitter, stubborn resistance."

Lowry's punishment was swift, and brutal. On March 28, just a day after he arrived in the Piney

Woods, he wrapped nooses around the necks of two Unionist leaders and left them dangling in the trees. A third man was shot down while trying to escape. Several others were arrested, including Hawkins, and held for trial.

Next, Lowry restored the Smith County sheriff to his office. Then, to make sure that the entire countryside was aware of his presence, he posted a stern notice to the citizenry. The following leaflet was distributed to the local villages.

"I came among you a few days since for the purpose of correcting evils which had well-nigh destroyed your county," Lowry wrote.

On my arrival I found your sheriff had been run from his home and duties, and that deserters and absentees had the ascendancy in your county. You are now free from this curse, and if you will now perform your duties as patriots and freemen you will remain so. Let each man feel that he has an individual duty to discharge and let him do it fearlessly and to the letter. When you find in your midst a deserter, secure and send him to his command. If loyal citizens are ordered from their homes by a band of marauders and house-burners, treat them as outlaws and common enemies to mankind. When our independence shall be gained and an unbiased history of this war written, do not have your children to feel disgraced because of the action of their sires. Your county has sent many

soldiers to the field. Numbers have won for themselves proud names and stand deservedly high in
their commands, and it is the imperative duty of
those at home to maintain good order, execute the
laws, and have a well-regulated community. Our
soldiers in the Army are enthusiastic and determined. All have the most perfect confidence in
the distinguished commander of this department,
Lieutenant-General Polk. Then let us work in concert together and we will soon again breathe the
pure air of liberty.

That Lowry meant to impose order, and was not to
be trifled with, was evident from his appearance. He
was a burly man who conveyed heavy-handedness as
he stalked and pranced on horseback across the countryside, the picture of rebel command in his fluttering
caped overcoat and slouch hat, elegant braided qua-
trefoil on his sleeves, and an oval of buttons glinting
on his double-breasted jacket. He wore his hair swept
well back from a thick-jowled face, and his cleft chin
was habitually upturned. But his most prominent
feature was the crooked M of his upper lip, which
seemed permanently twisted in an expression of disdain, accentuated with a dense, bristling mustache.
He exuded authority.

For three weeks, Lowry dashed about the Piney
Woods, chasing down men. In a sweep of Smith
County alone, he captured 350 prisoners. He found
the area teeming with missing conscripts, either shirk-

ing on their farms or hiding in the woods, and local rebels powerless over them. He observed "the entire demoralization of the whole country," he reported to headquarters. "Loyalty to the [Confederate] Government is punished by death or banishment from home, and the deserters are organized for defense against the cavalry or plundering upon good and loyal citizens."

Next, Lowry moved on the Jones County band. On April 12, Lowry's men trespassed on Newton Knight's territory for the first time. They were instantly repaid with gunshots. That evening, twenty of Lowry's men who had been patrolling stopped to dine at the home of a local physician. As the rebel troopers lounged on the piazza in the evening twilight, Daniel Reddoch, grandson of early Jones County settler William Reddoch and one of Newton's staunchest men, moved stealthily through the dusk. He raised his overpacked shotgun and brought down the hammers, with a blast that blanched the twilight. Men toppled out of their chairs with blood blossoming on their shirts. Reddoch had fired directly into the rebels' midst with a discharge so intense that it took out three men at once. A sergeant was killed outright, a lieutenant was mortally wounded, and a corporal badly injured.

It was the opening salvo in all-out war between Lowry and the Jones County Scouts, igniting a chain of violence that lasted almost a month. The deaths brought furious reprisals from Lowry. Three days later, on April 15, he thundered into the county at the head of his regiments, with packs of dogs baying like the noise of hell.

The slavering hounds flushed Daniel Reddoch and another member of the Knight band, Tucker Gregg, out of the woods and encircled them. As Reddoch stood ringed by the dogs, the rebels primed their Enfield rifles and executed him on the spot. Gregg tried to run but was cut down by bullets as he loped across a field and died of his wounds.

One night later, Newton's young neighbor Ben Graves was awoken by the sound of gun cracks. The distant sputtering of fire was from Lowry's men, who had descended on the home of Ben Knight, Newton's twenty-seven-year-old cousin. Ben was an absentee from the 7th Mississippi Battalion, a survivor of Corinth and a parolee at Vicksburg. The rebels may have mistaken him for Newton and believed they had the resistance leader trapped.

As rebel horsemen surrounded Ben's porch, the young man, still wearing his nightshirt, vaulted off the gallery and sprinted down a dirt path. He escaped the volley of gunfire and pelted across a narrow footbridge to Albert and Mason's old family property on the opposite bank of the Leaf River. He banged into the old cabin, perhaps hoping to find Newton. Instead he found his seventeen-year-old cousin Sil Coleman, asleep. Ben roused Sil, and together the two men hurtled across Mason Creek and into the swamps, pursued by dogs.

The first sets of teeth caught at their pants legs and sank into their calves, dropping them. Jaws clamped down on their flailing limbs like sprung game traps. Ben Knight managed to cut the throats of two or three dogs before he lost either his will or too much blood and succumbed to the mangling. When the rebels finally called the animals off, the prisoners had been badly ravened.

Rebels bound the bloody men, hoisted them into the back of a wagon, and drove back toward the old Knight place, to finish them off by lynching. As his executors wrapped the nooses, Ben pleaded for water. The soldiers stonily refused. Ben huddled in the wagon bed, gashed, pale, and slick with lost blood, and prayed for his grave to be filled with cool water.

A third prisoner was soon thrown into the wagon bed: Sil's younger brother, Noble. The boy was so young he still lived with his seventy-six-year-old grandmother, Mary Coleman, who had suffered the slaying of her son Tom years earlier by the local tyrant Nat Kilgore.

The rebels unfurled the ropes and flung them into the branches. The prisoners were yanked to their feet and the loops settled about their throats. The boys may have begged for mercy. One of the soldiers may have replied with a derisive remark about "crackers' necks." The wagon lurched. Three bodies twisted and spun, shoulders turning like clockweights, their heads at odd angles.

According to a Knight family account, when the prisoners had finished twisting on the ropes, the Confederates cut Ben Knight down and carried his corpse to the porch of the old Albert Knight home, where Serena was living, having returned to the county.

They threw the body on the steps, and a rebel offi-cer said, "Here's your husband. You will be obliged to bury him."

Serena replied, "My God man, that is not my hus-band. You have hung the wrong man."

Newton's youngest brother, Taylor, dug the grave, with the help of some of the local slaves. According to local slave legend, as the burying party shoveled earth out of the hole, water ran into it as Ben had prayed for. While the shovels plunged, Rachel carried the news of the hangings to Newton. He was said to be so grief stricken it made him sick to his stomach.

The Coleman boys were left hanging, shoulders slumped and feet still, until their sixteen-year-old sis-ter Cornelia came to find them. The girl sawed at the hemp and cut her brothers down.

To Newton the hangings were an atrocity, and some of Lowry's men agreed: one of them admitted Sil Coleman was a mere "lad," and another acknowl-edged that their cavalry had hanged a man "perhaps by mistake."

But Lowry was remorseless; it was his exact inten-tion and chief strategy to punish the guilty by pursu-ing the innocent. If Lowry couldn't catch Newton and his men, he could persecute their friends and relatives until the desperadoes showed themselves. A day later, Lowry rounded up still four more men for hanging. Tom Whitehead, twenty-one, and his younger brother Daniel, barely eighteen, were nephews of Newton's who had been raised in an antislavery home. Their mother was Mary Ann Knight, a sister of Albert's who like her brother had chosen to make her way in life without owning slaves. The other two men arrested were Jim Ates and his elder brother, Tom Ates, small farmers who had been conscripted into the 7th Mississippi Battalion and deserted after Corinth.

The four captured men were taken in irons to the village of Gitano, Mississippi, where their confessions were extracted. A so-called military court found them "guilty of desertion and of armed resistance to the civil and military law" and sentenced them to death by hanging. It was summary trial judgment—the young men were strung up just one day after their capture, in a crescent of the Leaf River swamp. Ever after it was called "Crackers' Neck."

The next to die was Newton's younger brother, twenty-year-old Franklin, apparently executed after a running gun battle. A week later, yet another Whitehead brother, twenty-six-year-old Noel, was seized and hanged. With that, the Whitehead family was virtually wiped out of sons, having lost four out of five. Their eldest, Emerson, had died after the battle of Iuka. Their only survivor was an eleven-year-old named George.

The toll of those two April days on Newton's company was severe: ten men killed by shooting or hanging, and five more wounded. More than fifty years later, the mention of Lowry's name made Newton's expression freeze. Meigs Frost observed the transformation in Newton's features when he introduced Lowry's name into their conversation.

"I'm told that General Lowry caught some of your men," he said.

Newton's smile vanished as if a light had gone out, replaced by a spasm of hatred, "a look of bitterness that showed the fires of a half century ago were not all dead, cold ashes," Frost wrote.

"He was rough beyond reason," Newton said. "He hanged some of my company he had no right to hang."

One of Lowry's men later bragged in an editorial to the **Mobile Evening News** that "terror was struck" by the Confederate campaign of vengeance. If so, the terrified were mostly women, boys, and old men. Lowry continued to seize blameless family members, young and old, to try to force guerrillas to turn themselves in. The **Jackson Mississippian** newspaper detailed his method: "He held the father as hostage until the son was brought forward, which rarely failed."

The Confederates rounded up local boys who were too young for conscription and put them in a stockade, called the bullpen, where they interrogated them and threatened them with hanging if they didn't tell all they knew about the Knight band. A twelve-year-old boy named W. B. Temples was nearly hanged three times in one day. The rebels put a noose around his neck, threw the end of the rope over a limb, and drew him up in the air until he choked, then let him down. When the terrified boy regained his voice, he was questioned again. When he again refused to answer, the procedure was repeated: the rope drew tight around his neck and he was jerked into the air. Finally, an officer intervened and freed the boy and told him to run on. As he tore across the countryside, some of the men fired after him.

Another boy named Richard Blackledge, whose brother rode with Newton, was picked up by the rebels for interrogation during a trip to the gristmill to grind some corn and held overnight in the bullpen. When the boy's father came looking for him, a rebel officer sarcastically informed him the child was in custody to "safeguard" him from the Knight band. The elder Blackledge replied hotly that he knew Newton Knight and other men in his company, but he never knew any of them "catching up boys and old men, and keeping them away from home." For his insolence the father was locked up with the son for the rest of the night.

Lowry arrested Newton's uncle, the elderly William H. Knight. The old man was threatened with hanging unless he revealed the whereabouts of his son William "Dickie" Knight, one of the most ardent Unionists in the Jones County Scouts. The slave Joe Hatton was sent into the swamps to tell Dickie that if he did not surrender, his father would be executed in his stead.

Dickie Knight sat on a rail fence, listening to Hatton. When Hatton had finished, Dickie spent a few agonized minutes thinking about what to do and then said, "You go back and tell the officer to just go ahead and hang Pap. He's getting to be an old man now, and they won't knock him out of many years. But they may knock me out of a good many."

Dickie Knight slipped back to his swamp hideaway,

where he informed the Jones County Scouts that he had decided to go to New Orleans to "join the Yankees." He and some of the men hatched a plan to build a boat to carry them down the Pearl River to the Crescent City.

Joe Hatton went home, not bothering to return to Lowry's men. Their bluff called, the rebels spared William Knight, and a few weeks later Dickie made it to New Orleans in his flat-bottomed boat and enlisted with the Union forces, with whom he proudly served out the war. As an old man, he would joke that he wanted to be "the only Yankee buried in Big Creek cemetery."

When Lowry's men weren't hanging boys or holding old men hostage, they perpetrated small meannesses on the yeoman wives, hoping to bait the Knight-company men into showing themselves. "It seems like they would take great delight in destroying what Knight's men had at home," Tom Knight recalled.

A woman named Mrs. Alzade Courtney, the mother of three small children, struggled to run her farm single-handedly, plowing all day and scrubbing all night. After darning and washing the homespun she would hang the clothes out to dry, only for the Confederates to snatch the garments. Each time she loaded her corn on a mule to take it to the mill she was waylaid by Confederate soldiers who seized it from her.

One afternoon she was working in a field when a

rebel horseman pulled up and demanded to know where her husband was. "Where is the man who has been plowing here?"

"There has been no man plowing here," she said.

"You are a liar; tell me where he is."

The officer dismounted and began stalking the field, looking for footprints. "Does them tracks look like men's tracks?" she asked bitterly.

Nancy Walters cringed in her cabin with her two youngest children as Confederates ransacked her farm and destroyed all of her stores. A host of mounted rebels rode into the yard and carefully hitched their horses to the shade trees and then tore open her corncrib and flung the contents on the ground for the horses to feed on. "It was a sight to see how they wasted our corn," the youngest son, Calvin Walters, remembered. Next, the soldiers caught all of the family's chickens, killed them, and plucked them in the yard. As the feathers drifted in the air they attacked the smokehouse too, dragging all of the meat out, slicing it into chunks, and throwing it into the dirt. As the men worked, Nancy bitterly wished aloud that Newton Knight and his men "could have known that they was here destroying our stuff that we had worked so hard for, but there was no way to get word to them."

At last the Confederates got ready to leave. As they were remounting, a rebel soldier stalked into the Walters pasture and put a bridle on her one good mare. This was too much for Nancy, who charged out of the house, seized a fence rail, and knocked the soldier flat with it. She led the horse back to the barn, wheeled around with the fence rail, and told another soldier "she would kill him if he didn't get out of the lot."

As Lowry's raids continued over the next three weeks, Newton and his men were powerless. They took shelter in the swamps, dodging their pursuers. "They fought men and dogs day by day about twenty days," according to one ally, B. A. Mathews, brother of one of the company members.

Lowry and his men dared not penetrate too deeply in the swamps after them, for fear of ambush. When some local Confederates wanted Lowry to mount a full-scale assault, Lowry replied that it would take several hundred more men than he had to clear out such treacherous combatants. Lowry wasn't afraid of the swamp, but he didn't mind admitting he was "afraid of them old shot guns that they had in their camps, and the way they used them."

The Jones County Scouts had the strategic advantage in the swamps, and they used it. Lowry's men lived in constant fear of ambush and surprise attack. One afternoon a yeoman wife was working on her farmstead when a squad of Confederates rode up to her porch and demanded to know the whereabouts of her son, a member of the company.

"I don't know where he is," she told them.

"Yes you know. Now, tell us where he is."

"Well," said she, "I told you the truth. I don't know where he is. But I can find out."

She unhooked a large drive horn from the wall,

stood up on the gallery, and blew a long note. After a moment, a distant blast answered. It was followed by another from a hillside and yet another from the brush. Soon the hills rang with a dozen answers.

The Confederate leader looked at his men. "Boys I guess we'd better get out of here," he said.

One old man named Reeves was picking pears on Sally Parker's property when rebel horsemen surrounded him and demanded to know if he had seen any of the guerrillas. Reeves decided to tease them. He replied, "Do you see that fence down yonder? Well there is two men in every corner of that fence ready to shoot."

In his later years, Newton boasted of how he and his men taunted Lowry's men, stealing up on them and scattering them with horn blasts and shotgun fire. On one such raid, a Confederate had trouble unhitching his horse and had been abandoned by his fellow troopers. As the rebel struggled with the tether, the Scouts teased him with gunfire, shooting to scare him but not to hit him, from different directions. When the rebel finally got his tether loose, horse and rider bolted down the road at a full gallop. "You could almost have rolled marbles on his coat tail behind him, he ran so fast," Newton joked.

But matters turned deadly serious again at the end of April. Newton received intelligence, perhaps from Rachel, that fifty of Lowry's men were to spend a night in Ellisville. Newton arrayed his men along the banks of Rocky Creek, where the Confederates were sure to cross. The guerrillas heard the rebels before they saw them cantering up the path and laughing in high spirits. Newton and his men rose up out of the creek bed and fired a volley that swept over the rebels like a lethal hailstorm. The front line of horses and men tumbled into the dust, screaming, while the rest of the men frantically wheeled around and galloped toward Ellisville. Newton counted fifteen wounded men and three dead horses in the road. He had his revenge for the hangings.

The ambush apparently finally moved Lowry to mount a large operation into the swamps. On April 25, he divided his men into squads of fifty and charged up the ravines and creek beds, searching out the guerrilla camps. Newton was encamped near the Jones-Jasper county line in a boggy triangle at the fork of two creeks, findable only by lifelong local woodsmen. With him were ten of his men, members of his innermost circle. They had just finished their breakfast when a watchman came sprinting down a narrow footpath breathlessly reporting that a large body of horsemen and dogs were crashing through the thickets straight toward their camp.

With just ten guns to meet fifty or sixty rebels and their dogs, Newton knew the Scouts couldn't stand them off. He decided they would try to run for it. "God be our leader," he told the men. They splashed through the bog and mire for nearly two miles, staggering through brush that raked at their faces, climbing over downed trees, and cutting through fields as the sound of dogs closed the distance behind them. Finally they cut into another obscure swampland called Clear Creek by crossing over some hidden foot-logs. As the last man stepped from the logs, Newton sprinkled them with red pepper. The men pushed deeper into the marsh, and to their relief, they heard the dogs coughing and sneezing as the red pepper blistered their snouts.

Newton believed he and his men had escaped thanks to divine protection. He had seen the Lord's will "demonstrated in his favor." It was only "God's power that delivered him from the enemy, the ones that were trying to take his life," he told his son.

But Jones County Scouts at other encampments had no such divine protection. Newton's muster roll recorded eighteen men captured by Lowry that day. Among them were some of his closest friends, men he had grown up with and fought alongside both in and out of Confederate uniform, men like John Valentine, William Welch, Younger Welborn Jr., Merida Coats, Dick Hinton, James Ewlen, and Lazrous Mathews. Most dishearteningly, several members of the Collins family were taken, including the man he designated his first lieutenant, forty-five-year-old Simeon Collins. He was in Lowry's custody with three of his sons. Newton would never see some of them again.

A smaller band of five men, among them Riley Collins and Prentice Bynum, were driven so deep into the swamps, and found themselves so isolated and cut off from home, that rather than risk a return they decided to keep moving. They floated via rivers to New Orleans and joined the Union forces there, as Dickie Knight had. They arrived in the Crescent City in May and enlisted in the 1st New Orleans Infantry under Lieutenant Colonel Eugene Tisdale, serving out the war in federal blue at Fort Pike, Louisiana.

Why didn't Newton go to New Orleans and join the army there? It was a hazardous journey, and it meant leaving his family—and Rachel—unprotected in the midst of an anarchical war zone. Union service in New Orleans was far from the front line of Newton's personal conflict. Though he respected those men who made the journey to serve in blue at Fort Pike, he believed their role there amounted to "guard duty." Nevertheless, they hazarded everything to serve their country and some would die for it. Riley Collins would die in August of 1864, at the age of thirty-nine, felled by dysentery.

Lowry and his men were triumphant: they had put the Jones County Scouts on the run. Newton's company of 125 men was surely shattered: 32 men had been killed, captured, or wounded by Lowry, and the rest were desperate and cut off in the bogs. Newton's own hat was riddled with bullets.

Years later, Newton recalled for journalist Meigs Frost how outnumbered and outgunned he and his men had been, with only their shotguns, against Lowry's men. Frost asked him if he was ever wounded.

"No—but they did their best. They shot off my hat and powder horn," he said. "All we had was muzzle loaders, shotguns mostly. They had these new re-peatin' rifles."

Lowry and his men finally wound up their work in Jones County on May 12. As they departed, "they destroyed all that Knight and his men had," accord-ing to Jones resident B. A. Mathews. They left be-hind them homes in flames and families in mourning. They took with them a line of captured men in irons, to be returned to duty.

They had ranged across seven counties in pursuit of deserters and arrested about five hundred men, while "several hundred more" had surrendered rather than risk capture. "We have changed the status of things in Jones, Perry, and Smith, and expect to reestablish in all South Mississippi a healthy loyalty to the powers that be," wrote one of Lowry's officers, Colonel Wil-liam N. Brown of the 20th Mississippi.

But Brown was somewhat troubled, too, and not entirely satisfied with what they had done. Brown was a privileged Confederate officer, the son of one of for-mer president James Polk's business partners and the owner of a seven-thousand-acre plantation in Bolivar County. He had risen to his colonelcy through se-niority, and he wasn't an especially gifted officer—his subordinate Walter Rorer seems to have believed him incompetent—but he was observant. Whatever satis-faction he felt at the completion of the mission in Jones County was tempered by an awareness of the deeper problems causing resistance in the Piney Woods.

Just before he left Jones County, Brown wrote a

long description of the expedition to Governor Clark. The yeomanry had good reason to be aggrieved by the Confederacy, Brown saw. Local women were reluctant to give up their husbands to conscription for fear of outright starvation. The rebel government had preyed upon everything they had. If the Confederacy would only send a load of corn to the conscripts' wives and children, Brown implored Governor Clark, it might improve the political sentiment. For one thing, "it would [convince] them that we have a government, a fact which they are inclined to doubt," he wrote.

Above all Brown believed the Piney Woods yeomanry was incited to open rebellion by the abuses they had suffered at the hands of crooked so-called Confederate tax officials, who had seized their livestock, crops, and goods. "These acts have done more to demoralize Jones County than the whole Yankee army," he wrote frankly.

His report summed up all he had observed in a month in the Piney Woods:

As you are perhaps aware my Regt comprises part of a detachment of Lorings Division now engaged in arresting and returning deserters to their commands from South Miss. and East La. under the command of Col Robt Lowry of the 6th Miss. we have been at this duty since the 23rd March and in that time have been over the country including Smith Co. Scott, Jasper, Jones and a part of Wayne, Perry and Covington counties. We have arrested and sent to Department Hd about 500 men. Several hundred more have eluded us or reported to their commands rather than be charged and sent under arrest. Lt. Gnl Polk estimates that 500 had reported to one Brigade alone and that this one success would no doubt do much towards determining and achieving the great object of the War (This information is a digression as my object is more particularly to refer to what is yet to do rather than boast of what has been done.)

From representations made to us we had expect[ed] to find [irregular] organizations among the disloyal for the purpose of resisting our authority. During the first five days operations we obtained a Flag from the family of one Hawkins who lives on the line of Smith and Scott Co, this led us to believe they had "Hung out the banners on the outer wall" and bitter stubborn resistance might be expected. In one or two cases this proved to be true. A small party under Lt. Evans of the 6th Miss was fired into and one man (Srgt Tillman) was killed, two others were wounded including Lt. Evans who we since have learned is dead. This was done by a single man, Daniel Reddoch who was afterwards caught and executed. Another party under Major Borden of the 6th Miss was ambushed and one man of my Rgt wounded this was done by Captain Newton Knight with 5 men two of which were captured and executed on the spot and Capt Knight narrowly made his escape.

At Knights Mill Jones Co on the 16th four men two brothers named Ates and two others named

Whitehead were found guilty of desertion and of armed resistance to the civil and military law and were sentenced to death by hanging before our military court. Accordingly the four men were executed. This made ten who have forfeited their lives for treason. All of them were clearly guilty and some of them had been wounded in skirmishes with the cavalry which had been sent to this country at different times. This for there has not been an example made from the citizens of the county, all have been soldiers and yet these men have often been mislead by some old and influential citizens perhaps their fathers or relatives who have encouraged and harbored them. We find great ignorance among them generally and many union ideas that seem to be [prompted] by demogauges of the agrarian class.

Among the women there is great reluctancy to give up their husbands and brothers and the reason alleged is the fear of starvation and disinclination to labor in the fields. More than half, I might say nearly all the soldiers wives are reduced to this strait.

Provisions are now scarce particularly corn. We estimated the supply inadequate for the maintenance of the poorer classes and particularly the females of such as are in the army. If something could be done to ameliorate their condition by State authorities it would be productive of a much improved moral and political sentiment. . . . A few wagons loads of corn distributed through this country from the most convenient depot on the

Mobile & O Rail Road would not only improve the political [tone] of the people here but would greatly encourage the men in the army from this quarter and in my opinion would greatly lessen desertion and the excuses to desert. Could not a train of wagons be organized for this purpose? I make the suggestion which I hope you will not take as [offensive] and will not pretend to argue the case to one of your [noble] administrative ability. Some complaint has been made of the commissioners whose duty it is to provide for the destitute families of soldiers. Of this I am not able to say except that very little seems to have been done by any one, and what was done is said to be for the families of particular favorites.

Another important item to which I would call the attention of your Excellency to the importance of [supplying] women of this country with cotton and woolen cards. The females are decidedly of the working part of the population and are greatly in want of these necessary articles. There seem to be considerable wool and enough cotton to keep them engaged, as they are now provided they manage to clothe the soldiers from this country and if encouraged would add greatly to the comfort of many more a good article of jeans sometimes sells for $6 per yard. I found today a widow of a soldier who was killed by the cavalry and having no cards she had taken to working [horn] combs. A specimen I send to you which for workmanship and ingenuity compares with the "yankee." The husband of this woman having been killed by our cavalry perhaps by mistake call to mind the many outrages that have been committed by many small commands of cavalry sent into this country on the duty now assigned to our command. Such at least are the many complaints we hear every day.

Brown was not the only officer of the 20th Mississippi with a troubled conscience. Walter Rorer had been left behind in Demopolis to sit on a military tribunal that heard court-martial cases of the captured deserters. Rorer had deep qualms about sitting in judgment on the absentees chased down by his unit. "A sad business it is, every day good men are tried and sentenced to infamy for going home to see wife and children," he wrote to his cousin Susan.

"I am weary of it," Rorer continued. "There is folly, mismanagement and meanness everywhere in the army . . . I have no heart to punish men for the disobeying of the orders of fools, still it must be done or we would have no army. If men could only be tried before Courts Martial for want of sense and common honesty I think our Court would have to try half the army."

If anyone in the high command followed Brown's commonsense suggestion that some food and relief from corruption would go a long way toward pacifying the Piney Woods farmers, there is no evidence of it. Lowry and his men left Jones on May 12 with their consciences unbothered. In the end, they chose to believe that the dissent and packed shotguns they had encountered were simply the expressions of a sullen peasantry. Lowry dismissed Newton as "an ignorant, uneducated man" and the action of his company as "bushwhacking."

Thirty years after the surrender, Dabney H. Maury devoted a lengthy passage in his memoirs to the Jones County Scouts, whom he depicted as malcontent serfs. Maury believed that "the worst class of our population was to be found in the vast region of piney woods that sweep along our seaboard from Carolina to the Sabine" and that these rabble "manifested the most vicious and cruel natures of a North American. Jones County, Mississippi, is in this piney woods belt, between Meridian and the lower Pearl River." Maury claimed that the Confederates had successfully invaded "this **imperium in imperio**" and reduced "these secessionists to order."

In fact, the Confederacy had not been able to stamp out the Union allegiance in Jones. Not three weeks after Lowry left the county, Newton and his men were actively reconstituting the company. The core of the band remained at large: Newton, Jasper Collins, William Wesley Sumrall, and about twenty others began once more to wreak havoc.

Confederate commanders were surely embarrassed by their inability to capture Newton, especially when the events in Jones made the Southern newspapers. Newton's elusiveness had become the subject of lore. On May 6, 1864, the **Mobile Daily Advertiser and Register** published an account from a rebel officer that suggested the extent of Newton's spreading fame.

"I see by your evening issue of the 2nd instant, that, under 'Mississippi Items' you say that Captain Newton Knight, of Jones, had sent in a flag of truce, etc., to Col. Lewis. This is not so," the correspondent reported, with obvious disappointment. A description of various actions followed, along with a comment on the "ignorance" of the impoverished people there. It concluded: "Newton Knight, it is thought, will report if he can be found."

He couldn't be found. Confederate officers never understood that horse soldiers were useless in the Piney Woods; success hinged on men well trained in the art of swamp fighting, not horseback riders who broadcast their arrival, got lost every half mile, and made for easy target practice. Although outnumbered, Newton and his men "knew every creek and footlog" in the Piney Woods, as Newton's son noted.

By June of 1864 Newton and his men were operating in force again, engaging in just the sorts of exploits Sherman might wish them to had he issued direct orders. They thwarted rebels' efforts to rebuild the railroads, confiscated Confederate supplies, and threatened impressment agents.

On June 14, 1864, just two months after the Lowry raids, local Confederate conscript officer Benjamin C. Duckworth wrote to Governor Charles Clark in despair that the area was still in Newton's control. The unionist guerrillas had wrecked or burned all of the local bridges and ferries, the local justices of the peace, constables, and commissioners refused to do public business, and "if a man is found dead the Civil authorities pays no attention to it any more than if it was a dog." Duckworth himself was "afraid to speak my sentiments on the account of the Deserters" and begged that Clark destroy his letter: "when you read those few lines commit the same to the flames."

On July 12, the Union-controlled **Natchez Courier** newspaper reported that "the county of Jones, State of Mississippi, has seceded from the State and formed a Government of their own, both military and civil." Although the story contained erroneous and even fanciful details, the gist of it was essentially true. "Numbers of deserters having congregated in the swamps of Jones County, determined to form a government for themselves. Colonel Mowry [**sic**], with a force was sent over to disband them, but they fought desperately, and in their strongholds defied the Colonel and his forces."

At the end of July, Lieutenant H. C. Kelley, a provost marshal stationed at Shubuta, Mississippi, about fifteen miles from Jones, wrote to his superiors with a plea for troops. The Jones County scouts had conducted yet another raid, liberating 150 cattle intended to feed the Confederate army. They turned them loose in the swamps where only they could find them and also destroyed corn standing in a field that was meant for the rebel troops.

"Colonel, I would call your attention to the situation of the county and Government property through this and Jones and Jasper Counties on account of the

(*Left*) Newton Knight in his prime, "just a fightin' fool when he got started." (*Middle*) An image of the slave woman believed to be Rachel Knight by some of her descendants. According to family oral tradition, she was part Choctaw. (*Right*) A possible alternative portrait of Rachel Knight. Some family members, however, believe the young woman in this image to be Rachel's granddaughter, Lessie.

Messmates shared the rituals of camp life.

A Confederate field hospital.

Confederate general Earl Van Dorn proposed to write his name in fire at Corinth.

General Sterling Price, CSA, in whose ranks Newton Knight served at Corinth before deserting.

Dabney Maury, the Confederate commander in Mobile, believed Newton and his fellow Piney Woods yeoman farmers to be the "worst class in our population."

The Tishomingo Hotel and depot served as a hospital in Corinth. Blood soaked the carpets, and surgeons pitched amputated limbs from the porch.

The battle of Corinth and the fight for Battery Robinett as rendered by *Harper's Weekly*.

The Confederate dead at Corinth. Colonel Rogers is visible in the foreground, his face blackened by powder.

A Union field hospital.

A meeting of clandestine Southern unionists, as envisioned
by *Harper's Weekly*.

The Deason house of Ellisville, where Confederate officer Amos McLemore was shot to death, allegedly by Newton Knight.

"Contrabands" streamed into Union positions.

Ulysses S. Grant, the tough-minded Union conqueror of Mississippi, about whom Newton would write an admiring line of poetry.

Union commander William Tecumseh Sherman reached to within twenty miles of Jones County on his Meridian campaign, and made contact with a band of Southern unionists, perhaps Newton's.

The siege caves at Vicksburg. Starved Southern soldiers ate soup of boiled shoestrings.

The destruction of Atlanta.

Adelbert Ames, the Union war hero and "Galahad" turned carpetbagger and Mississippi governor, and patron of Newton Knight. He watched helplessly as ex-Confederates effectively retook control of the state with violence and intimidation at the polls.

HARPER'S WEEKLY.
JOURNAL OF CIVILIZATION

Harper's Weekly illustrates the first black vote, November 1867.

Newton Knight and his grandson John Howard. "Do you know who I am?" he asked his mixed-race grandchildren. "I'm your grandfather."

An artist's rendering of the KKK's campaign of terror and intimidation against black voters in postwar Mississippi.

numerous quantity and boldness of the deserters," Kelley reported.

> Captain Fish, the Government quartermaster here for the impressment and purchase of beef cattle, has applied to me for assistance, but having no men can render him none. The deserters turned out over 150 head of cattle that he had collected for the Government the other day, and scattered them in the swamps, and threatened the lives of any of his agents who may go through those counties on business. Four of these deserters came in four miles of this town a few days ago and pulled a quantity of green corn, that they destroyed.

Newton had defied the combined efforts of Polk, Maury, and Lowry. All the Confederate cavalry, artillery, and crack infantry regiments had done was give him temporary pause. Nor had they solved the larger problem of desertion in the ranks: only 20 percent of the five thousand active deserters in Mississippi had been caught and returned to duty.

As Newton resumed his operations, once again there were signs that he was in contact with federal forces. A Yankee officer was rumored to be among the transients being harbored in Jones County. Also, every day more blacks liberated from plantations came into the swamps to join the struggle.

The Confederate brigadier general of the state militia, W. L. Brandon, wrote to Major General Dabney Maury on August 14:

A number of Yankees, in concert with deserters, both from Honey Island and that vicinity, have been committing serious depredations in the region of country bordering upon Jones and Jasper Counties, driving off large numbers of negroes and a great deal of stock. A Yankee lieutenant is now in Jones, entertained and protected by deserters, for the purpose, it is supposed, of concocting plans for the commission of further depredations. Probably a plan may be on foot for the cutting of the Mobile and Ohio Railroad simultaneously with the attack upon Mobile. Would it not be well to retain the force I have, as the contingency threatened may arise and no troops would be sufficiently near for concentration for the purpose of defeating their object?

But by now, Southern authorities had little time or manpower to devote to Newton Knight. Virtually every able-bodied soldier in buff and gray was needed to try to shore up the Confederacy against Sherman, who was again on the march, this time to Atlanta. Sherman intended to make Meridian look like only a rehearsal.

"All that has gone before is mere skirmishing," Sherman promised.

As Confederate troops streamed toward Atlanta to meet Sherman's advance, Robert Lowry, Walter Rorer, and William Nugent were among them. So too, unwillingly, were the foot-dragging men from

Jones County, impressed back into uniform in the 7th Mississippi Battalion.

The state was all but emptied of rebel forces. Leonidas Polk led his army into Georgia, first by rail and then the last seventy miles on foot, at the head of a divisional train that stretched for five miles. His headquarters alone required ten six-horse wagons to haul it. The departure left Mississippi largely undefended and in the hands of the deserters and Unionists who had so consistently eluded capture.

By the late summer of 1864, Jones County was again the center of a Union stronghold that extended throughout southeastern Mississippi. "The Free State of Jones" had become a battle cry, a statement of yeoman strength—and a warning to rebels.

The two armies grappled with each other across northern Georgia, columns of men scuttling along rugged red clay foothills that turned grease slick under their heels. The days were a punishing repetition of maneuver, dig, and march, while hundred-degree temperatures made bugs sing, and the air lay heavy as a quilt.

Sherman's men moved light and fast, carrying just five days of bacon. If the quartermaster's stores failed along the way, Sherman threatened, "We'll eat your mules up, sir; eat your mules up!" In just twelve days, the Yankees moved eighty miles, halfway toward Atlanta. But the pacing Sherman, unshaven, in muddy pants, a spur on one boot, slouch hat jammed over his quill-like hair, was unsatisfied. He remained frustrated by his inability to land a decisive blow or to break the will of his opponents.

"No amount of poverty or adversity seems to shake their faith," Sherman observed, "niggers gone, wealth and luxury gone, money worthless, starvation in view . . . yet I see no sign of let up—some few deserters, plenty tired of war, but the masses determined to fight it out."

The Southern strategy was to "resist manfully" to the last, as Robert E. Lee put it, with the hope that in the November 1864 election Lincoln would be replaced. If the South could just hold out until the election, Northern fatigue with the war would set in and a Peace Democrat, perhaps George B. McClellan, would negotiate a truce resulting in Southern independence. But U. S. Grant, now general in chief of the Union army, understood that the South was war weary too. He knew this from the constant stream of deserters who "come into our lines daily who tell us that the men are nearly universally tired of the war, and that desertions would be much more frequent, but they believe peace will be negotiated after the fall elections," Grant wrote.

Grant intended to settle the war not with peace negotiations, but with a series of aggressive blows that would break Southern will. He ordered Sherman, now in command of the west, to "get into the interior of the enemy's country as far as you can, inflicting all the damage you can against their war resources."

As Sherman pushed south across Georgia in a series of looping marches, the rebels under Generals Joe Johnston and Leonidas Polk continually parried and withdrew in a series of defensive actions. For weeks the two armies skirmished across rocky ridges of Georgia in asphyxiating heat and humidity, raking each other with artillery but never fully engaging, like two wary boxers dancing for position.

Confederate morale became uneven, men grew sick of walking backward, and hunger was a continual problem, rations so slim that William Nugent and his fellow cavalrymen received only a third of a pound of bacon a day. The army was plagued more than ever by desertions—not even another round of executions had stemmed the tide. Columbus Sykes, a colonel and a well-heeled planter in the 43rd Mississippi, whose wife continued to ride in her carriage though it had to be drawn by mules, wrote home at the end of April just before embarking for Georgia. His brigade had been forced to witness the deaths of two deserters, as a warning.

"Two men of the 31st Miss. Regt. and one of the 33rd Miss. are condemned to be 'Shot to death with Musketry' at 3 o'clock p.m. for desertion," he wrote. "The entire Brigade is ordered to witness the execution. What a solemn warning to those who are tired enough to desert their colors. The Government is determined to stop it by visiting upon the offender the extremest penalty known to military law."

A week later, Sykes was so affected by the episode that he wrote home again, this time describing the firing squad itself.

The execution took place between 3 and 4 o'clock. I need not tell you that it was a sadly solemn scene. To see men in the full tide of a vigorous manhood, sitting manacled on their coffins, hearing the sentence of the Court Martial read which, while it proclaimed their infamy to the assembled army, fixed the mode and hour of their death with the inexorable certainty of fate, to hear the last solemn prayer of the chaplain in their behalf, the order to stand up, have their arms bound behind them, eyes blindfolded, the last messages delivered for wife and children to the commanding officer, the command to the guard "ready, aim, fire," they fall on their backs lifeless corpses.

As for those impressed back to their units, loyal Confederates kept a wary eye on them and understood they couldn't be counted on. The apathy and evasions of reluctant soldiers such as Sim Collins in the 7th Mississippi Battalion were plain for all to see. While they wore the Confederate uniform, they had no intention of dying for the cause and were borderline insubordinate when shooting started. "The men who are caught and forced into the ranks cannot be relied on at all," Nugent observed. "Behind breastworks they may be induced to exchange shots with the enemy; in the open field they can never be brought to close quarters."

Nugent, encamped near Marietta, brooded over suspected disloyalty in one of his own soldiers, a lieutenant who seemed to duck battle and was likely preparing to defect to the "swamp, where he can have Yankee coffee and sundry parties to attend." Nugent's own devotion to duty was worn as thin as his clothes; he was matted and filthy as a ferret.

" 'Odds fish' how I would like to be five thousand miles from here now," he wrote to his wife. "Mud, filth, rain; every imaginable species of vermin crawling all around you; little sleep, hard work & fed like a race horse, constantly annoyed with stray bullets, whizzing shells & pattering grape; dirty clothes and not a change along; little or no time to wash your face and hands and very little soap . . . no comb for your hair."

The reluctant soldiers of 7th Mississippi Battalion were under almost continuous fire in June, as Sherman continued his artillery barrages and flanking movements along the ridgeline. On June 14, 1864, Leonidas Polk trudged up a steep hill known as Pine Mountain, near Marietta, for a view of the field. As he stood on the crest and studied the smoking and scored terrain below, a cannon shot whistled. It struck him square in the chest and tore a huge hole in him, "opening a wide door," according to his son, "through which his spirit escaped."

Though he was winning the war of attrition, Sherman himself was growing sick of the continual shelling with no definitive victory. On June 27, believing the Confederates close to the breaking point, and in a fit of impatience, he assaulted Kennesaw Mountain.

In the center of the rebel defenses was a brigade commanded by Robert Lowry. The daylong charges up steep slopes in broiling temperatures left Lowry and his men soaked in their own sweat, blood, and retching saliva. The Yankees were finally repelled with three thousand casualties, Lowry's line turning back two charges. Sherman accepted the defeat with a verbal shrug.

"I begin to regard the death and mangling of a couple thousand men as a small affair, a kind of morning dash," Sherman wrote to his wife.

In the superheated bedlam, the 7th Mississippi Battalion's position was overrun. Sixty men from the regiment went missing, eight of them members of the Knight band whom Lowry had towed back into service, including Sim Collins. These men were "captured" by Sherman's forces, though some of them later said they voluntarily turned themselves over to the Yankees. They refused to be exchanged or paroled, pleading to ride out the war as captives. They were eventually transferred to Midwest prison camps—Camp Morton in Indiana and Camp Douglas in Illinois—where they remained until surrender. But if prison was preferable to battle, it didn't necessarily mean escape from death; their health had been badly undermined, and some of them had been wounded. Sim Collins and James Ewlen would not see another summer. They died of their wounds and ailments in the winter-spring of 1865.

By mid-July Sherman had pushed to within six miles

of Atlanta, and Confederate president Jefferson Davis was uneasy. Davis wanted the Confederate army on the attack. On July 17 he made an intrusive error, removing the defensive-minded Joe Johnston from command and replacing him with the almost psychotically combative John Bell Hood. The change of command was a matter of "cold, snaky" second-guessing by the Confederate president, critics charged. But Davis was supercilious in matters of strategy; he was a great believer in his own stentorian oratory and coinlike visage, square jawed with almost no upper lip to speak of, just a grim line of self-certainty. He had "an exalted opinion of his own military genius," Grant wrote of him sardonically. "On several occasions he came to the relief of the Union army." The handing of command to Hood was one of those occasions. Hood immediately went on the offensive and played right into Union hands. It was "just what we wanted," Sherman wrote, "to fight on open ground."

The blond-maned, limpid-eyed, Viking-chested Hood had already fought crippled, his left arm incapacitated at Gettysburg and his right leg torn off at Chickamauga. He was physically indefatigable, riding into battle strapped to his horse, but he was "all lion, none of the fox," Robert E. Lee said of him. To diarist Mary Chesnut he exuded martyrdom with his "sad Quixotic face, the face of an old Crusader," and he had recently experienced a religious awakening. Shortly before Polk was killed, Hood asked the Episcopal bishop to baptize him. Polk conducted the ceremony in Hood's tent, using a tin wash pan to douse the young general, who braced himself upright on crutches. But religion had not gentled Hood's approach to battle, and he proceeded to do to the army what he had done to his own body.

Hood attacked, attacked, and attacked again—in three offensives over eight days, he took 15,000 casualties, all to no avail as Sherman continued his advance. Walter Rorer lost the use of a hand. During a respite in Decatur, the exhausted William Nugent and a captain from the 28th Mississippi Cavalry found an old bedstead under a pear tree. Nugent collapsed onto it, and the captain was about to join him when shrapnel exploded into the tree. The officer fell dead on top of Nugent, in a shower of bark. It seemed to Nugent that serving under Hood meant inevitable annihilation.

"He is for fighting all the time," Nugent wrote to his wife. "This sort of fighting, unless we meet with some more decided success will dissipate our army very soon. Eight more such fights and we will have no army at all."

Nugent's prediction came true. On September 1, battered and outflanked, Hood evacuated Atlanta, dynamiting all the manufacturing and industry in it as he left. "So Atlanta is ours, and fairly won," Sherman reported to Washington, an announcement that set off hundred-gun salutes. If Corinth and Vicksburg bent the spine of the Confederacy, Atlanta all but snapped it. Democratic peace candidate McClellan suddenly struggled not to sound faint voiced and defeatist. On

November 8, Lincoln would win the popular vote by roughly half a million and carry the electoral count by 212 to 21, on a platform calling for the constitutional end to slavery everywhere in the United States. Lincoln owed his victory in part to Sherman, whose successful campaign convinced Northern voters that the war would soon be over.

Jefferson Davis toured the South in a vain attempt to restore Confederate morale. He promised that the fierce Hood would yet force Sherman to retreat. But he also declared grimly, "We are fighting for existence." In fact, fighting was the only option left; there would be no merciful truce.

As Hood evacuated Atlanta, he burned anything that might be of value to the Union army. Sherman finished the destruction that Hood began. When the mayor of Atlanta protested his all-consuming policy, Sherman retorted, "War is cruelty, and you cannot refine it." Next, Sherman set out for the coast, intending to "make Georgia howl." In mid-December he wired Lincoln, "I beg to present you, as a Christmas gift, the city of Savannah."

Hood, meanwhile, presented the South with nothing but corpses. On November 30, he engaged another Union force under General John M. Schofield at Franklin, Tennessee. There, he all but murdered his own troops, many of the Mississippi regiments among them, with one of the most manifestly lunatic charges of the war.

Hood arrived at Franklin "wrathy as a rattlesnake"

at the Southern defeats and what he believed was the reluctance of the men to fight except in trenches. He stared out over two miles of flat, pleasant countryside at a heavily fortified Union position showing the black bores of cannon and decided that he would **make** his men fight. Almost as a punishment, Hood ordered a full frontal attack, unsupported. His generals protested—the ground was too open. He ignored them.

At 4:00 p.m., 22,000 obedient Southerners quick-stepped into the exposed fields, moving in a grand parade alignment, with their fixed bayonets shimmering. Advancing in formation were scores of Mississippians, previously far-flung men for whom Franklin would be a bloody crossroads: Lowry, Rorer, Brown, Sykes, and the Jones Countians of the 7th Mississippi Battalion. Riding in a cavalry force on the fringes of Franklin was William L. Nugent.

Regimental banners fluttered, and bands played martial airs like "Annie Laurie" and "Ben Bolt." Half a mile from the Yankee trenches, in full view of the gunsights, the Confederates paused and shifted into two battle lines. A few officers waved their hats. The men in line began to scream shrilly—and then charged.

As they ran, witnesses noticed strange flurries of movement along the ground. Rabbits and quail were scattering ahead of the pounding booted feet of the men in gray.

Yankee artillerymen yanked at their lanyards, and flames stabbed out of the mouths of the guns. Boiling smoke and plunging fire engulfed the rebel troops. The

Mississippi regiments were scythed down by repeating rifle fire from the front and canister that tore into them at close range from their right. As they pressed forward some of them stumbled into a thorny hedge of Osage orange, fifty yards from the Union line, on which they became hung up. The bullets and shrapnel were so thick that men imagined they could reach a hand up and grab pieces of lead from the air.

To get the troops moving again a thirty-nine-year-old Confederate brigade commander, General John Adams, spurred his bay horse toward Union gun emplacements. Just as his horse leaped onto the parapet, it was shot down. The horse sprawled dead, his hooves draped over the barricade, while Adams fell riddled with a half dozen Minié balls.

As Confederates continued to roll across the field in waves, whole outfits smashed into the ramparts and shattered in the smoke and flames. Men huddled, pinned down at the base of the Union emplacements. Generals and privates fought side by side, swinging whatever they could lay their hands on: picks, shovels, staves, and flagstaffs. Unit flags wavered and fell.

The blood pooled in ditches. "Many of the men were shot to shreds," one Mississippian wrote. "And I saw scores of [wounded] men . . . who had put their thumbs in their mouths and had chewed them into shreds to keep from crying, coward-like, as they lay exposed to the merciless fire . . . Franklin was the only battlefield I ever saw where the faces of the majority of the dead expressed supreme fear and terror."

The assaults continued for five hours, until past dark. Mississippians stumbled over their own dead and wounded, aghast to hear shrieks "as we trod on their mangled limbs." Men groped blindly forward in the night and smoke, only to be illuminated as if by lightning strikes when the big guns fired, white flame searing their faces.

Finally, the booming of guns and snapping of musketry ebbed. By 10:00 p.m., the firing ceased. Men peered over the entrenchments and saw the once flat field was covered by hillocks—the outlines of dead and wounded.

Hood had seven thousand casualties—a third of his army. He had slaughtered more men in five hours at Franklin than in two days at Shiloh. Lowry had survived, and so had William Nugent, wet from wading a river in retreat after a heavy firefight. But Walter Rorer was dead on the field—shot down while bearing the unit flag. His superior, Brown, had suffered two serious wounds. There were fifteen Confederate generals and fifty-four regimental commanders among the casualties.

Incredibly, Hood issued a statement declaring victory. His traumatized men received it stony eyed.

Next, Hood ordered yet another advance, this one to Nashville, where seventy thousand Union troops were garrisoned. Hood rationalized his decision by saying "the sinking fortunes of the Confederacy" had made retreat impossible. Wearily, the men lifted their gear for another march behind their homicidal commander. On December 16, Hood's skeletal lines were engulfed at Nashville by the Union forces under General George H. Thomas. Somehow, Lowry, who had taken over the slain Adams's brigade command, survived this battle too.

At last Hood led his tattered remnant of a force into retreat. He arrived back in Tupelo with no more than 15,000 infantrymen. Many of them were in bare feet, bloodied from walking in snow. Their thin shoulders shuddered from cold.

The men had never felt so beaten and seemed to know the end of the war was imminent. Henry St. John Dixon of the 28th Mississippi told his diary that he had "seen retreats before today but none to compare with this—Disorganization, straggling, dissatisfaction & disaffection bad—worse than bad . . . I confess my self to be discouraged, & sick at heart . . . Death, destruction & slavery only present themselves to view."

Hood had lost fully half his army in only two weeks. It took Confederate high commanders some time to realize fully the wreckage he had wrought—it was difficult to get a complete picture with so many officers dead or wounded and thus incapable of filing official reports.

But one way they assessed the campaign was by counting their flags. As the extent of the casualties became apparent, authorities took stock of their pennants, those symbols of inflamed patriotism. The surviving brigade leaders were ordered to report whether they still flew their colors, the standards men had charged behind and died for.

Lowry replied "with honor" that only one of his six regiments, the 15th Mississippi, had given up its banner. But he added this:

"Four men were shot down in bearing it," he wrote.

Mississippi fought on, though scourged, shell shattered, weed grown, and vandalized. There was no final catastrophe; the Confederacy didn't fall so much as it slowly disintegrated into piles of loose masonry and sagging neglected buildings, as deserters in stained and torn brown-gray flitted among the ruins like specters.

Yankees continued to ravage the state, destroying farms, railroads, and sometimes whole towns. They reduced Oxford to cinders and shards, burning thirty-four stores, the courthouse, the Masonic hall, the two best hotels, all of the carpenter and blacksmith shops, and the five finest homes. What was left looked like the prongs of a broken fork.

Skirmishes were tinged with vengefulness. Nehemiah Davis Starr, a Missourian who fought against Hood's army in Tennessee, reported that no Union soldier could hope to survive capture; every one caught was executed. "The Rebels are killing all they catch here whenever a man straggles from the army he is no longer." A quartermaster and a surgeon who paused to get dinner in a village were taken by Confederate guerrillas and shot through the head with pistols pressed so close that their hair was burned with powder.

Anson Hemingway of the 72nd Illinois was on picket duty on the Mississippi-Louisiana border in the summer of 1864 with a unit of colored troops. He had volunteered as a first lieutenant with the 70th U.S. Colored Infantry and was no longer a naïve private. Atrocity, he decided, should be met with atrocity.

"A scouting party was sent out from here, in which was a company of colored cavalry commanded by the colonel of a colored regiment," he wrote home. "After marching some distance, they came upon the party of whom they were in pursuit. There were seventeen prisoners captured and shot by the colored soldiers. When the guerillas were first seen, the colonel told them in a loud tone of voice to 'Remember Fort Pillow.' And they did: all honor to them for it. If the Confederacy wish to fight us on these terms, we are glad to know it, and will try to do our part in the contest. I do not admire the mode of warfare, but know of no other way for us to end the war than to retaliate."

It seemed as if the conflict would continue interminably, even as the end was inevitable. Grant had Lee under siege at Petersburg, and Sherman controlled the Deep South, that part of it he hadn't destroyed—still, surrender didn't come. Starr tried to gauge the progress of the war from the attitude of the Confederate prisoners taken at Franklin and Nashville. "Some say the war is near over some say it will never end," he wrote, ". . . some were tired of fighting and some others declared they meant to fight to the last men."

To Newton, it seemed like years since he had rested. His animal-like existence in the swamp had worn him down, and so had the weight of responsibility, of protecting so many people: his men, Rachel, his wife and children, the local slave community, and yeoman families who counted on him. He was more fugitive than free. "I have only the freedom of the air I breathe," he is supposed to have said to his cousin Alpheus. "I do not have the freedom of a slave, for a slave can lie down and sleep, unless his belly pinches to keep him awake."

Newton continued to plague the local Confederates. On September 1, 1864, Amos Deason and four other prominent loyals wrote to Governor Clark requesting a company of home guards for protection from his reprisals. Deserters continued to stream into the swamps by the hundreds, until Judge Robert S. Hudson lamented that Mississippi was "groaning under the flood of deserters" and estimated that the state was home to anywhere from five thousand to eight thousand of them. Newton's ranks swelled with disenchanted soldiers, freedmen, smuggled Yankees, and renegades.

Newton and his men had become so powerful that they actually hoped to overthrow the Confederates democratically, at the ballot boxes, in the county elections that October. On Election Day, men armed with guns, pistols, and bowie knives marched out of the woods to the precinct to cast ballots. But the effort to take back Jones County at the polls failed. Rebel cavalry guarded the ballot boxes and arrested four Unionists who tried to vote.

Newton and his men went back underground and kept fighting, but the worst of the war was over for the Jones County Scouts. Between the late fall of 1864 and January 10, 1865, Newton recorded just four more battles: in November, they fought an action against "a lot of Rebels sed to have belong to Forest's Caverle," near Reddoch's Ferry, where Newton captured and paroled twenty-one men. In December, Newton and his men were cornered by a company of cavalry under a Captain Gillis at a farm owned by the Gunter family on the Leaf River. Joe Gunter was caught and executed, according to one source shot in front of his wife, Selena, and their children, after which the cavalry forced her to build a fire and cook all of her chickens.

Also wounded in the firefight was Newton's corporal, S. G. "Sam" Owens, grandson of a legendary backwoods bare-knuckle brawler named Tom Sullivan. Owens was shot in the knee and the hip and only escaped capture by going limp and feigning his own death. The cavalry left him in the field, where Knight's men found him when they crept back from the thickets. They made a litter and carried him two miles to his mother's home and hid him in her loft. For weeks Owens lay in the attic convalescing, hidden behind a large trunk and peering through a small window to see what was going on outside. Owens's presence was a secret to everyone but his close family. When he was healed and able to move about, the sound of rustling and humming in the attic frightened a local slave, who took the sounds to be that of a ghost.

At the end of 1864, the Jones County Scouts finally had a happy event to celebrate: the marriage of Alpheus Knight. The twenty-year-old Alpheus had survived Corinth and Vicksburg and two perilous years of riding at Newton's side. He and his bride to be, Mary Powell, planned a small, clandestine ceremony during the Christmas week on his family's property on the Leaf River. In the wedding party were ten or so of the Knights' close relatives and comrades, including Newton, his sister Martha, and the wife of Dickie Knight, off serving the Union in New Orleans.

Somehow, a local Confederate wife learned of the wedding plans. She wrote out a message to the local rebel officers, informing them of the opportunity to capture the Knight band and handed it to her cook. "You take this message and don't you stop to eat or sleep until you've delivered it to the Confederate soldiers by Ellisville," she ordered. The kitchen slave dutifully delivered the message—but she also delivered a message to Newton via the grapevine that the Confederates had been tipped off. "Some folks that were friendly to me, they sent word about it," he recalled.

Newton urged Alpheus and Mary to go ahead with their celebration and offered to keep watch, though the temperature had plunged. Other members of the wedding party told him, "You'll freeze to death."

"The Lord lights a fire in a man to keep him warm when he's working for a good cause," he replied.

Newton stood sentinel on the banks of the Leaf River, peering into the dark for Confederates who might try to approach by ferry. Throughout the night he walked a half-mile beat, up and down the river-bank. The river was still until daybreak, when he heard a faint rattle of chains—the sound of a flatboat coming across the river. A moment later, he heard the noises of horse hooves stamping on the bottom of the flatboat. Newton turned and ran for the house, bursting through the door as the wedding breakfast was being laid out.

"You're just in time," a woman told him. "Sit down and eat."

"I've got no appetite," he said. "There's a fight coming. We've got to get out of here. There's about a hundred Confederates marching on this house."

As the others gathered their things, Newton bolted a cup of coffee and chewed on a piece of pie. The party rushed outside and scattered in four directions. Newton, Alpheus and Mary, his sister Martha, and two other women struck out over an open field. As they cut across it toward the woods, one of the women, who carried a small baby, struggled to keep up. "I can't carry this baby so fast," she gasped. Newton seized the child in one arm.

"I'll carry your gun," she said.

"No madam, you won't," he said. "Nobody carries my gun but me."

They had gone about two hundred yards when they

heard the beat of hooves. "Here they come!" Newton said. From out of the brush came a herd of colts, riderless. For a moment Newton was relieved—until the dashing of horses was followed closely by the rippling cracks of gunfire. About twenty Confederates had ridden behind the stampeding horses, using them as cover.

As Newton, Alpheus, and the women reached the tree line, Newton handed the baby to its mother and plunged into the brush. While the women pushed deeper into the woods, Newton and Alpheus swung around and kneeled to face the Confederates from the cover of the trees. The two men raised their weapons, and Newton cautioned Alpheus to fire only one barrel at a time. Then he drew aim on a captain riding straight for them.

"Lord God, direct this load," Newton said.

The blast kicked the gunstock into Newton's shoulder, and a fraction of a second later the rebel officer tumbled from his saddle. A moment later, Alpheus let go with one barrel, and another rebel flew from his mount. Alternating barrels, Newton and Alpheus dropped four men and a large gray horse before the Confederates reined to a halt.

Newton began to yell military orders from out of the timber. "Attention! Battalion! Rally on the right! Forward!"

The ears of the cavalrymen still rang from a half-dozen shotgun blasts. As they gazed at the thickets and heard Newton shouting orders it must have seemed that they had encountered an entire company. With four men bleeding on the ground, they were not inclined to press the attack against an unknown number in the woods. They turned their horses and galloped away.

The battle over, Newton and Alpheus exhaled with relief and moved out of the woods to skin the horse. They hauled the hide into the swamp and tanned it in a hole they dug in a log. They used the leather for shoes, a pair of which Newton gave to Martha. She wore them until they fell apart.

Two weeks later, the cavalry returned in search of Alpheus. When he heard the troopers approaching, he crawled up the chimney and ordered Mary to light a fire. His new bride was so nervous as the Confederates interrogated her that she continually fed more wood to the flames. As the troopers searched the rooms, under beds, and in the barn, Alpheus sweated and turned black in the smokestack. At last the soldiers left, and Alpheus climbed out of the chimney, his rear end roasted.

The Jones County Scouts fought their last engagement on January 10, 1865, near the place where they had first joined forces, Salsbattery. As a dual force of cavalry and infantry closed in on them from two sides, the Scouts delivered a mist of buckshot. After just a few of such volleys from the fringes of the woods, the rebels gave up the attack "as a bad job," Newton said. Years later, when a work crew cut a road through the area, they found buckshot dappled in the bark of the trees.

Twelve weeks later, the Confederacy toppled. On April 9, 1865, a surrounded and outnumbered Lee, his men starved into wraiths, wrote out a note of surrender at Appomattox and, though he would "rather die a thousand deaths," sent it across the line to the war-sick Grant, who awaited it racked by a migraine.

Two days later, Lincoln delivered a celebratory speech from the White House balcony in which he suggested that literate blacks, and those who had served the Union, should have citizenship. The speech outraged the ears of John Wilkes Booth. "That means nigger citizenship," Booth said. "Now, by God, I'll put him through. That is the last speech he'll ever make."

A day later, Mobile surrendered to Union forces. A week later, Lincoln was dead from Booth's bullet and Grant stood in disconsolate tears over his coffin as it lay in state at the White House.

Still, it was another month before the ceasefire reached Mississippi. On May 4, Confederate general Richard Taylor finally surrendered his remaining forces near Biloxi. On May 6, Governor Charles Clark yielded the capital at Jackson. When Jefferson Davis was captured while trying to flee in Georgia, the new U.S. president Andrew Johnson proclaimed the conflict was "virtually at an end."

For a brief and exultant time, Newton and the Jones County Scouts believed that they had helped win the war for the Union. The solidarity and resistant swamp tactics of Southern Unionists had dragged down the giant Confederacy, sapping its energy, manpower, and morale.

Newton and his men had fought for their homes and the principles for which they stood, Tom Knight recalled his father saying. "It made him feel good to know his men would fight and die by him for the cause they were fighting for and the interest they had in Jones County. He said he was never afraid to go into a fight when all the company was with him. He knew they would win; it made no difference with him how many cavalry were in the fight on the other side."

One month after the surrender, in early July of 1865, Newton and some of his men went to Meridian to meet the Union commander there, Major General William L. McMillen. The trusted subordinate of Sherman thanked them for their service and "recognized us as officers and soldiers," Newton recalled. Newton must have swelled with pride at the words from McMillen, impressive in his stiff, high-collared blue frock coat and gilt shoulder straps. McMillen was a veteran of bitter fighting with Mississippi cavalry during the long twilight months of the war. He remarked that the Jones County Scouts probably deserved pay as Union soldiers for their hazardous duty behind the lines, "as we were a great help to the Government in their defense." He authorized Newton to draw some rations for his men.

But Newton discovered that victory was a fleeting, ephemeral thing. Just because the Union had prevailed, it didn't mean Newton's foes had laid down their enmity for him. Ragged Southerners began to return home to find their fields destroyed, their traitorous enemy Newton Knight in a position of prominence, the local blacks impudent, and a new phrase, "The Free State of Jones," ringing in their ears, which made their sacrifices seem like a mockery. Conquered and no longer able to fight physically, they began to wage a more subtle political war to regain control of their state and redeem their Southern honor. They would dignify their treasonous actions under the rubric of a noble but Lost Cause.

William Nugent was among the troops who surrendered under General Richard Taylor in Mobile. Nugent was granted parole and amnesty at Vicksburg on May 22, after signing a "damned nasty oath" of loyalty to the U.S. government. Nugent began the long horseback ride home to Greenville, "disconsolate and weary." He arrived to find Greenville almost completely razed. As he turned down a lane toward Oakwood, his wife's family plantation, a neighbor greeted him and pointed him to a nearby field. There, he found his wife, Nellie, and his young sister, Evie, chopping weeds. The sight so undid him that he sat down on the ground and wept.

For months, Nugent had tried to forestall the Confederacy's imminent surrender and failed. But that did not mean Nugent accepted defeat. The South, he believed, would find other ways to continue the war. "I feel that we can never be subjugated, because even if our armies in the field are defeated there must be such a force kept among us 'to preserve the peace' that the Yankees' government will fall to pieces in the effort to keep it up," he predicted. Nugent added a second prediction, one in which he would be proven entirely correct.

"The greatest difficulty," he declared, "will arise after our armies are whipped."

Recollections of George Washington Albright, Holly Springs, Mississippi

I helped to organize the Negro volunteer militia, which was needed to keep the common people on top and fight off the organized attacks of the landlords and former slaveowners. We drilled frequently—and how the rich folks hated to see us, armed and ready to defend ourselves and our elected government!

Our militia helped fight off the Klan which was organized by the old slaveowners to try to make us slaves again in all but name.

I had a couple of narrow escapes from the Klan myself. When I began to teach school, the plantation owners said: "That Albright is a dangerous nigger. He's a detriment to the state." One day I got a warning from a friend that I'd better sleep away from home. I took the hint. Sure enough, that night the Klan came to the house and asked for me. My sister said she didn't know where I was.

Let me tell you also the story of a friend of mine by the name of Zeke House. Zeke House was a Negro Mail-carrier. One day, while he was carrying the mail from Holly Springs to Waterford, the Klan seized him and murdered him in the woods, and left him in a ditch. We found his body days later. That was in 1874.

Another friend of mine, Charles Caldwell, who

was a captain of the Negro militia and a member of the Mississippi Senate, was murdered by the Klan also.

The rich people regained control over Mississippi with the help of the Klan.

SEVEN

Reconstruction and Redemption

July 1865, Ellisville

Newton Knight had become the man to see in the Piney Woods. His new status in the first uneasy weeks of the so-called peace was plain in the sheen of the good horse he rode in open daylight down the broad streets of Ellisville and the authority with which he came and went from the Union headquarters, where officers jotted out orders for him and called him "Captain."

Ten thousand Union soldiers, many of them blacks who had mustered into U.S. Colored Infantry regiments during the war, occupied the towns and villages of Mississippi's interior to enforce order, a daily affront to rebels and a reminder of their defeat. A detachment of the 70th U.S. Colored Infantry set up camp in Ellisville in full view of the white portico of the Deason home. Local Confederates stared balefully at the occupiers, and at Newton, as he conducted his official business with them.

Their bitterness was heaped on top of scarcity—the state was prostrate. Whole villages had been burned to the ground, until even the roads were black with ash. In Lake Station, the destruction was so complete there was no sign it had ever been there. A resident tried "to get someone to make an affidavit that his town had existed" before the war. Corinth was a "bruised and battered village surrounded by stumpy fields, forts, earthworks, and graves," where "lonely white women crouched shivering over the hearth," according to one traveler. In Natchez, multimillionaires had become paupers. One planter, his sons killed and servants fled, chopped down the oak trees in front of his manse to sell as firewood to passing steamers. "I must live," he said. After five years of war Mississippi had become the poorest state in the Union. The whole town of Okolona could be purchased for five thousand dollars, and so many planters were ruined that in December the **Vicksburg Herald** advertised forty-eight plantations for sale or lease.

A third of Mississippi's Confederates, some 28,000 men, had died during the war. Entire companies had been slaughtered: Of the 123 men who had marched off with the Vicksburg Cadets, just 6 returned. In Aberdeen, the home of Walter Rorer, a visitor asked a local planter named Charles Langworthy the whereabouts of his five boys.

"Where is John, your oldest son?"

"Killed at Shiloh."

"Where is William?"

"Died of smallpox."

"And the other boys?"

"All were killed . . ."

Langworthy had two daughters; both were in mourning, their husbands dead as well.

Those who came back were maimed—more than half of Mississippi veterans had lost a leg or arm. Men hobbled home with sleeves and pants legs flapping, like scarecrows emptied of their straw, vacant cloth bunched and pinned to their sides. The male populace was so mutilated that in 1866 one-fifth of the state budget would be needed to purchase artificial limbs. As the sickened and disfigured veterans shuffled over the blackened roads on foot, many of them all the way from Atlanta or Mobile, still more of them died by the roadsides. Indeed, in some places it was more common to see a dead man than a squirrel or bird.

In Jones, it was rare to find a fence standing or a field with crops growing. The corn "was so rotten even the horses wouldn't eat it," according to a Piney Woods farmer. Local families were so penniless that yeoman wives clawed the soil from the floors of their smokehouses and boiled it for the salt. Small children tried to shove handfuls of dirt in their mouths. "After the war this country was as flat, I reckon, as ever one country could be," recalled Ben Graves.

Newton worked to get the county back on its feet. He emerged from his meetings with U.S. Army officers favored with an official appointment as "commissioner to procure relief for the destitute," which empowered him to requisition thousands of pounds of supplies from the federal supply depot at Meridian. On July 16, 1865, a Union captain signed a bill of lading for Newton, who shipped the following goods by the M&O Railroad:

2400 pounds bacon
2000 pounds of flour
1250 pds hard bread
400 pounds of beans
82 pounds of soap
82 pounds salt
Molasses

Newton delivered wagons full of the bacon, beans, flour, and salt to the starved citizens of Jones. Word of his role as a provider must have spread rapidly, because five days later a Union officer asked him to perform a similar service in Smith County. Captain John Fairbanks, a young Bostonian stationed with the 72nd U.S. Colored Infantry in the county seat of Raleigh, enlisted Newton's help there in aiding a local widow and her children, who were suffering badly from hunger:

Raleigh July 21 1865
Mr. N Knight
    I understand that you are commissioner to prove relief for the destitute in a part of Jones County and as Mrs. Davis has reported to me as being in

a very destitute condition I would request it of you as a favor if you would see that she is supplied as she has no one to look out for her and has a family to support. Yours respectfully, J. Fairbanks Capt. 72 commanding at Raleigh

Newton must have performed the errand without hesitation, because three days later Fairbanks turned to him again, this time with a more substantial mission. He wanted Newton to assist a local black family in re-claiming their children from a grudging former master.

A Smith County planter was holding two children against their will and preparing to move away with them. It was a common problem in the summer of 1865: ex-slaveholders refused to turn loose the men and women they still considered property, especially children. Under new federal regulations, whites were supposed to sign contracts with their black employ-ees, but some defiant planters resisted this transition to free labor and found a loophole in the fact that no contracts were required for children. Planters began to separate black children from their families so they could be worked as slaves.

It was a testament to Newton's muscle in the Piney Woods that the parents believed he could get their children back. Fairbanks gave Newton the military authority to do so in a written order:

Raleigh, Miss. July 24 1865
Mr. Knight,
    Sir this colored man informs me that you will get his two children for him and I hereby impower

you to do so as I am informed that the man they live with is about to leave the county and it is right that the families be kept together and as there is no written contract between them it is best that the two children be retained by their father.

Yours respectfully J. Fairbanks 72nd (USC Inf) comdg Raleigh

Newton delivered the children back to their parents, according to his son just one of many instances in which he settled sensitive matters between whites and former slaves. At around this same time, Newton received another entreaty to rescue a captive black child, this one held by a recalcitrant Smith County family named Mayfield. "I remember seeing an old Negro man and his wife come crying one day to see my father and to get his assistance in effecting the release of his boy," Tom Knight recalled. The couple begged Newton to help them; now that they were free they wanted to leave the plantation, but Mr. Mayfield refused to allow their boy to go.

The Mayfields, John and his son Tom, were ruined; their large prewar plantation once worth almost $25,000 was reduced to a stubbled wasteland valued at just $1,500. One can only imagine the unreasoning wrath of John and the humiliation of his heir to this spoil, teenager Tom—inheritance gone, position gone, authority gone—as the dirt-farming deserter Newton Knight prevailed in the matter of the boy.

"He [Mayfield] wanted to keep the boy as he was raised on his place and he felt he had a right to keep him," Tom Knight remembered. "But my father told him that as long as the Negroes were slaves he had a right to keep him, but since they had been freed he had no further right to hold the Negroes or their boy."

Newton's interference infuriated local Confederates, and he soon found that his new position as a government man and public protector of blacks was hardly less dangerous than his old one of fugitive. Confederate marauders continued to roam the state through the spring and summer of 1865, murdering freedmen and attacking Unionists. "Mississippians have been shooting and cutting each other . . . to a greater extent than in all the other states of the union put together," a federal inspector reported.

Newton had reason to fear for his life when he rode into Ellisville on business. According to one family account, his appearance in town one Saturday in the immediate postwar period nearly provoked a race riot. The usual white loiterers hung around outside the general store, sunburned men with plugs of tobacco in their cheeks, farmers in frayed homespun, and unrepentant veterans who persisted in wearing their gray. But also loafing and strolling along the sidewalk were newly freed blacks, "decked out in the best they had, and putting on an air of importance." Emotional crosscurrents collided in the street: Unionists and blacks were exultant, while the Confederates still choked on the bile of military surrender.

The sight of Newton and some of his men trotting down the street on horseback, showing off the fresh mounts and saddles they had been given as rewards for their Union loyalty, sent the blacks "into a state of jubilancy . . . song and laughter, and cheers broke out from the congregation." But not everyone in town was happy to see Newton, or his black friends, celebrating in the street. Suddenly, a pistol shot rang out. "The songs died, the grins vanished, and so did the Freedmen."

Newton further inflamed Confederate feelings against him when he used his influence to get rebel bureaucrats turned out of their jobs. He petitioned the new provisional governor, William Sharkey, to discard the results of the Confederate elections that had been held in October 1864, arguing that the rebels had denied citizens the right to vote. He proposed that all new county officers—loyal ones—be appointed. Newton reminded the governor that the Jones County Scouts had held "true and loyal to the Union," even when the name of Jones was "cast out as evil throughout the land," and had suffered for their allegiance.

"We stood firm to the Union when secession swept as an avalanche over the state," the petition said. "For this cause alone we have been treated as savages instead of freemen by the rebel authorities."

Newton's was the first signature. His was followed by sixty more, including those of Jasper Collins, Will Sumrall, and several other members of the guerrilla band. Their plea was successful: Sharkey followed Newton's recommendation and appointed Jasper's elder brother Vinson as judge of probate. He named another of Newton's allies, Thomas Huff, as the new Jones County sheriff.

The local rebels were beside themselves to see men

they considered low criminals gain ascendancy. A faction of Newton's old enemies soon retaliated. Joel E. Welborn, the secessionist surgeon John M. Baylis, and members of the Fairchild and McGilvery families wrote their own petition to Sharkey, smearing Newton and his men. They were nothing more than "outlaws who have been engaged in murder and pillage during the war, and who have stated frequently that they would not submit to authority of any kind." Vinson Collins, they contended, was "by relationships and sympathy . . . heart and hand with those who have been guilty of those acts of outlawry." Sharkey was not persuaded. He decided to let the appointments stand until new elections were held in the fall.

The feuding continued. Next, Newton wielded his authority against Amos Deason. Backed by an order from a Union officer, Newton impounded a sizable store of Confederate wool and denim cloth held by Deason, which the merchant no doubt hoped to sell for profit.

July 31, 1865 Headquarters Post at Raleigh
Capt. You will sease a civilian lot of wool and cloth that is in Jones Co. said to be Confederate property now in the [possession] of A Deason and report the same to thease headquarters without delay. I am sir
Very Respectfully your
Obd Servt
H. T. Elliot, Lieut. 50 USCI

It must have been a moment of exquisite justice for Newton, and an insult beyond galling for the merchant prince of Ellisville. Instead of sneaking around the side of the house as a guerrilla, Newton stalked up the elegant steps, and perhaps even across the pinewood floors that had been discolored by Amos McLemore's blood, and seized the cloth as the sanctioned arm of military power. For years, Confederates had seized goods from yeoman farmers and left them with nothing, and now the situation was reversed.

Deason challenged the seizure, and for the next three weeks charges and countercharges flew back and forth. Three different officers wrote out orders for Newton to hold the cloth in his possession until the question was legally settled. Finally, Newton's actions were upheld as proper under military orders, and the cloth became the property of the U.S. government.

But the Confederates exacted a unique form of payback. In the autumn of 1865 the unregenerate John Baylis and Joel Welborn launched a campaign to symbolically purge all traces of Unionism from Jones County. They petitioned the legislature to change the county name from Jones to Davis, and the county seat from Ellisville to Leesburg, in honor of the Confederate president and general. The gesture was plainly intended "for a slur on so many union people living here," said resident Maddie Bush.

Baylis, Welborn, and 104 other Confederate citizens, including a dozen men who had served with McLemore, declared themselves mortified by the county's Unionist activities. The county name had become "notorious if not infamous at least to sensitive ears." The signees asked that the petition be recorded by the legislature so there would be no doubt they were loyal Confederates.

> We therefore would petition your honorable body to change the name of our county seat to that of **Davis,** and the name of our county seat (Ellisville) to that of **Leesburg,** hoping that . . . its past history and name may be obliterated and buried so deep that the hand of time may never resurrect it, but by chance posterity should learn that there was a Jones county and the black part of its history, we would ask (not egotistically) that this petition, together with the names of those annexed, may be regarded by the Journals of both houses, that their mind (posterity) may be disabused of any on our part of any of its dark deeds, and it duty bound will ever pay.

The Confederates won the battle over names. In a disturbing sign of what was to come, in December of 1865 the legislature erased Jones County's name from the official record, and for the next three years, it was known for one of the most famous traitors in American history. That the legislature ratified the censure of Jones was a measure of resurgent Confederate political strength—and reflected the statewide view of Jones as a den of traitors and serfs.

The **Daily Picayune** newspaper noted the change sarcastically. "It is no very high compliment either to Mr. Davis or Gen. Lee. Jones is the poorest county in the State."

If Newton had allies among the Union officers, the Confederates had developed a more powerful ally in the North. Namely, President Andrew Johnson.

Johnson, sworn in as president on April 15, 1865, the day Lincoln died, initially seemed to identify with yeomen like Newton. A native of Tennessee and a tailor who had risen above meager beginnings, he had frequently lauded "honest yeomen" and had thundered against "the slaveocracy"—a "pampered, bloated, corrupted aristocracy." When he first took office as president, he declared: "I hold this: . . . **treason** is a crime, and **crime** must be punished." But Johnson's threats were empty. Though he verbally thundered against the South, he denied that the states had "surrendered their right to govern their own affairs." In fact, he enabled the states to resume their constitutional rights as quickly as possible and believed that the "old southern leaders . . . must rule the South."

Behind this Orwellian logic was Johnson's virulent racism and intractable personality. His mouth was grimly bowed and a pugnacious chin jutted from a weathered face, framed by coarse gray hair and eyebrows. He embraced emancipation only up to a point; he had owned a few slaves before the war, and he was wholly opposed to black suffrage, insisting that "white men alone" should manage government.

Johnson argued that blacks were the natural enemies of poor whites. "The colored man and his master combined kept the [poor white man] in slavery by depriving him of a fair participation in the labor and productions of the rich land of the country," he lectured a group of Northern blacks that included Frederick Douglass. Douglass countered by saying that blacks had far more in common with yeomen, and he envisioned a union of yeomen and former slaves in "a party among the poor." But Johnson, incapable of seeing other points of view, clung to the notion that the black man was inherently slavish and would "vote with his late master, whom he does not hate, rather than with the non-slaveholding white, whom he does hate." Given a choice between empowering blacks or forgiving the planter aristocracy, Johnson chose the latter.

Johnson had announced his plan for Reconstruction at the end of May 1865: he issued a general amnesty and restored all confiscated land to rebels who took an oath of allegiance to the Union and promised to support emancipation. About 15,000 Southerners were excluded from this general amnesty, mainly wealthy planters and senior Confederate officials. But these men could apply individually for pardons, and by the end of 1865, Johnson was granting them wholesale, "sometimes hundreds in a single day." He also appointed provisional governors in the rebel states who were sympathetic to his policy of general amnesty, and William Sharkey was one of these.

Sharkey, a planter and prewar anti-secessionist, filled his administration almost entirely with pardoned Confederate leaders in the belief that they would help restore order. Next, he called for a provisional legislature. The body that convened in July was also made up largely of former Confederates, and it promptly sought legal ways to return blacks to servitude, while debating whether they were obliged to recognize the Union at all.

Incredibly, Sharkey also allowed former rebels to rearm themselves and form military units. By mid-August of 1865, white Mississippians were nervously complaining of lawlessness and insolence among the four hundred thousand freed blacks in the state, many of whom roamed the countryside looking for food and work. Also, tensions were rising between white citizens and black occupying troops. "The negroes are bold in their threats, and the people are afraid," Sharkey said.

What seemed to threaten Mississippians the most was their loss of authority over a black population that outnumbered them. In November of 1865, the **Jackson Daily News** instructed the postwar state government: "We must keep the ex-slave in a position of inferiority. We must pass such laws as make him feel his inferiority."

Editorials in newspapers railed against the impudence of "idle darkies" who crowded the sidewalks and elbowed whites and who failed to tip their hats and show proper obeisance. "Take off your hat, you black scoundrel, or I'll cut your throat," a state legislator snarled at his former slave when he entered a room without doffing his cap. It was one more example of "the infernal sassy niggers."

The Confederate militias immediately started committing "outrages" against Southern Unionists and blacks. The vengeful mood against free blacks became such that a helpless federal official lamented that the lives of mules were more valued in Mississippi, because the "breaking of the neck of the free Negro is nobody's loss."

When Union general Henry Slocum, the federal commander of the Department of Mississippi, saw what was happening, he issued a general order prohibiting these armed companies, characterizing the men who formed them as "outlaws" who have "scarcely laid down the arms with which they have been opposing our Government." But Sharkey appealed to Andrew Johnson, who backed him and the Southerners. The military, Johnson declared, was in the state "to aid but not to interfere with the provisional government."

Thus, even though Mississippi was still under military occupation, federal soldiers like those stationed in the Piney Woods who were Newton's allies found their hands half tied in dealing with a surly, defiant citizenry, among whom the popular refrain was that they had not been beaten, only outnumbered. Midwestern boys enervated from the war and anxious to muster out were charged with preserving order in an atmosphere of strong drink and antagonism, even as they had been stripped of real authority by the president and the governor. At least in the war they had been able to do something about the wrongs they perceived.

An Iowan named Lewis F. Phillips stationed on the Mississippi- Alabama border described his postwar duty as a trial in which the local populace tried to poison him with a toxic mixture of "pine top" bootleg and buttermilk, local girls treated him spitefully, telling him "they would no more touch a blue sleeve than a rattlesnake," and the ex-planter class viciously persecuted former slaves.

One day when Phillips was on duty, a crew of black field hands came to the Union encampment from a distant plantation to show the soldiers the livid welts laid on their backs by a former master who still considered them his property. "Some of the old planters were now more savage with the Negroes than when they had a property interest in them and were cutting them up with the lash at a fearful rate," Phillips observed.

Phillips and a squad of soldiers decided to pay the planter a visit, "to read him the law." But the truth was that Phillips had no orders to make an arrest and could only hope to intimidate the planter. As the Yankees rode through the pleasant countryside, they stopped at various plantations along the way and found that virtually every man of the house had been slain, wounded, or captured. They spent half a day at the manor home of the lash-wielding planter, "telling him of the error of his ways and what would happen to him if he didn't be good." On the way back, Phillips and his men ran into a parade of bedraggled, emaciated Confederate soldiers making their way home. "They were not 'whipped,' " they informed the Yankees, but only "overpowered."

Phillips camped in the village of Uniontown, where the largest hotel still flew the Confederate Bonnie Blue flag, waving cheekily over Main Street. An irascible and inebriated Union colonel decided to teach the hotel proprietors a lesson and instructed his artillerists to wheel their guns directly in front of the hotel and fire a thundering salute. The explosions shattered every pane and teacup on the premises. "When we were done firing every glass that had been in that side of the house lay down on the ground," Phillips wrote.

There was nothing to do but drink. One evening Phillips watched a man stagger down the street and pause in front of a cigar store, where he tried to pry the cigar out of the hand of a wooden Indian. Phillips heard him muttering: "All the niggers were free and now By God he'd free the Indian." He tore the Indian down and kicked it into the street.

It was in this potent, uncertain environment that Newton and the Jones County Scouts were mustered out of service. On September 10, 1865, they followed orders and turned their arms over to Captain A. R. Smith of the 70th U.S. Colored Infantry in Ellisville, although they retained their personal shotguns.

The timing of the Jones County Scouts' disbanding could not have been worse; the white militias empowered by Sharkey were rampaging. Major General Carl Schurz, a former Union officer who would become secretary of the interior, took a trip to Mississippi to aid in Reconstruction. He observed that the armed bands of whites "indulged in the gratification of private vengeance, persecuted helpless Union people and freedmen, and endeavored to keep the Negroes in a state of virtual slavery."

In Mississippi's October elections, impenitent rebels were swept back into the state's highest offices. A former Confederate brigadier general, Benjamin G. Humphreys, who had fought in the peach orchard at Gettysburg, was elected governor. Humphreys still wore a torn and bullet-riddled Confederate army coat, which he ostentatiously bragged had been "thrice-perforated" by Yankee Minié balls. Humphreys won by a landslide. Three days after the election President Johnson approved his application for a pardon, allowing him to take office.

Humphreys and the legislature that convened on October 16 set about restoring the old antebellum order. The people of Mississippi had abolished slavery "under the pressure of federal bayonets," Humphreys said, and the Negro was free whether they liked it or not and entitled to certain protections. But that by no means meant the Negro deserved citizenship or equality. The "purity and progress" of Mississippi society depended on keeping blacks where they belonged according to the "law of God," Humphreys said: on the plantation where white bosses could guard against "the evils that may arise from their sudden emancipation."

One Delta planter put it less delicately. "I think God intended the niggers to be slaves. Now since man has deranged God's plan, I think the best we can do is keep 'em as near to a state of bondage as possible . . . My theory is, feed 'em well, clothe 'em well, and then, if they don't work . . . whip 'em well."

Mississippi's legislature began writing the notorious set of laws known as the "Black Codes." Though euphemistically labeled a "civil rights act," the laws collectively denied blacks their hard-won freedom and enslaved them again: freedmen were prevented from voting, assembling, renting or owning land, or quitting their jobs. Perhaps worst of all, under an "apprenticeship law" all blacks under age eighteen who were without means of support were required to be "apprenticed"—i.e., enslaved—to whites without pay.

A purposely overbroad vagrancy law defined any blacks whom whites might find troublesome or inconvenient as criminals: "All rogues and vagabonds, idle and dissipated persons, beggars, jugglers, or persons practicing unlawful games or plays, runaways, common drunkards, common night-walkers, pilferers, lewd, wanton, or lascivious persons, in speech or behavior, common railers and brawlers, persons who neglect their calling or employment, misspend what they earn, or do not provide for the support of themselves or their families, or dependents, and all other idle and disorderly persons, including all who neglect all lawful business, habitually misspend their time by frequenting houses of ill-fame, gaming-houses, or tippling shops, shall be deemed and considered vagrants." Insulting gestures and preaching without a license were also crimes. The penalty was imprisonment and a fine of fifty dollars, and those unable to pay could be hired out to whites.

The state legislature also refused to ratify the Thirteenth Amendment to the U.S. Constitution which abolished slavery, claiming it would empower "radicals and demagogues." The gesture sent a message to the rest of the country: Mississippi Confederates would govern their state without interference from federal law. (Not until 1995 would Mississippi ratify the Thirteenth Amendment.) Unionists like Newton must have wondered what the three hundred sixty thousand Union lives lost in the war had been sacrificed for.

By the end of 1865, in fact, Confederates had even distorted the meaning of "Unionism." Former Confederate officers, even generals like Humphreys, were claiming the mantle of Unionism as their own and twisting the term to describe themselves as moderates: "Union man" had come to mean simply someone who had opposed secession back in 1861, "regardless of subsequent service for the Confederacy." As one Union officer put it: "There is no such thing as loyalty here, as that word is understood in the North." The sophistry of those Confederates belittled men like Newton, who had suffered such wrath for pledging allegiance to the United States of America.

To a prominent Northern writer named John Townsend Trowbridge, who toured the state in the summer and winter of 1865–66 as part of a larger journey across the battlefields of the South, Mississippi's Confederates were remorseless. Trowbridge blamed the fact largely on Andrew Johnson's leniency. "The beautiful effect of executive mercy upon rampant Rebels was well illustrated in Mississippi," Trowbridge wrote.

Trowbridge arrived just as the Black Codes went into effect. One plantation owner told him, "I'd have been willing to let my plantation go to the devil for one year, just to see the free niggers starve."

During a midnight journey from Corinth to Memphis Trowbridge stumbled into an encampment of freedmen, a dozen or so people in "miserable conditions, wretchedly clad" who invited him to share a campfire that blew smoke in a circle and offered him what they had—an apple—which was more generous hospitality than any he had received from whites. The freedmen had worked all summer for a planter in Tishomingo who had refused to pay them.

As he rode a train to Memphis he gazed out of the window at more ragged freedmen and overheard fellow passengers remark, "They'll all be dead by spring" and "Niggers can't take care of themselves."

From Memphis, Trowbridge went to Vicksburg by riverboat, the parlor of which was so wreathed in tobacco smoke that it dimmed the light of chandeliers. The majority of passengers were planters going down-river to their estates, and Trowbridge found them to be "hard swearers, hard drinkers, inveterate smokers and chewers, wearing sad-colored linen for the most part, and clad in coarse 'domestic': slouching in their dress and manners, loose of tongue, free hearted, good humored, and sociable." They bought glasses of whiskey from decanters for twenty-five cents a shot, which they tossed down freely from noon until bedtime. Their talk was only of "mules, cotton, niggers, money, Yankees, politics, and the Freedmen's Bureau—thickly studded with oaths." There were a handful of Tennesseans onboard, who envied the Mississippians "their Rebel State government, organized militia, and power over the freedmen."

At one landing, Trowbridge saw a burned plantation reduced to nothing but fifty standing chimneys. "Yankee vandalism," a woman said. At another landing, he learned that four men in Confederate uniform carrying Spencer rifles had just robbed a store kept by a Union man and murdered a Negro.

But the strongest impression left by the riverboat trip came when a well-dressed, light-skinned black couple boarded the craft and asked for a stateroom. The captain exploded in rage: "God damn your soul! Get off this boat!" A chorus of furious passengers cried out, "Kick the nigger!" and "He ought to have his neck broke!" The couple disembarked, and their trunk was pitched to shore after them.

Along the way Trowbridge conversed with the planters, exchanging views on emancipation and free labor. By the end of the journey he had decided, "It was impossible to convince these gentlemen that the freedmen could be induced to work by any other means than by despotic compulsion."

The Union troops who had been Newton's allies were gradually mustered out of the state, leaving only a small federal presence in Mississippi, a few battalions of infantry, and agents from the Bureau of Refugees, Freedmen and Abandoned Lands, the division of the War Department that now governed the relationships between former slaves and white employers. The woefully understaffed and embattled head of the Freedmen's Bureau in Mississippi, Colonel Samuel Thomas, was overwhelmed by the size of the problem he faced.

Most Mississippi whites, Thomas reported, "cannot conceive of the negro having any rights at all. Men who are honorable in their dealings with their white neighbors will cheat a negro without feeling a single twinge of their honor; to kill a negro they do not deem murder; to debauch a negro woman they do not think fornication; to take property away from a negro they do not deem robbery. They still have the ingrained feeling that the black people at large belong to the whites at large."

To Newton, it must have suddenly seemed like the Confederacy had seized control of the govern-

ments in Jackson and Washington, D.C. He retired
to his hilltop acreage for much of 1865 and 1866 and
kept to himself, laying low, tending his crops, and re-
building his farm on the county border. For Newton
to continue fighting, surrounded as he was by rebels,
would have been useless, even suicidal. One of Newton's great talents as a soldier was that he had a sense
of when to go on the offensive and when to assume a
defensive strategy.

Newton persuaded Rachel to leave Jackie Knight's
old plantation and follow him, to help on the farm
and sharecrop. According to Rachel's granddaughter,
"After emancipation my grandmother and her family
moved from the old slave plantation in Jones County to
Jasper County . . . they went with one of the younger
Knights who did not believe in slavery."

Newton installed Rachel and her children in a barn
until he could complete a cabin for her, built of split
cypress boards. He raised the log-and-plank home not
far from the one he shared with Serena, and he gave
Rachel some acreage to work as her own.

Newton had another good reason to devote himself
to his farm: he had enmeshed himself in a tangled
domestic situation. Somehow, during his career as a
fugitive, he had found enough unguarded time to father children by the two women in his life at the same
time.

Newton had continued his wartime affair with Rachel, and sometime between 1863 and 1865 she had
his child, a daughter named Martha Ann, named,
presumably, after his loyal younger sister. Among the

freedmen Newton and Rachel's relationship was an open secret.

"Rachel was considered his woman," the former Knight slave Martha Wheeler said, "and he moved her to his place."

But on Serena's return to Jones County, Newton had reunited with her. In 1864 Serena too bore him a daughter, whom they also named after his sister Martha Ann. Serena shortly became pregnant again, and a son named Joseph Sullivan Knight was born in 1866. Newton seemed intent on following the Knight family tradition of leaving a double-digit number of heirs.

It's not clear how much Serena knew, or how she felt about Rachel's appearance on the farm as a sharecropper. But Newton's divided loyalties seem to have tilted in favor of his white family for a time—Rachel would not bear another child by Newton for four years, until 1869. She and Newton may have temporarily given up their affair as hopeless or simply too dangerous. Under the draconian Black Codes, interracial marriage was not only banned but penalized with a life sentence in the state penitentiary. Nevertheless, Rachel seems to have committed herself to Newton, and to working on his farm.

Newton's 170 acres became an informal if perhaps fraught collective. The Knights, black and white alike, went about the laborious job of reclaiming the land that had gone to weeds. Newton's farm had never been worth much, just $300 before the war, but now it wasn't even worth a third of that—it would only be valued at $120 in 1870. It would take him a decade of relentless clearing and cultivating to build it to 320 acres.

Foot by foot, the Knights cleared fields, felled trees and unearthed stumps, and turned the thorny undergrowth into neat furrows. They planted corn, and apple trees, because Newton loved the fruit. He raised a new plain log home with a large rock fireplace and a high-galleried porch, not far from the ashes of his first home.

But persistent droughts made recovery from the war hard. Newton's wartime neighbor Ben Graves recalled weather that seemed almost biblically punishing. "It seemed there came a drought every year . . . After the war the elements seemed to set in against us, for about 3 years the crops were a failure. We had 12 weeks of drought one year."

Newton's white children toiled side by side in the fields with Rachel's. His eldest sons did the same heavy work as Rachel's son Jeff. Clearing even a single new acre required the labor of the entire family: blacks and whites, adults and children alike, would bend over crosscut saws until a tree was felled, and then cut it into logs, after which the logs were rolled on top of sticks for carrying. It took a team of six or eight adults to lift the logs and carry them away, for hewing into boards or split rails for fences.

But not all of Newton's children were happy to be sharing the homestead with Rachel and her children as their equals. Tom grew increasingly resentful as he got old enough to understand the true nature of the arrangement, perhaps influenced by Serena's feelings on the matter. "The attitude of his mother caused Tom to have little, or no use for Rachel and her white daughters," a descendant observed. But Tom obeyed Newton's wishes and understood that they were there by virtue of "his will."

When the corn came in they would shuck it in the crib and then shell it at night by the fireside and put it in sacks, and the following day carry it on horseback to the mill, to be ground into meal. The nearest rail town was thirty-eight miles away, by ox wagon, so they did most of their marketing at an old post office—country store six miles away, where there was a water-powered gristmill. Sometimes, if there were a spare dozen eggs, Rachel would walk the six miles to the store to trade them for sugar or coffee.

There was never enough food to fill all of the bellies, just the lean game that Newton hunted, or the chickens they raised, with corn pone made with salt water in a skillet and garden vegetables. The Knight children were so perpetually famished that they searched the meadows for nut grasses, which they would chew to supplement their thin meals, along with muscadines, persimmons, and hickory nuts.

The new homestead sat on a spit of land above a verdant, heavily wooded hollow, and Newton wore a footpath down the hill to a cold spring that rushed at the foot of it. He would loft his shotgun into the crook of his elbow and wander off down the path to hunt alone for a day at a time. Or sometimes he simply strolled down to the spring, where he liked to go for the quiet. He tried "to forget the past" and forgive his grievances against his old enemies, he told his son Tom.

He wanted to "live peaceful with men as far as possible."

Mississippi's lawmakers had gone too far with the Black Codes. To Northerners they seemed to be trying to alter the outcome of the war, behaving as victors rather than the defeated. "The men of the North will convert [their] state into a frog pond before they will allow such laws to disgrace one foot of soil in which the bones of our soldiers sleep and over which the flag of freedom waves," wrote the **Chicago Tribune.** Congress agreed: it denied Mississippi readmission to the Union and placed the state under rigid federal military rule again.

Congress was also fed up with President Johnson, whose sore-headedness over black citizenship caused a total breach with the legislature. In April of 1867 lawmakers wrested Southern policy making away from him, passing a comprehensive new Reconstruction Act: Southern states were required to adopt black suffrage and to ratify the Fourteenth Amendment before applying for readmission to the Union. Also, Confederates were barred from holding office. The measure passed over the veto of an irate Johnson, who railed that it operated "in favor of the colored and against the white race" and that the South was being trodden underfoot "to protect niggers."

To Newton, the new radical Reconstruction policies at last seemed to promise "the end to rebel rule," as one Raleigh newspaper put it. But more than that, it was a breathtaking expansion of country, and Union. "We have cut loose from the whole dead past," wrote Wisconsin senator Timothy Howe, "and have cast our anchor out a hundred years."

As the climate became more favorable, Newton rode down from his hilltop to support his man in the 1868 presidential election, General U. S. Grant, who was running at the head of the Republican ticket against the unremarkable Democratic governor of New York, Horatio Seymour. Another fierce Grant supporter was Jasper Collins, who was such an ardent admirer of the Union general that he named one of his sons Ulysses.

But Newton and his fellow Republicans encountered furious resistance in a political season that was continually intemperate and even deadly. Mississippians had always been notorious for settling matters with violence, eye gouging, crotch kicking, stabbing, and shooting; one British tourist observed that even casual conversations had the "smack of manslaughter about them." The political stakes drove opponents to new levels of shrill contention: newspapers railed against "ranting niggers" and "stinking scoundrels," and the Ku Klux Klan and other white supremacist groups made their first appearance in the Piney

Woods, dedicated to foiling the "incredible scheme of granting suffrage to the half brutish blacks," which would be the "high water mark of political insanity."

The champions of Anglo-Saxon superiority, who posed as destroying angels, were men of all classes: planters, farmers, and merchants. They were men anchored in a tradition of slavery and soured by crop failures and the state's inability to recover from the war, and they scapegoated blacks for Mississippi's ills. Their ethic of vigilantism coupled with racial hatred led them to join rifle clubs named things like "Sons of the South." Their aim was to restore social order as they pictured it should be, and that meant punishing blacks for insolence and driving out the Northerners and radical Republicans who were the agents of change.

The Piney Woods had less Klan activity than many other areas, because of the relatively small population. Nevertheless, it was present. "It did not seem that the ku klux klan roamed around this country unless some Negro misbehaved," recalled Ben Graves. "They were organized to make Negros and carpetbaggers stay in their places. The carpet baggers were men that came here from the north, that come to put devilment in the negro's head. He would tell the Negro that he was as good as the white man . . . They thought the Negro and them would take the country . . . That was what organized the ku klux klan, to see that the carpet bagger and the Negro did not take the county. They were all that saved it."

In Covington County, a "White Cap Klan" meted out formal judgments against "objectionable negros" and polled the membership on whether an offender should be punished with violence or merely intimidated into "good behavior." They used ritualistic ceremonies to frighten superstitious local blacks: they would approach in a dead silence and ride in a circle around the victim, wordless but making mysterious motions. Some of their methods were no more than Halloween charades: a sheet-clad goblin would call for a drink of water and down a whole bucket, a sleight of hand performed with a rubber bag under the sheet.

In Paulding in Jasper County, a former slave named Jane Morgan who lived in a community of freedmen on an old ruined plantation watched as Klansmen kidnapped two of her friends. "Once de Ku Kluxes cum to our place and take two of our niggers off," she remembered. "We never knowed dey had done nuthin' but we sho never seen dem niggers no more—no sire we ain't."

The Klan activity was a response to the fact that in nearly every county, black Republicans and their white allies were forming grassroots Union Leagues or Loyal Leagues for the purpose of enlisting new members and organizing their vote. The clubs offered education in citizenship and protection in numbers. Their members were bound by political and sometimes religious affinity, often led by black preachers or educators, and fostered by white carpetbaggers or Southern abolitionists like Newton. Newton was almost cer-

tainly active in a Union League club. A Democratic
state senator, W. D. Gibbs, recalled that both Jones
and Jasper counties had Loyal Leagues and that one
political meeting of black voters in Jasper numbered
three hundred men.

"Of course the colored people up to that time were
thoroughly united under the loyal leagues, and under the influence of those men from the North, who
came down there and took part in the politics of the
state, and those southern men who joined with them,"
Gibbs said. ". . . They were as much subject to their
leaders in politics as to commands as they were subject to their masters before the war. It is their natural
disposition, being an ignorant people, to be led. They
were naturally attracted to these men, on account of
the gratitude they felt to the republican party of the
North for what they considered their actual enfranchisement."

The first meeting of the Loyal League Club of Jones
was probably held in secrecy in a barn or a church, or
perhaps even in a swamp hideout for reasons of safety.
Descriptions of other Union League clubs suggest
the scene: At the front of the darkened room stood a
pine table, and next to it a chair. Someone would have
brought copies of the Constitution and the Declaration of Independence, which were placed on the table
with a Bible. Beside the table stood an official United
States flag, attached to a pole whittled out of a tree
branch.

Newton would have been one of the few white men

at the meeting, if not the only one. It was a small congregation, and nervous, given the attitude of ex-Confederates toward blacks congregating in political meetings. The men in the room ranged from seventeen-year-old boys to old men, and most of them had likely helped the Jones County Scouts in one way or another during the war. Joe Hatton would likely have been there.

The meeting opened with a recitation from the Bible and a brief prayer. Then, in their first order of business, members may have voted to stockpile weapons and resume drilling in order to defend themselves against the KKK and rifle clubs, who were becoming increasingly antagonistic. New names were discussed for membership into the League, and there was a discussion, too, of which local men to beware of. Most of the meeting was devoted to political education. Newton might have read aloud from an old issue of a newspaper. They discussed their legal rights against white employers and the individual rights clauses of the Constitution and traded the names and whereabouts of sympathetic agents of the Freedmen's Bureau. The Leaguers agreed to convene monthly, and the meeting adjourned after everyone sang "Battle Cry of Freedom."

By Election Day, matters were so tense that Newton took his shotgun when he went to vote at Smith's Store, and so did a number of his men. They ran into a band of Democrats, and a murderous dispute threatened to break out. "I remember when there was an election once Newt belonged to the Republican party, he called himself a union man and was a full-fledged Republican," Ben Graves recalled. ". . . Him and his crowd carried their guns to this election. Very few Democrats voted. I thought they were going to have a fight at Smith's old store . . . Newt's crowd had their guns and hid them out when they could and they tot up a big argument and used pretty rough language." But they quashed the quarrel before any serious trouble could break out, probably thanks to the authoritative presence of old Vinson Collins.

Grant won with less than 53 percent of the vote—the Klan effectively suppressed the black vote in large swaths, but Unionist strongholds put him over the top. Newton's feelings on hearing of Grant's victory weren't recorded, but relief was surely one of them, and more than that, hope for his two families. Four days after the election another idealist dirt farmer, this one in South Carolina, expressed sentiments that Newton undoubtedly shared: "I am . . . a native borned . . . a poor man never owned a Negro in my life . . . I am hated and despised for nothing else but my loyalty to the mother government . . . But I rejoice to think that God almighty has given to the poor . . . [a] Gov. to hear to feel to protect the humble poor without distinction to race or color."

Grant's election meant a victory for Newton personally: he again became one of the most influential men in the Piney Woods. Grant appointed Adelbert Ames, a Union war hero, as Mississippi's provisional governor, and Ames began awarding state offices to Union loyalists and blacks. Newton's former comrade Will Sumrall became assistant U.S. marshal for Jones County. The onetime guerrilla and Unionist Prentice Bynum was named clerk of the circuit court. Another ally, B. A. Mathews, became a probate judge.

It seemed to Newton and his friends that they would be able to remake the state. In 1870 Mississippi at last approved a new constitution that abolished the Black Codes and upheld federal laws guaranteeing civil and voting rights. Blacks won election as sheriffs, mayors, and magistrates, and by 1873 there would be sixty-four black men occupying seats in the statehouse. The former slave John Roy Lynch became a justice of the peace in Natchez and would eventually rise to speaker of the Mississippi House of Representatives. The now heavily Republican state legislature also selected two new U.S. senators. One was the minister and teacher Hiram Revels, sent, in a spectacular bit of social justice, to complete the term Jefferson Davis had left unfinished. The other was Adelbert Ames.

Newton now had influential friends not just in the statehouse, but the nation's capital. He was confident enough of their backing that he devoted the next three years to pursuing some dangerously controversial public issues. The first was a small matter, but one that burned: he and his allies petitioned the state to restore the names of Jones County and Ellisville. The legislature approved and the short, inglorious reign of Davis County and Leesburg was over.

Next, Newton felt confident enough to press a case on behalf of himself and his men for compensation as Union soldiers. In 1871 three staunch Republicans in Washington personally took Newton's case to Congress and introduced bills in the Senate and House of Representatives in his behalf. The bills called for "the relief of Newton Knight and others, citizens of Mississippi" in return for their "services as officers and members of Knight's company, United States infantry." It requested payment of $21,150 for fifty-five men, first and foremost $2,000 for Newton.

Newton didn't include all of the 125 or so men who had fought with the Scouts. Instead he made a list of those he felt had served most reliably throughout the war, and perhaps those who were most needy. He left off some men because "they did not hold out faithful and the Capt would not send their names," according to Jones County probate judge B. A. Mathews, who helped Newton pursue the claim.

The legislators who took up Newton's cause in Congress were classic Republican abolitionists, or "carpetbaggers." They each saw something worthy in the plight of the Mississippi dirt farmer and "Southern Yankee" who had been so isolated among rebels during the war. Representative Legrand W. Perce was a Chicago lawyer and ex–Union colonel who had helped capture a supply train during the war and stayed in Mississippi after serving in the Gulf district to establish a law practice in Natchez, where he was elected to Congress for two terms. Albert Howe was a Massachusetts abolitionist and a Yale graduate and another Union officer who settled in Mississippi and won postbellum office; he was also a particular friend of Adelbert Ames's.

George Washington Whitmore's support of Newton was more coincidental; a lawyer and representative from the first congressional district in Texas and a former slaveholder, he had no apparent connection to Mississippi and introduced his bill because Perce had arrived on the floor too late to do it himself and handed the task off to his colleague. But Whitmore shared this much with Newton: he too had suffered persecution and imprisonment as a Unionist in the South, and therefore he understood the price the Jones County Scouts had paid for their loyalty. Whitmore had argued stridently against Texas secession as state legislator and remained such a voluble Unionist during the war that Confederate authorities finally arrested him in 1863 and jailed him for nearly a year—without formal charges or trial.

Parochial Republicans also supported Newton's case by writing letters in his behalf and attesting to his loyalty. Among them was a feisty, colorful judge named William M. Hancock, who kept his courtroom in order with a pistol. Hancock handwrote a letter in Newton's behalf to Perce, assuring him that the case was worth supporting. "He is an honest and clever man and is a staunch Republican and during the Rebellion was a union man and the recognized leader of the union party in this county and it was generally reported that he held a military office in the U.S. military service," Hancock wrote to Perce. "You may rely upon any statement he may make to you in regard to any matter he may write to you about."

Eventually even the illustrious Ames took a personal interest in Newton. Ames introduced yet another bill in Newton's behalf on the floor of the Senate on December 18, 1873. He would become so involved in the effort to recompense him that copies of Newton's roster and a flurry of communications still survive in his personal papers. But the Republican lawmakers failed to get the measure passed. It was shuffled from one committee to another—Judiciary, to Military Affairs, to Claims—with no action. Despite a raft of evidence—Newton provided General McMillen's name and the written orders he received from Union officers who occupied Jones just after the surrender—Northern legislators were simply dubious that a band of poor white Southern farmers had aided the Union.

Despite the federal government's failure to recognize his allegiance, Newton would demonstrate it again and again during Reconstruction—even at peril of his life. He would be one of the few white native Mississippians to remain loyal and useful to Ames during the next few years, years in which the federal government abandoned both men and unreconstructed Confederates sought to control the state with a campaign of murder and terror disguised as politics.

Newton's boldest public act in the years 1871 to 1873, and one on which he staked his personal safety, was a campaign to organize and build an integrated school. Newton's children were now of schooling age, and he was just as concerned with Rachel's family as Serena's. He had gradually come to feel as married to Rachel, if not more so, and they were in the midst of rapidly expanding their family. By 1875 Newton and Rachel would have five children together: Martha Ann (1865), Stewart (1869), Floyd (1870), Augusta Ann (1873), and Hinchie (1875).

For Klanners and white supremacists, black education was a focus of special fury. It was the generous Mississippian who viewed education for blacks as anything but useless, if not trouble. "A monkey with his tail off is a monkey still," the **Natchez Courier** opined.

In Okolona, an Episcopal minister who tried to teach some young blacks had four shots fired at him. On the night of March 9, 1871, in Aberdeen, a Northern teacher named Allen P. Huggins was called out of his house by a circle of white-robed men. They were "gentlemanly fellows, men of cultivation, well-educated, a much different class of men than I ever supposed I would meet in a K-Klux gang," Huggins said, but their message was not gentle. They told him they did not like his "radical ways" and the fact that he had instituted public schooling and was trying to "educate the Negroes." He had ten days to leave the state or they would kill him.

Huggins replied he would leave when he was ready. In response, one of the men undid a stirrup leather from his horse and began to beat Huggins with it, saying he was "just such a man as they liked to pound." On the seventy-fifth blow, Huggins passed out. He came to with pistols aimed at him and a chorus of voices warning him that if they laid eyes on him after ten days, he was dead. The beating left Huggins hobbled for a week but unbowed; he testified to the event before Congress and returned deputized as a U.S. marshal and began to round up Klanners for arrest.

In the summer of 1872 Newton was also deputized marshal, and though no record survives to tell us why, it's likely that Klan violence had visited the Piney Woods and that he acquired a badge to deal with it. A certificate shows that on July 6, 1872, he received an appointment as U.S. marshal for the "Southern District, Miss." His son Tom remembered that Newton "was appointed Provost Marshal . . . with authority to call out troops of the United States Infantry to put down riots or any other troubles he could not stop . . . he served for several years during these reconstruction days."

At first, Newton's neighbors had sought his advice and cooperation in building a new school. Every two or three miles in Jones and Jasper counties there was a family with children, including those of some of the men he had ridden with in the war. He and his old friends decided to split the cost and the work of raising the schoolhouse. "He was a kind-hearted man, and he was a man of good judgment, and was looked upon as being the leader of his community in matters of schools and other local affairs," Tom Knight remembered. Newton hewed beams and split logs for benches and contributed to the hiring of a teacher at a salary of ten dollars a month, the cost of which would be shared equally, along with his board.

On the first day of the term, Newton sent his children to school—and Rachel's children went with them. Parents who accompanied their young to the schoolhouse door were startled to see Rachel's son Jeff and daughters Georgeanne and Fannie file into the building. When some of the white parents angrily asked Rachel's children what they thought they were doing, they replied that their mother had sent them.

The teacher flatly announced that he refused to instruct them. Rachel's children were ordered out of the building. "Go home and tell your mother the school doesn't accept Negroes," they were told.

Newton was apparently outraged by the insult: he had put his sweat and labor into building the school for the common benefit of the neighbors' children, yet they refused the same benefits to his and Rachel's children. Rachel had protected the lives of some of those white men during the war. Their edict against race mixing in the classroom seemed the height of moral hypocrisy: plenty of Piney Woods yeomen had sired children with Negro blood—racial intermingling was surely all right with them when it came to sex. The difference was that they refused to take responsibility for their progeny, while Newton took care of his.

By one account, a day later the school, which still smelled of fresh-cut pine, went up in a bonfire. The embers were still glowing as word spread that Newton Knight had set the fire "because he wished the Negroes to have equal opportunity," according to one of his descendants.

Newton stopped talking to his neighbors over the school. It was the last straw for him—he had come to feel estranged from most local whites and more comfortable among blacks, with whom he shared an understanding of Unionism and democratic ideals. Martha Wheeler, the former Knight slave, said, "He had a complete break with the whites because he undertook to send several of his Negro children to a white school he had been instrumental in building."

In 1873 Ames ran for governor of Mississippi, campaigning on one part ambition and one part conviction that he had a "mission with a capital M" in protecting the rights of freedmen. "I found that the Negros who had been declared free by the United States were not free, in fact they were living under a code that made them worse than slaves," Ames said. ". . . They had no rights that were respected by white men." Ames believed that he could be of practical use "in securing their actual freedom."

His opponent in the gubernatorial election was James Lusk Alcorn, the sleek cotton trader and former Confederate whose pose as a conciliatory moderate had helped him to win the governorship in 1870. But Ames viewed Alcorn as a turncoat and an opportunist, evidence of which was his refusal to crack down on the Ku Klux Klan.

Ames shuddered at what had happened during one year of Alcorn's tenure alone: by his count, thirty Negro schoolhouses and churches were burned down and sixty-three men killed. One of the very worst outbreaks of Klan violence occurred in 1871 in Meridian, where a large population of ex-slaves had formed a strong Loyal League. The Klan used the trial of three blacks for arson as an excuse for a rampage, opening fire in the courtroom and killing the Republican judge as well as several spectators, throwing one defendant from a roof and slashing the throat of another. Over three days they cut down "all the leading colored men of the town with one or two exceptions." They left twenty-five black corpses in the street.

Ames ran on a state ticket that included three black candidates for high office, and he promised the safeguarding of rights, public education, and a program of public works. Black voters responded by sweeping him into office decisively. Alcorn's own field hands voted against him. They also elected ten new black state senators and fifty-five black representatives to the state legislature, along with fifteen carpetbaggers. White Republicans like Newton were crucial to the victory; they helped to organize and protect black voters. In Jasper County, Ames edged out Alcorn by eight votes, 642 to 634. "The negros did go up there and vote at the election just as the whites," remembered Ben Graves.

As Ames began his governorship, he must have seemed incapable of failure to Newton. He was just thirty-eight, but his record suggested enormous capabilities. The son of a Maine sea captain, he had graduated fifth in his class at West Point and served dauntlessly through sixteen major Civil War battles. He earned the Medal of Honor for his actions at Bull Run, where he fought to the point of fainting despite being shot through the thigh, and he was at Antietam, Fredericksburg, Chancellorsville, and Gettysburg, where he led a brigade on the front line for three straight days. By the end of the war he was a brevetted major general and "the closest thing to a Galahad" in the Union army.

An aide-de-camp said of him, "He was the beau ideal of a division commander, and as such there was no more gallant and efficient officer in the armies of the Union. Every one who rode with him soon discovered that Ames never hesitated to take desperate chances under fire. He seemed to have a life that was under some mystic protection. Although he never permitted anything to stand in his way, and never asked men to go where he would not go himself, still his manner was always cool, calm, and gentlemanly. Under the heaviest fire, when men and officers were being stricken down around him, he would sit on his horse, apparently unmoved by singing rifle ball, shrieking shot, or bursting shell, and quietly give his orders, which were invariably communicated in the most polite way, and generally in the form of a request."

Now Ames was the picture of a young statesman, with long brunet hair swept behind his ears, the luxuriant drooping mustache of a tycoon, and thought-shadowed eyes, perhaps the lingering effect of so much war. Though not strictly handsome, he cut a commanding figure, and he had swept up one of the belles of Washington, D.C., in Blanche Butler, the daughter of the Union general and conqueror of New Orleans Benjamin Butler. She began to visit the Senate gallery, where **Harper's Weekly** sketched Ames bending over her. As his wife she would support his political career devotedly though she despised Mississippi, which she considered the home of pestilence, lard, traitors, and socialite cats. "All are lynx-eyed, and one is always polite and kindly, but constantly on guard," she said.

But though Ames prevailed in the election, Republicanism was still under threat in the state. On the same day Ames and his allies were elected, Mississippi also sent the cinder-eyed Lucius Quintus Cincinnatus Lamar to the U.S. House of Representatives. The classic Mississippi Bourbon, a former Confederate general and defender of slavery, railed against "strangers" like Ames. Lamar labeled the new governor's Republican majority the "blackest tyranny that ever cursed this earth."

Lamar typified the long-held attitude of white conservatives to interfering outsiders. It was summed up by **The Nation,** which warned, "If any man from the North comes down here expecting to hold and maintain radical or abolitionist sentiments, let him expect to be shot down from behind the first time he leaves his home."

Newton was not a stranger, but he held radical and abolitionist sentiments, and for that, his enemies tried to assassinate him. As Ames took possession of the governor's office, Newton began to go to Jackson on state business for three and four weeks at a time. In addition to his duties as a U.S. marshal, according to his son Tom, he acquired a position as federal revenue collector, and it became a common sight to see him on the exchange platform at the Newton Station crossroad, waiting for the rail car to the capital. But his habits attracted attention.

As Newton idled on the platform one afternoon, two men eyed him, and he overheard them talking. "That's Newton Knight, let's go get some more men and take him out and kill him," one said. Certain they meant to return with a gang to waylay him, Newton hurriedly hid himself behind some cotton bales on the loading platform. When the train arrived he dashed out from behind the cotton and ran for the rail car like a hobo. Just when he leaped on the train, a half dozen men arrived to ambush him. As the train pulled away, he heard one of them say, "If we don't catch him this trip we'll get him on the return."

Newton related the episode to Ames, who gave him a pistol and advised him to buy a new double-barrel while he was in Jackson. Ames also suggested he trick his pursuers by getting a haircut and a shave. Newton did as Ames recommended: a barber cropped his long hair to his collar and removed his heavy whiskers, leaving just a mustache. The transformation in his appearance was startling. "When he stepped from the train at Newton with his new gun shining no one seemed to know him, neither did they ask any questions," his son recounted. Newton was so altered that when he arrived at home, even "we children did not know him," Tom wrote.

After this incident Newton began traveling incognito. For the first time in his life, Newton wore "store-bought shirts, finely tucked down the front," a gray fedora, and boots that shined like a pool of oil in the morning sun.

It seemed that every gun-packing backwoodsman with a grudge in the Piney Woods wanted to take him on. One of Newton's old foes paid a local tough to accost him, under the guise of offering him a drink. The fellow played drunk, waving a bottle of whiskey around his head as he invited Newton to partake. Newton declined—he didn't drink. But the man insisted, and kept waving the bottle, until Newton suspected he was looking for an opportunity to smash him with it. Newton stared the man down with his chill blue eyes, tracking the movements of the bottle. Unnerved, the man said, "God, Newt Knight, don't you ever wink your eyes?"

"Not when I'm looking at your sort of cattle," he said.

Newton believed one attempt on his life came close to succeeding. He was doing some trading at a general store in Ellisville when two men approached him, offering hearty handshakes and claps on the back. They were "mighty glad" to see the great Newton Knight, they said, who was talked about as the bravest man who had ever lived. They introduced themselves as photographers and said they had heard tales of his daring, how he had eluded the cavalry. They wanted to capture the famous man on film, and they had brought a camera to take his portrait. They suggested he pose for them in the woods where he had ranged. Newton, flattered, agreed. The men hiked over to the woods on the edge of town and pressed on into the thickets. Finally, they stopped and asked Newton to strike a pose. Newton, growing suspicious, cradled his shotgun while they set up the camera.

One of them suggested Newton pose without his gun. Why didn't the great man hand over the firearm?

"No, I'll give my gun to no man," Newton said, "but I will give you both barrels of what is in it if you don't leave here and do it now."

Newton drove his wagon back to his hilltop farm, where he told his family he wouldn't be going off into the swamp "to have his picture made no more." Too many so-called friends had betrayed him; from now on he would be mistrustful. He was becoming increasingly wary, and he cautioned his children against strangers who seemed overly friendly.

"Never allow any man to hug you . . . for he is likely

pretending to be your friend when he really intends to do you harm and deceive you," he said.

All that protected Newton was his lingering reputation as a dangerous man to deal with and his status as a federal agent. According to a descendant, "It was well known, and well understood, that if this man were openly slain, the Federal Government would take action, since he was an officer. Or a few of his old gang who remained faithful, would retaliate."

Still, Newton felt threatened and knew his life hung in the balance. He grew so guarded he even began to carry a pistol to church.

"It's best to go prepared for trouble," he told his son, "and not wait until you get into it, when it's too late."

In October of 1875, Governor Ames sat in his ornate, chandeliered office and read a letter in a scrawled, barely legible hand. The grammar was irregular and the spelling uneven—it was addressed to "Mr. Alebert Ames"—but the mistakes only conveyed the letter's sentiments more powerfully. It was from one of his black constituents in Newton's territory, Jasper County:

October 16, 1875
Mr. Alebert Ames, to your honor, Dear Sir: I write you these few lines to inform you that old Griffin Bender, a rank old Demicrit, reside in Jasper County. He was at Newton Station on that

day, and he remarked to Dempsey Bender, one of his old slaves, that the demicratic party was agoing to carry this election, and he said, with threght [threat] of violence and interdation [intimidation], that if they failed they intended to have blood— **blood;** and, Mr. Govner Ames, I don't think that you ought alouw such to go on in Mississippi; and, govner, the colard sitezens of Jasper County don't think that you'll let the demicrats trample on the rights of the republicans of Miss. in that kind of a manner because they are prencablely [principally] colard men. Now, govner, all we want is a fair chance in the world. To your honr you unacqunted colard frind,

    N. B. BLACKMAN

Ames was receiving hundreds of letters like it from all over Mississippi, and had been for weeks. They all reported the same thing: ex-Confederates and conservative Democrats were planning to retake the statehouse by force, using violence and intimidation against black voters. The Democratic campaign chairman, a former Confederate general named James Z. George, was turning the state elections of 1875 into a farce and doing it so successfully that it would become notorious as the "Mississippi Plan" and emulated by states throughout the South.

All over Mississippi white men were organizing, joining rifle clubs, and forming White Leagues pledged to preserve the color line. One of the more politically subtle groups was the taxpayers' league, a collection of planters and businessmen who blamed Ames for skyrocketing land taxes and the presence of blacks in office and vowed to rid the state of "Republican corruptionists." The movement was led by, among others, the ex-Confederate William L. Nugent, who had become a dedicated white supremacist. The subtext of the taxpayers' league was clear: it wanted to replace the Ames administration with what one pundit called "Ku Klux democracy."

Nugent had lost his wife, Nellie, whose health failed in 1866, but he had remarried and gradually rebuilt his life, launching such a prosperous law practice that in 1872 he moved into one of the largest mansions in Jackson, an edifice with pillars and wrought-iron balconies. In one of his most famous cases, Nugent defended a local theater that had denied seating to blacks. In January of 1875 Nugent helped organize a taxpayers' league statewide convention. Men pounded the lectern as they called for the ouster of Republicans who inflicted tax burdens on them, especially taxes that went to educating the Negro. To Ames's critics, Mississippi's problems came down to just two things, carpetbaggers and Negroes. Run the Yankees out of the state and restore the racial hierarchy, and all would be well. These "White Liners" could cloak their politics in discussions of tariffs, but Ames perceived their real cause: "The true sentiment of the assembly was 'the color line,' " he said.

Ames's government, like any, had its flaws. The

state's economy was bedeviled by chronic crop failures, and the Republican Party was rent by factionalism fueled by James Alcorn. Nevertheless, despite being met by opposition from antebellum leaders at almost every turn, Ames had accomplished much: he Johnny Appleseeded public education, built free hospitals, and was helping to lift Negroes from tenancy, and doing so in a state that was still razed by the war. If taxes were high, it was because every road and bridge needed to be rebuilt, and Mississippians desperately needed free schools and health care, without which they would never recover.

The first sign of serious trouble for Ames had come the previous summer in Vicksburg, where whites were livid over the marriage of a Negro legislator to the daughter of a local planter and the presence of several blacks on the Republican ticket in upcoming local elections. On July 4, 1874, a mob of Vicksburg White Leaguers shot up an Independence Day rally of black Republicans, killing several, and took over the city by force. Ames wrote to President Grant begging for federal troops to quell the riot. But Grant, fearful of political backlash, advised Ames to settle the matter locally and refused to interfere. Incredibly, on the very anniversary of his siege victory at Vicksburg, Grant effectively returned the city to his old enemies.

Six months later, emboldened white supremacists inflicted worse slaughter on Vicksburg. A mob forcibly turned the black Republican sheriff Peter Crosby out of office. The overthrown sheriff, on orders from

Ames, mustered a band of five hundred freedmen to help him take back his post, but as they marched on the town a heavily armed white militia headed by a Confederate cavalry colonel, Horace Miller, met them at a bridge on the outskirts. The leader of the black militia, a Union veteran named Andrew Owen, advised his outnumbered and outgunned men, "Boys, go back peaceable and quiet." As they turned their backs and began to disperse, a white fired into them. The shot touched off a massacre; for the next three days vigilantes hunted blacks down through the woods, where their bodies remained, their families too afraid to claim them.

Grant finally acted, dispatching a small unit of federal troops to restore order. But the damage was done: Ames's enemies now knew that he had weak backing from the federal government. They smelled blood. The Vicksburg riots had shown "the absence of all the elements of real authority" in the Ames administration, L. Q. C. Lamar said.

By March of 1875, Ames was convinced the Democratic Party in Mississippi had metastasized into a paramilitary organization that meant to retake the state with bullets. Anticipating trouble, Ames was able to get a bill through the legislature authorizing him to organize two regiments of militia and purchase four Gatling guns.

But Ames had trouble raising a trustworthy regiment of white men. Some refused to serve because they feared reprisals from the Klan. Others Ames didn't trust to side with blacks against their own race. Ames sought only the most deeply committed men. One of the few he trusted was the longtime Union man from the Piney Woods, Newton Knight. On March 18, Ames personally signed a commission appointing Newton a colonel in the 1st Infantry Regiment. As a white officer leading blacks Newton could expect bloody reprisals from his old foes; nevertheless, he took his place in the militia alongside black officers, who commanded about half the companies.

Newton may have tried to help raise other men to serve Ames's need. An undated fragment of a note from Ames's black lieutenant governor, A. K. Davis, to Newton suggests that he was responsible for some sort of mustering. "The governor wants you to appoint good men," it read.

All that summer and fall, gangs of heavily armed whites broke up political meetings, made threats, and generally terrified black communities.

Nov. 3, 1875
　　　　Miss., Noxubee County, Macon, Miss.
Governor Ames, Esq.:
　　Dear Sir: I write you a few lines on the state affairs of Nox. Co., Miss. Last Saturday, the 30th, the democrats was in Macon town in high rage, raring around and shooting off their cannons all up and down the street, and shooting all their pistols also . . . there was Richard Gray shot down walking on the pavements, shot by the democrats,

and he was shot five times, four times after he fell, and was said shot because he was nominated for treasurer, and, forther more, because he made a speech and said he never did expect to vote a demicratic ticket, and also advised the colored citizens to do the same. Although we had W. M. Connor for our sheriff, and he have never presented to do anything about it, and I would like to know if we colored republican population have not as much right to beat our drums in a civilization manner as the democrats is to shoot up and down the streets in Macon town, and shoot our colored population down when they gets ready, and nothing done about. I write to you to know where is the law, and what authority is for us, and I believe you are the man for just, and I do say we colored republican are very disgrossly emposed upon with protection, and all other violation of laws. The demicrats ranges through in house. I am not writing to you to be writing; I am speaking of what I know and see. Please read this and spend your opinion on it.

Respectfully,
THE COLORED PEOPLE

But the extent of Ames's powerlessness was being demonstrated almost daily. The sheriff of Yazoo City was Ames's good friend Albert Morgan, a carpetbagger and a valorous Union veteran from Wisconsin who had done the seeming impossible: he had helped three hundred or so black families buy their own land and opened schools for their children. Compounding these offenses, Morgan had married a beautiful mulatto schoolteacher from the North named Carrie Highgate, making him a special target of White Line ire. On the first day of September, the town bells began to ring, and Yazoo City was soon full of armed men on horseback. They poured gunfire into a Republican rally, wounding several people, and put Morgan on the run for his life. Bands of men galloped about with ropes hitched to their saddles, firing in the air, "and when the niggers would see the ropes tied to their saddle, that was enough for them, they did not want anything more." Morgan finally escaped after several days in hiding, thanks to a friend who met him in the woods with a horse waiting. Morgan rode away through the night and would not return to Mississippi.

"My friend, I fought for four years; was wounded several times; suffered in hospitals, and as a prisoner; was in twenty seven different engagements to free the slave and save our glorious Union—to save a country such as this!" Morgan wrote to Ames. "I have some love left for my country, but what is a country without it protects its defenders? . . . to be butchered here by this mob after all I have done here is too cruel."

To Ames, it seemed like the war all over again. "In '60 and '61 there were not such unity and such preparation against the government of the U.S. as now exist against the colored men and the government their votes have established," Ames remarked.

Just three days later another brutal assault took

place in Clinton, a small town just fifteen miles from the governor's mansion in Jackson. On September 4 a gang of white riflemen opened fire on a political rally of 1,200 Republicans led by a black state senator named Charles Caldwell. As Caldwell pleaded for calm, bullets tore through the crowd, and seven or eight people fell dead. This time, Republicans fought back, and two white men were killed in a blast of returned fire. Spectators screamed and fled into the woods, and for the next few days, periodic violence raged around Clinton. Large posses of armed white men arrived from surrounding counties by train, to join in chasing down blacks and shooting them. A black Republican named E. B. Welborn said, "They just hunted the whole country clean out, just every man they could see they were shooting at him just the same as birds."

A black Republican named Square Hodge was found dead in the swamp missing his entrails, one arm, and his head. Lewis Russell was marched a quarter mile into the woods and riddled with bullets by twenty guns. Nor were blacks the only ones to die. A band of fifty whites seized a carpetbagger who taught black schoolchildren, William Haffa, and executed him. Then they went next door and forced two black Republicans to stand on a tree stump and emptied their guns into them as if they were a firing squad.

Senator Caldwell escaped before they arrived at his door. His wife, Margaret Ann, was told by the men who stood on her porch, "We are going to kill him if it is two years, or one year, or six, no difference; we are going to kill him anyhow. We have orders to kill him, and we are going to do it because he belongs to this republican party, and sticks up for these Negroes . . . We are going to have the south in our own charge . . . and any man that sticks by the republican party, and he is a leader, he has got to die."

Margaret Caldwell testified that men were "shot to pieces" by the vigilantes. "They were around that morning killing people before breakfast," she said. The death toll was thirty. About five hundred survivors, including Caldwell, fled to Jackson, where they congregated around the federal buildings and pleaded for protection.

White Democrats openly celebrated Clinton as a great victory. The **Jackson Daily Clarion** declared: "This lesson of Anglo-Saxon supremacy, written in blood, will ever remain the most important of many lessons taught in the modest college town of Clinton to the rising young manhood of a proud and untrammeled Commonwealth."

Ames again beseeched the president for help. "A necessity of immediate action cannot be overstated," he wrote. There was a small force of five hundred or so U.S. troops in Mississippi, divided between posts in Jackson, Holly Springs, and Vicksburg. Ames begged to use them—they could not intervene without direct orders from Grant.

Grant declined. The victor in an epic war had become a tired, calculating politician. Grant sensed that the mood of the country had shifted, as had his own, to apathy. "The whole public are tired out with these annual autumnal outbreaks in the South," he complained. ". . . The great majority are ready now to condemn any interference on the part of the government. I heartily wish peace and good order might be restored without the issuing of a proclamation." What's more, a delegation of Ohioans had advised Grant that federal intervention in the South was so unpopular it could throw Ohio to the Democrats in the next election. Grant did the political math and decided that white Ohio, where Republican Rutherford Hayes was running for governor, was more important than black Mississippi.

Ames was alone with his troubles; there would be no federal troops to prop him up. Since the federal government lacked the will to protect Mississippi's blacks, they would have to protect themselves. Ames had hesitated to arm a black militia for fear of igniting a race war that would be "felt over the entire south." But now he ordered a thousand Springfield breech-loading muskets and authorized the mobilization of three Negro units. Among the columns were men who had been driven out of Clinton, including Charles Caldwell.

In early October, Caldwell led a small wagon train of men and armaments in a march across the countryside near Jackson. Word that black troops were armed with Springfields and bayonets so outraged whites that they threatened to hang Ames from a post in the governor's mansion. As the election approached, Ames feared that the small regiments of black troops would only be butchered. He flinched. A group of Democrats, led by James Z. George and including William L. Nugent, proposed a "peace" settlement and met with Ames at the mansion. He agreed to disband the black militia.

The peace was one-sided. County by county, Ames lost control of the state. In Jasper County, a black activist named Sandy McGill was slain by the Klan when he refused to cease political organizing, despite threats. "He was a leader among the negros and they killed him because he defied them and made his boast," Ben Graves remembered. McGill and his brother-in-law, a man named Bill Henderson, were on McGill's porch and waiting when the Klan rode into his yard. A white neighbor watched the riders stalk past the house, "one horse right after the other," in a slow procession. McGill and Henderson refused to flee. Instead, they raised their weapons and triggered off a round. "They didn't wait for the Ku Klux to fire; they fired on them," Graves said. The two men were quickly overrun on their porch. Henderson managed to get away into the woods, but McGill was caught. "I think they beat him dead with a mall," Graves remembered.

How Newton reacted to these atrocities is conjecture; there is no record of his feelings. But they must have cut him deeply—and implanted a cold fear for Rachel and her family.

The Democratic activist W. D. Gibbs campaigned through Jasper and Jones counties in 1875, pausing in Paulding to deliver what must have been a speech loaded with meaning before the Loyal League. Later, during an investigation of the election by the U.S. Senate, Gibbs denied terrorizing blacks and insisted the only guns Democrats had brandished were for squirrels.

Gibbs claimed that his appeal to black voters was perfectly free of intimidation. "I satisfied them, to the best of my knowledge and ability, the interests of the white man and the black man in Mississippi were identical." Senate investigators asked:

Q: That was the line of your argument?
A: That was the line of my argument.
Q: You made no threats at all?
A: No threats at all.
Q: So far as you saw in that county, did you see any violence?
A: I did not see any violence.
Q: Did you see any intimidation?
A: I did not hear of any intimidation.

In Paulding, Gibbs claimed, there were even "a good many colored people out to hear me."

But Ames's friend Albert Morgan drew a different portrait of W. D. Gibbs's "canvassing." Gibbs had menaced Morgan during a conversation about the election, in which Gibbs made clear the true nature of his Democratic activism.

"No one objects to the nigros votin' now," Gibbs told Morgan. "But the white man objects to nigro rule, and won't submit to it any longer. It's time for yo' to quit yo'r ship. It is sinking mighty fast, and it'll keep on till it reaches bottom. With yo'r support we could carry the county without any trouble at all. But, with or without it, we have made up our minds that we can, and by the Eternal, we will carry the county next time . . . We won't harm you all unless yo' get in ou' way."

"Who do you mean by you all?" Morgan asked.

"Why! Yo' all Yankees and nigros—yo' party."

Gibbs continued: "I hope yo'll all stand from under. It'll save we all a heapo' trouble. I tell yo' we all white people have made up ou' minds that we can, and we are going to carry this county next time. Peaceably, if we can, but fo'cibly if we must."

To reinforce the point, Democratic leaders paraded not with squirrel guns, but with cannon. In Meridian on the day registration began, voters were informed that if they didn't vote the right way, the siege guns would be turned on them. In Noxubee, Oktibbeha, and Colfax counties the cannon were detonated "very often, as a means to annoy, frighten, and intimidate those opposed to them," until in Colfax County there was almost "a reign of terror." In Monroe County, Democrats boasted that "there will be no U.S. soldiers to protect the voters, and they will have it all their own way."

As matters grew worse, the Republican majority splintered and voter support faltered. A Republican ally named J. B. Allgood wrote to Ames advising him that the Republican league there was dissolving. "If we can have no protection, it is to the interest of us to disband our organization," he wrote. "The negro is unable to protect himself; ignorant, illiterate, poor, and dependant as he is, he is at the mercy of the white man. I would like to know if we can get any protection; if not, we should know it, and shape our course accordingly."

By now Ames didn't need to read letters to know what the Democrats were doing. They threatened to do violence to Ames himself. One night in Jackson a group of belligerent Democrats marched through the streets with a cannon drawn by mules and paused at the governor's mansion. They jeered and roared at the windows—and then fired pistol shots at them. They disappeared for a time, but returned in the early hours of the morning, thoroughly drunken, and began firing again, and also detonated the cannon, rattling the windows. They debated whether to storm the manse and kill Ames on the spot, but decided not to. Instead they went to the offices of the Republican newspaper, the **Jackson Pilot,** and shattered the windows.

On November 1, 1875, the day before the election, Ames wrote to his wife, "The reports which come to me almost hourly are truly sickening. Violence, threats of murder, and consequent intimidation are co-extensive with the limits of the state. Republican leaders in many localities are hiding in the swamps or have sought refuge beyond the borders of their own counties."

The Democrats won in a landslide. In Columbus, Mississippi, vigilantes set fourteen fires and killed four black voters, and mobs greeted others and made them vote Democratic at the end of gun barrels. In Claiborne County, a cluster of black voters had to pass through a gauntlet of eighty White Liners carrying Remington breechloaders; they opened fire on them at a blast from a bugle, wounding six. When a report of the incident was wired to General James Z. George, he responded approvingly, "Your dispatch satisfactory. Push on the column, but keep quiet." The Republican vote count in Claiborne was expected to be more than 1,800. It was just 496.

In Aberdeen, a hundred mounted and uniformed men under former Confederate general Reuben Davis guarded the polls and threatened to "cover the yard with dead niggers in fifteen minutes" if any blacks tried to vote. Those who did were pistol-whipped, and the crowd dispersed. There were 1,400 Republicans in Aberdeen; just 90 cast votes. In Yazoo County, the Negro population was 12,000. There, Republicans got just 7 votes.

In Jones County, they got just 4.

As the returns came in on election night, Democrats carried sixty-two of seventy-four counties. A brass band led a parade to the house of James Z. George, who declared "the redemption of our common mother, Mississippi." By the time all the votes were counted, the Democrats controlled the state legislature with a four-to-one majority.

The killing didn't stop with the election. All over

Mississippi jubilant White Liners continued to drive Republicans out of office by force and did violence to blacks who had defied them. They had a particular score to settle with State Senator Charles Caldwell, who had displayed such militancy during the Clinton affair.

They assassinated him at Christmastime. A group of vigilantes invited him to have a drink, and the clinking of glasses was the prearranged signal: he was shot through the back from a window. He was then dragged to the sidewalk, where he lay bleeding as a Clinton street mob fired thirty to forty more bullets into him. When the town bells pealed to announce his death, his wife Margaret took to her bed in grief. When Caldwell's brother Sam rode into town to find his brother's body, he too was shot dead.

Blanche Ames wrote her mother: "Those who have seen Caldwell's corpse report that the body had to be tied together, while on his head and neck there was not a space where one could lay a hand."

Ames too feared assassination. He hardly knew a man in Jackson who hadn't either taken part in the terrors or sat idly by as they occurred. Vigilantes liked to demonstrate how defenseless he was by firing their guns near the mansion. "At night in the town here, the crack of the pistol or gun is as frequent as the barking of dogs," Blanche wrote. "Night before last they gave us a few shots as they passed the mansion yard, by way of reminder."

Ames barely lasted past the New Year. In February

of 1876 the state legislature drew up thirteen articles of impeachment against him. One of them accused him of fomenting a race war by naming Charles Caldwell to the militia. James Z. George formed a committee of prominent men to press Ames for his resignation, and among them was William L. Nugent. The delegation confronted Ames and threatened him with removal. Rather than prolong the state's agony, he resigned.

Newton left no record of his mood after the election of 1875, but it can be guessed at: Mississippi Republicans had lost all faith in politics. Grant's refusal to send in troops had left them "to the tender mercies of the Ku Klux Klan," as one Mississippian put it. The Reconstruction project had collapsed, and the state was in the hands of the same antebellum leaders who had driven the South into desolation. As the presidential race of 1876 approached, Newton had no hope that the law would protect him, or his friends and loved ones.

"The Negroes are now almost ready to take to the swamps, and unless the government send troops here at least a month before the election, the Negroes will not go to the polls," one Republican activist wrote to Washington. "We look for the Government to stand by us and if it does not it can take these Southern States and do what it pleases with them."

Ames departed for Washington, where he announced to anyone who would listen that Mississippi had been violently overthrown. A Senate select committee was convened to inquire into voting conditions

in the state, headed by George Boutwell of Massachusetts. Ames, stiff with dignity yet seething, testified
that James Z. George's so-called Redeemers had won
the state "due wholly to fraud, violence, and murder
to such an extent and degree that the northern mind
seems incapable of comprehending it."

In the spring and summer of 1876 members of the
Boutwell committee went to Mississippi to collect testimony firsthand, but they found many Republicans
so traumatized they refused to cooperate. A party man
from Macon named E. Stafford wrote a letter declin-
ing to appear, using searing language that surely reflected some of Newton's own feelings.

"Very few from this county will go voluntarily
before your committee, for two important reasons,"
Stafford wrote.

> First, they have no money to pay expenses . . .
> Secondly, they believe—not without reason—that
> it would not be safe to return, if they did go . . .
> Abandoned by the administration, and those
> whom we have fought the battles of the party to
> elevate to position and influence, this "conclusion"
> has its advantages—we may at least save our scalps,
> which are worth more to us and our families than
> the broken faith of a pack of ingrates. I have been
> brick batted, ku-kluxed, and struck by lightning,
> in the service of reconstruction in this state, and
> still live to see my bitter political enemies walk
> off with the rewards. I want no "committee" in
> mine.

Still, after devoting months to the task, the committee collected two volumes of documentary evidence, including testimony from witnesses such as Albert Morgan and Margaret Caldwell, the wife of the assassinated legislator. Stacks of pages described in gruesome detail the tactics that had been employed in the election of 1875. The report ended with a succinct conclusion that stated in unmistakable language that militants had retaken by force what Grant and Sherman had fought so bloodily for.

"The state of Mississippi is at present under the control of political organizations composed largely of armed men whose common purpose is to deprive the negroes of the free exercise of the right of suffrage and to establish and maintain the supremacy of the white-line democracy, in violation alike of the constitution of their own state and of the Constitution of the United States," it read.

Not that it did any good. Even while the report was being written, Mississippi's Democrats were once again employing gun blasts and suppression to sway the 1876 presidential race between Rutherford Hayes and Samuel J. Tilden. Mississippi's White Line legislature issued a new decree aimed at black voters: they were required to disclose where they lived and were employed. Once again, thousands of fearful black voters stayed away from the polls. In Yazoo County exactly two Republicans cast votes. In Tallahatchie, the total was one.

When the national votes were tallied, it was the closest election in U.S. history. The deadlock created a constitutional crisis that lasted for months and was only settled, after protracted negotiation, by the Compromise of 1877. Democrats agreed to give Hayes the presidency, in exchange for his concession that federal troops would no longer intervene in the South. There would be no more meddling in Dixie's domestic matters; Southern whites would settle "the Negro question" for themselves without any further federal help.

It had been a decade since the Civil War, and yet to Rachel, Newton, their children, and other freedmen it seemed that "the whole South—every state in the South—had got into the hands of the very men that held us as slaves," as one black leader bewailed. **The Nation** magazine announced, "The Negro will disappear from the field of national politics. Henceforth the nation, as a nation, will have nothing more to do with him."

For men like Newton and Ames, the dirt farmer and the patrician governor alike, it was a disaster, the wreck of all they had hoped for from Reconstruction. In fact, it was more than that: it was the true end of the war. "A revolution has taken place—by force of arms," Ames had declared, as he watched events helplessly, "and a race are to be disenfranchised—they are to be returned to a condition of serfdom—an era of second slavery." The Mississippi election of 1875 had been merely a continuation of the conflict they had fought a decade earlier and thought they had won. They were wrong. They had lost.

Testimony of Thomas J. Knight in *The State of Mississippi v. Davis Knight,* Ellisville, Mississippi, December 1948

Q: Mr. Knight, when was the last time you visited your father's grave?

A: I ain't visited it.

Q: You never have visited it?

A: No, sir.

Q: Did Rachel die before he died, or after he died?

A: Yes, sir, Rachel died before he did.

Q: Rachel died before he died?

A: Yes, sir.

Q: Mr. Knight, don't you know as a matter of fact that Captain Newton Knight and Rachel are both buried out there on Mr. B. L. Moss's place?

A: Well, now, you want to know? I don't know.

Q: You don't know.

A: That's some of that supposed business.

EIGHT

The Family Tree

Autumn 1876, Jasper County, Mississippi

Newton retreated to his farm, but he didn't surrender. Instead, to the frustration and disgust of his enemies, he propagated. What few ideals Newton had left, he lived out privately, devoting himself to his acreage and his ever-burgeoning families. He said there was "no time to try to attend to other men's business, that he had plenty to do to attend to his own business," his son Tom recalled.

His "own business" was indeed plentiful: By 1876, the Knight homestead teemed with sixteen children and infants, most of them Newton's. It almost seemed as if he was determined to colonize a separate mixed-race society.

One bit of business Newton had was pressing: a month after the presidential election, he deeded Rachel 160 acres of land. The deed, handwritten and dated December 3, 1876, was an almost unheard-of gesture for a white man in Mississippi, and it bespoke Newton's partnership with Rachel, whom he had come to regard as his "second wife." It also suggested how much he wanted to secure her independence. Most whites sought to virtually re-enslave blacks, to drive them from land, or use them as tenants and cheap laborers, not to promote their independence. The title to her own land would protect Rachel in the event something happened to him.

According to the deed, Newton gave Rachel the land for less than a dollar an acre, a fraction of what it was worth. The "fea simple" came to $150, and we can't know whether Rachel actually paid Newton, but if she did have that kind of money, it means she was hugely industrious and that Newton had treated her with generosity in their sharecropping arrangement. In any case, the possession of her own land was a great day for Rachel. Land was the irreplaceable American prerequisite for social standing and autonomy. Land was what so many blacks believed was promised to them as compensation for slavery after the Civil War— forty acres and a mule—and had been lost by the broken promises of Reconstruction. Land was freedom itself. "What's de use of being free," one black asked, "if you don't own land enough to be buried in? Might as well stay slave all yo days." Land was everything— and the vast majority of blacks were landless. A survey of seventeen Mississippi counties in 1870 found that not one in a hundred blacks owned the land on which they worked. Fifteen years after the Civil War, only 7.3 percent of blacks in the entire rural Cotton South owned farms. Rachel now owned four times forty acres, and the land would shelter her from the neo-Confederate ascendancy that had swept the state and release her from the "iron grip" of the sharecropping system.

How Serena felt about the deed is lost to history. But with so many mouths to feed, Newton, Rachel, and Serena weren't left with much time to argue over domestic emotional dramas. There was just too much work, and too little privacy.

In all, eleven bodies jostled for space in Rachel's log home, the children so numerous they always seemed to be "in the way, constantly shoved and pushed around," her granddaughter Anna Knight remembered.

The cabins in which Newton's dual families dwelled were packed with hungry-mouthed youngsters in coarse hand-me-down homespun. He now had seven children with Serena ranging in age from their eldest boy, Mat, born before the war, to a toddler named Cora. Rachel's five children by Newton, meanwhile, were all under the age of eleven. Also living in Rachel's cabin were her teenaged children by Davis Knight, Jeff and Fannie, and the two eldest who had been purchased with her in slavery, the boy Edmund, and Georgeanne, now a full-grown woman. Lastly, there were two more babies. These were Georgeanne's own infants, a daughter named Anna and a son named John Howard.

The Knights, white and black alike, worked in an endless circle of arm-wearying, hand-callousing toil, plowing and chopping cotton. The youngest did their part by ferrying water in tin buckets up and down the hill from the spring and carting jugs to their elders in the fields. As soon as a child was big enough, he or she took a place in the line, hoeing or chopping weeds with an old pickax. The Knight children picked the cotton in the late, hot summers; one child remembered picking a row every half hour, filling her sack. The family together could make a bale in a day. When they weren't working cotton fields they tended to crops of turnip greens, mustard greens, string beans, and tomatoes.

Often, it was work without much recompense. When the crops didn't fail, they fetched paltry prices: Mississippi was locked in an agricultural depression that lasted from the mid-1870s until the 1890s. Cotton, once king, sold for just six to eleven cents a pound depending on the year. Pay for a field hand was twelve dollars a month, but nobody had cash. Mansions buckled and peeled, while sharecropper families starved in dogtrot cabins. Mississippians were worth only $286 per capita in 1877, compared to an average of $1,086 in the North.

Nevertheless, over the next ten years other members of Rachel's family also became independent. Georgeanne eventually purchased eighty adjoining acres and moved her children into a one-room hewn-log cabin there. In time Newton also deeded land to Rachel's eldest son, Jeffrey. This meant that

Rachel and her children were part of a tiny class of independent, landed black yeomen, while so many others were trapped in the stasis of tenant farming. By 1890, the proportion of blacks who owned their own farmsteads in Mississippi would still be just 11.4 percent.

The white and black Knight families were now neighbors and equals in all but one respect. Their children worked and played alongside one another, but Rachel's children and grandchildren still could not attend school. Instead they picked up their education secondhand from the books the white Knights brought home, poring over their copies of the **Blue Back Speller,** or McGuffey's reader, and learning by drawing words in the sand in the yard.

On Sundays the neighboring families would gather and hold their own church services. Afterward they held dances, or card games, or spelling bees for adults and children alike as entertainment. For a blackboard, they nailed boards together and painted them with soot, and they dug out natural white chalk from the mud banks. After the spelling matches, they had ball games, or threw stones, or had country sing-alongs from an old beloved songbook, **The Sacred Harp,** voices rising in the choruses of "Awake, My Soul" and "A Charge to Keep."

As the homestead grew by the acre, it became less rustic and more gracious. An apple tree stood in Rachel's yard, with a bench in the shade, where she would do her hair. A yard full of flowers, spikes of iris and herbs, was enclosed by a picket fence. A cedar pinwheel hung on the gate and spun when there was a breeze. Flowering vines twined up the porch to the gallery, and a cedar water bucket and gourd hung by the door for the thirsty.

There were more tragedies over the years for both families. Two children died: Serena's son Billy was trapped in a fire, and Rachel's son Edmund would not see 1880. The cause of Edmund's death is uncertain, but he was probably a casualty of an epidemic of yellow fever in 1878 that took several lives in the area.

Newton grieved; he was a tender parent, and an attentive one when he wasn't too tired from work. His daughter Molly had vivid memories of tussling and giggling with him, and stories of his gentleness with children survived for generations. But he was also burdened and could become laconic and morose. He called these "thinking" periods and would shoulder his shotgun and wander off down the hill toward the spring and disappear for a day or more at a time. He may have been visiting Rachel, with whom he "was forever having business." There is some evidence that Serena complained about these solitary trips.

Newton's loyalty to Rachel was becoming a well-known scandal in the county. Ben Graves, his old neighbor, was appalled by rumors that Newton "took a Negro as a wife." Accounts of Newton's behavior circulated among the black community, too: Martha Wheeler, the former slave who had worked for Jackie Knight, heard that Newton had begun to live almost entirely "among the Negroes" and that his children with Rachel "were given advantages."

Neighbors began to shun them, and some of Newton's relatives and oldest friends refused to have anything to do with him. His old guerrilla compatriot Dick Yawn, who had married his loyal younger sister, Martha, announced that he would no longer visit Newton's farmstead, even though they had fought in the war together. Cousins denied they were kin with him. "So many vile things were said of Newt" that even one of his own brothers, James, supposedly refused to acknowledge him because he had "married" a black woman and "mixed the blood of the races."

There would be more intermingling as the combination of social pressures and political dangers drove the Knights inward. Increasingly isolated in the hilltop enclave, they began to intermarry. In 1878 Rachel's son Jeffrey courted and married Newton and Serena's white daughter Molly. Shortly afterward, Newton's eldest white son, Mat, wed Rachel's daughter Fannie. The couples shared mutual experiences and sympathies and had been encouraged to view each other as equals. Socially cut off from their peers, they perhaps also shared a sense of loneliness, in which affection grew.

The couples moved to land adjoining Newton's and started their own homesteads. By 1880 Jeffrey and Molly were farming 140 acres and had the first of their seven children, a daughter they named Altimirah after their aunt, the antebellum mistress who had cared for so many slave children. Mat and Fannie were next door farming 48 acres. The Knight households had become so interrelated that it was hard to keep straight who lived where, and with whom. A federal census taker in 1880 tried to get a headcount of the people living in the cabins that now dotted the Knight acreage but became hopelessly confused, getting their relations wrong and scribbling some names down twice.

As the young marrieds started their own families, Newton and Rachel seem to have hoped that their children and blended grandchildren would inherit a world with fewer racial classifications. It was a fantasy. Instead, Mississippi was becoming ever more obsessed with racial purity and blood quantum. New Jim Crow laws erected impassable barriers between white and black and defined even a fractional trace of slave heritage as an intolerable pollutant. The Knights weren't becoming safer and more racially invisible to the rest of the world. On the contrary.

The Redeemers asserted their political will with statutes reminiscent of the Black Codes. Sweeping new vagrancy laws took effect: Rachel's son Jeffrey could be jailed simply for not having a job, or for leaving one before his contract expired. Rachel was liable to wind up in prison if she herded the wrong hog under Mississippi's new "pig law," passed in early 1876, which defined the theft of any farm animal worth more than ten dollars as grand larceny and made it punishable by five years in the penitentiary.

The statutes were calculated to bend the sweating backs of freedmen on behalf of planter-merchants again. Under a draconian convict-lease system petty offenders found themselves in bondage, hired out for involuntary hard labor and whipped by overseers for "slow-hoeing." The number of state convicts quadrupled. Men and women were thrown into jail and then had their sentences extended when they were unable to pay bureaucratic fines. Newton's family didn't have to look far to see the abuses of the convict-lease program: Covington County had its own chain gang. One small-time thief in that county found his servitude lengthened to a lifetime when he couldn't pay the sixty cents a day board he was charged while working on it.

But it was the extralegal justice system that worried Newton most. He continued to fear for his own safety, and for that of his family. He played the role of watchman, habitually sitting on his galleried porch with his shotgun across his knees. He became a fitful sleeper and insisted windows and doors be barred at night, the latchstring pulled inside. He was so on guard against an attack from his old enemies that he took to camping in the woods like a guerrilla again. Once, he climbed into a treetop to spy on a group of white men who called at the farm for him. When they were finally satisfied he wasn't at home and left, Newton called out to a relieved Rachel and Georgeanne. He seemed to be ever alert and kept anyone who addressed him in front of him.

A description of Newton in these years suggests how uneasy he was living in the midst of his old adversaries. He was "never seen outside his house without his trusty revolver and rifle, and though he seeks no quarrel with any one, he would be a bad man with whom to debate," wrote a historian who published an early account of Jones County Unionism. "His home is some distance from Ellisville, where he has lived in retirement since his dethronement, working industriously on his farm . . . He has lived in the midst of his enemies in defiance of their threats, almost under the shadow of the revolver. His past is as a sealed book with him, and nothing will induce him to talk of the war."

It was a sign of the times that Robert Lowry was back in a position of power again. In 1881, Lowry, now a graying, heavily mustachioed corporate lawyer and father of eleven, became the Democratic candidate for governor. Lowry was the ultimate Confederate company man, a friend to railroad magnates and to L. Q. C. Lamar, and no friend to blacks. He ran on a platform that stressed big business and white supremacy. Political equality between whites and blacks, he declared, was unworkable and would "ruin both races."

Lowry's opponent was an independent named Benjamin King, whose supporters were a coalition of dissident farmers, Republicans, and blacks. Lowry viewed this opposition as gutter trash, and his stump speeches reawakened all the old rivalries and internal strife of Reconstruction. "As the stream could not rise above its source, neither can the candidate rise above his constituency," Lowry sneered.

A Democratic newspaper urged the party to stuff ballot boxes, "stuff them, cram them, shake them down with votes for Robert Lowry." Democrats again conducted a campaign of fraud and political terrorism, using, as they later acknowledged, "repression, intimidation, and other . . . illegal devices . . . to overcome the Negro majority." Lowry won by 17,000 votes after 68 percent of all registered blacks stayed away from the polls. Even some in Lowry's own party were appalled by the campaign. "We have won, but I am disgusted, and never again will I make such a fight," one man wrote to the **Greenville Times.**

Yet in an inaugural speech that must have soured Newton's stomach, Lowry bragged that it was an election Thomas Jefferson would be proud of, because there had only been one case of "criminal violence." In the very opening words of his address after taking the oath of office, Lowry launched straight into a racial tirade, recruiting Jefferson into his argument. The founding father had believed the two races "could not live equally free under the same government and shuddered to contemplate such an experiment."

Lowry's administration, which lasted for two terms, was undistinguished and so marked by corruption that one Mississippi newspaper branded it "weak and wicked." His main agenda was to enable industry while maintaining white social stability. Farmers like Newton resented him bitterly as a lackey for the railroads and enemy of agriculture. And that was on top of his actions during the war. It was said that Lowry never dared campaign in the Piney Woods, where the yeomen hadn't forgotten the hangings. Newton's old friend Jasper Collins was still so embittered that he said he would "get up on the coldest night he ever saw to kill Lowry if he ever knew he was passing through Jones County."

Newton felt the same. At the end of his life, asked if it was true that Lowry never came into Jasper County for fear of meeting him, Newton replied, "I don't know about that. But I do know that I never saw Lowry knowingly." The implication was clear: if he had seen him, he might have killed him.

Lowry's presence in the governor's mansion stirred Newton to what seems to have been his last act of political involvement. In November of 1884, Newton won an appointment in circuit court as an election supervisor for Jasper County. Presumably, he fought for the appointment so he could try to guard against fraud in Lowry's campaign for reelection. He may also have been agitated, as so many Mississippi farmers were, by Lowry's generous tax exemptions to industry, while the state's farm economy remained depressed.

Newton plowed all day just to sell a bushel of corn for less than a dollar, thanks to Lowry's policies, which gave huge breaks to railroads and textile mills, while small farmers were bent double under taxes, crop liens, shipment levies, etc. Life remained interminably hard for the yeoman farmer. Torrential rains ruined half of Newton's crop in 1886. He lost a grandchild and several neighbors to the yellow fever epidemic. His elder brother Albert died of age and exhaustion in the winter of 1887 and was buried with honor by the Freemasons. Through it all, Newton struggled to cadge his small living from the ground. Corn went for seventy-five cents a bushel, bacon twelve cents a pound, potatoes fifty cents a bushel, peas one dollar. Meanwhile coffee cost him twenty cents a pound and molasses fifty cents a gallon.

Lowry's political success was also galling because it was evidence of the degree to which ex-Confederates had reintegrated into public life. Everywhere Newton turned, it seemed that old rebel "colonels" were publicly congratulated as patriots who had defended states' rights. Southern veterans built war memorials to themselves on every village lawn, including Ellisville's, where there was a marble statue of a rebel with a gun. They wrote self-justifying memoirs in which they revised history and the war's causes, conveniently omitting slavery. Much of their "corrected" history would make its way into textbooks in Southern public schools.

Some of Newton's former comrades—men who had pledged allegiance to the Union—now treated Lee, Jackson, and Forrest as heroes and hung Confederate flags from their porches. These men had even become Confederate sentimentalists, collecting prints with such titles as "First Interview between Lee and Jackson"; "Last Interview between Lee and Jackson"; "Jackson Introducing Himself to Lee"; "Jackson Accepting Lee's Invitation to Dinner." These Southern Unionists moved closer to Southern conservatives to preserve their sense of honor and their sense of difference from Negroes as a class.

The worshipful Confederate revival reached its height when Lowry escorted Jefferson Davis to the state legislature to give an address on the condition of wounded and indigent ex-rebels. Davis, who had retreated to his estates in Vicksburg and the magnificent mansion of Beauvoir on the Gulf, was greeted with reverence by Mississippi's lawmakers. As Lowry led him into the statehouse chambers, "cheer after cheer resounded through the building." Lowry would eventually serve as a pallbearer at Davis's funeral.

Even as Mississippi was trapped in the antebellum past politically, in the 1880s new industry dramatically altered the state's landscape and especially ravaged the primeval forest area around Newton. The Southern Railroad arrived in 1883, and crossties began to lace the countryside. One Jones County woman who had never ridden on a train before marveled at the whistling and chugging. "I bet that thing is tired, it is puffing so," she said.

The Piney Woods experienced a lumber boom. Sawmills and logging camps sprang up all through the woods and toppled large swaths of the great forests for their yellow pine and turpentine. Newton could hear the buzzing even on his hilltop. Next, iron mines opened in Jasper and Clarke counties. The noise of all the new mechanization bothered Newton, but the machinery intrigued him, as he wrote in a letter to his elder brother John.

"I lie in herren of 4 steam sawmills, and can hear the cars at a still time when they pass Talahoma Creek," Newton scrawled. "I tell you they are sla'en them big pines. Know they have cut them all from Ellisville to the Buffalo Hill along the Old Mobile Road."

As trains made the Piney Woods more accessible, missionaries arrived bringing new doctrines, while preaching against an old enemy, the thriving back-woods whiskey business. "The stills is too numerous to talk about," Newton wrote. Proselytizers knocked on farmhouse doors, talking of martyrs and temperance and seeking to reform worshippers, especially blacks. The notion of a "social gospel" had become popular, and revival meetings lit up the countryside. "John, I tel you our county is filling up with all sorts of people and Missionaries from everywhere and skillet-head doctors, and you can gess at the balance," Newton wrote.

What Newton neglected to add was that the religious makeup in his own family had begun to change. The Knights, whose devotions had been makeshift for so long, were open to these visits from interesting strangers who offered fresh thoughts as well as company. They began to experience sudden conversions.

Rachel listened intently to the Mormon elders who regularly came to Jones and Jasper counties preaching the revelations of Joseph Smith. The proselytizers from the Church of Jesus Christ of Latter-day Saints traveled in pairs through the Mississippi hill country, pausing wherever they found a welcome. Although the Mormons taught that dark skin was a curse from God, the missionaries emphasized that all souls were of the same spirit family. The Book of Mormon specifically stated that the Lord "denieth none that come unto him, black and white, bond and free, male and female; and he remembereth the heathen; and all are alike unto God, both Jew and Gentile."

The Mormon missionaries told Rachel that their saints did away with pride and with class distinctions and dwelt in righteousness, with no poor or rich among them. According to Joseph Smith all those who converted were brothers and sisters, all socially equal, and all would be grafted onto the chosen family of Abraham. The light and dark skinned alike would join the house of Israel to build a new world. What's more, these Mormon missionaries saw no obstacles to intermarriage between the races, or to polygamy in the case of a responsible male provider such as Newton.

The Mormon missionaries found a willing listener in Rachel, and perhaps also shelter and protection in her home. Blacks shared mutual sympathies with the Mormons over persecution from the Klan. The Mormons received hostile welcomes in Jones and Jasper counties from Klansmen, who sought to whip the blasphemers out of the area. Two elders named John William Gailey and William H. Crandall were set on and beaten by a mob in Jasper County. The elder Crandall and his fellow missionary Thomas Davis were "fired on" while traveling in Jones County.

In July of 1881, Rachel was baptized into the Church of Latter-day Saints. An elder named William Thomson Jr. recorded Rachel's baptism in a logbook, as well as the name of her father, so that she could be "sealed" to her family in heaven. Within a year, Rachel's daughters Fannie and Martha Ann also converted to Mormonism and submitted the names of their fathers for sealing and endowments: Fannie put down Davis Knight, and Martha Ann named Newton. Fannie was so enthusiastic a Mormon that she may have named a child for John William Gailey, one of the men beaten by the mob in Jasper. In 1884, she and Mat Knight had a son and called him William Gailie.

It is not hard to understand why Mormonism appealed to Rachel, given the nature of the Knight farm. Her baptism as Mormon would allow both the white and black members of her Knight family to be integrated in heaven, after they had been severed on earth owing to segregation. Also, marriage to Newton was prohibited on earth, but the Mormon Church would allow them to be married in the afterlife. And, possibly, she converted because it helped reconcile her to Newton's polygamy.

Newton himself did not convert to the Mormon

Church, and it's impossible to know what he made of Rachel's Mormon awakening, whether he considered it "skilletheaded" or not. He remained a devout Baptist, and according to his son, in 1885 or 1886 he joined a new Primitive Baptist church that was built about three miles from Ellisville.

But it makes sense that Newton would have accepted Rachel's Mormonism, given its vision of community and of the role of a male leader whose chief duty was to protect and provide. Newton and Rachel embraced many Mormon-similar values even before Rachel converted. Their daily ethic was Mormon-like: they not only abstained from alcohol, they practiced industry, frugality, and charity with neighbors. Mormonism sanctified their love and reflected their notion of community as sacred and defined by sharing and faith.

Newton demonstrated tolerance in the face of another religious conversion in the family. Young Anna Knight, daughter of Georgeanne, was an intellectually starved girl who read a pamphlet given to her by Seventh-Day Adventists and became captivated. She began to question her family's approach to religion, especially after a cyclone tore through the area, stunning her with its force and the damage it wrought. She became a full-fledged convert who forswore dancing and work on Saturday. This provoked a fierce battle with Georgeanne, who tried to force her to plow, but Newton apparently supported the girl and told her to follow her conscience. Anna eventually used savings from the sale of a bale of cotton to buy a ticket to Chattanooga, Tennessee, where she enrolled in a missionary school. She would spend the rest of her life as a Seventh-Day Adventist missionary, a calling that took her to Asia and India. But she did her most important work at home, returning to the Piney Woods in 1898 to build a school for the community's black children, an accomplishment that must have been deeply gratifying to Newton.

The Knights may also have been open to religious conversion simply because these non-mainstream missionaries treated them as brethren. It was obvious to Rachel that she would have to wait until the afterlife before most Mississippi whites viewed her and her children as anything but servile. The state's color line was growing ever more rigid.

Jim Crow statutes already decreed the races eat, drink, travel, study, and even get sick separately, but as the 1880s wore on, a series of determined attempts by blacks to organize for self-protection convinced white supremacists that even stricter laws were needed to govern black behavior. In 1886 in Carroll County, ten black citizens had the temerity to accuse a white of murder. For that transgression, supremacists opened fire on them in open court when they showed up to testify. A Colored Alliance sprang up in Leflore County in 1889, dedicated to fostering economic independence. The members dared to bear arms, threatened to organize a cotton-pickers' strike, and boycotted certain stores. In response the local sheriff, backed by troops dispatched by the governor, massacred twenty-five of them and broke the organization.

Once again, James Z. George organized the political response, calling for a convention to draft a new state constitution, where the main business would be to deprive blacks of voting rights. Democrats dominated the convention—any other nominees were threatened or murdered. In Jasper County, a prominent white Republican named M. F. B. "Marsh" Cook, a farmer known for "speaking words of prudence, wisdom, and calmness," announced his candidacy for delegate. Democrats warned him to withdraw. He refused. A few days later his body was found riddled with bullets on a deserted country road. The **Clarion-Ledger** celebrated his death and assured readers that he was not missed.

"At the time of his death he was canvassing Jasper County as a Republican candidate for the Constitutional Convention, and was daily and nightly denouncing the white people in his caucuses and speeches . . . Then one or more persons decided that Cook must die. The Clarion-Ledger regrets the manner of his killing, as assassination cannot be condoned at any time. Yet the people of Jasper are to be congratulated that they will not further be annoyed by Marsh Cook."

The special convention neatly circumvented the Fifteenth Amendment and reversed black enfranchisement. Under a new polling requirement, any voter had to be able to read a section of the state constitution and give a reasonable interpretation if asked. This meant that examining registrars had the discretion to disallow black voters, which they proceeded to do in monumental numbers.

But Rachel didn't live to witness this last, ultimate indignity. In 1889, not yet fifty years of age, she died suddenly of an unexplained cause. It's possible that her constitution was weakened by so many years of child-bearing, servitude, and hard work. There is a vague family tradition that she died of having too many children, having given birth to at least nine between 1856 and 1875. An observation by another woman who was born into slavery in the Knight family household, Martha Wheeler, sheds some light on Rachel's wearying existence: she "never knew such slavery as she experienced as the mother of thirteen children."

Rachel left behind a color-proscribed world the Confederacy still governed, and race divided every realm, including death—in 1890 the first separate cemetery for Negroes would be dug in Jackson. Lowry's election and the etching of the Jim Crow laws across every aspect of Mississippi life had meant that in her last years she lived in a far more segregated world than the antebellum one she'd grown up in. No wonder she stepped into the grave early.

Hymns were sung over Rachel's grave in a small family cemetery on Newton's hillside in a copse of oaks, privet, and sweet gum trees. She lay among other family members who had died untimely deaths, the children taken by fire and epidemic. At the rear of the little cemetery there was a row of unmarked graves, some ill-fated travelers stricken by typhoid as they passed through the county, who had been taken in by Newton. Still other markers in the graveyard were said to belong to two of Newton's guerrillas and six Confederates he and his men had killed in battle.

Her headstone was a plain gray tablet that read "In Memory of Rachel Knight, Born March 11, 1840, Died February 11, 1889." It was one of the few documentary or physical traces of her existence, along with a thin sheaf of slave and census records. It could not adequately explain who she was, or the dynamic role she had played as a lover, soldier, mother, and self-liberator who shed the heavy encumbrances of her enslavement, only to be caught in the dissonant fugue that was postbellum Mississippi. Whites outside of her immediate family, scandalized by her liaison with Newton, chose to render her nonexistent, omitting her from their versions of local history. Newton's son Tom, who had seen his mother cast aside in favor of Rachel, would be so ashamed of her he would write an entire memoir of Newton without directly mentioning her. On the one occasion when he **was** forced to speak of Rachel publicly, he tried to deny his father's relationship with her and derided her as "just an old Negro woman."

Nevertheless, impressions of Rachel lived on in the deeper fathoms, in the memories of her children and grandchildren and their oral traditions passed down in the family. She had conjuror's eyes. She was "extraordinarily intelligent and industrious"; she was independent even in slavery; she was captivating. She was Newton's woman and he had loved her, and he had been more hers than anyone else's.

Newton carried on with his seasonal plowing and harvesting, but with Rachel's death the fragile interracial community he called a family began to splinter. At some point in the next few years, Serena left him.

According to the vague, tangled story passed along by the gossips in the county, Newton "ran his wife who was old man John Turner's daughter, away from home and took a Negro as a wife." It's not clear exactly when Serena finally gave up on the husband who had been partly absentee for years, but she was no longer in his house sometime after 1890. As he coped with Rachel's death Newton was probably more inattentive and neglectful than ever, and he may have abandoned Serena altogether in favor of his black family, whose claims on him had possibly become greater. He had his two youngest children with Rachel, Augusta Ann, sixteen, and Hinchie, fourteen, to comfort and finish rearing.

By then, Serena's own children were grown and she may have felt no longer needed in Newton's home. The final straw perhaps came when she realized that Newton had no intention of severing his relationship with Rachel's family and was instead closer than ever with them—especially with Georgeanne, with whom he all but set up house. According to Martha Wheeler, after Rachel died, Georgeanne took Rachel's place "and separated him from his wife."

Newton's relationship with Georgeanne was that of an aging, solitary man who needed someone to care for him and his children, and perhaps more. For years he had divided himself between Rachel and Serena, and now he found himself without either of them. Georgeanne became his caregiver, and in 1891, after a sixteen-year hiatus in childbearing, Georgeanne became pregnant and delivered a daughter, Grace. In 1894, she had a second daughter, Lessie. Who fathered Georgeanne's children was an unanswered question, but they may well have been Newton's.

Serena moved in with Molly and Jeffrey Knight, the young couple who had fused Newton and Rachel's families by intermarrying and who now had a thriving farm and five children. Whatever Serena's feelings about Rachel and Newton, she seems to have made her peace with her daughter's marriage and accepted Jeff as her son-in-law, which was a testament to the sheer affableness of the man. A photograph of Serena shows her seated in the front yard of their cabin, a galleried plank home enclosed by a picket fence, surrounded by Jeff and Molly's family. Jeff was a tall, tawny man with cheekbones so prominent they seemed hewn by a knife, and a disposition so pleasant that even Newton's withdrawn, taciturn son Tom liked him. Tom and his brother Mat both had "a certain respect for Jeff, because he was good and honest in his dealings, and was nice to them."

But race increasingly divided the family. Tom also

bolted from the farm, aggrieved by his father's relationships and tired of impoverished yeomanry and of being unwanted by white society. He moved to Ellisville, where he ran a small store that sold candy and newspapers, and refused to acknowledge his relationship to Rachel's family.

Mat's feelings on race also turned sharply and ruined his marriage with Rachel's daughter Fannie. In 1895, after more than fifteen years, Mat deserted his wife and their several children, the youngest of whom was just a year old, because he wanted to live as a white man. Mat was so determined to shuck his interracial bonds that he left with nothing but the clothes on his back. Fannie was left to work the eighty-acre farm, which was heavily mortgaged, on her own. Fannie rarely saw him again, though he married a white woman (a Knight fourth cousin) and lived on in the area.

Mat was not alone in his desire to escape painful racial definitions. As the mixed-race Knight children and grandchildren grew into adulthood, many of them sought to separate themselves from the darker-skinned side of the family. Fannie, too, would attempt to redefine herself later in her life. When she was asked during a real-estate court proceeding in 1914 if she was black, she described her racial makeup instead as "Choctaw and French," which is perhaps what she believed her heritage from Rachel to be. When a lawyer insisted she was black, she replied, "Well, you will have to do your own judging."

Those who tried to evade their family history did so for the simple reasons that it was stigmatic and dangerous to be a Knight. It was the lynching era. Statistics on lynchings are unreliable; only those that got press attention were counted. But Mississippi led the nation in documented hangings with 581 between 1882 and 1962—and those were just the ones reported.

Some of the highest citizens and officials in the state condoned lynching as a method of controlling blacks. A longhaired, withered-armed haranguer named James K. Vardaman, a prominent lawyer and newspaper publisher, would be elected to the governorship in 1903 by championing violence against blacks. Vardaman called the Negro a "lazy, lying, lustful animal" and urged white citizens to take the law into their own hands, which they did with heinous consequences. Vardaman would defend a notorious incident in Rocky Ford, near Tupelo, when a man named Jim Ivy, accused of raping a white woman, was burned to death without a trial. Ivy was captured by a mob, wrapped in heavy chains, and staked to a knee-deep woodpile as six hundred spectators looked on. Three men tapped gasoline cans, dousing him and the wood, and set him on fire. "Oh, God!" Ivy cried. "Oh God damn!" A journalist who was an eyewitness to the burning wrote: "His scream . . . was the only sound from a human voice that I thought might, by sheer strength alone, reach heaven . . . Jim screamed, prayed and cursed; he struggled so hard that he snapped one of the log chains that bound his ankles to the stake."

One public official did attempt to contain the violence. Governor Andrew H. Longino devoted much of his inaugural address in 1900 to lynching, decrying it as "the most demoralizing, brutalizing, and ruinous species of lawlessness known to any brave and free people," he declared. The stance cost him his career—he never won office again.

In 1900, the Census Bureau again visited the Knights. This time, the sprawling mixed-race family living in the hills on the Jones-Jasper county line did not confuse the census taker. Everyone who lived there was simply classified as black, including every last child and grandchild, and Newton himself. He had officially become a Negro. They were the "white negros" or the "Knight Negroes," as the locals called them. Or just the "Knight Niggers."

Despite this, one member of the Knight family chose to come back to the farm instead of leaving it: Anna Knight had grown into a forceful, bell-voiced young missionary who felt called to improve her Mississippi hill country people. She had spent six years training as a nurse, teacher, and missionary in Seventh-Day Adventist boarding schools in Chattanooga and Battle Creek, Michigan, and she had a tough mind and unbreakable will. In 1898 she built her private school for black children, a project that excited the hostility of local whites, as did her preaching against moonshiners.

The school began as a dilapidated old cabin on one of her uncles' farms. After a year, with profit from four acres of cotton she planted herself and the broadax labor of Knight men like Newton and Jeff, she was able to build a new schoolhouse of plank wood with glass windows. She taught twenty-four pupils at eight grade levels and charged them one dollar a month. Even so, only one parent could afford to pay in cash; the rest worked it off.

Anna taught adults as well as children, holding tutorials in penmanship, reading, and arithmetic, as well as hygiene, nutrition, and temperance. She taught women how to can fruit and on a biological chart showed them what liquor did to their kidneys. Soon local moonshiners sent her a message to quit preaching or "they would put me out of business." Anna, who was nothing if not a Knight, sent back word that "I covered the ground I stood on, and when they got ready to shoot, I was ready." Her family and friends urged her to shut the school down, but she replied that she was not "a quitter."

Anna began traveling armed with both revolver and shotgun, which she kept close by even in her classroom. On one occasion after teaching a Sunday school class, she had to race on horseback through a gauntlet of white men who stood in the road and fired their guns in the air. Soon afterward, three glaring men entered her schoolhouse while she was teaching and took seats on the back bench. They listened to her lesson for several minutes, boring holes into her with their eyes. One of them deliberately spat on the floor. Then they stood up and left, walking into the woods.

Certain that they meant trouble, Anna dismissed the class and summoned two of her male relatives. When the three angry whites returned, they were drunk, and a pitched fight resulted. "They soon found that the two 'Knights' were too much for the three of them, and finally gave up and left," Anna wrote. After that incident, various Knight males stood watch over the school building every night, while Anna "took my books and guns each day and carried on the work." Still, despite tireless efforts to protect the building, in 1902 someone burned it to the ground.

The flames devoured the pine board structure, burning to black ash every joist and window sash that they had painstakingly fashioned with their own hands. With her work destroyed, Anna left for missionary work in Calcutta, India, where she spent the next five years. But Mississippi was never out of her thoughts. When she returned from overseas in 1908, her relatives implored her to return to teaching. She built a new school in the village of Gitano in Jones County, and this time it stood, providing a generation of Knights with the only education they would receive.

Only Newton's protection and his repute as a dreaded enemy saved the Knights from worse persecutions. Even as he neared seventy, with his once-dark beard turned white, Newton remained capable of fearsome acts of violence if circumstances demanded it, especially where his family was concerned. Any neighbors who were tempted to harass the black Knights thought twice after an incident in a churchyard one morning, when Newton demonstrated that he still possessed a killer's disposition in defense of his sons.

As Tom Knight tells the story, Newton had just attended Sunday services near his home with Tom and one of his younger brothers when some local toughs accosted them. Tom doesn't say whether the "younger brother" in question was white or black, but given that the incident took place late in Newton's life, it almost certainly concerned a mixed-race son. One of the toughs had a dispute with the young Knight boy over some hogs. As the Knights left church, the antagonist approached the boy and feigned friendliness, saying to him, "I want to talk with you a minute." He walked the boy to a corner of the churchyard, where he began to curse him and then struck him from behind with a pine limb.

With that, the rest of the Knights charged across the yard. A melee ensued, as men windmilled their fists at one another and rolled on the ground. As they churned up the dust, the attacker lashed out with a boot and caught Newton squarely in the shin, peeling off some of his skin.

Newton didn't utter a cry. Instead he reacted silently. There was a glitter of metal and an almost imperceptible wave of his hand, and an instant later the man was gurgling from his throat and covered in his own blood. Newton sheathed his knife, the fight over. Newton said, "He would learn him that it was Newt Knight he was kicking."

Newton had slashed the man's throat—if he'd have cut an eighth of an inch deeper, the man would have been dead. As it was, he wounded the victim so badly a doctor had to be summoned to stop the bleeding, and the man would be in bed for a month.

"So my father said it looked to him like it was a free for all fight and he was old and had been crippled up and he just did not feel like being kicked about by anyone and especially by a big young man," Tom Knight related.

But though Newton continued to travel well armed, in general he avoided quarrels; any fight he was involved in was bound to end with bloodshed, and so he sidestepped confrontation and tried to live quietly. He particularly avoided the subject of the war; there were no fond reminiscences from Newton, or condemnations and indictments either. It remained a dangerous matter in a small community in which so many families were cross-knitted to one another and everyone had lost something. Also, Newton knew too much.

"He toats his old gun," said the ex-Confederate Maddie Bush in 1912. "I think Newt could make big money if he would just tell what he knows about it, but he won't. I don't reckon he is to blame for it, as there are a good many people living here that have kinsmen that were killed and might want to get revenge."

Even if Newton's old foes were tempted to forgive him for his sins in the war after a half century, his continued crossings of the color line were fresh offenses. For instance, Newton sat proudly for a studio photograph with one of his mixed-race grandsons, a strict taboo for a white man. The old man, stern faced and upright in his clean white shirt and jacket, posed with a handsome boy of about twelve leaning against his shoulder.

Newton's grandchildren would always remember the kindness of the old man, who refused to disown them. One granddaughter would sit in his lap and comb his long white beard. At Christmastimes, Newton loaded his wagon with fresh fruit and drove around to hand it out to the smallest children in the family. A boy named Amos, the son of Martha Ann, Newton's eldest daughter with Rachel, recalled the quiet old man with a wagonload of gleaming apples, drawn by a light-colored horse. "Do you know who I am?" he said gently, as he gave Amos the apples. "I'm your grandfather."

His family remained frighteningly vulnerable. A fresh tide of racism swept the country after World War I, as the trigger-tempered men who hung around drugstore counters found new subjects for outrage in immigrants, godless evolutionists, and uppity blacks. After the war black veterans who had tasted more liberal society in France returned home to find that Southerners intended to put them back in their place. In 1915 D. W. Griffith's blockbuster film **The Birth of a Nation** glorified the Klan as an American institution rescuing the South from savages, and by the 1920s the Klan would grow to between 3 and 4 million members. In one incident during the era, white-capped Klansmen paraded into Baptist churches in Jones County, swearing to protect the "purity of womanhood and 100 percent Americanism."

The "Knight Negroes" lived with the knowledge that their closest neighbors were capable of racial bloodthirstiness. In 1919, one of the most vicious lynchings in the history of the South took place right in downtown Ellisville. John Hartfield, accused of assaulting a white woman, was pursued through the woods of three counties for ten days before he was caught. A committee of vigilantes announced they intended to hang Hartfield outside of the courthouse, and the state's biggest newspaper, the **Jackson Daily News,** advertised the event in an eight-column front-page streamer of a headline. "John Hartfield Will Be Lynched by Ellisville Mob This Afternoon at 5 P.M.," it read. "Negro Jerky and Sullen As Burning Hour Nears." Other papers picked up the news, and correspondents made the journey to Ellisville for the event, including a writer named Hilton Butler, who recorded his memories for **The New Republic.**

Six thousand spectators congregated in a pasture near the town courthouse, many of them with picnic baskets. District Attorney T. Webber Wilson of Laurel, later elected to Congress, stood on the running board of a car and gave a speech to the mob.

When the hour reached 5:00 p.m., Hartfield, clad in nothing more than a pair of olive drab pants, was dropped from a sycamore—the same tree, according to locals, from which Robert Lowry had hanged three of Newton's men. As Hartfield's body twisted on the rope, men in the crowd began shooting at it, and the journalist Butler had to scramble down from another tree to escape the hail of fire. "Every time a bullet hit an arm, out it flopped like a semaphore," Butler wrote. The writer estimated not less than two thousand bullets were fired into the body. "One of them finally clipped the rope. John's body fell to the ground, a fire was built around it, and John was cremated."

That night, as Butler strolled through the town of Laurel, he encountered a ghoulish exhibition on the sidewalk. A grinning man exhibited a quart jar filled with alcohol, in which bobbed a finger cut jaggedly from a Negro's hand. "I got a finger, by God," the man said. "And I got some photographs, too." He was selling the pictures for twenty cents each.

"We 'orter kill more of 'em around here," he said. "Teach 'em a lesson. Only way I see to stop raping is to keep on lynching. I'm goner put this finger on exhibition in my store window tomorrow, boys, and I want you to drop around."

Just a few months after the Hartfield lynching, Newton's efforts to safeguard his family failed. In November 1920, Newton and Rachel's son Stewart was found murdered. Stewart Knight was an industrious farmer and businessman, dapper in a dark mustache and suit with vest and watch chain. A neighbor found his body: an ax had been sunk into the back of his head, which was also partly shot off. A white man from nearby Stringer named Sharp Welborn was arrested and convicted—of manslaughter. The apparent motive was robbery, but Stewart's family believed an incident with a white woman was the real cause of the attack.

We can only surmise Newton's grief and anger over the murder of his son; there is no record of his feelings, or his reaction. But it's safe to say that the terrible events of 1919 and 1920 made the insomniac old man, now nearing 85, more vigilant than ever.

One of his granddaughters, a child of Fannie and Mat's, remembered sitting on the porch with "Grandpa Newt" as he stared out over the fields at the road, his rifle at his side.

"If you see anybody coming, don't say anything," he said. "Just touch me."

By the time Meigs O. Frost made his way up the dirt road to Newton's farm, the old man had become reclusive. He preferred to wander alone through the woods for days, rather than venture into society. In his forest retreat he seemed to Frost a figure of almost mythic isolation.

"In simplicity primeval he has lived, and in simplicity primeval he will die," Frost observed.

Newton still farmed, growing the peas and sweet potatoes that had always sustained him, and he remained strong enough to fell an oak tree by himself. He carved ax handles, which he sold to friends. He was hearty; he needed only the old Civil War remedies he had always used: blue moss, castor oil, and calomel.

In his seclusion he had quit following the progress of the larger world. He had only made three trips in his life to Laurel, which had become the biggest town in Jones County with a population of 14,000. Newton marveled that such a place had grown up in what was once the thickest forest and brush where he had ranged as a guerrilla.

He confessed to Frost that he had never ridden in a trolley car, or used a telephone, or seen electric lights at night.

As the two men talked through the morning, Newton finally allowed himself to reminisce about his actions during the great conflict. He remembered sixteen sizable fights, he told Frost. Then, too, he recalled, "There was a lot of skimishin' that you couldn't properly call battles." He kept track of the dead, but he hadn't counted the wounded—they were too numerous. "I used to treat their gunshot wounds myself," he said. "There were a number of those."

He remembered being conscripted, and the Twenty Negro Law. He remembered the swamp hideouts, and the hounds—forty-four of them had once come tearing through the woods after him. He remembered the Lowry hangings and the battle that he had fought after Alpheus Knight's marriage. "Not that I ain't heard that lots of other weddings ended up in battles, too," he said, grinning.

He had almost been killed twice, on one occasion

when a bullet tore through his coat, and another time, when his gun jammed. "I remember once when a big fellow was coming at me, and my gun hammer spring wouldn't work. It was a homemade spring I made after the first one broke. He pretty nearly got me." His voice drifted off. He didn't want to dwell on the encounter.

Was it true that he and his men had executed a Baptist preacher who told the Confederates about one of their hiding places? Frost asked. Again, Newton lapsed into silence.

There were other details Newton refused to divulge. He remained circumspect about the makeup of his company—most of his old compatriots were long dead anyway, he told Frost mournfully. Just seven were still alive that he knew of, and he was the only officer. "I keep my old muster rolls out here in the woods in one of my old places," he said. "Whenever I hear one of the boys has died, I mark him off on the rolls."

He was reluctant to name names when so many descendants still lived in Jones, some of them prominent. It could lead to nothing but trouble. "Who are the ones left? I'm not tellin' that," he said. "No use naming a lot of names and getting people worked up again."

He sighed. "The Civil War's over long ago. No use stirring up that old quarrel this late day, is there?"

Frost reluctantly guessed not. He rose to go. Newton walked him out into the yard and cordially told him to "drop in again" sometime. Then Newton gestured to "one of the folks" who dwelled on the place. A sack of peanuts appeared out of an old log storehouse, and Newton pressed it on Frost as a gift.

The two men shook hands, and Frost climbed into his car. As he drove away, "the gnarled old figure stood erect by the hand hewn picket fence, waving good bye."

Less than a year later, on February 16, 1922, Newton passed away. He went, he told friends, to a truer life in the hereafter. He supposedly left instructions for how he wished to be buried: with his head elevated above his feet, ever at the alert. His son Mat and his grandson Amos placed Newton's body in the casket and closed the lid. Then they sat up with Newton all night, passing the time by playing cards, because Newton had always watched over them so faithfully at night.

He was buried in the small family graveyard, near Rachel, under a cedar tree. It was said that just two whites attended his funeral. One of them was his cousin, George "Clean Neck" Knight, the son of Jesse Davis Knight. Somehow Newton and the son of the old Confederate planter had remained close, perhaps because Clean Neck understood his familial connection to Rachel's children. The mulatto Knight relations, children and grandchildren, cousins and second cousins, stood around the gravesite as Newton was lowered in the ground, the only white man buried among former slaves. Knight's stone was a simple gray tablet etched with his name and vitals: b. 1829, d. 1922. Fittingly, even the stone would become a source of debate: the birth date was probably wrong.

His engraved epitaph, however, was simple and true: "He lived for others."

Newton had so withdrawn from white society that it took almost a month for the news of his death to make it into Ellisville. On March 16, 1922, his obituary finally appeared in the **Ellisville Progress,** and even then, the details of his passing were vague, and the newspaper apologized for not having brought the story to readers sooner.

"A unique character of national repute passed away at his home several miles north of Soso, Mississippi about three weeks ago," the obit read. "For some unaccountable reason the newspapers failed to hear of his death or else the account would have been given wide publicity. Newt Knight was about ninety years of age when he died. His claim to notoriety was due to the fact that he walked off from the Confederate army sometime after enlisting, and organized a band of deserters which held together until the close. Capt. Knight and his followers held that after the Twenty Negro Law was passed during the war they had no interest in the fortunes of the Confederacy." The newspaper observed that "there was a great deal of truth" in the position taken by Newton and his men.

But it added in closing, "Knight ruined his life and future by marrying a Negro woman."

Newton was not at rest in the ground. Over the years his tombstone was stolen, replaced, vandalized, and, according to oral tradition, perhaps even moved so that it would not be too close to Rachel's, the woman for whom he'd fought his Civil War. Few whites in the county ever visited his grave, including his own son, Tom.

With Newton dead and buried, the Klan targeted the black Knights who remained on the hilltop. Word went around that the KKK had decided to "burn them out." Fannie Knight's granddaughter, Ardella, was taught early how to shoot a Smith and Wesson .32. One evening in 1923 white men surrounded her home and threatened to torch it. She and her mother fled into the night to an uncle's home.

The Knights survived, but their community became increasingly cut off and split from within and without by racial divisions. They existed in a social netherworld, disdained by whites—but neither were they accepted by other blacks. When they went into town they were stared at, and pointed at, like anthropological specimens. So they stayed to themselves, worshipped by themselves, schooled themselves at Anna Knight's schoolhouse, and even delivered their children by midwife. One of Newton and Rachel's great-granddaughters would grow up without a birth certificate or without ever having formal education other than the lessons she got from Anna Knight. Her family history was a matter of virtual secrecy. "Back then it was just taboo," she says. "It was just hurt."

Decades passed. Knights were born and died, and the genealogy of the family grew ever more tangled, even as branches of the family spread. Some stayed in Mississippi in the places they were born, others struck out for Texas or California and passed as white. Mat and Fannie's son George Monroe went to Texas, where he lived as a white man and even sought to escape the Knight name, eventually changing it to McKnight. He never told his own children who their grandparents were.

Some Knight branches grew lighter, and some grew darker. Classifications developed. There were the "fair Knights" and "not-so-fair Knights." The fair Knights were also called "half-white Knights." The whitest Knights proudly did their family trees, guarded the family's history and secrets, and tended to its Confederate dead. The other Knights feared the Klan, wrote names in a family Bible, traded oral histories, and kept secrets, too. Some Knights ignored others in an attempt to keep the color line. Some never knew they were Knights at all.

But on December 13, 1948, the Knight family's mixed-race heritage became the subject of open discussion in Jones County. With the bang of a gavel, Newton Knight's conduct with Rachel effectively went on trial in a courtroom in Ellisville. Sitting at the defendant's table was his twenty-three-year-old great-grandson, Davis Knight, charged with the previously unspoken offense of his ancestor. Davis was under indictment by the state of Mississippi for the crime of miscegenation, the mixing of racial blood. Davis had married a white woman.

Davis Knight was the grandchild of Jeff and Molly

Knight. Newton Knight had never been properly punished in his lifetime for crossing the color line and producing children of mixed races, and now Davis Knight was going to be held accountable for him.

Davis Knight, lean-facedly handsome with a pencil mustache, looked no different from all the other chain-smoking, prematurely worldly young men who returned from World War II to start their peacetime lives. In 1946, he had received his honorable discharge from the navy after a three-year stint and come home to wed June Lee Spradly, a blond, blue-eyed eighteen-year-old, in the presence of her mother and a civil clerk. The clerk had not thought to ask him his race, and Davis considered himself, and passed as, white. According to **Time,** "a relative, irked by an old family feud" had dug up Davis's genealogy and reported him. "In Mississippi," **Time** noted, "that kind of marrying was against the law." County police arrested him.

For four days, **The State of Mississippi v. Davis Knight** was heard in the courthouse in Ellisville, Mississippi. The seat of Jones County was now a dowdy old whistle-stop with a few galleried Victorian buildings, such as a slant-floored relic called the Hotel Alice, built in the 1880s, where gossipers lounged on the porch. At Ward's Pharmacy, a turn-of-the-century fixture with a soda fountain and a brass cash register, thick-bellied white men sat drinking coffee, cup after cup, as they discussed the case so controversial that even **Time** magazine had taken notice of it.

The county courthouse was just around the corner

from Ward's and the Alice, a cream- and redbrick redoubt with wide steps anchored by two water fountains, one for whites and one for "coloreds." Fronting the lawn was a white marble Confederate monument with a rebel sentry perched at attention. Inside, polished banisters of facing twin staircases gleamed dimly in the bureaucratic light as they ascended to the main courtroom. White citizenry, businessmen in Arrow shirts and wide-striped neckties and farmers in bib overalls, craned to see around women in padded shoulders and pancake hats, packed in rows of comfortable drop-seats bolted to the floor as in a movie theater. A smaller set of stairs continued upward to a stifling, low-ceilinged gallery. This was where the coloreds sat. Whites were loath to admit it, but there were Knights in each of these divided audiences, as testimony would make clear.

The crime Davis was charged with, racially polluting a white woman, was no mere misdemeanor to the many Mississippians who still carried a sense of outrage at the betrayal of Newton Knight. They were further disquieted by a series of headline-making events in 1948 that challenged their social order. The Supreme Court had ruled that religious instruction in public schools violated the Constitution. Scientists Ralph Alpher and George Gamow published a paper describing an agnostic theory of creation, called the Big Bang. The House Un-American Activities Committee was rooting out "subversives" in the first political hearings ever held on TV. Emboldened blacks home from the war agitated for social justice with acts of civil disobedience, moving President Harry Truman to issue a pair of executive orders ending discrimination in the armed services and federal employment.

But there wasn't a more threatening or distasteful topic to Jim Crow Southerners than interracial sex. According to Mississippi's senator Theodore G. Bilbo, intermingling meant nothing less than the ruin of civilization. **Take Your Choice: Separation or Mongrelization** was the title of Bilbo's book. In 1946 Mississippians had reelected the five-foot-two bantam, cigar-biting Ku Kluxer Bilbo, nicknamed "The Man," to a third term in the Senate as reward for a career of race-baiting. He had filibustered against an antilynching bill, promising "the blood of the perpetrators of these crimes that the red-blooded Anglo-Saxon white Southern men will not tolerate."

Bilbo didn't just rail against blacks, he also inveighed against "farmer murderers," "poor-folks haters," "shooters of widows and orphans," "international well-poisoners," "charity hospital destroyers," "spitters on our heroic veterans," "rich enemies of our public schools," "European debt cancelers," "unemployment makers," pacifists, Communists, and "skunks who steal Gideon Bibles from hotel rooms." Bilbo had at last stopped babbling in 1947, when he contracted, appropriately enough, mouth cancer. Five thousand people attended his funeral.

Most Mississippians in the Ellisville courtroom believed, like Bilbo, that African blood was quantifiable, and as different from pure white blood as a muddy creek was from a stream of spring water. Mississippi legally defined anyone with one-eighth or more African ancestry as a Negro. If found guilty, Davis could be sentenced to five years in Mississippi's Parchman Farm, the hell hole of the South.

It was the job of District Attorney Paul Swartzfager to establish just how black Davis Knight was. In order to make the case that Davis was a fractional one-eighth Negro he had to prove that Rachel must have been of full African ancestry. That necessarily meant that both Rachel's racial identity, and her liaison with Newton, be discussed in open court.

Day after day, Swartzfager grilled witnesses about Rachel's features and her relationship to the Knights. Was she more Creole, Indian, or African? And what did that make Davis?

Testimony of Knight neighbor H. V. Welch:

Q: Do you know Davis Knight's general reputation in the community in which he lives as to his Race?
A: He goes just like his daddy goes.
Q: And what is that.
A: Folks call them "The Knight Negroes."

Representing Davis Knight was a prominent Mississippi defense attorney named Quitman Ross, a good lawyer with a sure sense of the illogic of the entire proceeding. He struggled to cast doubt on Rachel's racial classification, as hostile witnesses described her dark skin, the thickness of her lips, the flatness of her nose, the texture of her hair. Among the most hostile witnesses was Newton's eighty-eight-year-old white son Tom Knight, still ashamed of and embittered by his father's defection. Tom, who had refused to go to his father's funeral, seemed intent on preventing Davis Knight from passing as a white man, as he described Rachel's "wooly head."

To many witnesses, just living in close proximity to Rachel's family seemed to mean they might have tainted blood. A witness named D. H. Valentine, descended from one of the old Jones County Scouts, responded defensively when asked if his father had been a friend of Newton Knight's. "Not so much friends as associates—my father was a White man, altogether." He added, "I was raised white myself."

Ross continued his cross-examination of Valentine:

Q: What do you call the Negro graveyard?
A: Where they bury Negroes.
Q: Well, if there are any White folks buried there you wouldn't call it a Negro graveyard, would you?
A: Yes, if they class themselves to be buried there.
Q: Did you know Newton Knight?
A: Yes.
Q: Was he a white or a Negro?

A: He was as white as you or I.

Q: Then if Rachel Knight was buried in the same graveyard as Newt Knight, how would you class it, would that change the color?

A: I wouldn't class it, but his character forced him to be buried there.

Q: I didn't ask you that.

A: I don't even know if they was buried in the same graveyard.

Q: Well, if you don't, how would you class it?

A: I wouldn't class it. I would go around it.

Relatives called Rachel "ginger cake," and friendly witnesses strove to emphasize her "white" features. The friendliest was a local physician named Dr. John W. Stringer, who had traded hogs and syrup with Rachel, given the Knights medical care, and shared family meals with them. He described Rachel as a woman of indeterminate race, perhaps Indian looking, "of a brown color, with long hair hanging down on her shoulders, long hair hanging down her back."

Another defense witness, Rachel and Newton's grandson Henry Knight, denied that she had any Negro blood whatsoever, calling her part Creole and part Indian. He said, "Her hair was curly, wasn't no kinky about it." While he was on the stand, Henry, the son of Mat and Fannie, acknowledged that his grandfather was indeed Newton Knight. Asked if Newton was white, he replied, "He was a thoroughbred."

The jury found Davis Knight guilty.

But on November 14, 1949, the Mississippi Supreme Court overturned the conviction. Quitman Ross asked that the verdict be reversed on the grounds that the statute was unconstitutional and threatened to appeal. Fearful that such an appeal would invite federal interference in Mississippi's segregation laws, the court reversed the verdict, using the excuse that it was impossible, sixty years after Rachel's death, to establish her racial identity. Prosecutors "failed to prove beyond all reasonable doubt" whether Davis Knight was one-eighth Negro. Essentially, the court ruled that everyone had just been dead for too long.

The trial solved nothing; various Knights continued to take different paths, some lived as blacks, some whites. Despite winning his case, Davis Knight lost everything else. His marriage and his business failed. He moved out to the old Knight family area near Soso, Mississippi, at the Jones County line, where he lived much of his life among Newton and Rachel's people. He drowned in a fishing accident in Houston in 1959.

In 1960, Davis's sister Louvenia Knight launched a five-year battle with the state over whether her children were white and thus could attend white schools. The Mississippi State Sovereignty Commission viewed the case distastefully—these "white Negroes" presented a dilemma. If the children were allowed to go to a white school, they would taint it. Yet, if they were forced into a black school, Jasper County would be unintentionally integrated—the last thing Mississippi officials wanted. During a lengthy investigation of Knight genealogy, the commissioner identified Rachel as the "villain" and source of all the trouble. She was the one who "infused Negro blood into the white blood of the descendants of Newton Knight," he wrote. In the end, state officials swallowed hard and decided the children should be enrolled in a white school—in order to preserve segregation.

It was just one more mixed verdict on the life of Newton Knight.

Over the years, memory, and the need to revise a too-painful past, blurred the facts of history. Mementos were scattered, keepsakes disappeared, pictures went into lockboxes or into attics, stories were forgotten or altered. Newton's gun disappeared. No one was quite certain what Rachel looked like anymore.

Knights continued to marry, and intermarry. Cousins married cousins, grandchildren married great-grandchildren, family lines and generations crisscrossed, and gradually the racial classifications became ever more ambiguous. One "black" descendant of Newton and Rachel's from Biloxi recalled being taken to the country to see her grandmother and wondered, "What is that picture of a bearded old white man doing on the mantel?" Her parents explained who Newton Knight was, and the Knight history. When her brother cursed whites for the way they had treated his family, their mother marched him to a mirror. "Look at that," she said. "How can you hate something that's in you?"

Some Knights married descendants of his old enemies. "Newt's seed is all over this county," remarked his great-granddaughter Vermell Moffett, in 1977. The difference between white and black Knights grew ever more vague and indiscernible. And in that, finally, was a victory for Newton and Rachel, who lay in the small graveyard on the hill, moss covering their tombstones. "We'll all die guerillas, I reckon," he said.

Genesis 22:17: "I will indeed bless you, and I will make your offspring as numerous as the stars of heaven and as the sand on the seashore. And your offspring shall possess the gate of their enemies."

Generation succeeded generation, blood poured through old veins and pulsed in new heartbeats. Still the genetic matter of Newton and Rachel Knight spun on, twined and parted, and then intertwined again, dual spirals and strands, parallels and anti-parallels, in a never-ending hourglass shape, running like ribbons through the whole country.

ACKNOWLEDGMENTS

The origin of this project was unusual—ordinarily the film comes after the book. In this case, the opposite was true: there would not be a book without film director and screenwriter Gary Ross, who brought the powerful narrative of Newton and Rachel Knight to us as a gift, and shared his vision of them as forgotten American patriots. It was Gary who introduced us to each other and proposed that we work together on a book, and it was Gary who presented the idea to Phyllis Grann at Doubleday. Along the way he became our great friend, and proved a brilliant scholar of the Civil War and Reconstruction era. His screenplay, **The Free State of Jones,** based on his own penetrating original research and his determination to tell the truth about Newton and Rachel, was our impetus and inspiration.

These pages could also not have been written without the contributions of the descendants and scholars of Newton and Rachel Knight, who shared their knowledge, family history, and in some cases their possessions with us. Kenneth Welch is an immensely generous and learned archivist whose Knight collection is simply unrivaled. Knight great-granddaughter Barbara Blackledge opened her heart and her family's past to us and shed a light on the subject no one else could have. Martha Welborn shared her extensive genealogy files and stunning photos of the Knight family. Other Knight family members who gave us their time and invaluable insights were Dorothy Knight Marsh, Jules Smith, Catharine McKnight (who was extraordinarily helpful in copying files we couldn't have obtained any other way), Caroline Ramagos Kelly, and Kecia Carter, all of whom contributed precious oral history or archival material.

Perhaps our greatest single intellectual and archival debt is to Jim Kelly, vice president of instructional affairs at Jones County Junior College, who was our guide on two separate visits to Jones County, leading us to rare documents we wouldn't have found, introducing us to descendants, taking us for coffee at Ward's Pharmacy, and sharing every scrap of his knowledge, becoming a dear friend and colleague in the process.

The people we met in Jones County were so kind they gave new meaning to the term "Southern hospitality"; chief among them were Charles and Bunny Windham of Laurel, who hosted us in their home, and Wyatt Moulds, the extraordinary teacher of history at Jones County Junior College.

We received indispensable aid from the archivists at the following libraries: the Mississippi Department of Archives and History in Jackson, Mississippi; the Lauren Rogers Museum in Laurel, Mississippi; the University of Southern Mississippi's McCain Library and Archives; the Smith College Libraries; the New York Public Library; the Houghton and Widener Libraries at Harvard University; the Military History Institute in Carlisle, Pennsylvania; Oakwood University in Huntsville, Alabama; and the National Archives and Records Administration and the Library of Congress in Washington D.C.

Harvard scholars Jamie Jones and Zoe Trodd were simply dazzling in their ability to uncover important documents, and Natalie Jacoby went to heroic lengths to retrieve rare volumes, saving us incalculable hours. In New York, Christine McKay gave us crucial help in piecing together a documentary picture of the Knight family.

We also would like to extend our deep thanks to Jim Engell, Henry Louis Gates Jr., Evelyn Brooks Higginbotham, and Christine McFadden of Harvard University, and to the editors of the **Washington Post** for their unwavering support and their flexibility in allowing us to research and write this book amid numerous other obligations.

A number of scholars provided critical encouragement and advice: Skip Gates, David Brion Davis, William Freehling, John Wood, James M. McPherson, Rich Newman, Alan Trachtenberg, Walter Johnson, Susan O'Donovan, Vernon Burton, Jeff Ferguson, Tim McCarthy, Deborah McDowell, Martha Hodes, David Von Drehle, and Joel Achenbach.

There simply would not have been a book without the tireless efforts and guidance of Jackie Montalvo and the production team at Doubleday, who worked through nights and holidays to create this volume.

Neither one of us would be authors without the great agents and editors who help us find work we love and pay us for it, and who do multiple duty as friends, angels, advisers, and handholders: Jon Karp, Esther Newberg, and Phyllis Grann.

Lastly, love and thanks to the people who come first in our lives: Deb, Erik, and Nicole.

NOTES

We often do not include endnotes in every paragraph or after every quotation, since we sometimes quote the same source in multiple paragraphs. To find the source for a quotation that lacks an immediate citation, refer to the next endnote.

ABBREVIATIONS

MDAH: Mississippi Department of Archives and History

OR: The War of the Rebellion: A Compilation of the Official Records of the Union and Confederate Armies

MHI: Military History Institute

NARA: National Archives and Records Administration

PROLOGUE: THE SOUTH'S STRANGEST SOLDIER

Page

2 **"Just a fightin' fool when he got started":** Meigs O. Frost, "The South's Strangest Army Revealed by Chief," **New Orleans Item,** March 20, 1921.

3 **"I believe in giving the devil his due":** B. D. Graves, address to the Hebron Community, June 17, 1926, Lauren Rogers Museum, Laurel, Miss.

3 **"like George Washington, with his long white hair":** "Captain Knight's Life Remains Controversy," **Laurel Leader Call,** October 21, 1967.

3 **"What he did after the war was worse than deserting":** Interviews with Knight descendants Barbara Blackledge, March 28, 2008, and Jules Smith, April 6, 2008; conversations with Knight genealogists Ken Welch and Martha Welborn, March 28–29, 2008; quotation from B. D. Graves, address to the Hebron Community, June 17, 1926, Lauren Rogers Museum, Laurel, Miss.

4 **remained loyal against all odds:** In the 1860 presidential election, almost all disunionists voted for John Breckinridge, who received only 44 percent of the Southern popular votes. More Southerners voted for John Bell, the Unionist Southern candidate. Breckinridge campaigned to protect slavery, but he trusted "that the time may never come" either to secede or to demand that the federal government "interfere for the protection" of our rights. After Lincoln's election, Breckinridge denied that the time had come for secession. In the state secession conventions, only one state (Texas) allowed a popular vote. In all the other Southern states, delegates voted on secession, and many of them defied their constituencies by voting in favor. See William W. Freehling, **The Road to Disunion,** vol. 2, Secessionists Triumphant, 1854–1861 (New York: Oxford University Press, 2007), pp. 339–40, 495–96; quotation from p. 339. See also Georgia Lee Tatum, **Disloyalty in the Confederacy** (1934; reprint, Chapel Hill: University of North Carolina Press, 1999); Carl N. Degler, **The Other South: Southern Dissenters in the Nineteenth Century** (Boston: Northeastern University Press, 1982); Jon L. Wakelyn, ed., **Southern Unionist Pamphlets and the Civil War** (Columbia: University of Missouri Press,

1999); Richard N. Current, **Lincoln's Loyalists: Union Soldiers from the Confederacy** (Boston: Northeastern University Press, 1992); Phillip S. Paludan, **Victims: A True Story of the Civil War** (Knoxville: University of Tennessee Press, 1981); Daniel W. Crofts, **Reluctant Confederates: Upper South Unionists in the Secession Crisis** (Chapel Hill: University of North Carolina Press, 1989); John C. Inscoe and Robert C. Kenzer, eds., **Enemies of the Country: New Perspectives on Unionists in the Civil War South** (Athens: University of Georgia Press, 2001); Margaret M. Storey, **Loyalty and Loss: Alabama's Unionists in the Civil War and Reconstruction** (Baton Rouge: Louisiana State University Press, 2004).

4   **formally enlisted in the Union army in New Orleans:** Mark A. Weitz, **More Damning than Slaughter: Desertion in the Confederate Army** (Lincoln: University of Nebraska Press, 2005), p. ix. Records of the Adjutant General's Office, Record Group 92, Compiled Service Records of Volunteer Union Soldiers Who Served in Organizations from the State of Louisiana, 1st New Orleans Regiment, "Tisdale's," microfilm (M396), NARA. Also copies of Jones County Union pension records, courtesy of archivist Kenneth Welch. William W. Freehling, **The South vs. The South: How Anti-Confederate Southerners Shaped the Course of the Civil War** (New York: Oxford University Press, 2001).

4   **eroded its fierce will to fight:** While most scholars today acknowledge the role of blacks in the Confederacy's defeat, they downplay or ignore the role of poor Southern whites. There are a few exceptions: as Steven Hahn notes, yeoman farmers "pushed the Confederacy to the edge of internal collapse as the Yankees pressed to victory on the battlefield." See Steven Hahn, **The Roots of Southern Populism: Yeoman Farmers and**

the Transformation of the Georgia Upcountry, 1850–1890
(1983; reprint, New York: Oxford University Press, 2006), p.
131; and Weitz, **More Damning than Slaughter,** pp. ix–x. On
the role of Southern blacks **and** yeoman whites in defeating
the Confederacy, see Albert Bushnell Hart, "Why the South
Was Defeated in the Civil War," **New England Magazine** 11:3
(November 1891): 372–376. On the role of blacks leading to the
South's defeat, see Freehling, **The South vs. The South,** part 3;
and Joseph T. Glatthaar, "Black Glory: The African-American
Role in Union Victory," in **Why the Confederacy Lost,** Gabor
S. Boritt, ed. (New York: Oxford University Press, 1992), pp.
133–62. The authors are especially grateful to Kenneth Welch
for sharing his insights into Jones County's Unionism, as well
as his authoritative knowledge of Knight family genealogy.

4   **"hidin' out and bushwhackin' ":** Frost, "The South's Strangest Army Revealed by Chief."

5   **"how many men they killed or wounded":** Thomas J. Knight,
**The Life and Activities of Captain Newton Knight and
His Company and the Free State of Jones** (Ellisville, Miss.:
printed by the **Progress Item,** c. 1934), p. 19. Despite their difficult relationship, Tom published an admiring if spare account
of his father's life.

5   **predisposition toward silence on the subject:** Newton
Knight filed claims for Union compensation through Congress in 1871, 1872, 1873, 1875, 1895, and 1900. Four bills
with identical wording were introduced in the U.S. Congress
on behalf of Newton Knight from 1871 to 1873. H.R. 2775
was introduced on January 16, 1871, by Representative George
Washington Whitmore. H.R. 1814 was introduced on March
4, 1872, by Representative Legrand W. Perce. And H.R. 822
was introduced by Albert Howe on December 18, 1873. In
addition, Senator Adelbert Ames introduced the same bill as

S.219 in the U.S. Senate on December 18, 1873. **Congressio-nal Record,** Library of Congress. See **Journal of the Senate of the United States of America, Being the First Session of the Forty-third Congress, Begun and Held at the City of Washington, December 1, 1873, in the Ninety-Eighth Year of the Independence of the United States** (Washington: Government Printing Office, 1873), p. 85.

5   **"the true facts about Jones County during the war":** J. M. Arnold to Dunbar Rowland, January 15, 1920, Newton Knight subject file, M.D.A.H.

6   **in an age when the average male height was about five feet seven:** On average heights we've relied on Richard H. Steckel, "A History of the Standard of Living in the United States," especially the table "Average Height of Native-Born American Men and Women by Year of Birth," in EH.Net Encyclopedia, online at http://www.eh.net/encyclopedia/?article=steckel.standard.living.us.

7   **one friend remarked:** Frost, "The South's Strangest Army Revealed by Chief." On backwoods fighting see Elliott J. Gorn, " 'Gouge and Bite, Pull Hair and Scratch': The Social Significance of Fighting in the Southern Backcountry," **American Historical Review** 90:1 (February 1985): 18–43.

8   **exposing his scandal-ridden administration:** "Noted Author Meigs O. Frost Dies," **New York Times,** June 10, 1950.

8   **"What is it you want me to tell you?":** Frost, "The South's Strangest Army Revealed by Chief."

CHAPTER 1: CORINTH

Page

9   **"the evacuation of Corinth":** Peter Cozzens, **The Darkest Days of the War: The Battles of Iuka and Corinth** (Chapel Hill: University of North Carolina Press, 1997), p. 33.

9   **"chiggers, fleas, and niggers":** Ibid., pp. 19–22.

10   **just outside the front porch:** Ibid., p. 18.

10   **"I shall ever be an advocate of peace":** James M. McPherson, **Ordeal by Fire,** vol. 2 (New York: McGraw-Hill, 2001), p. 50; James M. McPherson, **Battle Cry of Freedom** (New York: Oxford University Press, 1988), p. 413; Herman Melville, "Shiloh. A Requiem," in **Battle-Pieces and Aspects of the War** (1866; reprint, New York: Da Capo Press, 1995), p. 63.

10   **caused some of the doctors and nurses to pass out:** McPherson, **Battle Cry of Freedom,** pp. 477, 479; Cozzens, **The Darkest Days of the War,** pp. 19, 22; Richard B. Harwell, ed., **Kate: The Journal of a Confederate Nurse** (1959; reprint, Baton Rouge: Louisiana State University Press, 1988), pp. 9–40.

11   **"The Bloody Sixth":** General Clement A. Evans, ed., **Confederate Military History,** vol. 9 (1899; reprint, Wilmington, Del.: Broadfoot Publishing, 1987), pp. 263–64.

11   **home to his wife:** Letter from William L. Nugent to his wife, Eleanor, June 22, 1862, quoted from William M. Cash and Lucy Somerville Howorth, eds., **My Dear Nellie: The Civil War Letters of William L. Nugent to Eleanor Smith Nugent** (Jackson: University of Mississippi Press, 1977), p. 90.

11   **" 'Our fathers were at the battle of Corinth' ":** "General P. G. T. Beauregard to his soldiers, May 2, 1862," **OR,** series 1, vol. 10, part 2 (Washington, D.C.: Government Printing Office, 1880–1901), p. 482; "How the Rebels Win Victories," **Harper's Weekly,** May 3, 1862, p. 288.

12   **"The salt sparkled and glistened in it":** Diary of Joseph K. Nelson, Civil War Collection, MHI, U.S. Army History and Education Center, Carlisle Barracks, Pa.

12   **his latest was typical:** Cozzens, **The Darkest Days of the War,** p. 7.

12   **cavalier general named Dabney H. Maury:** Ibid., p. 137.

13   **It was a testament to Knight's sheer vigor:** Rudy H. Leverett, **The Legend of the Free State of Jones** (Jackson: University of Mississippi Press, 1984), p. 50, citing records of the 7th Mississippi Battalion.

13   **hard didn't bother him:** Quotation from Frost, "The South's Strangest Army Revealed by Chief."

13   **"rather than be conscripted":** Ibid.; quotation from the address of M. P. Bush before the meeting of the DAR, February 17, 1912, Lauren Rogers Museum, Laurel, Miss.; Victoria E. Bynum, **The Free State of Jones** (Chapel Hill, London: University of North Carolina Press, 2001), p. 99.

14   **"I did organize the men as conscripts":** Deposition of Joel E. Welborn in Congressional Case 8013-8464, **Newton Knight et al. v. United States.** Knight appealed three times to Congress for payment for service to the Union; this was his last try, and the Court of Claims denied him. Although some neo-Confederate historians have contended that Knight was a Confederate volunteer, the testimony of Welborn, who was no ally, makes clear he was a draftee.

14   **like-minded men who shared their wretched experiences:** Gary Fisher, **Rebel Cornbread and Yankee Coffee** (Birmingham: Crane Hill Publishers, 2000), p. 10.

14   **"Buzzards would not eat it at any season of the year":** Bell Irwin Wiley, **The Life of Johnny Reb** (1943; reprint, Baton Rouge, London: Louisiana State University Press, 1993), p. 98.

15   **"a more regular issue of rations":** Notation by Captain Walter A. Rorer, Company B, 20th Mississippi Infantry, October 23, 1862, **Supplement to the Official Records of the Union and Confederate Armies,** part II, **Record of Events, Missis-**

sippi (Conf.), vol. 33, p. 569; Wiley, **The Life of Johnny Reb,** pp. 104–105.

15   **The canteen would split open and flatten:** Wiley, **The Life of Johnny Reb,** p. 98.

15   **refused to be conscripted:** Knight, **The Life and Activities of Captain Newton Knight,** p. 60; Bynum, **The Free State of Jones,** p. 59.

16   **"on all the face of the earth":** T. J. Knight identified his father as a Primitive Baptist in his memoir (p. 18). Rachel Knight's granddaughter, Anna Knight, stated that Newton "did not believe in slavery" in her memoir of her childhood, **Mississippi Girl** (Nashville, Tenn.: Southern Publishing Association, 1952), p. 1. On some Primitive Baptists' antislavery views (especially yeoman farmers'), see Randy J. Sparks, **On Jordan's Stormy Banks: Evangelicalism in Mississippi, 1773–1876** (Athens: University of Georgia Press, 1994), pp. 87–90, 109–11, 115–25, 132–34, 137, 142, 144.

16   **"help nurse sick soldiers if they wanted":** Frost, "The South's Strangest Army Revealed by Chief."

16   **"the captain threatened to have him shot":** Deposition of O. C. Martin, **Newton Knight et al. v. United States,** Congressional Case 8013-8464, November 29, 1890.

16   **land and resell it:** 1860 United States Federal Census, Jones County; Bynum, **The Free State of Jones,** p. 65.

17   **as his neighbors:** Letter from William L. Nugent to his wife, Eleanor, August 22, 1863, in Cash and Howorth, **My Dear Nellie,** p. 129; Dabney Herndon Maury, **Recollections of a Virginian in the Mexican, Indian and Civil Wars** (1894; reprint, New York: Scribners and Sons, Kessinger Publishing's Legacy, Reprint 2007, p. 246; Leverett, **The Legend of the Free State of Jones,** p. 18.

17   **"damnable despotism as governs the army":** Letter from James D. Shows to his wife, James D. Shows Collection, University of Southern Mississippi, McCain Library and Archives; James M. McPherson, **For Cause and Comrades: Why Men Fought in the Civil War** (New York: Oxford University Press, 1995), p. 48; John K. Bettersworth, **Mississippi in the Confederacy: As They Saw It** (1961; reprint, New York: Kraus Reprint Company, 1970), p. 65.

17   **mortification at his own appearance:** Henry Steele Commager, ed., **The Civil War Archive: The History of the Civil War in Documents** (New York: Black Dog and Leventhal Publishers, 2000), p. 221.

18   **basic drill commands:** War Department Collection of Confederate Records, Record Group 109, Compiled Service Records of Confederate Soldiers Who Served in Organizations from the State of Mississippi, 7th Battalion, Mississippi Infantry, microfilm (M269), NARA; Leverett, **The Legend of the Free State of Jones,** p. 50.

18   **"all the medicine we had then":** Frost, "The South's Strangest Army. Revealed by Chief."

18   **induce calm and sleep:** "The Regimental Hospital," in Henry Steele Commager, ed., **The Civil War Archive** (New York: Black Dog and Leventhal Publishers, 2000), pp. 537–38; George Worthington Adams, "Confederate Medicine," **Journal of Southern History** 6:2 (May 1940): 154–55.

19   **a wounded soldier's best friend:** McPherson, **Battle Cry of Freedom,** pp. 477, 486; on field hospital orderlies, see Walt Whitman, "Specimen Days," in **The Portable Walt Whitman,** Mark Van Doren, ed. (New York: Penguin Books, 1977), pp. 420, 421, 427, 432; Harwell, **Kate: Journal of a Confederate Nurse,** pp. 9–40; Harold Elk Straubing, ed., **In Hospital**

and Camp: The Civil War Through the Eyes of Its Doctors and Nurses (Harrisburg, Penn.: Stackpole Books, 1993), pp. 27–37; H. H. Cunningham, Doctors in Gray: The Confederate Medical Service (1958; reprint, Baton Rouge: Louisiana State University Press, 1986), pp. 71–98; Wiley, The Life of Johnny Reb, pp. 244–69. Rorer is quoted from a typescript of a letter to his cousin Susan, December 20, 1863, Civil War Collection, MHI. The original of Rorer's letter, one of several to his cousin describing camp life, is in the papers of James M. Willcox, 1831–71, Duke University, Special Collections Library.

19 at Iuka two weeks earlier: A division consisted of three brigades. A brigade included four regiments (or three battalions) of ten companies, with each company constituting between forty-five and one hundred men, according to McPherson, Ordeal by Fire, pp. 172–73.

19 exile in Mexico over surrender: For a description of Price and his actions at Iuka see Cozzens, The Darkest Days of the War, pp. 75–103; letter from Lieutenant Colonel Columbus Sykes of the 43rd Mississippi Infantry to his wife, Pauline, September 18, 1862, Civil War Collection, MHI, Carlisle Barracks, Pa.

19 "the impudence to come near": Letter from Lieutenant Colonel Columbus Sykes to his wife, Pauline, September 18, 1862, Civil War Collection, MHI, Carlisle Barracks, Pa.

20 tramping back the way they came: Cozzens, The Darkest Days of the War, pp. 75–133.

20 "a more foolhardy expedition than the last": Ibid., p. 135.

20 "the confidence of all his soldiers": Letter from Lieutenant Colonel Columbus Sykes to his wife, Pauline, September 29, 1862, Civil War Collection, MHI, Carlisle Barracks, Pa.

21 charges of negligence: Shelby Foote, The Civil War, A Narrative, part 1 (1956; reprint, New York: Vintage, 1986), p. 725.

Van Dorn was rumored to be licentious and would be shot to death the following May by physician George Peters over a supposed adulterous affair, although some suspected Peters of disloyalty. For the Confederate official reports of the battle of Corinth see **OR,** series 1, vol. 17, part 1, pp. 375–414.

22 **"Had grape pie for supper":** Cozzens, **The Darkest Days of the War,** p. 33; diary of John McKee, 2nd Iowa Infantry, Civil War Collection, MHI, Carlisle Barracks, Pa.

22 **"You must be a mind reader":** Memoir of Hugh Carlisle, 81st Ohio Infantry, Civil War Collection, MHI, Carlisle Barracks, Pa., p. 157.

22 **"whenever they get a chance":** McPherson, **For Cause and Comrades,** p. 119.

23 **"before we got niggers":** Ibid.

23 **"reproduce their kind":** Memoir of Joseph K. Nelson, 81st Ohio, Civil War Collection, MHI, Carlisle Barracks, Pa.

23 **"take better care of them":** Diary of George C. Burmeister, 35th Iowa Infantry, November 27, 1862, Civil War Collection, MHI, Carlisle Barracks, Pa. To a certain extent, Burmeister has internalized proslavery rhetoric, which assumed that masters and slaves lived together peacefully and that slaves were well treated. Even someone as sophisticated as Nathaniel Hawthorne could assert that in the South, masters and slaves lived "together in greater peace and affection . . . than had ever elsewhere existed between the taskmaster and the serf." See Nathaniel Hawthorne, **Life of Franklin Pierce** (1852; reprint, Honolulu: University Press of the Pacific, 2002), p. 90.

23 **informed the Northern soldiers:** Memoir of Lewis F. Phillips, 4th Iowa, Civil War Collection, MHI, Carlisle Barracks, Pa.

24 **"a just retribution":** Bobby Leon Roberts and Carl Moneyhon, eds., **Portraits of Conflict: A Photographic History of Mis-**

sissippi in the Civil War (Fayetteville: University of Arkansas Press, 1993), p. 275.

24   **it seemed they might overlap:** Memoir of Hugh Carlisle, 81st Ohio Infantry, Civil War Collection, MHI, Carlisle Barracks, Pa.

24   **one had just missed:** Memoir of Lewis F. Phillips, 4th Iowa, Civil War Collection, MHI, Carlisle Barracks, Pa.

24   **to clean the wound:** Commager, "The Regimental Hospital," in **The Civil War Archive,** pp. 537–38; memoir of Hugh Carlisle, Civil War Collection, MHI, Carlisle Barracks, Pa.

25   **rallying them onward:** Diary of John McKee, 2nd Iowa Infantry, Civil War Collection, MHI, Carlisle Barracks, Pa.; **OR,** series 1, vol. 17, part 1.

25   **He went to the rear:** Memoir of Hugh Carlisle, 81st Ohio Infantry, Civil War Collection, MHI, Carlisle Barracks, Pa.

25   **sparing their lives:** Memoir of Hugh Carlisle, 81st Ohio Infantry, and diary of William Burge, 11th Iowa Infantry, Civil War Collection, MHI, Carlisle Barracks, Pa.

26   **"and spiked the big guns":** The eyewitness account of Terral's death is from Roberts and Moneyhon, **Portraits of Conflict,** p. 168.

27   **overcome in a single day: OR,** series 1, vol. 17, part 1, p. 379.

27   **were suddenly cold:** Cozzens, **The Darkest Days of the War,** pp. 230–32.

27   **to keep him alive:** This scene is drawn from McPherson, **Battle Cry of Freedom,** p. 477; Ambrose Bierce, "The Coup de Grâce," in **Civil War Stories** (New York: Dover Publications, Inc., 1994), pp. 79–80.

27   **invariably suppurated:** Commager, "The Regimental Hospital," in **The Civil War Archive,** pp. 537–38.

28   **not only hollow, but obscene:** Ibid.

28   **"into the street"**: Memoir of Hugh Carlisle, 81st Ohio Infantry, Civil War Collection, MHI, Carlisle Barracks, Pa.

29   **reinforcements arrived via train: OR,** series 1, vol. 17, part 1, p. 431.

29   **"her bells rang out"**: Letters of Nehemiah Davis Starr, 21st Missouri Volunteers, Leslie Anders Collection, MHI, Carlisle Barracks, Pa.; Foote, **The Civil War,** part 1, p. 723.

30   **"on the wagons"**: Letters of Nehemiah Davis Starr, 21st Missouri Volunteers, Leslie Anders Collection, MHI, Carlisle Barracks, Pa.

30   **"from under our feet"**: Memoir of Lewis F. Phillips, 4th Iowa, Civil War Collection, MHI, Carlisle Barracks, Pa.

31   **or even orders: OR,** series 1, vol. 17, part 1, pp. 385–92; Cozzens, **The Darkest Days of the War,** p. 235.

31   **raining down on them:** Letter from Lieutenant Colonel Columbus Sykes to his wife, Pauline, August 31, 1862, Civil War Collection, MHI, Carlisle Barracks, Pa.; **OR,** series 1, vol. 17, part 1, pp. 389–92.

32   **charge at the "double-quick": OR,** series 1, vol. 17, part 1, pp. 385–92.

32   **"The very atmosphere seemed filled": OR,** series 1, vol. 17, part 1, pp. 385–92; Cozzens, **The Darkest Days of the War,** pp. 268–69.

32   **"until I stopped!":** McPherson, **For Cause and Comrades,** p. 42.

32   **"trampled underfoot"**: Quoted in Cozzens, **The Darkest Days of the War,** p. 241.

32   **through the jaw:** Leverett, **The Legend of the Free State of Jones,** p. 56. It's not clear exactly when Harper and Reddoch were wounded in the action, but this was the heaviest fighting the 7th Battalion was involved in.

33 **"old women":** Diary of Joseph K. Nelson, 81st Ohio, Civil War Collection, MHI, Carlisle Barracks, Pa.

33 **"in the <u>bakeries</u> and <u>stores</u>":** Memoir of Lewis F. Phillips, 4th Iowa, Civil War Collection, MHI, Carlisle Barracks, Pa.; the Civil War diary of Cyrus F. Boyd, as quoted in Bettersworth, **Mississippi in the Confederacy,** p. 98.

34 **"din of battle":** Diary of Edward Dean, 4th Wisconsin, Civil War Collection, MHI, Carlisle Barracks, Pa.

34 **"snow in thaw":** OR, series 1, vol. 17, part 1, pp. 385–92; Cozzens, **The Darkest Days of the War,** pp. 268–69.

34 **"intense meaning of that term":** OR, series 1, vol. 17, part 1, pp. 385–92; Cozzens, **The Darkest Days of the War,** pp. 268–69; Bettersworth, **Mississippi in the Confederacy,** p. 97.

35 **"like pitch forks":** General description of the action at Robinett is from Cozzens, **The Darkest Days of the War,** p. 268; the diary of William Burge, 11th Iowa Infantry, Civil War Collection, MHI, Carlisle Barracks, Pa.; quotation is from the Civil War diary of Cyrus F. Boyd, 15th Iowa Infantry, as quoted in Bettersworth, **Mississippi in the Confederacy,** pp. 95–98.

35 **"My God, my boys are running!":** Cozzens, **The Darkest Days of the War,** p. 270.

35 **"running from my mouth":** McPherson, **For Cause and Comrades,** p. 42.

35 **and Rogers's horse:** The photograph of Rogers and Battery Robinett is reproduced in Roberts and Moneyhon, **Portraits of Conflict,** p. 175; description of those found there is from the diary of William Wade, 11th Iowa, Civil War Collection, MHI, Carlisle Barracks, Pa.

36 **as at parade rest:** Diary of Edward Dean, 4th Wisconsin, and diary of Joseph K. Nelson, 81st Ohio, Civil War Collection, MHI, Carlisle Barracks, Pa.

36   **refused to move:** Diary of Edward Dean, 4th Wisconsin, Civil War Collection, MHI, Carlisle Barracks, Pa.

37   **one long, thin coffin:** Cozzens, **The Darkest Days of the War,** pp xi–xii, quotation from p. xii; "The Battle of Corinth," **Harper's Weekly,** November 1, 1862, quotation from p. 699; Earl Van Dorn, "Report of the Battle of Corinth, October 20, 1862," **OR,** series 1, vol. 17, part 1, p. 379; Leverett, **The Legend of the Free State of Jones,** p. 56.

37   **"sustained a death-blow":** Ulysses S. Grant, **Memoirs and Selected Letters** (New York: Library of America, 1990), p. 281; William Tecumseh Sherman, **Memoirs of General W. T. Sherman** (New York: Library of America, 1990), p. 284.

37   **lay uncared for: OR** and Court Martial of Van Dorn, **OR,** series 1, vol. 17, part 1, pp. 460–75.

37   **by happenstance:** Ibid.

38   **with their own money:** Ibid.

38   **reported for duty:** War Department Collection of Confederate Records, RG 109, Compiled Service Records, 7th Battalion, Mississippi Infantry, microfilm (M269), NARA; Bynum, **The Free State of Jones,** pp. 101–102; Leverett, **The Legend of the Free State of Jones,** p. 56.

38   **at about this time:** War Department Collection of Confederate Records, RG 109, Compiled Service Records, 7th Battalion, Mississippi Infantry, microfilm (M269), NARA; Leverett, **The Legend of the Free State of Jones,** p. 56; Welborn deposition, **Newton Knight et al. v. United States,** Congressional Case 8013-8464.

39   **"a thousand wrongs":** Lord Byron, "The Siege of Corinth" (1816), in **Selected Poems,** eds. Susan J. Wolfson and Peter J. Manning (New York: Penguin Books, 1996), p. 363. On ancient Greek stories being in circulation in the antebellum South, see Michael O'Brien, **Conjectures of Order: Intellectual Life**

and the American South, 1810–1860 (Chapel Hill: University of North Carolina Press, 2004), pp. 606–22, 636–52; Michael O'Brien, ed., **All Clever Men, Who Make Their Way: Critical Discourse in the Old South** (Athens: University of Georgia Press, 1992), pp. 398–419; Caroline Winterer, **The Culture of Classicism: Ancient Greece and Rome in American Intellectual Life, 1780–1910** (Baltimore: Johns Hopkins University Press, 2002), pp. 44–98; Caroline Winterer, **The Mirror of Antiquity: American Women and the Classical Tradition** (Ithaca: Cornell University Press, 2007), pp. 165–90.

Iphicrates was the Athenian general who in 390 BCE liberated Corinth from the siege by the Spartan king Agesilaus. He thus abandoned longheld loyalties to Sparta. He later assisted Sparta, and eventually turned traitor again, and this time tarnished his fame, when he sided with his father-in-law in a battle against his hometown of Athens. Newton would not have known all of these details.

In a later classical siege of Corinth, the Achaean general Diaeus controlled an army "swelled with emancipated slaves." After establishing his headquarters in Corinth in 147 BCE, Mummius led a successful siege on Corinth. In 146 BCE Diaeus abandoned Corinth to Mummius and fled home to Megalopolis, where he killed his wife to prevent her from being captured by enemies and then killed himself with poison.

See William Smith, ed., **Dictionary of Greek and Roman Biography and Mythology,** vol. 1 (Boston: Little, Brown, and Company, 1867), quotation from p. 997; William Smith, ed., **Dictionary of Greek and Roman Biography and Mythology,** vol. 2 (Boston: Little, Brown, and Company, 1867), pp. 616–18, 1119–120; Simon Hornblower and Antony Spawforth, eds., **The Oxford Classical Dictionary,** 3rd ed. (New York: Oxford University Press, 1996), pp. 765, 1405.

On Byron being read in the Confederacy, see Kate Cuming, **Kate: The Journal of a Confederate Nurse,** ed. Richard Barksdale Harwell (1866; reprint, Baton Rouge: Louisiana State University Press, 1987), p. 14; O'Brien, ed., **All Clever Men,** p. 69; Michael O'Brien, **Rethinking the South: Essays in Intellectual History** (Athens: University of Georgia Press, 1998), pp. 28, 51, 70, 106–9.

39 **fed the Confederacy:** Leverett, **The Legend of the Free State of Jones,** pp. 56–57; McPherson, **Battle Cry of Freedom,** p. 184.

39 **rest of the war:** Frost, "The South's Strangest Army Revealed by Chief."

39 **without leave:** Thomas J. Knight, **The Life and Activities of Captain Newton Knight,** p. 60.

40 **"did more to injure the Southern case":** Platt and Womack to Pettus, November 7, 1862, and Saffold to Pettus, November 3, 1862, quoted from John K. Bettersworth, **Confederate Mississippi: The People and Policies of a Cotton State in Wartime** (Baton Rouge: Louisiana State University Press, 1943), p. 191.

40 **"for o tha care":** Eric Foner, "The South's Inner Civil War," **American Heritage** 40:2 (March 1989), online at http://www.americanheritage.com/articles/magazine/ah/1989/2/1989_2_46.shtml.

40 **"so far above him":** B. D. Graves, address to the Hebron Community, June 17, 1926, Lauren Rogers Museum, Laurel, Miss.

40 **forced back:** Leverett, **The Legend of the Free State of Jones,** pp. 56–58.

40 **as AWOL:** Bettersworth, **Confederate Mississippi,** pp. 198, 202–3, 218–19. Bettersworth notes that "when the troops evacuated Corinth, 3,792 men were absent without leave; and by the time the army reached Tupelo, 2,919 more were missing." During the remainder of the year, hundreds more desertions occurred (pp. 202–3).

41   **soldiers home:** Bettersworth, **Confederate Mississippi,** pp. 198, 202–3, 218–19.

41   **"even houses":** Ibid., pp. 82, 110–11, 199–200, quotation from p. 82.

41   **"This was too much for my father":** Knight, **The Life and Activities of Captain Newton Knight,** pp. 21, 60.

41   **"when I got ready":** Frost, "The South's Strangest Army Revealed by Chief"; Leverett, **The Legend of the Free State of Jones,** pp. 43, 57. In his crisis, Newton resembled Huck Finn, who had to decide between remaining loyal to his slave-owning society, which continually spurned him, or becoming an outlaw by helping his friend Jim find freedom. And like Huck, Newton chose to remain true to himself and follow his heart.

41   **into the woods:** War Department Collection of Confederate Records, RG 109, Compiled Service Records, 7th Battalion, Mississippi Infantry, microfilm (M269), NARA.

41   **"duty here at home":** Knight, **The Life and Activities of Captain Newton Knight,** p. 57.

42   **"knocks and signs and passwords:** George P. Rawick, **The American Slave: A Composite Autobiography,** supplement, series 1, vol. 6, **Mississippi Narratives,** part 1 (Westport, London: Greenwood Press, 1977), pp. 10–19.

CHAPTER 2: HOME

Page

43   **"and polygamous":** Faulkner as quoted in **Plain Folk of the South Revisited,** Samuel Hyde Jr., ed. (Baton Rouge and London: Louisiana State University Press, 1997), p. 74.

44   **"I am ruined, I am ruined":** Rawick, **The American Slave,** supplement, series 1, vol. 10, **Mississippi Narratives,** part 5, interview with Martha Wheeler, former slave belonging to Jackie

Knight, pp. 2262–71. Wheeler described the unusual layout of the Knight plantation; normally slave cabins were in the back, not the front.

44   **"ole master's" tobacco:** Ibid.

44   **on a spread with ten slaves:** U.S. Federal Census, Jones County, 1860; U.S. Federal Slave Schedule, Jones and Covington Counties, 1860; Rawick, **The American Slave,** vol. 10, **Mississippi Narratives,** part 5, interview with Martha Wheeler, pp. 2262–71.

44   **underlying the secession crisis:** Jackie may also have grieved over secession because his father died establishing the nation. According to family oral tradition, Jackie's father fought in the Revolutionary War. However, Knight genealogists have been unable to trace his identity. Jones County archivist and genealogist Ken Welch believes he may indeed have died prematurely—perhaps killed in that war—given that the Knights tended to have extremely large families, yet Jackie Knight and his brothers James and Lewis were their mother's only children, suggesting that her husband died young.

45   **last will and testament:** According to family descendant and genealogist Earle W. Knight, Albert Knight was opposed to the Confederacy; see Victoria E. Bynum's notes on interviews for **The Free State of Jones,** Mississippi Oral History Project, McCain Library and Archives, University of Southern Mississippi. Jackie Knight's will is in Probate Court Record 3, June 1860–1865, Covington County, copy in possession of the authors. A typescript is reprinted in Winnie Knight Thomas, Earle W. Knight, Lavada Knight Dykes, and Martha Kaye Dykes Lowery, **The Family of John "Jackie" Knight and Keziah Davis Knight** (Magee, Miss: n.p., 1985), pp. 11–12, 327–33. For further discussion of whether the Albert Knight family were anti-

slavery, see Leverett, **The Legend of the Free State of Jones,** p. 11.

45   **fathers for their sins:** A strain of dissidence seemed to run among the younger, poorer members of the Knight family. Fourteen of Jackie's grandchildren would ally themselves with Newton in opposing the Confederacy. Victoria E. Bynum in **The Free State of Jones** identifies those relatives who were allies in a useful genealogical chart, p. 192.

45   **cotton and slaves:** The description of Jackie Knight's arrival in Jones County is from Thomas, et al., **The Family of John "Jackie" Knight and Keziah Davis Knight,** pp. 11–12. Jackie Knight's cotton and rice production is from Bynum, **The Free State of Jones,** p. 63.

46   **buy more slaves:** According to Martha Wheeler, Jackie Knight was a slave trader as well as planter. Rawick, **The American Slave,** vol. 10, **Mississippi Narratives,** part 5, interview with Martha Wheeler, pp. 2262–71. A Knight descendant, Earle W. Knight, also believed that Jackie did some slave trading. See Bynum, notes on interviews with Earle Knight, Mississippi Oral History Project, University of Southern Mississippi.

46   **"fields of mimic snow":** Bettersworth, **Mississippi in the Confederacy,** pp. 4–5.

46   **"Bought him by weight":** Eugene R. Dattel, "Cotton in a Global Economy: Mississippi (1800–1860)," from Mississippi History Now, an online publication of the Mississippi Historical Society, October 2006, http://mshistory.K12.ms.us/articles/161/cotton-in-a-global-economy-mississippi-1800-1860; Bettersworth, **Mississippi in the Confederacy,** pp. 4–5; quotation is from B. D. Graves, address to the Hebron Community, June 17, 1926, Lauren Rogers Museum, Laurel, Miss. On converting antebellum money into 2008 currency, we multiply by a factor

of 75. We arrive at this figure by comparing a skilled laborer's wage of roughly $500 in the 1840s to an average annual family income in 2000 of around $37,500: 37,500 / 500 = 75. See U.S. Bureau of the Census, **Historical Statistics of the United States: Colonial Times to 1970, Part I** (Washington, D.C.: U.S. Department of Commerce, Economics and Statistics Administration, 1995), p. 224; **idem, Statistical Abstract of the United States, 1994: The National Data Book** (Washington, D.C.: U.S. Department of Commerce, Economics and Statistics Administration, 1995), pp. 487–88. See also John Stauffer, **The Black Hearts of Men: Radical Abolitionists and the Transformation of Race** (Cambridge, Mass.: Harvard University Press, 2002), p. 322, n. 84. We are grateful to the economist of slavery Stanley Engerman for helping with these figures.

46   **"sell for that":** Bettersworth: **Mississippi in the Confederacy,** pp. 4–5.

47   **"Have they any Negroes?":** According to Knight family slave Martha Wheeler, Jackie gave two slaves to each child when they married. See Rawick, **The American Slave,** vol. 10, **Mississippi Narratives,** part 5, interview with Martha Wheeler, pp. 2262–71. Quotation is from B. D. Graves, address to the Hebron Community, June 17, 1926, Lauren Rogers Museum, Laurel, Miss.

47   **his children could read and write:** Jackie Knight's possessions were detailed in the records of his estate auction, Probate Court Records for Covington County, 1860–1865. His home was also described by Martha Wheeler in Rawick, **The American Slave,** vol. 10, **Mississippi Narratives,** part 5, pp. 2262–71. In addition to his two cases of books, Jackie had a stable of eight horses, an expensive buggy, several teams of oxen, and a vast array of bed and table linens, counterpanes, and crockery.

47   **personal estate worth $8,900:** U.S. Federal Slave Sched-
ules, Jones and Covington Counties, 1840, 1850, 1860; Jackie
Knight's will is in Probate Court Record 3, June 1860–1865,
Covington County, copy in possession of the authors.

48   **All of her children received some education:** Rawick, **The
American Slave,** vol. 10, interview with Martha Wheeler, pp.
2262–71; Bynum, notes on interviews with Earle W. Knight,
Mississippi Oral History Project, University of Southern Mississippi. On the 1850 U.S. Federal Census for Jones County,
Albert and Mason listed themselves as literate and all of their
children above the age of ten as receiving schooling in the past
year. Knight family genealogist Ken Welch has an interesting
conjecture on Mason's unusual name: perhaps she was named
for famous antislavery patriot George Mason.

48   **"too poor to raise a fuss on":** Quotations from James Street,
Look Away!: A Dixie Notebook (1936; reprint, Westport,
Conn.: Greenwood Press, 1977), pp. 43, 53, 54, and B. L. Moss,
essay on "Jones County's Agricultural and Industrial Develop-
ment," Lauren Rogers Museum, Laurel, Miss. Piney Woods is
also called the "Long Leaf Pine Belt" and "Pine Barrens." See
Herbert Weaver, **Mississippi Farmers, 1850–1860** (Nashville:
The Vanderbilt University Press, 1945), pp. 10, 20.

49   **"forests are all my own":** Street, **Look Away!,** p. 55.

49   **Most families owned none at all:** U.S. Federal Census for
Jones County, 1860, and U.S. Federal Slave Schedules, 1860;
Leverett, **The Legend of the Free State of Jones,** pp. 11, 35.
Most of the Knight family slaves were listed in the Covington County census rather than Jones, including the twenty-two
held by Jackie. Still, he was among the largest slaveholders in an
area in which it was rare to own slaves at all.

49   **"settled gloom":** J. F. H. Claiborne, "A Trip Through the Piney

Woods," **Publications of the Mississippi Historical Society,** vol. 9, 1906.

49   **wild game for the table:** B. D. Graves, address to the Hebron Community, June 17, 1926, Lauren Rogers Museum, Laurel, Miss.

50   **a single horse:** Samuel C. Hyde Jr., **Plain Folk of the South Revisited** (Baton Rouge, London: Louisiana State University Press, 1997), p. 207; Weaver, **Mississippi Farmers,** pp. 87, 88, 96; Horace Greeley, **What I Know of Farming . . .** (New York: G. W. Carleton & Co., 1870), p. 87; Gorn, " 'Gouge and Bite,' " pp. 18–43.

50   **children could crowd around it:** John Melton Knight, address to the Rainey Community Meeting, June 10, 1926, Lauren Rogers Museum, Laurel, Miss. J. M. Knight was Newton's cousin and contemporary. He was the son of Jesse Davis Knight.

50   **oars and a pull-rope:** U.S. Federal Census, Jones County, 1840, 1850; B. D. Graves, address to the Hebron Community, June 17, 1926, Lauren Rogers Museum, Laurel, Miss.

51   **bushels of them that year:** Addie West, "A Brief History of Jones County," unpublished Works Progress Administration collection for Jones County, record group 60, vol. 315, MDAH; J. M. Knight, address to the Rainey Community Meeting, June 10, 1926, Lauren Rogers Museum, Laurel, Miss. Statistics on livestock are from Leverett, **The Legend of the Free State of Jones,** p. 35.

51   **about as long as a boy:** J. M. Knight, address to the Rainey Community Meeting, June 10, 1926, Lauren Rogers Museum, Laurel, Miss.

51   **mightier than the mouth:** On Piney Woods literacy and reading practices, see O'Brien, **Conjectures of Order,** pp. 709, 721, 722, 725, 728, 739, 740, 741, 750, 1079; Michael O'Brien, **Re-**

thinking the South, pp. 28, 51, 70; O'Brien, **All Clever Men Who Make Their Way,** p. 69; Grady McWhiney, "Antebellum Piney Woods Culture: Continuity over Time and Place," in **Mississippi's Piney Woods: A Human Perspective,** Noel Polk, ed. (Jackson: University Press of Mississippi, 1986), pp. 40–58; J. F. H. Claiborne, "A Trip Through the Piney Woods," **Publications of the Mississippi Historical Society,** 1906; Frank Lawrence Owsley, **Plain Folk of the Old South** (Chicago: Quadrangle Books, 1949), pp. 142–49; Lawrence Levine, **High Brow/Low Brow: The Emergence of Cultural Hierarchy in America** (Cambridge, Mass.: Harvard University Press, 1988), pp. 29–30. On **Dilworth Spelling-Book** being read by yeomen, see David Herbert Donald, **Lincoln** (New York: Simon & Schuster, 1995), pp. 29–30. See also **The Columbian Orator . . . , Bicentennial Edition,** David W. Blight, ed. (New York: Columbia University Press, 1997).

51 **any boy around:** Philip Henry Gosse, **Letters from Alabama, Chiefly Relating to Natural History** (London, 1859), pp. 130–33, reprinted in Owsley, **Plain Folk of the Old South,** p. 120. Newton's adeptness with a gun was described by his descendant Barbara Blackledge in her interview with the authors, March 28, 2008.

52 **chairs in the back:** J. M. Knight, address to the Rainey Community Meeting, Lauren Rogers Museum, Laurel, Miss.

52 **"round up the corn":** Owsley, **Plain Folk of the Old South,** p. 113.

52 **"call it a fine house":** Thomas J. Knight, in **The Life and Activities of Captain Newton Knight,** p. 2, describes his father as belonging to a Primitive Baptist congregation.

52 **homespun in a day:** Mrs. J. W. Moss, "Essay on the History of the Union Line Community," Lauren Rogers Museum, Laurel, Miss.

52   **the nature of the faith:** "Primitive Baptists" later became known as "hard-shell Baptists." See Randy J. Sparks, **On Jordan's Stormy Banks: Evangelicalism in Mississippi, 1773–1876** (Athens and London: University of Georgia Press, 1994), pp. 88–90.

53   **"with Christ forever shared":** Stephen Marini, **Sacred Song in America: Religion, Music, and Public Culture** (Urbana: University of Illinois Press, 2003), pp. 68–81; Sparks, **On Jordan's Stormy Banks,** pp. 29, 88–90, 116–22; Cushing Biggs Hassells, **History of the Church of God, from the Creation to AD 1885** (Middletown, N.Y.: Gilbert Beebe's Sons, 1886), pp. 840, 844; Benjamin Griffin, **History of the Primitive Baptists of Mississippi** (Jackson, Miss.: Barksdale and Jones, 1853).

53   **"also in the body":** Acts 10:34; Hebrews 13:3.

53   **God's authority:** Sparks, **On Jordan's Stormy Banks,** p. 89.

53   **"tongue of the learned":** Primitive Baptist Association, quotation from Sparks, **On Jordan's Stormy Banks,** p. 89.

53   **purity of simple living:** Primitive Baptist Association, quotation from Sparks, **On Jordan's Stormy Banks,** p. 90.

54   **Old Union:** For a fuller portrait of Norvell Robertson, see Bynum, **The Free State of Jones,** pp. 65, 75–76; B. D. Graves, address to the Hebron Community, June 17, 1926, Lauren Rogers Museum, Laurel, Miss.

54   **trips to Mobile:** Dona Broom and John Wood, "Outlaw Days," unpublished WPA Collection, Covington County, MDAH.

55   **mutual protection:** M. P. Bush, address to the meeting of the DAR, February 17, 1912, Lauren Rogers Museum, Laurel, Miss.

55   **roosted in the trees at night:** Details of the Knights at market in Mobile are from J. M. Knight's address to the Rainey Community Meeting, Lauren Rogers Museum, Laurel, Miss.

55   **"pretty costumes":** Whitfield Community Meeting, June 4, 1926, Lauren Rogers Museum, Laurel, Miss. For a vivid description of Mobile, see David W. Blight, **A Slave No More: Two Men Who Escaped to Freedom** (New York: Harcourt, Inc., 2007), p. 77.

56   **passed directly through Jasper:** Claiborne, "A Trip Through The Piney Woods." On the Piney Woods farmers' commute to local commercial centers, see Hyde, **Plain Folk of the South Revisited,** p. 86. A homemade keelboat was excavated on the Leaf River a mile from New Augusta in 1990, with barrel staves suggesting it carried cargo and that farmers must have tried to access market towns via the waterways.

56   **obstreperous wife: Jackson Daily News,** August 21, 1941.

57   **pair of farming shears:** J. M. Knight, address to the Rainey Community, Lauren Rogers Museum, Laurel, Miss.

57   **"The Free State of Jones":** Leverett, **The Legend of the Free State of Jones,** p. 13.

57   **"defied them": New Orleans Picayune,** July 17, 1864.

58   **"primitive areas of the state":** Leverett, "A Biographical Sketch of Amos McLemore," **Clarion-Ledger,** November 29, 30, 1977, and Leverett, **The Legend of the Free State of Jones,** pp. 64–67.

58   **Confederate legislature:** U.S. Federal Census, 1860; Bynum, **The Free State of Jones,** pp. 67–73.

59   **gone for protection:** Bynum, **The Free State of Jones,** p. 73.

60   **without a quiver:** On reading portraits, and portrait conventions for white men, see Alan Trachtenberg, **Reading American Photographs: Images as History, Mathew Brady to Walker Evans** (New York: Hill and Wang, 1989), pp. 3–70; John Stauffer, **The Black Hearts of Men: Radical Abolitionists and the Transformation of Race** (Cambridge, Mass.: Harvard

University Press, 2002), ch. 2; and Stauffer, "Daguerreotyping the National Soul: The Portraits of Southworth and Hawes," **Prospects: An Annual of American Cultural Studies** 22 (1997): 69–107.

60 **"a nice, smooth way":** Donald, **Lincoln,** p. 575; Street, **Look Away!,** p. 49; quotation from Knight, **The Life and Activities of Captain Newton Knight,** p. 36.

60 **"any more than she would a Negro":** B. D. Graves, address to the Hebron Community, June 17, 1926, Lauren Rogers Museum, Laurel, Miss.

60 **"rigid in economy":** U.S. Federal Census, Jasper County, 1860; Frederick Douglass, **Life and Times of Frederick Douglass** (1892; reprint, New York: Collier Books, 1962), p. 272.

60 **his life with Serena would be difficult:** Knight, **The Life and Activities of Captain Newton Knight,** p. 4.

61 **entire life working:** On reading portraits, see Trachtenberg, **Reading American Photographs,** and Stauffer, "Daguerreotyping the National Soul," pp. 69–107.

61 **mesmeric quality:** One image said to be of Rachel is privately held by Martha Welborn of Jones County. Welborn's husband, Herman, amassed a formidable collection of material on Newton and Rachel, much of it directly from Knight descendants Lacy and Idell Knight, who were both grandchildren of Rachel and Newton. Their daughter, Barbara Blackledge, gave the picture to the Welborns. The other photograph is held by Florence Knight Blaylock and Dorothy Knight Marsh. Blaylock and Marsh, sisters, are also great-granddaughters of Newton and Rachel Knight.

61 **partly Creek or Choctaw:** Rachel's daughter Fannie Knight described herself as "Choctaw and French." Deposition of Fannie Knight Howze in the case of **Martha Ann Musgrove et al.**

v. J. R. McPherson et al., January 27, 1914, copy in possession of the authors, courtesy of the family of Harlan McKnight, grandson of Mat Knight.

62   **household she came from:** According to her headstone, Rachel was born March 11, 1840. The ages and birth dates of Rachel's children are from the U.S. Federal Census for 1870 and headstones in the Knight graveyard in Jasper County, Miss. Georgeanne's headstone lists her birth date as October 14, 1855, which would make her less than a year old when she was purchased by Jackie.

Rachel's background is described briefly in a memoir by her granddaughter; Anna Knight, **Mississippi Girl** (Nashville: Southern Publishing Association, 1954), p. 4. Anna Knight, the daughter of Georgeanne, became a prominent Seventh-Day Adventist missionary. In her memoir, she stated, "My mother was born a slave in Macon, Georgia." The name of Rachel's father, Abram, is contained in the records of the Church of Jesus Christ of Latter-day Saints, Southern States Mission Records of Missionaries, Records of Admissions, 1878–1888, to which she converted late in life.

According to the files of Knight family genealogist Herman Welborn, courtesy of Martha Welborn, Rachel was bought with not one but two small children: a daughter Rosette was born in 1854. However, there is no other confirmable record of a Rosette. Rachel's son Edmund appears to have died as a boy; he does not appear on the 1880 census.

62   **"family could colonize":** Jan Sumrall and Ken Welch, in **The Knights and Related Families** (Denham Springs, La.: n.p., 1985), traced Jackie's younger brother James Knight to Monroe, Ga., just north of Macon. The notion that Rachel was personally bought by Jackie at a public slave auction comes primarily

from Ethel Knight. Jackie's advanced age did not prevent him from buying slaves. In 1857 Jackie purchased an eleven-year-old boy named William for one thousand dollars in Jones County, the deed of which is reprinted in Thomas, et al., **The Family of John "Jackie" Knight and Keziah Davis Knight,** p. 331.

62 **"jet black negroes":** Blight, **A Slave No More,** pp. 57–59.

63 **"whip, pistol and knife":** William Kaufman Scarborough, **The Overseer: Plantation Management in the Old South** (Athens: University of Georgia Press, 1966); John Hill Aughey, **Tupelo** (1888; reprint, Chester, N.Y.: Blyany Press, 2005), p. 203.

63 **"the cruelty of slavery":** Frederick Law Olmsted, **The Cotton Kingdom: A Traveller's Observations on Cotton and Slavery in the American Slave States, 1853–1861** (1861; reprint New York: Da Capo Press, 1966), pp. 451–55.

63 **"till one day he died":** Rawick, **The American Slave,** supplement, series 1, vol. 6, **Mississippi Narratives,** part 1, pp. 308–310.

64 **"one stiffened joint": Memphis Daily Appeal,** January 1, 1859.

64 **"you ain't got no mo' chance than a bullfrog":** Rawick, **The American Slave,** supplement series 1, vol. 8, **Mississippi Narratives,** part 3, p. 937.

64 **"Let that be an example to you":** Rawick, **The American Slave,** supplement series 1, vol. 7, **Mississippi Narratives,** part 2, pp. 529–31.

64 **"kind and good":** Rawick, **The American Slave,** supplement series 1, vol. 10, **Mississippi Narratives,** part 5, pp. 2262–71; a classic example of masters who treated their slaves with relative decency was Thomas and Hugh Auld, the masters of Frederick Douglass.

65 **largest slaveholders for miles:** U.S. Slave Schedules, 1860, Covington and Jones Counties; Bynum, notes on interview with Ethel Knight, Mississippi Oral History Project, University of Southern Mississippi.

65 **perhaps she was simply kind:** For a genealogical chart of Rachel's children and grandchildren, see Bynum, **The Free State of Jones,** pp. 206–207. Jackie Knight's deeds of slaves to his children are found in Thomas, et al., **The Family of John "Jackie" Knight and Keziah Davis Knight,** pp. 337–38.

65 **"eight or ten of them when my grand-daddy was alive":** U.S. Federal Census, 1860; quotation from the address by J. M. Knight to the Rainey Community Meeting, June 10, 1926, Lauren Rogers Museum, Laurel, Miss.; Bynum, notes on interview with Ethel Knight, Mississippi Oral History Project, University of Southern Mississippi.

66 **near to him in age:** Typescripts of deeds found in Thomas, et al., **The Family of John "Jackie" Knight and Keziah Davis Knight,** pp. 337–38.

66 **That which commands admiration:** Deborah Gray White, **Ar'nt I a Woman** (New York: W. W. Norton and Co., 1999), p. 96.

66 **The whites who truly ruled Rachel's life:** Ibid., pp. 6, 97–100, 114; Elizabeth Fox Genovese, **Within the Plantation Household** (Chapel Hill: University of North Carolina Press, 1988), p. 103.

66 **As Rachel's children grew old enough:** Genovese, **Within the Plantation Household,** pp. 150–52.

67 **as Newton would discover:** Steven Hahn, **A Nation Under Our Feet** (Cambridge, Mass.: Belknap Press of Harvard University, 2003), p. 4.

67 **"suited their purpose to do so":** John Blassingame, ed., **Slave**

Testimony: Two Centuries of Letters, Speeches, Interviews, and Autobiographies (Baton Rouge: Louisiana State University Press, 1977), pp. 373–79.

67 **bartering and selling her goods:** Hahn, **A Nation Under Our Feet,** p. 4.

67 **There was a lingering hint:** Genovese, **Within the Plantation Household,** p. 116. Information on Rachel's independence and her ability as a folk doctor is from the authors' interview with Dorothy Knight Marsh, Washington, D.C., June 28, 2006. The notion that Rachel dabbled in spells is from the authors' phone interview with Knight descendant Kecia Carter, January 22, 2008. "They used to tell weird stories about Rachel," she said. "They tried to say she voodooed Newt." Also, from Ethel Knight, **Echo of the Black Horn,** p. 263.

67 **lumps of cornmeal to stretch it:** Rawick, **The American Slave,** supplement series 1, vol. 10, **Mississippi Narratives,** part 5, William Wheeler, Leflore County, p. 2272.

68 **a slave from Monroe County remembered:** Hahn, **A Nation Under Our Feet,** pp. 7, 41, 55.

68 **fear of violent slave revolts:** Hahn, **Roots of Southern Populism,** pp. 116–17, quotation from p. 117; Thomas D. Cockrell and Michael B. Ballard, eds., **Chickasaw: A Mississippi Scout for the Union: The Civil War Memoir of Levi H. Naron as Recounted by R. W. Surby** (Baton Rouge: Louisiana State University Press, 2005), p. 19; Harvey Wish, "The Slave Insurrection Panic of 1856," **The Journal of Southern History** 5:2 (May 1939): 206–22.

69 **seized a whip and flogged him:** Aughey, **Tupelo,** p. 199.

69 **"different political parties":** Hahn, **A Nation Under Our Feet,** p. 65.

69 **Jeffrey was the issue:** On the 1880 U.S. Federal Census manu-

script for Jasper County, Rachel gave her age as forty, and Jeff
E. Knight gave his age as twenty-one. This information is consistent with all other census reports save for 1870.

70   **If so, he had good reason:** Last will and testament of John
"Jackie" Knight; it was perhaps a sign of Jackie's esteem that
Jesse Davis Knight was named co-executor of the estate, along
with Altimirah's husband, George Brumfield. The suggestion
that Newton first took an interest in Rachel before the war
comes from Knight family genealogist Martha Welborn, who
heard it from Rachel's descendants; interview with authors,
March 29, 2008.

70   **as cash property:** Last will and testament of John Knight.
Fanny Knight in 1882 identified her father as Davis Knight
when she joined the Church of Latter Day Saints; see Records
of the Church of Jesus Christ of Latter Day Saints, Southern
States Mission Records of Missionaries, Records of Admissions,
1878–1888, a copy of which is in the possession of the authors.
The fact that Jesse Davis was Jeffrey Knight's father was also
publicly suggested during the 1948 trial of a younger Davis
Knight, this one a grandson of Newton and Rachel, for the
crime of miscegenation, details of which are contained in the
final chapter of this book. Defense attorney Quitman Ross asserted to Henry Knight, son of Jeffrey and grandson of Rachel,
"Your grandfather was old Davis Knight, wasn't he?" Henry
Knight appeared ignorant as to his white Knight lineage. However, he did testify that Jeffrey and younger sister Fannie were
full brother and sister. See transcript of **The State of Mississippi v. Davis Knight,** December 13, 1948, Circuit Court of
the First Judicial District of Jones County.

70   **for, or against, secession:** Claiborne, in "A Trip Through the
Piney Woods," describes a political rally in the town of New
Augusta.

70   **"in Judea":** Bettersworth, **Confederate Mississippi,** p. 1; Bettersworth, **Mississippi in the Confederacy,** pp. 21–22.

71   **"Lord deliver us!":** Bettersworth, **Mississippi in the Confederacy,** p. 341.

72   **glares and murmurs:** The examples of fire-breathing secession speeches are quoted from Aughey, **Tupelo,** pp. 5–6.

72   **"they were all anti secession":** Knight, **The Life and Activities of Captain Newton Knight,** p. 87; testimony of Joel E. Welborn in **Newton Knight et al. v. United States,** Congressional Case 8013-8464.

72   **sex with a marc:** Bynum, **The Free State of Jones,** pp. 6, 83–84.

72   **"cannot stand":** Interview with Ben Sumrall, August 21, 1936, WPA Collection, Jones County, record group 60, vol. 315, MDAH. On Lincoln's paraphrasing the Bible and Aesop's fables in his "House Divided" argument, see John Stauffer, **Giants: The Parallel Lives of Frederick Douglass and Abraham Lincoln** (New York: Twelve, 2008), p. 211.

73   **tell the convention so:** Knight, **The Life and Activities of Captain Newton Knight,** p. 87.

73   **politics and the state convention:** Bettersworth, **Mississippi in the Confederacy,** pp. 4–5; Freehling, **The Road to Disunion,** pp. 338–41, 445–62.

73   **"commerce of the earth":** "A Declaration of the Immediate Causes Which Induce and Justify the Secession of the State of Mississippi from the Federal Union," **Journal of the Minutes of the Mississippi Secession Convention,** January 1861, p. 3.

74   **second state to secede, after South Carolina:** For a summary, see McPherson, **Battle Cry of Freedom,** pp. 234–75, map on p. 236.

74   **field of blue:** Bettersworth, **Confederate Mississippi,** pp. 7–11, 30–33; James W. Silver, ed., **Mississippi in the Confed-**

eracy as Seen in Retrospect (Baton Rouge: Louisiana State University Press, 1961), pp. 16–21, quotations from pp. 17, 21; Bynum, **The Free State of Jones,** p. 98; Leverett, **The Legend of the Free State of Jones,** pp. 38–41. Bynum refers to Powell as "John H. Powell," Leverett as "J. D. Powell." We follow Bynum, whose sources are much better documented.

75   **"Single Star!":** Bettersworth, **Mississippi in the Confederacy,** pp. 31–32; Bettersworth, **Confederate Mississippi,** pp. 9–12.

75   **"cause in which they believed":** Frost, "The South's Strangest Army Revealed by Chief"; interview with Ben Sumrall, August 21, 1936, WPA Collection, Jones County, record group 60, vol. 315, MDAH.

75   **disloyalists, and traitors:** Leverett, **The Legend of the Free State of Jones,** p. 39; Bynum, **The Free State of Jones,** pp. 103–4.

75   **defend federal property:** Lincoln, "First Inaugural Address, March 4, 1861," in **Great Speeches** (New York: Dover Publications, 1991), p. 61; William M. Wiecek, **The Sources of Antislavery Constitutionalism in America, 1760–1848** (Ithaca: Cornell University Press, 1977), pp. 276–77; McPherson, **Battle Cry of Freedom,** pp. 246–75.

76   **"would like to shoot a Yankee":** William L. Nugent to Eleanor Smith Nugent, August 19, 1861, in Cash and Howorth, **My Dear Nellie,** p. 46.

76   **"get the big guns on":** M. P. Bush, address to the meeting of the DAR, February 17, 1912, Lauren Rogers Museum, Laurel, Miss.

76   **two men to desertion:** War Department Collection of Confederate Records, RG 109, 27th Mississippi Infantry, microfilm (M269), NARA; Leverett, **The Legend of the Free State of Jones,** pp. 64–67.

77   **"no contrary opinion":** Aughey, **Tupelo,** p. 25.

78   **no husbands to help:** The Piney Woods farewell barbecue is described by former slave Elsie Posey in Rawick, **The American Slave,** supplement series 1, vol. 10, **Mississippi Narratives,** part 4, p. 1735.

78   **prison in Virginia:** M. Shannon Mallard, "I Had No Comfort to Give the People," **North and South** 6:4 (May 2003), pp. 78–85; Foner, "The South's Inner Civil War."

79   **"into their hands":** Aughey, **Tupelo,** p. 106.

79   **"towards the national government":** Foner, "The South's Inner Civil War."

79   **"Such be the doom of all traitors":** Aughey, **Tupelo,** p. 27.

80   **"as long as a southren lives":** McPherson, **For Cause and Comrades,** p. 23.

80   **enrollment can be guessed at:** Jean Strickland and Patricia Edwards, eds., **Records of Jasper County** (Moss Point, Miss: n.p., 1995), pp. 131–32.

81   **"under guard":** Testimony of B. F. Moss in **Newton Knight et al. v. United States,** Congressional Case 8013-8464. Moss testified against Newton in his attempt to be recompensed as a Union soldier. Newton's lawyer recited the story of the horse while cross-examining Moss and asked him if Knight was brought into the company "under guard." Moss said he didn't recall either incident.

81   **"burned by his enemies":** Deposition of W. M. Welch in **Newton Knight et al. v. United States,** Congressional Case 8013-8464.

81   **"left his family destitute":** Sworn deposition of John Mathews, H. L. Sumrall, Allen Valentine, James Hinton, and Madison Harrington, October 15, 1870, Accompanying Papers, H.R. 1814, Newton Knight File, record group 233, box 16, NARA.

81 **urgent family matter:** Strickland and Edwards, **Records of Jasper County,** pp. 131–32; testimony of B. F. Moss, **Newton Knight et al. v. United States** congressional case 8013-8464. During the questioning of Moss, Knight's lawyer contended that the discharge was the result of a special plea from back home. Moss could not recall the reason for it, but this is the most plausible explanation.

81 **twelve-year-old Taylor:** U.S. Federal Census, Jones County, 1860.

82 **"other people's business":** Knight, **The Life and Activities of Captain Newton Knight,** p. 36.

82 **"Everybody was afraid of him":** B. D. Graves, address to the Hebron Community, June 17, 1926, Lauren Rogers Museum, Laurel, Miss.; U.S. Federal Census, Jones County, 1860. Graves referred to Martha's husband as "Bill Morgan" but he was probably mistaken about the name. According to Victoria Bynum in **The Free State of Jones,** there were two William Morgans in the area, father and son, but the elder Morgan was a married, forty-year-old farmer in 1860, and the son lived until 1926. Kenneth Welch believes the only "Morgan" in the county who fit the age and criminal description of Martha's husband is Morgan Lines.

82 **"my mother got tired of it and told my father":** Knight, **The Life and Activities of Captain Newton Knight,** pp. 36–37.

82 **"slip up on him and kill him":** B. D. Graves, address to the Hebron Community, June 17, 1926, Lauren Rogers Museum, Laurel, Miss.

83 **"we never were whipped any more":** Knight, **The Life and Activities of Captain Newton Knight,** pp. 36–37.

83 **didn't see who fired the shot:** B. D. Graves, address to the Hebron Community, June 17, 1926, Lauren Rogers Museum, Laurel, Miss.

83 **"He was a desperado":** Ibid.

84 **he demanded killing:** U.S. Federal Census, Jones County, 1870.

85 **"steer clear of the burning masses":** Wickham Hoffman, **Camp, Court and Siege** (New York: Harper and Brothers, 1877), pp. 35–37.

CHAPTER 3: THE SWAMP AND THE CITADEL

Page

86 **full of tadpoles:** Description is from Aughey, **Tupelo,** p. 203. Although we do not have explicit evidence that Newton walked rather than took a train or rode a horse back to Jones County, our interpretation of him walking back is consistent with accounts from other fugitives in the Deep South at the time. See John H. Aughey, **Tupelo;** Aughey, **The Iron Furnace: Or, Slavery and Secession** (1865; reprint, New York: Negro Universities Press, 1969); Surby, Chickasaw; Storey, **Loyalty and Loss;** John Roy Lynch, **Reminiscences of an Active Life: The Autobiography of John Roy Lynch,** John Hope Franklin, ed. (Chicago: University of Chicago Press, 1970); William Baxter, **Pea Ridge and Prairie Grove, or, Scenes and Incidents of the War in Arkansas,** William L. Shea, ed. (1864; reprint, Fayetteville: University of Arkansas Press, 2000); Inscoe and Kenzer, eds., **Enemies of the Country,** essays by Keith S. Bohannon, Thomas G. Dyer, and William Warren Rogers Jr., pp. 97–120, 121–47, 172–87; Blight, **A Slave No More.**

87 **"What shall I do with them?":** David W. Blight, **A Slave No More,** p. 73.

87 **"Kill, slay & murder them":** Cash and Howorth, **My Dear Nellie,** p. 74.

87 **"yelping dogs":** Aughey, **Tupelo,** p. 130.

88 "wondrous kind": Ibid., p. 126.

88 eluding the dogs: Ibid., p. 203.

88 "one and inseparable": Ibid., pp. 22–25.

89 "loud . . . and deep": Ibid., p. 83.

89 clandestinely fed and cared for: Ibid., p. 47.

90 crossed trails with a runaway slave: Ibid., p. 131.

90 "run it's almost day": Ibid., p. 120.

90 "God carved in ebony": Ibid., p. 147.

91 shot on the spot: Blight, **A Slave No More,** p. 70.

91 "they gloried in my spunk": Ibid., p. 58.

91 use him for target practice: Ibid., p. 75; Turnage made multiple unsuccessful attempts to escape to Union lines. His owner finally took him to Mobile and left him in a slave trader's yard, where he was auctioned to the highest bidder and sold for two thousand dollars, to Collier Minge, nephew of former president William Henry Harrison. Turnage ran away yet again and this time made it to Union lines near Mobile. He served as a cook in the Union army and after the war moved to New York.

91 lice even in his beard: Lice and lack of decent clothing were the most common complaints of Confederate soldiers other than the quality of their food. See Bell Irvin Wiley, **The Life of Johnny Reb,** p. 250, and Commager, **The Civil War Archive,** p. 221.

92 no quick end in sight to the war: From 1861, when the Confederate Congress authorized the issue of treasury notes, to the beginning of 1861, inflation devalued Confederate currency by a factor of 7.62. We estimate a threefold devaluation by mid-1862. See McPherson, **Ordeal by Fire,** p. 202.

93 overworked old deadhead: Knight, **The Life and Activities of Captain Newton Knight,** pp. 42, 58.

93 "stand for such conduct and not resent it": Knight, **The Life and Activities of Captain Newton Knight,** pp. 57–60.

93   **less profitable food crops:** Foner, "The South's Inner Civil War"; the prime example of planters insulating themselves economically was James Lusk Alcorn, who served eighteen months in uniform before returning to his plantation to smuggle cotton and invest in Union currency. Alcorn sacrificed in other ways, however: he would lose two sons in the war.

93   **"permits their wives and children to starve":** Bettersworth, **Mississippi in the Confederacy,** p. 101.

94   **"encouraging these things":** War Department Collection of Confederate Records, RG 109, Compiled Service Records, 7th Battalion, Mississippi Infantry, microfilm (M269), NARA; Bynum, **The Free State of Jones,** p. 103.

94   **"they'd really shoot me?":** Weitz, **More Damning Than Slaughter,** p. 233; Bynum, Notes on Interviews with Earle Knight, Mississippi Oral History Project, University of Southern Mississippi; Robert E. Lee to Jefferson Davis, April 13, 1864, quoted in Commager, **The Civil War Archive,** pp. 348–49.

94   **to punish chattel:** McPherson, **For Cause and Comrades,** p. 51.

95   **and then a long wail:** Bettersworth, **Confederate Mississippi,** pp. 257–60; Simon Winchester, **The Professor and the Madman: A Tale of Murder, Insanity, and the Making of the Oxford English Dictionary** (New York: Harper Perennial, 1999), pp. 57–61, quotation from p. 61.

95   **enfeebled shuffle:** Aughey, **Tupelo,** p. 72.

95   **routine part of camp life:** Commager, "A Confederate Surgeon's Letters to His Wife," **The Civil War Archive,** p. 347.

95   **return to their units:** Weitz, **More Damning than Slaughter,** pp. 203–204; Bynum, **The Free State of Jones,** p. 104.

95   **"for my services or not":** Quoted from Bynum, **The Free State of Jones,** p. 104.

96   **AWOL soldiers in Newton's unit:** Leverett, **The Legend of the Free State of Jones,** p. 58.

96   **reserved for the most defiant resisters:** Deposition of John Mathews, H. L. Sumrall, Allen Valentine, James Hinton, and Madison Harrington, October 14, 1870, Accompanying Papers, H. R. 1814, Newton Knight file, record group 233, box 16, NARA.

96   **"he wept—he wept!":** On treatment of those who resisted see Commager, "Punishments in the Union and Confederate Armies," **The Civil War Archive,** pp. 343–46; Aughey, **Tupelo,** pp. 106–112; Leverett, **The Legend of the Free State of Jones,** p. 58; and McPherson, **For Cause and Comrades,** p. 53.

96   **"uniformly" as the war went on:** Bynum, notes on interviews with Earle Knight, Mississippi Oral History Project, University of Southern Mississippi; Robert E. Lee to Jefferson Davis, April 13, 1864, quoted in Commager, **The Civil War Archive,** pp. 348–49.

97   **was then filled with earth:** Aughey, **Tupelo,** p. 112. For other firsthand accounts of Confederate executions in 1863, see Commager, "Executing Deserters," **The Civil War Archive,** p. 346.

97   **loose from the Southern cause:** War Department Collection of Confederate Records, RG 109, Compiled Service Records, 7th Battalion, Mississippi Infantry, microfilm (M269), NARA.

97   **punching through the Chickasaw Bayou: OR,** supplement, part 2, Record of Events, vol. 33 (Mississippi, Conf.), pp. 101–109; Michael Ballard, **Vicksburg, The Campaign That Opened the Mississippi** (Chapel Hill, London: University of North Carolina Press, 2004), p. 133.

98   **But the Yankees would be back:** For a fuller account of Sher-

man's expedition against the bluffs, see Ballard, **Vicksburg,** pp. 132–46.

98   **"hardly a friend left, except myself":** Bettersworth, **Mississippi in the Confederacy,** p. 251; Harry J. Maihafer, **War of Words, Lincoln and the Civil War** (Washington, D.C.: Brassey's Inc., 2001), p. 91; McPherson, **Ordeal by Fire,** vol. 2, p. 337.

98   **straight into the main entrenchments:** Ballard, **Vicksburg,** p. 213.

99   **seems plausible that he did too:** For detailed reports and descriptions of Confederate movements, see **OR,** series 1, vol. 24/2; War Department Collection of Confederate Records, RG 109, Compiled Service Records, 7th Battalion, Mississippi Infantry, microfilm (M269), NARA. There is no absolute proof that Newton was in Vicksburg, and a case can be made that he was not. In his few statements after the war he made no reference to it. However, Newton was purposely vague on the subject of his Confederate experiences—he never talked about Corinth or his first enlistment either. It was in his best interest to minimize his rebel service as he pursued a federal pension as a Union soldier, and he tended to be purposely vague about the facts of his stay in the Confederate army. "I left it pretty soon after they got me, but I cannot remember the date," he said. "I never served any more." Deposition of Newton Knight in **Newton Knight et al. v. United States,** Congressional Case 8013-8464. The recollections of others are hardly more helpful. Joel E. Welborn, in his testimony in the pension case, recalled that Newton deserted in "August 1862." This was impossible; Newton had only just been conscripted into the unit, and his record shows him present and receiving regular promotions until after Corinth. Welborn may well have meant August of 1863.

Another acquaintance in the 7th Mississippi Battalion, O. C. Martin, believed Newton left from Snyder's Bluff. But Martin served in a different company, and his knowledge of Newton's service was sketchy at best, and at times erroneous. The most persuasive evidence that Newton deserted before Vicksburg is a deposition provided by some of Newton's friends in his Union pension case stating their belief that he came home in May. But they may have wanted to aid him by understating his time in rebel uniform. See the deposition of John Mathews, H. L. Sumrall, Allen Valentine, James Hinton, and Madison Harrington, October 15, 1870, Accompanying Papers, H. R. 1814, Newton Knight file, record group 233, box 16, NARA. We believe, given his arrest, the strategic conditions, the difficult landscape and number of troops around Vicksburg, and the fact that all of his friends and relatives were there, that he too suffered through Vicksburg. The Vicksburg trauma might also explain his subsequent psychological transformation from a passive deserter to a violent anti-Confederate guerrilla.

99   **"a sort of waste heap":** Ballard, **Vicksburg,** p. 1.

100   **drowned 129 of them in the river:** Ibid., p. 4.

100   **"two halves together":** Ballard, **Vicksburg,** pp. 1–4; Vicksburg National Military Park, http://www.nps.gov/archive/vick/vcmpgn/key.htm; William L. Shea and Terrence Winschel, **Vicksburg Is the Key: The Struggle for the Mississippi River** (Lincoln: University of Nebraska Press, 2003), p. vii.

101   **"I never could see the end clearly until now":** Shelby Foote, **The Civil War,** vol. 2, p. 380; McPherson, **Battle Cry of Freedom,** p. 631.

101   **it sounded disconsolate:** McPherson, **Battle Cry of Freedom,** p. 630.

102   **he would come to the rescue:** Ballard, **Vicksburg,** p. 86; Bettersworth, **Mississippi in the Confederacy,** p. 137.

102 **backbreaking victories of the war at Vicksburg:** Ballard, **Vicksburg,** p. 308; Foote, **The Civil War,** vol. 2, pp. 381–82.

103 **"works built of timber":** Civil War diary of George C. Burmeister, 35th Iowa, Civil War Collection, Military History Institute, Carlisle Barracks, Pa.

103 **mood of the blue troops:** Foote, **The Civil War,** vol. 2, p. 381.

104 **"lopped gently upon us":** Ibid., pp. 381–82.

104 **administering just 200 or so:** Ballard, **Vicksburg,** p. 330.

104 **"I would say one week":** Foote, **The Civil War,** vol. 2, p. 388.

105 **a penchant for war reporting:** "Anson Hemingway, A Legacy of War Reporting," **Military Images,** January–February 2000, online at http://find articles.com/p/articles/mi_qa3905/is_/ai_n8887767; Lydia Minturn Post, **Soldiers' Letters from Camps, Battlefields and Prisons** (New York: Bunce and Huntington, 1865), p. 366.

105 **"why don't they order us to charge":** McPherson, **For Cause and Comrades,** p. 38.

105 **fuses rolled down upon them:** Civil War diary of George Burmeister, Civil War Collection, MHI, Carlisle Barracks, Pa.

105 **There would be no more assaults:** Ballard, **Vicksburg,** pp. 338–48; Foote, **The Civil War,** vol. 2, p. 385.

106 **"God save him":** Ballard, **Vicksburg,** p. 349; Civil War diary of George Burmeister, Civil War Collection, MHI, Carlisle Barracks, Pa.

106 **a gigantic swarming anthill:** Roberts and Moneyhon, **Portraits of Conflict,** p. 262.

106 **"I feel dirty and lazy":** Civil War diary of George Burmeister, Civil War Collection, MHI, Carlisle Barracks, Pa.

107 **"your beans have gone to hell":** Roberts and Moneyhon, **Portraits of Conflict,** p. 262.

107 **"dodge the shells":** "A Woman's Diary of the Siege of Vicksburg," **The Century Illustrated Monthly Magazine,** vol. 8, May–October 1885, pp. 768–74.

107 **cool the guns:** "A Woman's Diary of the Siege of Vicksburg," pp. 768–74; Civil War diary of George Burmeister, Civil War Collection, MHI, Carlisle Barracks, Pa.

107 **"$50 bills anywhere in camp":** "A Woman's Diary of the Siege of Vicksburg"; Memoirs of Lewis F. Phillips, Civil War Collection, MHI, Carlisle Barracks, Pa.

108 **printed on strips of wallpaper:** Ballard, **Vicksburg,** pp. 349–50; "A Woman's Diary of the Siege of Vicksburg," pp. 768–74.

108 **faux restaurant menu:** Commager, **The Civil War Archive,** pp. 449–50.

109 **"jest on such fare":** Ibid.

110 **tasted like green dust:** Allan Nevins, **The War for the Union: The Organized War, 1863–1864** (New York: Charles Scribner's Sons, 1971), p. 72; Bettersworth, **Mississippi in the Confederacy,** p. 134.

110 **Men were so emaciated:** Victoria Bynum, notes on interviews with Earle Knight, great-grandson of Newton Knight, June 28–30, 1994, Mississippi Oral History Project, University of Southern Mississippi, vol. 698; Ballard, **Vicksburg,** p. 399.

110 **"unless it can be fed":** MANY SOLDIERS to General J. C. Pemberton, June 28, 1863, **OR,** series 1, vol. 24, part 3, pp. 982–83.

110 **"their bodies are worn out":** Hébert to Major-General Forney, July 2, 1863; **OR,** series 1, vol. 24, part 3, pp. 982–93.

111 **"Sleek horses, polished arms":** Roberts and Moneyhon, **Portraits of Conflict,** p. 221; "A Woman's Diary of the Siege of Vicksburg," pp. 768–74.

111 **the long siege was over:** Shelby Foote, **The Civil War,** vol. 2, p. 427.

111   **goods in both arms:** Grant, **Personal Memoirs,** p. 278; Roberts and Moneyhon, **Portraits of Conflict,** p. 290.

112   **clothes would have to be burned:** Diary of Edward Dean, 4th Wisconsin, Civil War Collection, MHI, Carlisle Barracks, Pa.

112   **"Grant is my man":** Foote, **The Civil War,** vol. 2, pp. 623–25; Brooks D. Simpson, **Ulysses S. Grant: Triumph Over Adversity, 1822–1865** (New York: Houghton Mifflin, 2000), p. 215.

112   **"we had a fool for a general":** Ballard, **Vicksburg,** pp. 398–99; "A Woman's Diary of the Siege of Vicksburg," pp. 768–74.

112   **equal number of Union prisoners:** Grant, **Personal Memoirs,** p. 313.

113   **to prison camps:** McPherson, **Ordeal by Fire,** pp. 330–31; Grant, **Personal Memoirs,** pp. 308–10.

113   **"much account again, as an army":** Foote, **The Civil War,** p. 625.

114   **didn't wait for papers:** Leverett, **The Legend of the Free State of Jones,** p. 58.

114   **"precisely what I expected":** Grant, **Personal Memoirs,** p. 314.

114   **repeated Confederate orders:** Grant, **Personal Memoirs,** p. 377; Arnold, **Grant Wins the War,** pp. 298–99.

114   **finally returned to uniform:** McPherson, **Ordeal by Fire,** pp. 330–31; Lincoln's Emancipation Proclamation did not emancipate all the slaves. But by the summer of 1863 the federal government was taking steps to end slavery in every state. See for example McPherson, **Ordeal by Fire,** pp. 292, 300–301, 309–15, 330–34, 346–53, 358–67; McPherson, **Battle Cry of Freedom,** pp. 490–510, 684–88; Bynum, **The Free State of Jones,** p. 105.

115   **"when they met of Gen. Grant":** Knight, **The Life and Activities of Captain Newton Knight,** p. 88.

115 **"I am his the rest of the war"**: McPherson, **Ordeal by Fire,**
quotation from Lincoln on p. 332. See Knight, **The Life and
Activities of Captain Newton Knight,** pp. 97–98.

116 **"incompetence of our officers"**: Letters of Walter A. Rorer,
Civil War Collection, MHI, Carlisle Barracks, Pa.

CHAPTER 4: THE HOUNDS

Page

117 **feather mattress in a swamp:** Civil War diary of George C.
Burmeister, Civil War Collection, MHI, Carlisle Barracks, Pa.

118 **"perish beneath its waters"**: Bettersworth, **Mississippi in the
Confederacy,** p. 150.

118 **"a great amount of the stock"**: Roberts and Moneyhon, **Portraits of Conflict,** p. 275.

119 **curtains for tents:** Bettersworth, **Mississippi in the Confederacy,** pp. 210–12.

119 **"dear to every man in the regiment"**: **OR,** supplement, part
2, vol. 33, p. 598. Walter Rorer was promoted steadily throughout the war from captain to lieutenant-colonel.

119 **"now worth nothing"**: Walter A. Rorer to his cousin Susan,
June 13, 1863, Civil War Collection, MHI, Carlisle Barracks,
Pa.

120 **"our beloved country is bleeding"**: Walter A. Rorer to his
cousin Susan, August 25, 1863, Civil War Collection, MHI,
Carlisle Barracks, Pa.

121 **"given to the flames"**: **OR,** series 1, vol. 24, part 2, p. 517.

121 **Her continual physical exhaustion:** Bell Irvin Wiley, **The
Plain People of the Confederacy** (Baton Rouge: Louisiana
State University Press, 1944), pp. 67–69.

121 **"The ways of Zion"**: Ibid., p. 62.

122 **"I set down to rite you afew lins"**: Ibid., p. 42.

122 **Instead of aid from the government:** Storey, **Loyalty and Loss,** pp. 84, 106–7.

123 **"that her god dam'd Yankee husband":** Storey, **Loyalty and Loss,** pp. 106–7.

123 **"Yankees have unhinged things terribly":** Cash and Somerville, **My Dear Nellie,** p. 137.

123 **"no room for them":** Arnold, **Grant Wins the War,** p. 299; Bettersworth, **Confederate Mississippi,** pp. 204–205, 220; **OR,** series 4, vol. 2, p. 717.

124 **the officer noted with alarm:** Weitz, **More Damning than Slaughter,** p. 275.

124 **self-described Unionists:** Arnold, **Grant Wins the War,** p. 299; Bettersworth, **Confederate Mississippi,** pp. 204–212.

124 **"shot down from the wayside":** Letter to Governor Pettus from Henry Carre and D. W. Johnston, April 29, 1863, as quoted in Suzanne Spell, "A History of Jones County" (n.p., 1961), Special Collections, Mitchell Memorial Library, Mississippi State University.

125 **"stealing everything they can get their hands on":** Lieutenant Harmon Mathis to his Excellency John J. Pettus, June 1, 1863, as quoted in Spell, "A History of Jones County."

126 **smears of blood on the ground:** Wiley, **The Life of Johnny Reb,** pp. 116–18.

126 **Measles disabled men:** Ibid., pp. 250–51.

126 **"Oaths, blasphemies, imprecations":** William L. Nugent to his wife, May 2, 1863, Cash and Somerville, **My Dear Nellie,** pp. 110–17.

127 **"my own personal ruin":** Cash and Somerville, **My Dear Nellie,** pp. 117, 168; for a riveting survey of the motivations of soldiers on both sides, see McPherson, **For Cause and Comrades.**

127   **many of them needed socks:** William L. Nugent to his wife,
       March 24, 1863, Cash and Somerville, **My Dear Nellie,** p. 95;
       Walter A. Rorer to his cousin Susan, November 12, 1863, Civil
       War Collection, MHI, Carlisle Barracks, Pa.

128   **"Everybody thought you were dead!":** Recollections of an un-
       named Jones County soldier, WPA Collection, Jones County,
       box 10729, MDAH.

128   **"I'm feeling for a furlough":** Wiley, **The Life of Johnny Reb,**
       p. 131.

128   **until the war ended:** Knight, **The Life and Activities of Cap-
       tain Newton Knight,** p. 51.

129   **firing squads were causing comment:** For a summary of the
       Confederate desertion epidemic, see Weitz, **More Damning
       than Slaughter,** pp. 204–206.

129   **"before the trouble can be stopped":** Commager, **The Civil
       War Archive,** p. 347.

130   **"If I had captured him":** Foote, **The Civil War,** vol. 1,
       p. 214.

130   **bring the men in by force:** Leverett, **The Legend of the Free
       State of Jones,** p. 62.

131   **McLemore was rewarded with a promotion:** Rudy H. Lever-
       ett, "Biographical Sketch of Amos McLemore," **Clarion-Ledger,**
       November 29–30, 1977.

131   **he knew many of the missing men personally:** Leverett, **The
       Legend of the Free State of Jones,** p. 62. To back up Mc-
       Lemore, the Conscription Bureau detached Company F of the
       26th Mississippi Infantry, known as the Ann Terry Guards, for
       special duty to arrest and guard "deserters, stragglers, absentees
       and conscripts" in the Piney Woods.

131   **for return to their regiments:** Leverett, **The Legend of the
       Free State of Jones,** pp. 63–65.

132   **"for the intention of speculation":** Bettersworth, **Mississippi in the Confederacy,** p. 290; Wiley, **The Life of Johnny Reb,** p. 135.

133   **"he kept on carrying news":** Knight, **The Life and Activities of Captain Newton Knight,** pp. 73–74.

133   **"I expect to attend to it":** Ibid.

133   **"I can stop that":** Leverett, **The Legend of the Free State of Jones,** pp. 64–65; Bynum, notes on interviews with Earle Knight, grandson of William Knight, who was cousin to Newton and a member of the Knight band, as well as a Union soldier, June 28–30, 1994, Mississippi Oral History Project, University of Southern Mississippi; Knight, **The Echo of the Black Horn** (1951; reprint, Ellisville, Miss., 1976), p. 166.

133   **the rude farmhouses:** Bynum, **The Free State of Jones,** p. 67; Leverett, **The Legend of the Free State of Jones,** pp. 63–64.

134   **McLemore's voice:** Bynum, notes on interviews with Earle Knight; Knight, **The Life and Activities of Captain Newton Knight,** pp. 73–74.

134   **Confederates conversing:** Bynum, notes on interviews with Earle Knight, Mississippi Oral History Project, University of Southern Mississippi.

134   **into the squalling night:** Bynum, notes on interviews with Earle Knight, Mississippi Oral History Project, University of Southern Mississippi; Leverett, **The Legend of the Free State of Jones,** p. 64. Leverett's version of McLemore's killing comes from a letter by T. C. Carter, a fellow soldier and former student of McLemore's who was with him when he was wounded at Perryville. Carter wrote a brief sketch of McLemore for the **Hattiesburg American** newspaper in 1914 and confirmed that he was shot by the fireside in Deason's home while visiting with officers and friends.

135 **"gathering up conscripts and deserters"**: The Daily Dis-patch, October 21, 1863; The Louisville Daily Journal, November 11, 1863.

135 **"One of the three shot him"**: Knight, The Life and Activities of Captain Newton Knight, pp. 73–74.

135 **visiting with fellow officers**: " 'Robin Hood' Traitor Newt Legend Lives On," Clarion-Ledger, October 5, 1977.

136 **"I think it's the hinge"**: Ibid.

136 **"the killing of a senior Confederate officer"**: Leverett, The Legend of the Free State of Jones, p. 65.

136 **"a quasi-political force"**: Ibid., p. 65. By the summer of 1863 the federal government was taking steps to end slavery in every state. See for example McPherson, Ordeal by Fire, pp. 292, 300–301, 309–15, 330–34, 346–53, 358–67; McPherson, Battle Cry of Freedom, pp. 490–510, 684–88.

138 **"putting down the rebellion"**: Depositions of Newton Knight and Jasper Collins in Newton Knight et al. v. United States, Congressional Case 8013-8464; interview with Ben Sumrall, August 31, 1936, WPA Collection, Jones County, record group 60, vol. 315, MDAH.

138 **Unionists offering assistance**: Cockrell and Ballard, Chicka-saw, pp. 169–73.

138 **unanimously elected captain**: Depositions of Newton Knight and Jasper Collins in Newton Knight et al. v. United States, Congressional Case 8013-8464; interview with Ben Sumrall, August 31, 1936, WPA Collection, Jones County, record group 60, vol. 315, MDAH.

138 **"to stay together and obey all orders"**: Newton Knight depositions, Newton Knight et al. v. United States, Congressional Case 8013-8464.

139 **"a cause in which they believed"**: Interview with Ben Sum-

rall, August 31, 1936, WPA Collection, Jones County, record group 60, vol. 315, MDAH.

139 **"for the defense of the union":** Depositions of Jasper Collins, R. N. Blackwell, and J. M. Valentine in **Newton Knight et al. v. United States,** Congressional Case 8013-8464. It was in the best interest of these men to stress their Unionism, given that Newton was seeking to have himself and his men compensated as Union soldiers.

139 **"best men in our Country":** General affidavit, February 10, 1898, **Newton Knight et al. v. United States,** Congressional Case 8013-8464.

140 **"organization of such character":** As quoted in Leverett, **The Legend of the Free State of Jones,** p. 17.

140 **"men of honest conviction":** Deposition of Joel E. Welborn in **Newton et al. v. United States,** Congressional Case 8013-8464. Welborn, Newton's Confederate commander, was called to testify in the pension case. Welborn's long enmity with Newton made his assertion that the Knight band were Unionists from principle the more persuasive. "I was inclined to believe and think this from my acquaintance with several of his men," Welborn said, "from intimate neighborship, from men who were regarded as men of honest conviction, and Gentlemen."

140 **"I am a friend to you":** Newton Knight muster roll, circa 1870, Ames Family Papers, Sophia Smith Collection, Five Colleges Archives and Manuscript Collection, Smith College, collection number MS-3; interview with Ben Sumrall, August 31, 1936, WPA Collection, Jones County, MDAH.

141 **sang anthems of the federal cause:** Ethel Knight, **The Echo of the Black Horn,** p. 146. Ethel Knight was one of those neo-Confederates who tended to characterize the Knight band as criminal rather than political, so it's interesting that she as-

serts the men sang Union songs. She also states that the songs were often led by Jasper Collins, which, given his family's ardent Unionism, seems plausible.

141 **"army of the Lord"**: Knight, **The Echo of the Black Horn,** p. 146; John Stauffer, **The Problem of Evil: Slavery, Freedom, and the Ambiguities of American Reform** (Amherst: University of Massachusetts Press, 2007), pp. 288–89; Franny Nudelman, **John Brown's Body: Slavery, Violence, and the Culture of War** (Chapel Hill: University of North Carolina Press, 2004), pp. 1–3.

142 **shoot at the dogs first:** W. C. Morrow, "The Bloodhounds," in **Confederate Battle Stories,** Martin H. Greenberg, Frank D. McSherry, Jr., and Charles G. Waugh, eds. (Little Rock, Ark.: August House Publishers, 1992), pp. 135–47.

142 **through the hill country:** Knight, **The Life and Activities of Captain Newton Knight,** p. 23; Newton Knight deposition, **Newton Knight et al. v. United States,** Congressional Case 8013-8464.

143 **Deserter's Lake:** Knight, **The Echo of the Black Horn,** p. 106; Addie West's notes on the Reddoch section of Jones County, WPA Collection, Jones County, record group 60, vol. 315, MDAH.

143 **evaporated back into the swamps:** Knight, **The Life and Activities of Captain Newton Knight,** p. 23.

143 **shot him down in the yard:** Knight, **The Life and Activities of Captain Newton Knight;** p. 52; Bynum, **The Free State of Jones,** p. 111.

144 **"two severely wounded":** War Department Collection of Confederate Records, RG 109, Compiled Service Records, 26th Mississippi Infantry, microfilm (M269), NARA; deposition of Joel E. Welborn, **Newton Knight et al. v. United States,** Congressional Case 8013-8464; **OR,** supplement, vol. 33, part 2, p. 761.

144   **rounding up deserters:** Bettersworth, **Confederate Mississippi,** p. 260.

145   **"millions of living things":** Solomon Northup, **Twelve Years a Slave** (Stillwell, Kan.: Digireads Books, 2005), p. 59; Knight, **The Echo of the Black Horn,** p. 106.

145   **"those of wild beasts":** Frederick Douglass, "The Heroic Slave," in **Violence in the Black Imagination: Essays and Documents,** ed. Ronald T. Takaki (New York: Oxford University Press, 1993), p. 50.

145   **"laws they so much need":** Letter from H. C. Clock to his brother Warren, February 15, 1863, Leslie Anders Collection, MHI, Carlisle Barracks, Pa.

146   **other fugitive memoirs:** According to the volume of Knight genealogy collected by his descendants, **The Family of John "Jackie" Knight and Keziah Davis Knight,** Joe Hatton belonged to Newton's uncle William Knight and also aided William's son Dickie Knight, an ardent Unionist who eventually went to New Orleans to join the Union army. Ethel Knight similarly describes Joe Hatton as helping Newton survive in the swamps and considering himself a fellow soldier of Newton's in **The Echo of the Black Horn,** p. 122.

146   **"more fatal than that of the rattlesnake":** Northup, **Twelve Years a Slave,** pp. 58–59. We have drawn from numerous sources to describe the experience of living in the Piney Woods swamps; the most important are Northup, **Twelve Years a Slave,** pp. 55–66; and Street, **Look Away!,** pp. 39–51. Northup notes that slaves had a competitive advantage in the swamps since whites had not learned how to survive in them.

146   **"in a crooked race":** Northup, **Twelve Years a Slave,** pp. 58–59; Knight, **The Echo of the Black Horn,** p. 106.

147   **"preferred dog flesh":** Commager, **The Civil War Archive,** p. 541.

147 **door would fall shut:** Northup, **Twelve Years a Slave,** p. 81.

147 **to secure her freedom:** Interview with Barbara Black-ledge, great-granddaughter of Newton and Rachel, March 29, 2008, Ellisville, Miss., interview with Dorothy Knight Marsh, great-granddaughter of Newton and Rachel, Washington, D.C., June 28, 2008; phone interview with Jules Smith, great-granddaughter of Newton and Rachel, April 6, 2008; Bynum, notes on interviews with Earle Knight, Mississippi Oral History Project, University of Southern Mississippi.

148 **his eyes and ears:** Interviews with Barbara Blackledge, Dorothy Knight Marsh, Jules Smith.

148 **poisons in the dog food:** Ethel Knight, **The Echo of the Black Horn,** p. 174.

148 **"lead poisoning":** For more on slaves collaborating with white fugitives, see Aughey, **Tupelo,** p. 124; Knight, **The Echo of the Black Horn,** p. 174; Frost, "The South's Strangest Army Revealed by Chief."

148 **free slaves from bondage:** Knight, **The Echo of the Black Horn,** p. 75. Although Ethel Knight's account is at times unreliable and some of her scenes clearly fictionalized, it's difficult to dismiss her as a source altogether on the subject of Rachel. She alone among historians acknowledged the relationship between Newton and Rachel, and she also recognized that women and blacks aided and in some cases fought alongside the Jones County band.

148 **armed with pistols:** Blight, **A Slave No More,** p. 70.

149 **"Many a god bless you":** Diary of George C. Burmeister, May 11, 1863, Civil War Collection, MHI, Carlisle Barracks, Pa.

149 **Another woman demanded wages:** "A Woman's Diary of the Siege of Vicksburg," pp. 768–74.

150 **"don't you forgit it":** Rawick, **The American Slave,** sup-

plement, series 1, vol. 10, **Mississippi Narratives,** part 5, p. 2003.

150   **"by the loyal public":** Quoted from Martha M. Bigelow, "The Significance of Milliken's Bend in the Civil War," **Journal of Negro History** 45:3 (1960): p. 158.

151   **"usage of a civilized warfare":** Cash and Somerville, **My Dear Nellie,** p. 90.

151   **"washing for the company":** As quoted in McPherson, **For Cause and Comrades,** p. 119.

151   **at the double-quick:** Hoffman, **Camp, Court and Siege,** pp. 59–60.

153   **"employment of Negro troops":** Bigelow, "The Significance of Milliken's Bend in the Civil War," p. 163.

153   **a fellow soldier of Newton's:** Knight, **The Echo of the Black Horn,** p. 122; Thomas, et al., **The Family of John "Jackie" Knight and Keziah Davis Knight.**

153   **"run back to the house":** Rawick, **The American Slave,** vol. 9, **Mississippi Narratives,** part 4, pp. 1801–1802.

153   **"dey would be near by":** Rawick, **The American Slave,** vol. 8, **Mississippi Narratives,** part 5, p. 2065.

154   **"treachery to freedom":** Frederick Douglass, "The Heroic Slave," p. 47.

154   **"You find out who you are":** W. H. Auden, **Lectures on Shakespeare** (Princeton: Princeton University Press, 2000), p. 48.

155   **Newton came to belong more to Rachel:** Authors' interviews with Barbara Blackledge, Dorothy Knight Marsh, Jules Smith; Bynum, notes on interviews with Earle Knight, Oral History Project, University of Southern Mississippi.

155   **a comrade of blacks:** Bynum, **The Free State of Jones,** p. 100.

155 **spared their sexual attentions:** Bynum, **The Free State of Jones,** pp. 86–87; Sumrall and Welch, **The Knights and Related Families.** Fannie Knight's birth date is taken from census records.

156 **"faithful, loyal, and true":** These quotes are drawn from ex-slaves who acknowledged the love between white men and black women: William Wells Brown, **Clotel; or, The President's Daughter** (1853; reprint, Boston: Bedford/St. Martin's, 2000), p. 100; John Roy Lunch, **Reminiscences of an Active Life: The Autobiography of John Roy Lynch** (Chicago: University of Chicago Press, 1970), p. 6.

156 **"seduction under the implicit threat of force":** Eugene Genovese, **Roll, Jordan, Roll: The World the Slaves Made** (New York: Vintage Books, 1976), p. 428.

156 **"as it is known in other countries":** Albert T. Morgan, **Yazoo; Or, On the Picket Line of Freedom in the South: A Personal Narrative** (1884; reprint, Columbia: University of South Carolina Press, 2000), p. 212.

156 **"than to submit to compulsion":** Harriet A. Jacobs, **Incidents in the Life of a Slave Girl, Written by Herself,** Jean Fagan Yellin, ed. (Cambridge, Mass.: Harvard University Press, 1987), p. 55. As the scholar Eugene Genovese notes, even relationships whose initial overtures were exploitive often developed into more. "They were not supposed to, but they did—and in larger numbers than they or subsequent generations of black and white southerners have ever wanted to admit." See Genovese, **Roll, Jordan, Roll,** p. 413.

For our understanding of Newton's relationship with Rachel, we have also benefited from the following sources: White, **Arn't I a Woman;** Stephanie M. H. Camp, **Closer to Freedom: Enslaved Women and Everyday Resistance in the Planta-**

tion South (Chapel Hill: University of North Carolina Press, 2004); Thavolia Glymph, **Out of the House of Bondage: The Transformation of the Plantation Household** (New York: Cambridge University Press, 2008); Catherine Clinton, **Tara Revisited: Women, War, and the Plantation Legend** (New York: Abbeville Press, 1995); Marie Jenkins Schwartz, **Born in Bondage: Growing Up Enslaved in the Antebellum South** (Cambridge, Mass.: Harvard University Press, 2000); Virginia Elise Lemire, **"Miscegenation": Making Race in America** (Philadelphia: University of Pennsylvania Press, 2002); Annette Gordon-Reed, **The Hemingses of Monticello: An American Family** (New York: W. W. Norton, 2008); David J. Libby, Paul Spickard, and Susan Ditto, eds., **Affect and Power: Essays on Sex, Slavery, Race, and Religion in Appreciation of Winthrop D. Jordan** (Jackson: University Press of Mississippi, 2005); Randall Kennedy, **Interracial Intimacies: Sex, Marriage, and Adoption** (New York: Pantheon, 2003); Carl Plasa and Betty J. Ring, eds., **The Discourse of Slavery: Aphra Behn to Toni Morrison** (New York: Routledge, 1994); Martha Hodes, ed., **Sex, Love, Race: Crossing Boundaries in North America** (New York: New York University Press, 1999); and Martha Hodes, **White Women, Black Men: Illicit Sex in the Nineteenth-Century South** (New Haven: Yale University Press, 1997).

157   **"tortured as well as degraded":** Genovese, **Roll, Jordan, Roll,** p. 419.

157   **"Amalgamation is incest":** Ibid., p. 418.

158   **"marry our daughters to the niggers":** McPherson, **For Cause and Comrades,** p. 109.

158   **"a long train of evils":** Cash and Somerville, **My Dear Nellie,** p. 129.

158 **"there's lots of ways I'd ruther die"**: Frost, "The South's Strangest Army Revealed by Chief."

160 **"mustered into the U.S. service"**: Deposition of Joel E. Welborn in **Newton Knight et al. v. United States,** Congressional Case 8013-8464.

CHAPTER 5: THE THIRD FRONT
Page

161 **"army in the woods"**: Frost, "The South's Strangest Army Revealed by Chief."

162 **until the horns sounded:** Leverett, **The Legend of the Free State of Jones,** pp. 82–83; this account of the wagon raid is based on Leverett's excerpt from a private unpublished memoir by William Fairchild's descendants, titled "The House of Fairchild." Although the account contains some errors, it generally conforms to other accounts of a raid by Newton on a Confederate wagon train in early 1864, including Newton's own, and mentions contained in official reports.

162 **"they cut and run"**: Frost, "The South's Strangest Army Revealed by Chief."

163 **brazenness of the attackers:** Leverett, **The Free State of Jones,** p. 83.

163 **"an old buck"**: Knight, **The Life and Activities of Captain Newton Knight,** pp. 82–83.

163 **"killed them both"**: Ibid.

164 **"Newt pluged him"**: Leverett, **The Legend of the Free State of Jones,** p. 84, excerpts from "The House of Fairchild."

164 **rode out behind his animals:** Tom Knight refers to McGilvery as "Angus," apparently mistaking him for his son. William McGilvery owned half a dozen slaves and $5,480 in land and stated his personal wealth at $18,910, according to U.S. Federal

Census Records for 1860. Amos Deason was the executor of his estate, according to Bynum, **The Free State of Jones,** p. 253, n. 66.

165 **he died that night:** Knight, **The Life and Activities of Captain Newton Knight,** p. 30.

165 **John Carlyle:** Interview with J. C. Andrews, in Jean Strickland and Patricia N. Edwards, eds., **Miscellaneous Records of Jones County** (Moss Point, Miss: n.p., 1992), p. 99; there is a reference to Rushton being shot "in his bed by a deserter" in "Points of Interest in Jones County," WPA Collection, Jones County, record group 60, vol. 315, MDAH; M. P. Bush, address to the meeting of the DAR, February 17, 1912, Lauren Rogers Museum, Laurel, Miss.

165 **Their houses began to burn:** Devall to Governor Charles Clark, March 21, 1864, as quoted in Leverett, **The Legend of the Free State of Jones,** p. 81; letter from James Hamilton, CSA Major and Controlling Quartermaster Tax in Kind for Mississippi and East Louisiana, to Col. T. M. Jack, Assistant Adjutant-General, March 31, 1864, **OR,** series 1, vol. 32, part 3, pp. 727–28.

165 **"There was no sheriff":** Interview with J. C. Andrews, in Strickland and Edwards, **Miscellaneous Records of Jones County,** p. 99; M. P. Bush, address to the DAR, February 17, 1912, Lauren Rogers Museum, Laurel, Miss.

166 **"at the risk of my life":** James W. Silver, ed., "The Breakdown of Morale in Central Mississippi in 1864: Letters of Judge Robert S. Hudson," **Journal of Mississippi History** 16 (1954): 99–104; Leverett, **The Legend of the Free State of Jones,** pp. 73–74.

166 **across five counties:** Knight, **The Life and Activities of Captain Newton Knight,** p. 68.

166   a "strong force" to their aid: Silver, "The Breakdown of Morale in Central Mississippi in 1864," pp. 99–104; Leverett, **The Legend of the Free State of Jones,** pp. 73–74.

167   **Polk labeled them:** Polk coined the descriptive term "Southern Yankees" in a report to Jefferson Davis, March 21, 1864, **OR,** series 1, vol. 32, part 3, pp. 662–63.

167   **"No time should be lost":** Polk to Dabney Maury, February 7, 1864, **OR,** series 1, vol. 32, part 2, pp. 688–89.

168   **"lamentation of distant families":** McPherson, **Battle Cry of Freedom,** p. 744.

168   **"these terrible hardships of war":** William Tecumseh Sherman, **Memoirs** (1875; reprint, New York; London, Ontario: Penguin Books, 2000), p. 495.

169   **"for their special benefit":** Ibid., p. 311.

169   **"quicker by such a course":** Ibid., p. 316; McPherson, **Battle Cry of Freedom,** pp. 808–809; Buck T. Foster, **Sherman's Mississippi Campaign** (Tuscaloosa: The University of Alabama Press, 2006), p. 31.

170   **drive south from Memphis:** Sherman, **Memoirs,** p. 422; Sherman's report, March 7, 1864, **OR,** series 1, vol. 32, part 1, pp. 173–79.

170   **"a preeminent man":** Letter from Walter A. Rorer to his cousin Susan, January 28, 1864, Civil War Collection, MHI, Carlisle Barracks, Pa.

171   **"I could scarcely ride":** Letter from Walter A. Rorer to his cousin Susan, February 24, 1864, Civil War Collection, MHI, Carlisle Barracks, Pa.

171   **"neither traitors nor deserters":** Roberts and Moneyhon, **Portraits of Conflict,** p. 308.

172   **"almost starving children":** Ibid., p. 309.

172   **only the dresses on their backs:** "A Woman's Account of the Doings at Meridian," **New York Times,** March 27, 1864.

173 **"no longer exists":** Sherman's report, March 7, 1864, **OR,** series 1, vol. 32, part 1, p. 175.

173 **"northern mud sills":** McPherson, **For Cause and Comrades,** p. 155.

173 **indiscriminately for firewood:** Foster, **Sherman's Mississippi Campaign,** p. 109.

174 **"10 miles of negroes":** Sherman to Halleck, **OR,** series 1, vol. 32, part 2, pp. 498–99.

174 **seized wagons and vehicles:** "United States," **Harper's New Monthly Magazine** 28:168 (May 1864): 848; Sherman's report, March 7, 1864, **OR,** series 1, vol. 32, part 1, p. 175; Sherman to Halleck, **OR,** series 1, vol. 32, part 2, pp. 498–99.

174 **"for such action as you please":** "Sherman to Halleck, February 29, 1864," **OR,** series 1, vol. 32, part 2, p. 499.

175 **"this great game of war":** Sherman, **Memoirs,** p. 311.

176 **up in Lauderdale County:** Foster, **Sherman's Mississippi Campaign,** p. 103; for a description of the Piney Woods as a destination for fugitives, see Leverett, **The Legend of the Free State of Jones,** p. 68. According to Ethel Knight in **The Echo of the Black Horn,** p. 106, not only did some of Aughey's associates collaborate with the Jones Scouts, but by the war's end, blacks and escaped Yankee soldiers also belonged to the company. Although she is the only source for a connection between Aughey and the Knight band, other accounts attest to the itinerant nature of deserter and Unionist bands in interior Mississippi; see especially Aughey's memoir **Tupelo** and Silver, "The Breakdown of Morale in Central Mississippi in 1864."

176 **address in Columbus, Ohio:** Newton Knight depositions, 1890, 1895, in **Newton Knight, et al. v. United States,** Congressional Case 8013-8464; **OR,** series 1, vol. 32, part 1, p. 403. Newton and McMillen could not have met during the Meridian campaign, as at the time McMillen was traveling with Gen-

eral William Sooy Smith's cavalry, which never made it farther south than West Point, Miss., ninety miles to the north. Smith departed late and encountered General Nathan Bedford Forrest's Confederate cavalry and thus never linked up with Sherman as planned, to the wrath of Sherman, who believed that with cavalry he could have caught and destroyed Polk's entire army. However, McMillen might have encountered Piney Woods Unionist guerrillas on other assignments. In 1870, an advocate representing Newton in his pension case forwarded McMillen's name and post office address as a favorable witness and acquaintance of Newton's: "You will find enclosed the post office address of Genl WL. McMillen you can confer with him he had an interview with Capt. Knight," wrote Probate Judge B. A. Mathews to Congressman Legrand W. Perce on December 8, 1870. However, McMillen was unreachable; he had moved to Louisiana, where he became a planter and served for a time in the state legislature. See Accompanying Papers, H.R. 1814, Newton Knight file, record group 233, box 16, NARA. For biographical information on McMillen, see Stewart Sifakis, **Who Was Who in the Civil War** (New York: Facts on File, Inc., 1988), pp. 421–22.

177 **"11 times with rifle bullets":** Frost, "The South's Strangest Army Revealed by Chief"; Knight, **The Life and Activities of Captain Newton Knight,** p. 52.

178 **underbrush and reed brakes:** Frost, "The South's Strangest Army Revealed by Chief"; Knight, **The Life and Activities of Captain Newton Knight,** pp. 31–32; interview with J. C. Andrews, Strickland and Edwards, **Miscellaneous Records of Jones County,** p. 99.

179 **"They are becoming very troublesome":** A. S. Polk, CSA Acting Assistant Inspector General, to Lt. Col. T. F. Sevier, Asst.

Inspector General, March 3, 1864, **OR,** series 1, vol. 32, part 3, pp. 579–80.

180 **"they were free":** The report of the Augusta raid, written by Captain A. F. Ramsey of the 3rd Mississippi to CSA Major J. C. Denis, the regional provost marshal, on March 8, 1864, is quoted from Leverett, **The Legend of the Free State of Jones,** p. 74. Thomas Landrum's name does not appear on Newton's roster of men, but he went on to enlist in the 1st New Orleans Infantry under Lieutenant Colonel Eugene Tisdale, as did a number of other men from the Knight Company, in the late spring of 1864.

180 **to help protect it:** Major-General General Dabney Maury to James A. Sedden, Secretary of War, March 3, 1864, **OR,** series 1, vol. 32, part 1, p. 403; Weitz, **More Damning than Slaughter,** pp. 206–8.

180 **he would hang on the spot:** March 21, 1864, CSA Lieut-General L. Polk to His Excellency President Davis, **OR,** series 1, vol. 32, part 3, pp. 662–63.

181 **yielded few returns:** A cavalry trooper under Maury wrote a description of the expedition to his father, and the letter was reprinted in the **Mobile Advertiser and Register,** March 19, 1864. Leverett reprints it in **The Legend of the Free State of Jones,** p. 90.

181 **"we had better return to camp":** Leverett, **The Legend of the Free State of Jones,** p. 90.

181 **killed in the exchange:** Knight, **The Life and Activities of Captain Newton Knight,** p. 38.

181 **buckshot for their shotguns:** Frost, "The South's Strangest Army Revealed by Chief."

181 **holding baskets of provisions above her head:** Bynum, **The Free State of Jones,** p. 109.

182   **calling for hogs:** Ibid., p. 122.

183   **"from such retreats":** William L. Nugent to his wife, Nellie, January 22, 1864, in Cash and Howorth, **My Dear Nellie,** p. 154.

183   **lasted for generations:** Ethel Knight, no sympathetic portrayer of Newton Knight, acknowledged that "many descendants of these people tell until this day that Newt Knight kept them from starvation, which he did, but nothing is ever mentioned about how he acquired help for these families." Knight, **The Echo of the Black Horn,** p. 94.

183   **"ground's too poor to sprout them":** Addie West, "A Brief History of Jones County," WPA Collection, Jones County, MDAH.

183   **"were launched into eternity":** Interview with J. C. Andrews, Strickland and Edwards, **Miscellaneous Records of Jones County,** p. 99; Leverett, **The Legend of the Free State of Jones,** p. 90.

184   **all but 20 or so:** March 12, 1864, from CSA Colonel Henry Maury to Major-General Dabney H. Maury, **OR,** series 1, vol. 32, part 3, pp. 632–33.

184   **company would be wiped out:** Ibid.

185   **"opposition to the Confederate Government":** Daniel P. Logan to CSA Maj. J. C. Denis, April 7, 1864, **OR,** series 1, vol. 32, part 3, p. 755.

185   **cached it in Devil's Den:** There are numerous references in official Union and Confederate reports to Honey Island as a haven for deserters (see **OR,** series 1, vol. 32, part 2, pp. 522–23, and **OR,** series 1, vol. 32, part 3, pp. 632–33), which make Ethel Knight's description of Newton transporting arms by flatboat plausible (**The Echo of the Black Horn,** p. 152).

185   **hiding out there: OR,** series 1, vol. 34, part 1, pp. 869–70.

186 **fend for themselves:** Jasper Collins interview with Goode Montgomery, as recounted in Montgomery's essay "Alleged Secession of Jones County," **Publications of the Mississippi Historical Society** 3 (1904): p. 13–23. Montgomery was a local historian and resident of Ellisville. Also see the depositions of Jasper Collins and Newton Knight in **Newton Knight, et al. v. United States,** Congressional Case 8013-8464. There was only one organized foray of Yankee troops into Jones County, and it was not to aid Unionists. It took place in June of 1863, when a detachment of forty-five mounted raiders under Captain Calvin A. Mann was ordered by Grant to tear up bridges and railroads in southern Mississippi. The Yankee raiders destroyed some rail cars at Brookhaven but were ambushed by local Confederates. Four were killed, four wounded, and thirty-seven taken prisoner. The incident suggests that Jones was at the time still very much under the control of Confederate loyalists and that Newton was either not yet home from the Vicksburg area or was home but in deep hiding and not yet effectively resisting. For more on Mann's raid, see James G. Hollandsworth Jr., "Mann's Foray: A Grierson-like Raid That Failed," **The Journal of Mississippi History** (March 2005): p. 29–43.

186 **"speak out against them":** Silver, "The Breakdown of Morale in Central Mississippi in 1864," p. 104.

187 **"resolved not to pay any tax":** Devall to Governor Charles Clark, March 21, 1864, as quoted in Leverett, **The Legend of the Free State of Jones,** p. 81.

187 **"risk of his life and property":** Letter from James Hamilton, CSA Major and Controlling Quartermaster Tax in Kind for Mississippi and East Louisiana, to Col. T. M. Jack, Assistant Adjutant-General, March 31, 1864, **OR,** series 1, vol. 32, part 3, pp. 727–28.

187 **"sent there to arrest them"**: As quoted in Leverett, **The Legend of the Free State of Jones,** p. 75.

188 **"hearts of stone"**: Silver, "The Breakdown of Morale in Central Mississippi in 1864," p. 102.

188 **"this hellish tide"**: Ibid., pp. 102–4.

188 **"disloyal men and women"**: Walter A. Rorer to his cousin Susan, April 8, 1864, Civil War Collection, MHI, Carlisle Barracks, Pa.; Roberts and Moneyhon, **Portraits of Conflict,** p. 301; Silver, "The Breakdown of Morale in Central Mississippi in 1864," p. 102.

190 **"well drilled infantry troops"**: CSA Captain W. Wirt Thomson to Hon. James A. Seddon, Secretary of War, C.S. Army, March 29, 1864, **OR,** series 1, vol. 32, part 3, pp. 711–13.

190 **"all efforts to capture them"**: March 21, 1864, CSA Lieut-General L. Polk to His Excellency President Davis, **OR,** series 1, vol. 32, part 3, pp. 662–63.

190 **for deserters:** Weitz, **More Damning than Slaughter,** pp. 203–10.

190 **"necessary to correct these evils"**: April 13, 1864, CSA Colonel Robert Lowry to Col. T. M. Jack, Assistant Adjutant-General, **OR,** series 1, vol. 52, part 2, pp. 657–58.

191 **"build a fire under us"**: Frost, "The South's Strangest Army Revealed by Chief."

CHAPTER 6: BANNERS RAISED AND LOWERED

Page

192 **the letters "U.S.A.":** "Letter from Mississippi," **Mobile Advertiser and Register,** May 6, 1864, as reprinted in Leverett, **The Legend of the Free State of Jones,** pp. 98–99. The number of stars on the handmade federal flag—thirty-seven—was rich

with symbolism, reflecting the Jones County Scouts' political sophistication. At the time there were only thirty-five states in the Union. But Nevada had already applied for statehood, and the Scouts knew that Republicans in Washington were rushing the process to help ensure Lincoln's reelection. The thirty-sixth star anticipated Nevada's statehood. The thirty-seventh star was probably for Jones County, suggesting that Newton and his men had declared independence from the treasonous governments of Mississippi and the Confederacy. The thirty-seven stars together emphasize that the Scouts refused to dignify rebel states as a separate and distinct nation. Like Lincoln, Grant, and other Republicans, they believed that secession and the founding of the Confederacy constituted treason against the United States, and they were helping to suppress it and preserve the peace. For a photograph of the flag, see Leverett, **Legend of the Free State of Jones,** pp. 69–70.

193 **"getting their little banner back again":** McPherson, **For Cause and Comrades,** p. 85.

193 **"bitter, stubborn resistance":** Letter from Col. William N. Brown to Governor Charles Clark, Comp. 20th Miss. Regt. Knights Mills Jones Co. Miss., Governors' Papers, record group 27, vol. 56, box 949, MDAH.

193 **distributed to the local villages:** April 13, 1864, CSA Colonel Robert Lowry to Col. T. M. Jack, Assistant Adjutant-General, **OR,** series 1, vol. 52, part 2, pp. 657–58.

194 **"pure air of liberty":** Ibid., p. 658.

195 **"good and loyal citizens":** Ibid., pp. 657–58.

195 **a corporal badly injured:** Ibid.; see also Leverett, **The Legend of the Free State of Jones,** pp. 98–99.

196 **filled with cool water:** B. D. Graves, address to the Hebron Community, June 17, 1926, Lauren Rogers Museum, Laurel,

Miss. Graves was the son of the Leaf River farmer who heard the sound of guns in the night.

197   **sick to his stomach:** Knight, **The Echo of the Black Horn,** pp. 137–38.

197   **cut her brothers down:** Bynum, **The Free State of Jones,** p. 119.

197   **"perhaps by mistake":** "Letter from Mississippi" as quoted in Leverett, **The Legend of the Free State of Jones,** pp. 98–99; May 5, 1864, Letter from Col. William N. Brown to Governor Charles Clark, Comp. 20th Miss. Regt. Knights Mills Jones Co. Miss., Governors' Papers, record group 27, vol. 56, box 949, MDAH. Some of Ben Knight's relatives claimed he was legally absent from the 7th Mississippi Battalion because he was officially paroled after Vicksburg. See Bynum, **The Free State of Jones,** pp. 118–20.

198   **"Crackers' Neck":** Letter from Col. William N. Brown to Governor Charles Clark, Comp. 20th Miss. Regt. Knights Mills Jones Co. Miss., Governors' Papers, record group 27, vol. 56, box 949, MDAH; letter from Quitman Ross, Knight family attorney, to A. L. Hopkins, Mississippi State Sovereignty Commission, December 3, 1963, MDAH, copy in possession of authors.

198   **eleven-year-old named George:** Ben Graves, address to the Hebron Community, Lauren Rogers Museum, Laurel, Miss.; interview with Ben Sumrall, August 31, 1936, WPA Collection, Jones County, MDAH; Bynum, **The Free State of Jones,** p. 121n.

198   **"no right to hang":** Frost, "The South's Strangest Army Revealed by Chief"; Montgomery, "Alleged Secession of Jones County," pp. 13–23.

198   **mostly women, boys, and old men:** Leverett, **The Legend of the Free State of Jones,** p. 99.

198 **"He held the father as hostage":** As quoted in Leverett, **The Legend of the Free State of Jones,** p. 100.

199 **men fired after him:** Knight, **The Life and Activities of Captain Newton Knight,** p. 72.

199 **the father was locked up:** Ibid., p. 73.

200 **"Big Creek cemetery":** Thomas et al., **The Family of John "Jackie" Knight and Keziah Davis Knight.**

200 **"take great delight in destroying":** Knight, **The Life and Activities of Captain Newton Knight,** p. 52.

200 **"look like men's tracks?":** Ibid., pp. 53–55.

201 **"she would kill him":** Ibid., p. 53.

201 **"They fought men and dogs":** Letter from B. A. Mathews to L. W. Perce, December 8, 1870, Accompanying Papers, H.R. 1814, Newton Knight file, record group 233, box 16, NARA.

201 **"afraid of them old shot guns":** Knight, **The Life and Activities of Captain Newton Knight,** p. 41.

202 **"we'd better get out of here":** Frost, "The South's Strangest Army Revealed by Chief."

202 **"ready to shoot":** Knight, **The Life and Activities of Captain Newton Knight,** p. 42.

202 **"rolled marbles on his coat tail":** Ibid., p. 76.

203 **revenge for the hangings:** Ibid., p. 26; interview with Ben Sumrall, WPA Collection, Jones County, MDAH.

203 **red pepper blistered their snouts:** Knight, **The Life and Activities of Captain Newton Knight,** pp. 28–29.

203 **"God's power that delivered him":** Ibid., p. 49.

204 **never see some of them again:** Newton Knight muster roll, c. 1870, Ames Family Papers, Smith College, collection number MS-3.

204 **Fort Pike, Louisiana:** Records of the Adjutant General's Office, Record Group 92, Compiled Service Records of Volunteer Union Soldiers Who Served in Organizations from the State of

Louisiana, 1st New Orleans Regiment, "Tisdale's," microfilm (M396), NARA; Newton Knight muster roll, c. 1870, Ames Family Papers, Smith College, collection number MS-3.

204   **felled by dysentery:** The Union pension claims of the families of these men are documented in Jean Strickland and Patricia N. Edwards, **Miscellaneous Records of Jones County** (n.p., Moss Point, Miss., 1992) and Strickland and Edwards, **Records of Jasper Co. Mississippi,** WPA source material, Will Abstracts 1866–1914 (n.p., Moss Point, Miss., 1995). Also, Jones County archivist Kenneth Welch has amassed a formidable collection of pension materials on Jones County Unionists, which he was kind enough to provide copies of to the authors.

204   **riddled with bullets:** Newton Knight's muster roll, c. 1870, Ames Family Papers, Smith College, collection number MS-3. Newton did not list all of the men who served as guerrillas with him on his muster roll, omitting those who he felt did not "hold out faithful" to the Union cause throughout the war, according to his advocate B. A. Mathews. See Letter from B. A. Mathews to Rep. Legrand W. Perce, Ellisville Miss. December 8, 1870, Accompanying Papers, H.R. 1814, Newton Knight file, record group 233, box 16, NARA.

204   **"new repeatin' rifles":** Frost, "The South's Strangest Army Revealed by Chief."

205   **captured men in irons:** Letter from B. A. Mathews to Rep. L. W. Perce, December 8, 1870, Accompanying Papers, H.R. 1814, Newton Knight file, record group 233, box 16, NARA.

205   **Colonel William N. Brown:** April 13, 1864, Lowry to Jack, **OR,** series 1, vol. 52, part 2, pp. 657–58; May 5, 1864, Letter from Col. William N. Brown to Governor Charles Clark, Comp. 20th Miss. Regt. Knights Mills Jones Co. Miss., Governors' Papers, record group 27, vol. 56, box 949, MDAH; Leverett, **The Legend of the Free State of Jones,** p. 100.

205   **resistance in the Piney Woods:** Allardice, **Confederate Colonels,** pp. 79, 257.

208   **"the many complaints we hear every day":** Letter from Col. William N. Brown to Governor Charles Clark, Comp. 20th Miss. Regt. Knights Mills Jones Co. Miss., Governors' Papers, record group 27, vol. 56, box 949, MDAH.

208   **"try half the army":** Letter from Walter A. Rorer to his cousin Susan, March 31, 1864, Civil War Collection, MHI, Carlisle Barracks, Pa.

209   **"bushwhacking":** Leverett, **The Legend of the Free State of Jones,** p. 18.

209   **"these secessionists to order":** Maury, **Recollections of a Virginian,** p. 246.

210   **"knew every creek and footlog":** Knight, **The Life and Activities of Captain Newton Knight,** p. 75.

210   **threatened impressment agents:** H. C. Kelley to T. H. Taylor, July 30, 1864, **OR,** series 1, vol. 39, part 2, pp. 736–37; other information in this paragraph comes from **OR,** series 1, vol. 32, part 2, pp. 688–89; and **OR,** series 1, vol. 32, part 3, pp. 579–80, 580–81, 711–13, 727–28.

210   **"commit the same to the flames":** June 14, 1864, Letter from B. C. Duckworth to Governor Charles Clark, Governors' Papers, record group 27, vol. 56, box 949, MDAH.

210   **"defied the Colonel and his forces":** "The Republic of Jones," **Natchez Courier,** July 12, 1864.

211   **"pulled a quantity of green corn":** H. C. Kelley to T. H. Taylor, July 30, 1864, **OR,** series 1, vol. 39, part 2, pp. 736–37; Weitz, **More Damning than Slaughter,** pp. 208–232.

211   **liberated from plantations: OR,** series 1, vol. 39, part 2, pp. 568, 570, 571, 777; **OR,** series 1, vol. 32, part 3, pp. 755, 820–21.

212   **"defeating their object?": OR,** series 1, vol. 39, part 2, p. 777.

212 **"mere skirmishing"**: Knight, **The Echo of the Black Horn,** pp. 204–205; Mallard, "I Had No Comfort to Give the People," p. 81; Ella Lonn, **Desertion During the Civil War** (1928; reprint, Lincoln: University of Nebraska Press, 1998), pp. 62, 68, 70–72, 75–76.

212 **impressed back into uniform: Newton Knight, et al. v. United States,** Congressional Case 8013-8464; War Department Collection of Confederate Records, RG 109, Compiled Service Records, 7th Battalion, Mississippi Infantry, microfilm (M269), NARA.

213 **the will of his opponents:** McPherson, **Battle Cry of Freedom,** p. 722; Foote, **The Civil War,** vol. 3, p. 319.

213 **"determined to fight it out":** Foote, **The Civil War,** vol. 3, p. 323.

213 **"after the fall elections":** McPherson, **Battle Cry of Freedom,** pp. 718–21, 803.

213 **"against their war resources":** Ibid.

215 **"lifeless corpses":** Letters from Columbus Sykes to his wife, Pauline, April 23, 1864, April 30, 1864, Civil War Collection, MHI, Carlisle Barracks, Pa.

215 **"brought to close quarters":** Cash and Howorth, **My Dear Nellie,** p. 203.

215 **"no comb for your hair":** Ibid., p. 182.

215 **"his spirit escaped":** Clement A. Evans, ed., **Confederate Military History,** vol. 1, p. 665.

216 **"a kind of morning dash":** Albert Castel, "The Life of a Rising Son, Part III, the Conqueror," **Civil War Times Illustrated** 18:6 (October 1979): 13.

216 **winter-spring of 1865:** Depositions in **Newton Knight, et al. v. United States,** Congressional Case 8013-8464; Bynum, **The Free State of Jones,** p. 125.

217 **"to fight on open ground":** Grant, **Personal Memoirs,** p. 363; McPherson, **Battle Cry of Freedom,** pp. 753–54.

217 **what he had done to his own body:** Foote, **The Civil War,** vol. 3, p. 330; McPherson, **Battle Cry of Freedom,** p. 753.

217 **"no army at all":** Cash and Howorth, **My Dear Nellie,** p. 189.

218 **no merciful truce:** McPherson, **Battle Cry of Freedom,** pp. 774, 804–6.

218 **"the city of Savannah":** Ibid., pp. 804–6.

219 **Riding in a cavalry force:** James Lee McDonough and Thomas L. Connelly, **Five Tragic Hours: The Battle of Franklin** (Knoxville: The University of Tennessee Press, 1983), appendix. There were thirty-three Mississippi infantry regiments and five Mississippi cavalry regiments at Franklin.

219 **feet of the men in gray:** McDonough and Connelly, **Five Tragic Hours,** pp. 104–6, 146–49; Wiley Sword, **Embrace an Angry Wind, The Confederacy's Last Hurrah: Spring Hill, Franklin and Nashville** (New York: HarperCollins, 1992), p. 246.

220 **"supreme fear and terror":** Sword, **Embrace an Angry Wind,** p. 267.

220 **flame searing their faces:** Ibid., pp. 226–27, 246.

220 **commanders among the casualties:** McDonough and Connelly, **Five Tragic Hours,** p. 154.

221 **shuddered from cold:** Sword, **Embrace an Angry Wind,** p. 279.

221 **"present themselves to view":** McPherson, **For Cause and Comrades,** p. 161.

221 **"Four men were shot down":** OR, series 1, vol. 45, part 1, p. 714.

222 **prongs of a broken fork:** Roberts and Moneyhon, **Portraits of Conflict,** p. 283.

222 **burned with powder:** Nehemiah Davis Starr letters, Leslie Anders Collection, MHI, Carlisle Barracks, Pa.

222 **"I do not admire the mode of warfare":** "Anson Hemingway, A Legacy of War Reporting."

223 **"fight to the last men":** Nehemiah Davis Starr letters, Leslie Anders Collection, MHI, Carlisle Barracks, Pa.

223 **"keep him awake":** Knight, **The Echo of the Black Horn,** p. 185.

223 **smuggled Yankees:** Roberts and Moneyhon, **Portraits of Conflict,** p. 281.

223 **four Unionists who tried to vote:** Bynum, **The Free State of Jones,** p. 127; Silver, "The Breakdown of Morale in Central Mississippi in 1864," pp. 99–106.

224 **paroled twenty-one men:** Letter from Amos Deason to Governor Charles Clark, September 1, 1864, Governors' Papers, series 768, box 950, MDAH; Knight, **The Life and Activities of Captain Newton Knight,** p. 23; Leverett, **The Legend of the Free State of Jones,** pp. 113–14.

224 **cook all of her chickens:** Bynum, **The Free State of Jones,** p. 127.

224 **frightened a local slave:** Rawick, **The American Slave,** supplement, series I, vol. 10, **Mississippi Narratives,** part 5, interview with Martha Wheeler, pp. 2262–71.

224 **serving the Union in New Orleans:** Frost, "The South's Strangest Army Revealed by Chief"; Bynum, **The Free State of Jones,** p. 127.

226 **They used the leather for shoes:** Frost, "The South's Strangest Army Revealed by Chief"; Knight, **The Life and Activities of Captain Newton Knight,** p. 35.

227 **his rear end roasted:** Thomas, et al., **The Family of John "Jackie" Knight and Keziah Davis Knight,** p. 128.

227   **buckshot dappled in the bark:** Knight, **The Life and Activities of Captain Newton Knight,** p. 64.

227   **lay in state at the White House:** McPherson, **Battle Cry of Freedom,** pp. 851–52.

227   **"virtually at an end":** McPherson, **Ordeal by Fire,** p. 485; Jay Winik, **April 1865: The Month That Saved America** (New York: HarperCollins, 2001), p. 320. On May 26, the last of the trans-Mississippi Confederates surrendered, which officially ended the war.

228   **energy, manpower, and morale:** According to official records, tallied by Mark Weitz in **More Damning than Slaughter,** 103,400 men deserted Confederate service by the end of the war. Of those, 11,604 were Mississippians. For more on the effects of desertion on the army, see Weitz, **More Damning than Slaughter,** p. ix; Mallard, "I Had No Comfort to Give the People," pp. 78–86.

228   **"in the fight on the other side":** Knight, **The Life and Activities of Captain Newton Knight,** p. 63.

228   **rations for his men:** Deposition of Newton Knight, **Newton Knight, et al. v. United States,** Congressional Case 8013-8464.

229   **a noble but Lost Cause:** David W. Blight, **Race and Reunion: The Civil War in American Memory** (Cambridge, Mass.: Harvard University Press, 2001), pp. 1–30.

229   **"after our armies are whipped":** Cash and Howorth, **My Dear Nellie,** p. 211.

230   **"with the help of the Klan":** Rawick, **The American Slave,** supplement, series I, vol. 6, **Mississippi Narratives,** part 1, pp. 10–19.

CHAPTER 7: RECONSTRUCTION AND REDEMPTION

Page

231 **official business with them:** Accompanying Papers, H.R. 1814, Newton Knight file, record group 233, box 16, NARA; it does not appear that Anson Hemingway was in Ellisville. Beginning on July 25, 1865, he was on detached service in Natchez as a subcommissioner in the Bureau of Refugees, Freedmen and Abandoned Lands, the agency in charge of protecting blacks and ushering them to emancipation. Hemingway remained in Mississippi until he was honorably discharged on March 19, 1866, when he returned to Chicago and became "an easygoing real estate man with much more interest in outdoor living than in making money," according to his descendants. He marched every year with his comrades in the Army of the Republic parades. In 1909, he gave his grandson Ernest a twenty-gauge shotgun. He died in 1926 at the age of eighty-two. Anson Hemingway file, Compiled Service Records, 70th U.S. Colored Infantry, RG94, NARA; "Anson Hemingway: A Legacy of War Reporting."

232 **forty-eight plantations for sale or lease:** William C. Harris, **Presidential Reconstruction in Mississippi** (Baton Rouge: Louisiana State University Press, 1967), pp. 18–36, quotation from p. 19; John Townsend Trowbridge, **The South: A Tour of Its Battlefields and Ruined Cities** (1866; reprint, Ann Arbor: The University of Michigan University Library Historical Reprint Series), p. 377; David M. Oshinsky, **"Worse than Slavery," Parchman Farm and the Ordeal of Jim Crow Justice** (New York: Free Press Paperbacks, 1997), p. 13.

232 **their husbands dead as well:** Walter Lord, "Mississippi: The Past That Has Not Died," **American Heritage** 16:4 (June

1965), online at http://www.americanheritage.com/articles/magazine/ah/1965/4/1965_4_4.shtml.

233 **more common to see a dead man:** Oshinsky, **"Worse than Slavery,"** p. 12.

233 **"this country was as flat":** Harris, **Presidential Reconstruction in Mississippi,** pp. 18–36, quotation from p. 19; notes on the Whitfield Community Meeting, June 4, 1926, Lauren Rogers Museum, Laurel, Miss.

233 **"Molasses":** Bill of Lading, Accompanying Papers, H.R. 1814, Newton Knight file, record group 233, box 16, NARA.

234 **"I understand that you are commissioner":** Letter from Capt. J. Fairbanks, 72nd USCI to Newton Knight, July 21, 1865, Accompanying Papers, H.R. 1814, Newton Knight file, record group 233, box 16, NARA.

234 **"Sir this colored man informs me":** Letter from Capt. J. Fairbanks, 72nd USCI to Newton Knight, July 24, 1865, Accompanying Papers, H.R. 1814, Newton Knight file, record group 233, box 16, NARA.

235 **allow their boy to go:** Knight, **The Life and Activities of Captain Newton Knight,** pp. 4–5.

235 **"hold the Negroes or their boy":** Ibid., p. 4.

235 **"Mississippians have been shooting":** Oshinsky, **"Worse than Slavery,"** p. 24.

236 **a pistol shot rang out:** The account of Newton's ride through Ellisville is from Ethel Knight, **The Echo of the Black Horn,** p. 233. That Newton stirred strong emotions when he appeared in public, and that political and racial violence threatened to erupt around him, is verified by other sources, including T. J. Knight and Jones County resident Ben Graves. See B. D. Graves, address to the Hebron Community, June 17, 1926, Lauren Rogers Museum, Laurel, Miss.

236 **new Jones County sheriff:** Jones County Mississippi to his Excellency William L. Sharkey, July 15, 1865, Governor's Papers, Sharkey, Letters, Petitions, Telegrams July 15–18, 1865, series 771, box 955, MDAH.

237 **He decided to let the appointments stand:** Bettersworth, **Mississippi in the Confederacy,** p. 148; Bynum, **The Free State of Jones,** p. 132.

237 **"Capt. You will sease a civilian lot of wool":** Letter from Lt. H. T. Elliot to Newton Knight, July 31, 1865, Accompanying Papers, H.R. 1814, Newton Knight file, record group 233, box 16, NARA.

238 **property of the U.S. government:** Letter from Capt. A. R. M. Smith, 70th USCI, to Newton Knight, August 19, 1865, and letters from Lt. Simon Smith, 70th USCI, to Newton Knight, Sept. 2, Sept. 8, 1865, Accompanying papers, H.R. 1814, Newton Knight file, record group 233, box 16, NARA.

238 **"duty bound will ever pay":** "To the Senate and House of Representatives of the State of Mississippi, Oct. 16, 1865," in Bettersworth, **Mississippi in the Confederacy,** p. 148; M. P. Bush, address to the meeting of the DAR, February 17, 1912, Lauren Rogers Museum, Laurel, Mississippi; **The Daily Picayune,** December 3, 1865; Bynum, **The Free State of Jones,** p. 135.

239 **"poorest county in the State":** Daily Picayune, December 3, 1865.

239 **"must rule the South":** Foner, **Reconstruction: America's Unfinished Revolution, 1863–1877** (New York: Harper and Row, 1988), pp. 176, 177, 276.

240 **Johnson chose the latter:** Foner, **Reconstruction,** pp. 179, 180, 181.

240 **recognize the Union at all:** Harris, **Presidential Reconstruc-**

tion in Mississippi, pp. 38, 52–58; Roberts and Moneyhon, **Portraits of Conflict,** pp. 334–35; Oshinsky, **"Worse than Slavery,"** p. 24.

241   **"the people are afraid":** Harris, **Presidential Reconstruction in Mississippi,** pp. 71–72.

241   **"make him feel his inferiority":** Lord, "Mississippi: The Past That Has Not Died."

241   **"the infernal sassy niggers":** Oshinsky, "Worse than Slavery," p. 18.

241   **"breaking of the neck of the free Negro":** Harris, **Presidential Reconstruction,** pp. 104–140; Oshinsky, "Worse than Slavery," p. 25.

241   **"to aid but not to interfere":** Foner, **Reconstruction,** pp. 190–91, quotation from p. 191; "General Slocum at Vicksburg," **Harper's Weekly,** October 21, 1865, p. 658 (quoted); Harris, **Presidential Reconstruction,** pp. 16, 71–76, 61 (quoted).

243   **He tore the Indian down:** Memoirs of Lewis F. Phillips, Civil War Collection, MHI, Carlisle Barracks, Pa.

243   **their personal shotguns: Newton Knight, et al. v. United States,** Congressional Case 8013-8464.

243   **"a state of virtual slavery":** Harris, **Presidential Reconstruction,** p. 72.

243   **allowing him to take office:** Oshinsky, "Worse than Slavery," p. 20.

244   **"their sudden emancipation":** Harris, **Presidential Reconstruction,** p. 134; Oshinsky, "Worse than Slavery," p. 20.

244   **"whip 'em well":** Oshinksy, "Worse than Slavery," p. 11.

244   **hired out to whites:** The complete text of Mississippi's Black Codes can be found online at http://afroamhistory.about.com/library/blmississippi_blackcodes.htm.

245   **allegiance to the United States of America:** Storey, **Loyalty**

and Loss, pp. 175–76, quotation from p. 176; Foner, **Reconstruction,** p. 185.

245   **"see the free niggers starve":** Trowbridge, **The South,** p. 365.

246   **"despotic compulsion":** Trowbridge, **The South,** pp. 330–37.

247   **"belong to the whites at large":** Foner, **Reconstruction,** p. 150.

247   **"did not believe in slavery":** Knight, **Mississippi Girl,** p. 2; Rawick, **The American Slave,** supplement, series 1, vol. 10, **Mississippi Narratives,** part 5, interview with Martha Wheeler, former slave belonging to Jackie Knight, pp. 2262–71.

247   **acreage to work as her own:** Knight, **The Echo of the Black Horn,** pp. 253–54; the U.S. Census for 1870 shows Rachel living next door to Newton and Serena and lists her occupation as "keeping house." She has six children and a net worth of fifty dollars.

248   **"he moved her to his place":** Knight, **Mississippi Girl,** pp. 11–14; Rawick, **The American Slave,** supplement, series 1, vol. 10, **Mississippi Narratives,** part 5, interview with Martha Wheeler, former slave belonging to Jackie Knight, pp. 2262–71; Bynum, **The Free State of Jones,** pp. 144–45 and Knight family genealogical chart, p. 206; U.S. Federal Census Records, 1870.

248   **a double-digit number of heirs:** Bynum, **The Free State of Jones,** Rachel Knight genealogical chart, pp. 206–7.

248   **life sentence in the state penitentiary:** The Mississippi miscegenation law, enacted in 1865, was repealed for ten years beginning in 1870, owing to federal pressure during congressional Reconstruction. The miscegenation law was restored in 1880, with penalties of up to a $500 fine and ten years imprisonment, until 1967, when the U.S. Supreme Court, in **Loving v.**

Virginia, struck down all bans against miscegenation because they violated the due process and equal protection clauses of the Fourteenth Amendment. See Peter Wallenstein, "Reconstruction, Segregation, and Miscegenation: Interracial Marriage and the Law in the Lower South, 1865–1900," **American Nineteenth Century History** 6:1 (March 2005): 58–59.

248 **working on his farm:** U.S. Federal Census, 1870.

249 **ashes of his first home:** Ibid.

249 **"We had 12 weeks of drought":** B. D. Graves, address to the Hebron Community, June 17, 1926, Lauren Rogers Museum, Laurel, Miss.

249 **by virtue of "his will":** Knight, **The Echo of the Black Horn,** p. 285. Ethel Knight claimed to have gotten much of the material for her book from Tom Knight and likely understood his feelings about Rachel and her children. See Bynum's notes on her interview with Ethel Knight, Mississippi Oral History Project, University of Southern Mississippi.

249 **trade them for sugar or coffee:** Knight, **Mississippi Girl,** pp. 18–19.

250 **persimmons, and hickory nuts:** Ibid., p. 12.

250 **"live peaceful with men":** The description of the Knight homestead is from Knight, **The Echo of the Black Horn,** pp. 263–69, and from Knight, **Mississippi Girl,** pp. 11–14, as well as the authors' visit to the site. According to Ethel, Newton "was forever having business" at Rachel's house and Serena voiced her suspicions that Newton was "keeping her," pp. 264–66. On Newton's forgiving frame of mind after the war, see Knight, **The Life and Activities of Captain Newton Knight,** p. 82.

250 **federal military rule again:** Oshinsky, "Worse than Slavery," p. 22.

251 **"to protect niggers":** Foner, **Reconstruction,** p. 276.

251   **"have cast our anchor out":** Oshinsky, "Worse than Slavery," p. 22; Foner, **Reconstruction,** p. 280.

251   **"high water mark of political insanity":** Oshinsky, "Worse than Slavery," pp. 22–25; Eric Foner and Olivia Mahoney, **America's Reconstruction** (New York: HarperCollins, 1995), p. 88; Dona Broom and John Wood, "Outlaw Days," WPA files, Covington County, MDAH.

252   **agents of change:** Oshinsky, "Worse than Slavery," pp. 25–26.

252   **"They were all that saved it":** B. D. Graves, address to the Hebron Community, June 17, 1926, Lauren Rogers Museum, Laurel, Miss.

252   **under the sheet:** Broom and Wood, "Outlaw Days," unpublished WPA Collection, Covington County, MDAH.

252   **"no sire we ain't":** Rawick, **The American Slave,** supplement, series 1, vol. 9, **Mississippi Narratives,** part 4, pp. 1573–75.

253   **"actual enfranchisement":** Testimony of W. D. Gibbs, Congressional Records, 44th Congress, 1st Session, Senate Report 521, pp. XLIX–LI.

253   **whittled out of a tree branch:** Foner, **Reconstruction,** pp. 281–85; Albion Tourgée, **A Fool's Errand,** John Hope Franklin, ed. (1879; reprint, Cambridge, Mass.: Harvard University Press, 1961), pp. 113–27; Bynum, **The Free State of Jones,** p. 134; McPherson, **Ordeal by Fire,** p. 523; Steven Hahn, **A Nation Under Our Feet,** pp. 177–98.

254   **"Battle Cry of Freedom":** Foner, **Reconstruction,** pp. 281–85; Tourgée, **A Fool's Errand,** pp. 113–27; Bynum, **The Free State of Jones,** p. 134; McPherson, **Ordeal by Fire,** p. 523; Hahn, **One Nation Under Our Feet,** pp. 177–98.

254   **old Vinson Collins:** B. D. Graves, address to the Hebron Community, June 17, 1926, Lauren Rogers Museum, Laurel, Miss.

255 **"without distinction to race or color":** Statistics and quotation from Foner, **Reconstruction,** pp. 344–45.

255 **became a probate judge:** Bynum, **The Free State of Jones,** p. 160.

255 **The other was Adelbert Ames:** Foner, **Reconstruction,** pp. 352–53.

255 **short, inglorious reign:** Bynum, **The Free State of Jones,** p. 135.

256 **helped Newton pursue the claim:** Four bills with identical wording were introduced in the U.S. Congress on behalf of Newton Knight from 1871 to 1873. H.R. 2775 was introduced on January 16, 1871, by Representative George Washington Whitmore. H.R. 1814 was introduced on March 4, 1872, by Representative Legrand W. Perce. And H.R. 822 was introduced by Albert Howe on December 18, 1873. In addition, Ames introduced the same bill in the U.S. Senate on December 18, 1873, S. 219. All bills available at NARA. Quotation is from the Letter of B. A. Mathews to Rep. L. W. Perce, December 7, 1870, Accompanying Papers, H.R. 1814, Newton Knight file, record group 233, box 16, NARA.

257 **without formal charges or trial: New York Times,** March 18, 1911, obituary of Legrand W. Perce; biographical information on George Washington Whitmore is from his entry in The Handbook of Texas Online, Texas State Historical Association, http://www.tshaonline.org/handbook/online/articles/WW/fwh43.html.

257 **"You may rely upon any statement":** Letter from Wm. Hancock to Legrand Perce, December 10, 1870, Accompanying Papers, H.R. 1814, Newton Knight file, record group 233, box 16, NARA.

257 **Southern farmers had aided the Union:** Similar skepticism

would doom Newton's future attempts with the Southern Claims Commission. Ames's and Perce's communications with B. A. Mathews can be found in the Ames Family Papers, Smith College, collection number MS-3. A copy of Newton's roster and Mathews's notation with McMillen's address can be found in the Accompanying Papers, H.R. 1814, Newton Knight file, record group 233, box 16, NARA.

258   **Hinchie:** Interview with Knight genealogist Ken Welch; Bynum, **The Free State of Jones,** genealogical chart on pp. 205–6; interview with Newton and Rachel's great-granddaughter, Barbara Knight Blackledge, March 28, 2008.

258   **"A monkey with his tail off":** Lord, "Mississippi: The Past That Has Not Died."

258   **round up Klanners for arrest:** Stephen Budiansky, **The Bloody Shirt: Terror after Appomattox** (New York, Viking Penguin, 2008), p. 2.

259   **"during these reconstruction days":** A copy of the certificate is in the collection of Knight archivist Ken Welch, and also of Jim Kelly, Knight scholar and vice president of instructional affairs at Jones County Junior College, who shared it with the authors.

259   **"the school doesn't accept Negroes":** Bynum, **The Free State of Jones,** p. 145; Knight, **The Echo of the Black Horn,** p. 266.

260   **"he wished the Negroes to have equal opportunity":** Bynum, **The Free State of Jones,** p. 145; Knight, **The Echo of the Black Horn,** p. 266.

260   **"he had been instrumental in building":** Rawick, **The American Slave,** supplement, series 1, vol. 10, **Mississippi Narratives,** part 5, pp. 2268, 2269; Knight, **The Echo of the Black Horn,** pp. 266–72.

260   **"in securing their actual freedom":** Nicholas Lehmann, **Redemption** (New York: Farrar, Straus and Giroux, 2006), p. 55.

261   **twenty-five black corpses in the street:** Oshinsky, "Worse than Slavery," pp. 27–28.

261   **"The negros did go up there and vote":** Lehmann, **Redemption,** p. 49; B. D. Graves, address to the Hebron Community, June 17, 1926, Lauren Rogers Museum, Laurel, Miss.; Foner, **Reconstruction,** pp. 538–39.

262   **"in the form of a request":** Lehmann, **Redemption,** p. 32; Budiansky, **The Bloody Shirt,** p. 66.

262   **"All are lynx-eyed":** Lehmann, **Redemption,** p. 64.

262   **"blackest tyranny":** Ibid., p. 69.

262   **"first time he leaves his home":** Lord, "Mississippi: The Past That Has Not Died."

263   **"we children did not know him":** Knight, **The Life and Activities of Captain Newton Knight,** pp. 5–6; Tom Knight does not name Ames, he merely states that Newton went to see the "Governor" on state business and told him of the assassination attempt. Ames appears to be the only Mississippi governor with whom Newton corresponded.

263   **pool of oil in the morning sun:** Knight, **The Echo of the Black Horn,** pp. 245–46, quotation from p. 246.

264   **"your sort of cattle":** Frost, "The South's Strangest Army Revealed by Chief."

265   **"do you harm and deceive you":** Knight, **The Life and Activities of Captain Newton Knight,** pp. 11–12.

265   **"a few of his old gang":** Ibid., p. 6.

265   **"when it's too late":** Ibid.

265   **"Mr. Alebert Ames, to your honor, Dear Sir":** Letter from N. B. Blackman to Adelbert Ames, October 16, 1875, in George Sewel Boutwell, **Report of the Select Committee to Inquire**

into the Mississippi Election of 1875, with the testimony and documentary evidence, vol. 2 (Washington, D.C.: Government Printing Office, August 1876), p. 44.

266 **"Mississippi Plan":** For the most in-depth description of the Mississippi Plan and James Z. George's role, see Lehmann, **Redemption,** pp. 100–155; for a briefer summary see Oshinsky, **"Worse than Slavery,"** pp. 37–40.

267 **" 'the color line' ":** William C. Harris, **The Day of the Carpetbagger: Republican Reconstruction in Mississippi** (Baton Rouge: Louisiana State University Press, 1979), p. 626; Bradley Bond, **Political Culture in the 19th Century South, Mississippi 1830–1900** (Baton Rouge: Louisiana State University Press, 1995), pp. 174–75; Cash and Howorth, **My Dear Nellie,** pp. 240–41. Nugent would become president of the state bar in 1887.

267 **they would never recover:** Walter Lord, writing from the perspective of 1965 and in the midst of the civil rights movement, makes a compelling case for the worthiness of Ames's administration in "Mississippi: The Past That Has Not Died" and even argues that the victory of the Democrats over Ames left the state locked in an isolated past and impoverished for years to come. "The state's landed leaders," he observes, ". . . owed their authority to an odd combination of ante-bellum nostalgia and redemption heroics—certainly not new ideas."

267 **Grant effectively returned the city:** Lehmann, **Redemption,** pp. 73–75; Oshinsky, **"Worse than Slavery,"** p. 38.

268 **too afraid to claim them:** Lehmann, **Redemption,** p. 91.

268 **"absence of all the elements of real authority":** Oshinsky, **"Worse than Slavery,"** p. 38; Foner, **Reconstruction,** p. 558.

268 **four Gatling guns: Congressional Record,** 44th Congress, 1st Session, Senate Report 521, pp. XLIX–LI; 465–66.

268 **about half the companies:** Ibid.; copy of Newton Knight's appointment is in the possession of the authors, courtesy of the files of Jim Kelly, Vice President of Instructional Affairs, Jones County Junior College.

268 **"appoint good men":** Ames Letter Books, letter to Newton Knight from Lt. Gov. A. K. Davis, series 802, box 986, Letter Box C, #757, MDAH.

269 **"Dear Sir: I write you a few lines:" Congressional Record,** 44th Congress, 1st Session, Senate Report 521, p. LXXIII.

270 **would not return to Mississippi:** Lehmann, **Redemption,** p. 147.

270 **"be butchered here by this mob":** As quoted in Lehmann, **Redemption,** p. 111.

270 **"their votes have established":** Budiansky, **The Bloody Shirt,** p. 200.

271 **pleaded for protection:** Lehmann, **Redemption,** p. 116–20.

271 **"untrammeled Commonwealth":** As quoted in Oshinsky, **"Worse than Slavery,"** p. 39.

271 **without direct orders from Grant:** Lehmann, **Redemption,** p. 121.

272 **more important than black Mississippi:** Ibid., pp. 136–37.

272 **disband the black militia:** Ibid., pp. 114–27.

273 **"beat him dead with a mall":** B. D. Graves, address to the Hebron Community, June 17, 1926, Lauren Rogers Museum, Laurel, Miss.

273 **"a good many colored people out to hear me":** Testimony of W. D. Gibbs, **Congressional Record,** 44th Congress, 1st Session, Senate Report 521, pp. XLIX–LI.

274 **"but fo'cibly if we must":** Albert T. Morgan, **Yazoo; or, On the Picket Line of Freedom in the South: A Personal Narrative** (1884; reprint, Columbia: University of South Carolina

Press, 2000), pp. 451, 452. In the narrative, Morgan refers to Gibbs as "Major," and in his chapter descriptions in the table of contents, he includes the heading: "What Major Gibbs said about it—'Peaceably if we can, fo'cibly if we must' " (p. x).

274   **"have it all their own way":** Boutwell, **Report of the Select Committee to Inquire into the Mississippi Election of 1875,** vol. 2, pp. 44, 53, 70.

274   **"shape our course accordingly":** Ibid., p. 70.

275   **shattered the windows:** Lehmann, **Redemption,** pp. 147–48.

275   **"their own counties":** Ibid., p. 148.

275   **It was just 496:** County election statistics and details are from Boutwell, **Report of the Select Committee to Inquire into the Mississippi Election of 1875, see appendix charts.** Also Lehmann, **Redemption,** pp. 140–56.

276   **they got just 4:** Ibid. The lack of Republican support in Jones was not surprising—the county was solidly Democratic—but four paltry votes nevertheless suggests Republicans stayed home. In Jasper County Republicans apparently voted safely, and the party actually amassed 835 votes. Nevertheless Jasper, a county that had been solidly Republican two years earlier, swung to the Democrats, who commanded 1,163 votes.

The degree of intimidation, murder, and warfare against blacks and Republicans was heaviest in the wealthy planter counties with high black populations; those counties (Adams, Claiborne, Hinds, Holmes, Washington, Yazoo) showed the most dramatic swings to Democratic victories, owing to the success of the Mississippi Plan. Republicans like Newton clearly did not pose as much of a threat in Jones and Jasper as they did in the Black Belt. These inferences are supported by the fewer incidences of violence against Republicans in Jones and Jasper, though there were some. Newton Knight, with his Republican and interracial ideals, could be tolerated by whites in Jones and Jasper counties in a way that he never would have been had he lived near Natchez or in Yazoo or another predominantly black (and Republican) county. It's safe to say that had Newton Knight lived in Adams County (near Natchez) or in Yazoo, near Albert Morgan, he would have either been killed, run out of town, or forced to vote Democratic in exchange for his life.

276 **four-to-one majority:** Foner, **Reconstruction,** pp. 558–63; Lord, "Mississippi: The Past That Has Not Died."

276 **"not a space where one could lay a hand":** Lehmann, **Redemption,** pp. 159–60.

276 **"by way of reminder":** Ibid., pp. 163–64.

277 **Rather than prolong the state's agony:** Ibid.; Somerville and Howorth, **My Dear Nellie,** pp. 240–41.

277 **As the presidential race of 1876 approached:** Foner, **Reconstruction,** p. 569.

277 **"do what it pleases with them":** Lehmann, **Redemption,** p. 171.

277 **"incapable of comprehending it":** Ibid., p. 165.

278 **"I want no 'committee' in mine":** Records of the Select Committee to Inquire into the Mississippi Election of 1875, microfilm, New York Public Library, Manuscript and Archives Division.

278 **"the Constitution of the United States":** Boutwell, **Report of the Select Committee to Inquire into the Mississippi Election of 1875,** vol. 2, conclusion.

279 **without any further federal help:** Foner, **Reconstruction,** p. 582; Lehmann, **Redemption,** p. 166.

279 **"nothing more to do with him":** Quotes are from Foner, **Reconstruction,** p. 582.

279 **They had lost:** Foner, **Reconstruction,** p. 562.

280 **"that supposed business":** Transcript of **The State of Mississippi v. Davis Knight,** Circuit Court of the First Judicial District, Jones County, p. 20.

CHAPTER 8: THE FAMILY TREE
Page

281 **a separate mixed-race society:** Knight, **The Life and Activities of Captain Newton Knight,** p. 12. Bynum, in **The Free State of Jones,** p. 144, observes that even as redeemers regained control of the state, Newton again defied them, "not just politically but personally."

282 **The title to her own land:** A copy of Newton's deed to Rachel is in the files of the authors, who received it from Jim Kelly, Newton Knight scholar and vice president of instructional affairs at Jones County Junior College. It stated that Rachel paid Newton a "fea simple" of $150 for the land, which he declared free of "incubance." The price of less than a dollar an acre was extremely cheap; the average price of unimproved land in the South in those years was two dollars to eight dollars, according to Loren Schweninger, **Black Property Owners in the South 1790–1915** (Champaign: University of Illinois Press, 1997), p. 148. Newton pledged to "warrant and defend the title of the Said Richel Knight and to her heirs and assigners." Rachel was referred to as Newton's "second wife" by Vermell Moffett, granddaughter of Newton and Rachel, in a newspaper interview, "Knight Legend Lives on in Mulatto Offspring," **Clarion-Ledger,** October 6, 1977.

282 **"iron grip" of the sharecropping system:** Statistics on black land ownership in the state are from Vernon Lane Wharton, **The Negro in Mississippi 1865–1890** (New York: Harper Torchbooks, 1965), p. 61. Statistics on land ownership in the

Cotton South and description of the white "iron grip" on real estate are from Schweninger, **Black Property Owners in the South,** p. 163.

282   **"constantly shoved and pushed around":** Knight, **Mississippi Girl,** p. 12.

283   **a son named John Howard:** U.S. Federal Census, 1870; also see Bynum, **The Free State of Jones,** pp. 206–7, for a genealogical chart. Who fathered Georgeanne's children was an open question. Some said they were the offspring of neighboring white farmers, and as an adult, Anna Knight suggested her father was an unnamed sharecropper who worked on Newton's land; see Knight, **Mississippi Girl,** p. 11. There were also disquieting rumors that they were Newton's; see Bynum, **The Free State of Jones,** p. 272n. No one would ever know for sure. The parentage of the infants hardly mattered from a practical standpoint; Newton helped to rear and provide for all of the children on the farm, who treated him as a father.

Knight descendants do not tend to believe that Georgeanne's children were Newton's, according to the authors' interviews and Bynum's notes on her interviews of Knight descendants. Genealogists are split on the matter. Martha Welborn, operating on oral history passed down from Rachel's grandchildren, believes they were the progeny of neighboring yeomen. Kenneth Welch, however, is convinced they are Newton's.

Anna Knight applied for a Social Security card in 1963, and on it, she listed her father as "Newton Knight." (A copy is in possession of the authors.) However, it's possible that Anna regarded Newton as her father simply because he raised her. In her memoir **Mississippi Girl,** p. 11, Anna refers to her father only obliquely and suggests he farmed on Newton's property. "Although my parents were no longer slaves, they were poor and had little of this world's goods and were compelled, by circumstances, to work as sharecroppers on the white man's land until they were able to buy land for themselves," she writes. But Anna may have been purposely circumspect since her memoir was that of a devout Seventh-Day Adventist missionary and meant for a young audience.

Georgeanne would have two more children, daughters Grace and Lessie, born in 1891 and 1894 respectively. According to Welch, and to Bynum (**The Free State of Jones,** p. 272n), Grace and Lessie's death certificates also list Newton Knight as their father. Again, they may have considered him a father simply because he provided for them.

Welch, operating on the belief Newton indeed fathered them, offers an interesting theory. He notes a seventeen-year gap between the births of Georgeanne's two sets of children and speculates that Newton may have become involved with Georgeanne in 1875 or 1876, but that Rachel put a stop to it. Newton then resumed his relationship with Georgeanne after Rachel's death. It's worth noting that the only woman with whom Newton seems to have fathered any children between 1875 and 1889 was Rachel. It seems possible that Newton honored Rachel's wishes and remained faithful to her until her death.

According to Welch, and to Bynum (**The Free State of Jones,** pp. 206–7), Newton's children with Rachel were: Martha Ann (1865), Stewart (1869), Floyd (1870), Augusta Ann (1873), and John Madison (1875). Newton's children with Serena were: George Mathew "Mat" (1859), Thomas Jefferson (1860), Martha Ann "Molly" (1864), Joseph Sullivan (1866), Susan A. (1868), Keziah (1871), and Cora Ann (1873). In addition, Newton and Serena buried two small boys, Billy, twin of

T. J., apparently killed in a fire just after the war (see Knight, **The Echo of the Black Horn,** p. 255), and Leonard (b. 1875), who died in infancy.

283 **mustard greens, string beans, and tomatoes:** Authors' phone interview with Jules Smith, granddaughter of Hinchie Knight, youngest son of Rachel and Newton Knight, April 6, 2008.

283 **an average of $1,086 in the North:** Lord, "Mississippi: The Past That Has Not Died."

284 **just 11.4 percent:** U.S. Federal Census, 1870, 1880; Bynum, **The Free State of Jones,** p. 145; Knight, **Mississippi Girl,** p. 12; Wharton, **The Negro in Mississippi,** p. 61.

284 **"A Charge to Keep":** Knight, **Mississippi Girl,** pp. 16–17.

284 **for the thirsty:** Knight, **The Echo of the Black Horn,** p. 258.

284 **took several lives in the area:** U.S. Federal Census, 1880; "Spotlight on Ellisville," **Jackson Daily News,** August 1, 1949.

285 **these solitary trips:** Knight, **The Echo of the Black Horn,** p. 263.

285 **"were given advantages":** B. D. Graves, address to the Hebron Community, June 17, 1926, Lauren Rogers Museum, Laurel, Miss.; Rawick, **The American Slave,** supplement, series 1, vol. 10, **Mississippi Narratives,** part 5, interview with Martha Wheeler, former slave belonging to Jackie Knight, pp. 2262–71.

285 **"mixed the blood of the races":** Bynum, **The Free State of Jones,** p. 160; Knight, **The Echo of the Black Horn,** pp. 281–328, quotation from p. 281. Ethel Knight was descended from James Knight's side of the family.

286 **scribbling some names down twice:** U.S. Federal Census, 1880; Bynum, **The Free State of Jones,** p. 144.

287   **sixty cents a day board:** Foner, **Reconstruction,** p. 594; Oshinsky, **"Worse than Slavery,"** p. 42.

287   **He seemed to be ever alert:** Victoria Bynum's notes on interview with Knight descendants Florence Blaylock, Olga Watts, Dorothy Marsh, Lois Knight, and Annette Knight, Soso, Mississippi, July 22, 1996, for **The Free State of Jones,** Mississippi Oral History Project, University of Southern Mississippi; Knight, **The Echo of the Black Horn,** p. 259.

287   **"nothing will induce him to talk of the war":** G. Norton Galloway, "A Confederacy within a Confederacy," **Magazine of American History** 16:4 (July–December 1886), p. 389. Galloway's version of the Jones County guerrillas was highly inaccurate in places, but his description of Newton is validated by other descriptions that suggest he indeed felt threatened. See Knight, **The Life and Activities of Captain Newton Knight,** pp. 5–6; Bynum's notes on interviews with Florence Blaylock and Dorothy Knight Marsh; as well as the authors' interview with Barbara Blackledge, March 28, 2008.

288   **"ruin both races":** "Inauguration of Robert Lowry," **Vicksburg Daily Appeal,** January 9, 1882.

288   **"As the stream could not rise above its source":** Bond, **Political Culture in the 19th Century South,** p. 274.

288   **"We have won, but I am disgusted":** Cincinnati Daily Gazette, September 22, 1881; Stephen Cresswell, **Rednecks, Redeemers, and Race: Mississippi After Reconstruction, 1877–1917** (Jackson: University Press of Mississippi, for the Mississippi Historical Association, 2006), p. 111; "Inauguration of Robert Lowry," **Vicksburg Daily Appeal,** January 9, 1882.

288   **"contemplate such an experiment":** "Inauguration of Robert Lowry," **Vicksburg Daily Appeal,** January 9, 1882.

289   **he might have killed him:** A. D. Kirwan, **Revolt of the Red-**

necks: Mississippi Politics 1876–1925 (Lexington: University of Kentucky Press, 1951), p. 56; Montgomery, "Alleged Secession of Jones County," pp. 13–23; Frost, "The South's Strangest Army Revealed by Chief."

289 election supervisor for Jasper County: Copy of appointment in the files of Knight archivist and scholar Kenneth Welch, provided to authors by Jim Kelly, vice president of instructional affairs at Jones County Junior College.

289 molasses fifty cents a gallon: Letter from Newton Knight to his brother John, April 3, 1887, reprinted in Thomas et al., The Family of John "Jackie" Knight and Keziah Davis Knight.

290 conveniently omitting slavery: Roberts and Moneyhon, Portraits of Conflict, p. 335.

290 difference from Negroes as a class: Ethel Knight, The Echo of the Black Horn, pp. 245–78; Mark Twain, Life on the Mississippi, James M. Cox, ed. (1883; reprint, New York: Penguin Books, 1984), pp. 315–16; John M. Coski, The Confederate Battle Flag: America's Most Embattled Emblem (Cambridge, Mass.: Harvard University Press, 2005), pp. 45–50.

290 Davis's funeral: Evans, Confederate Military History, vol. 9, p. 263; Ames's quotation is from Lehmann, Redemption, p. 79.

290 The Piney Woods experienced a lumber boom: Notes on the Whitfield Community Meeting, "Historical Events in Whitfield," June 4, 1926, Lauren Rogers Museum, Laurel, Miss.

291 "along the Old Mobile Road": Letter from Newton Knight to his brother John, April 3, 1887, the family of John "Jackie" Knight.

291 "you can gess at the balance": Letter from Newton Knight to his brother John, April 3, 1887, the family of John "Jackie" Knight.

292 **a responsible male provider such as Newton:** Thomas W. Murphy, "From Racist Stereotype to Ethnic Identity: Instrumental Uses of Mormon Racial Doctrine," **Ethnohistory** 46:3 (Summer 1999): 451–80; Paul K. Conkin, **American Originals; Homemade Varieties of Christianity** (Chapel Hill: University of North Carolina Press, 1997), p. 216.

292 **while traveling in Jones County:** William Whitridge Hatch, **When Push Came to Shove: Mormon Martyrs in an Unrelenting Bible Belt, 1831–1923** (Portland, Ore.: Inkwater Press, 2005), pp. 13, 29.

292 **recorded Rachel's baptism in a logbook:** Church of Jesus Christ of Latter-day Saints, Records of the Conference of Southern States Mission, Records of Missionaries, 1867–1888, Record of Admissions, 1878–1886, Historical Record 1842–1886. Knight genealogist and archivist Kenneth Welch originally discovered the records of the conversions of Fannie, Rachel, and Martha Ann, and we thank him and Knight scholar Jim Kelly of Jones County Junior College for sharing the information with us.

293 **he joined a new Primitive Baptist church:** Knight, **The Life and Activities of Captain Newton Knight,** pp. 18–19. Tom Knight was in error about the name of the church Newton joined, "Mt. Zora." No such church seems to have existed. However, he may have joined another Primitive Baptist Church in the area.

293 **deeply gratifying to Newton:** Knight, **Mississippi Girl,** pp. 34–35. According to Dorothy Knight Marsh, in an interview with the authors, June 28, 2008, Newton supported Anna and admired her firm conscience, and told her, "Do what you have to do."

294 **massacred twenty-five of them:** Cresswell, **Rednecks, Redeemers and Race,** pp. 62–63, 112.

294   **James Z. George organized the political response:** Ibid., pp. 114–15; Wharton, **The Negro in Mississippi,** pp. 210–11.

295   **"annoyed by Marsh Cook":** Wharton, **The Negro in Mississippi,** p. 211.

295   **"mother of thirteen children":** Bynum, **The Free State of Jones,** pp. 159, 272; Rawick, **The American Slave,** supplement, series 1, vol. 10, **Mississippi Narratives,** part 5, interview with Martha Wheeler, pp. 2262–71.

295   **he and his men had killed in battle:** Knight, **The Echo of the Black Horn,** p. 255.

296   **"just an old Negro woman":** Testimony from the transcript of **State of Mississippi v. Davis Knight,** 1948, p. 65.

296   **he had been more hers:** Author interviews with Barbara Blackledge, March 28, 2008, and Dorothy Knight Marsh, June 28, 2008, great-granddaughters of Rachel and Newton Knight; quotation from Knight, **The Echo of the Black Horn,** p. 45.

297   **to comfort and finish rearing:** B. D. Graves, Address to the Hebron Community, June 17, 1926, Lauren Rogers Museum, Laurel, Miss.

297   **"separated him from his wife":** Rawick, **The American Slave,** supplement, series 1, vol. 10, part 5, interview with Martha Wheeler, pp. 2262–71; Bynum, **The Free State of Jones,** pp. 206–207.

297   **A photograph of Serena:** Photograph found in Bynum, **The Free State of Jones,** p. 156; quotation from Knight, **The Echo of the Black Horn,** p. 285.

298   **"do your own judging":** The account of Fannie's marriage is from the deposition of Fannie Knight Howze in the case of **Martha Ann Musgrove et al. v. J. R. McPherson et al.,** January 27, 1914, copy in possession of the authors, courtesy of the family of Harlan McKnight, grandson of Mat Knight. The case was a legal dispute over the estate of Mat Knight. Mat

and Fannie's son, George "Mat" Knight, moved to Texas and changed his name to McKnight and lived the rest of his life as a white man. Harlan McKnight is his son.

298 **led the nation in documented hangings:** Cresswell, **Rednecks, Redeemers, and Race,** p. 63.

299 **"he struggled so hard":** Hilton Butler, "Lynch Law in Action," **The New Republic** 67, (July 22, 1931): pp. 256–57.

299 **he never won office again:** Cresswell, **Rednecks, Redeemers and Race,** pp. 63–66.

299 **Or just the "Knight Niggers":** U.S. Federal Census, 1900; Bynum, **The Free State of Jones,** p. 144.

301 **only education they would receive:** Knight, **Mississippi Girl,** pp. 81–88.

302 **"especially by a big young man":** Knight, **The Life and Activities of Captain Newton Knight,** p. 16.

302 **"might want to get revenge":** M. P. Bush, address to the meeting of the DAR, February 17, 1912, Lauren Rogers Museum, Laurel, Miss.

303 **leaning against his shoulder:** Copy of photograph in the files of Martha Welborn, who showed it to the authors.

303 **"I'm your grandfather":** Victoria Bynum's notes on interview with Florence Blaylock, Olga Watts, Dorothy March, Lois Knight, and Annette Knight, Soso, Mississippi, July 22, 1996, for **The Free State of Jones,** Mississippi Oral History Project, University of Southern Mississippi; also Bynum, Notes on Interview with Yvonne Bevins and Anita Williams, July 4, 1996, for **The Free State of Jones,** Mississippi Oral History Project, University of Southern Mississippi.

303 **"purity of womanhood":** Bynum, **The Free State of Jones,** pp. 143–44, 152, 165–66, 172.

304 **Other papers picked up the news: The Crisis,** June 26, 1919,

reprinted the front pages of the **Jackson Daily News** and the **New Orleans Item.**

304   **"I want you to drop around":** Hilton Butler, "Lynch Law in Action," pp. 256–57.

305   **the real cause of the attack:** Bynum, **The Free State of Jones,** p. 165.

305   **"Just touch me":** "Knight Legend Lives On in Mulatto Offspring," **Clarion-Ledger,** October 6, 1977. The story was told to the newspaper by Vermell Moffett, granddaughter of Mat and Fannie Knight, and great- granddaughter of Newton and Rachel.

305   **"In simplicity primeval":** Frost, "The South's Strangest Army Revealed by Chief."

306   **"No use stirring up that old quarrel":** Ibid.

307   **so faithfully at night:** Victoria Bynum's notes on interview with Florence Blaylock, Olga Watts, Dorothy March, Lois Knight, and Annette Knight, Soso, Mississippi, July 22, 1996, for **The Free State of Jones,** Mississippi Oral History Project, University of Southern Mississippi.

307   **the birth date was probably wrong:** On the 1900 U.S. Federal Census, Newton Knight gave his year of birth as 1837. All of the available documentary evidence conforms to this date, save for his headstone, according to Bynum.

308   **"Knight ruined his life":** "Passing of Newt Knight," **Ellisville Progress,** Thursday, March 16, 1922.

308   **Newton was not at rest:** Knight's marker has a fraught history, as does Rachel's. On one occasion in the 1970s, Knight's stone disappeared, only to reappear a short time later. On another occasion Rachel's marker was actually placed **closer** to Knight's, according to Barbara Blackledge, great-granddaughter of Newton and Rachel Knight, who was interviewed by the au-

thors March 28, 2008, Ellisville, Miss. Blackledge personally retrieved Rachel's tombstone from one thief who claimed he wanted to clean it. The notion that Knight's stone was moved to separate him from Rachel persists among some members of the Knight family. Others, including Blackledge, believe it is accurately placed.

308 **to an uncle's home:** Bynum, **The Free State of Jones,** p. 173.

309 **"It was just hurt":** Authors' interview with Barbara Knight Blackledge, March 28, 2008. Blackledge is a Knight on both sides; her father Lacy was the son of Charley Knight, one of Jeff and Molly's sons. Her mother Idell was a daughter of Hinchie Knight, the youngest of Rachel's children. Blackledge grew up in a racial netherworld on the old Knight property, midwived, without a birth certificate, and frustrated by her lack of formal schooling after the third grade. "I might as well be alien, I fell from the sky," she says. She finally got her GED when she was forty years old. She also received her master's degree and is now a licensed social worker in Jones County.

309 **who their grandparents were:** Authors' telephone interview with Catharine McKnight, wife of the late Harlan McKnight, son of George Monroe Knight, April 29, 2008.

309 **Some never knew they were Knights:** "Knight Legend Lives On in Mulatto Offspring," **Clarion-Ledger,** October 6, 1977.

309 **the crime of miscegenation:** The term "miscegenation" entered the English language in late 1863 as part of the Democratic campaign against Abraham Lincoln's Republican Party. Copperhead Democrats, many of whom received support from Confederates, attacked the Emancipation Proclamation, arguing that Lincoln and his party had turned the war into a "nigger crusade" that would lead to blood mixing and the mongrelization of the white race. Shortly before Christmas 1863, a

Democratic editor issued a seventy-two-page pamphlet entitled **Miscegenation: The Theory of the Blending of the Races, Applied to the American White Man and Negro.** It passed as scholarship. Attacking Republicans for advocating miscegenation proved a powerful weapon for the Democrats in the 1864 campaign. McClellan might well have won had not Sherman's victory in Atlanta convinced Northerners that the war would soon be over. For sources see Sidney Kaplan, "The Miscegenation Issue in the Election of 1864," in **American Studies in Black and White: Selected Essays** (Amherst: University of Massachusetts Press, 1991), pp. 47–100; Elise Virginia Lemire, **"Miscegenation": Making Race in America** (Philadelphia: University of Pennsylvania Press, 2002); Werner Sollors, **Neither White nor Black but Both: Thematic Explorations of Interracial Literature** (New York: Oxford University Press, 1997), pp. 285–335; Peter Wallenstein, "Reconstruction, Segregation and Miscegenation: Interracial Marriage and the Law in the Lower South, 1865–1900," **American Nineteenth Century History** 6:1 (March, 2002): 57–76; Walter Wadlington, "The Loving Case: Virginia's Anti-Miscegenation Statute in Historical Perspective," **Virginia Law Review** 52:7 (November 1966): 1189–223.

310 **County police arrested him:** "The Children's Children," **Time,** December 27, 1948.

311 **"white Southern men will not tolerate":** Miscegenation laws specifically opposed marriages and sexual relationships between white women and black men. Such relationships threatened racial "purity" of the white woman, on which white supremacy depended. It was all too common for white men to have sex with black women, and thus "mix blood," but the offspring were defined as blacks and not acknowledged as kin of the

white man. Some white Southern men were even proud of such practices. One Mississippi planter, running for the state senate before the Civil War, canvassed for votes by bringing with him a black girl named Sal and an "ample supply" of whiskey and tobacco so that voters could "choose" among these "creature comforts." "That did the business for me," the planter recalled; "I was the first Whig Senator ever sent to the legislature from this county." The tradition that treated black women as objects of sexual pleasure for white men persisted through most of the twentieth century. See Morgan, **Yazoo,** pp. 33–34.

311   **attended his funeral: A Current Biography,** 1943 (New York: H. W. Wilson, 1943), pp. 47–50.

312   **"Folks call them 'The Knight Negroes' ":** Transcript of **State of Mississippi v. Davis Knight.**

314   **"He was a thoroughbred":** Ibid.

314   **He drowned in a fishing accident:** "Knight Legend Lives On in Mulatto Offspring," **Clarion-Ledger,** October 6, 1977.

315   **in order to preserve segregation: Report of Mississippi Sovereignty Commissioner Erle Johnston Jr. on the case of Louvenia Knight Williamson, December 12, 1963,** MDAH.

315   **"How can you hate something that's in you?":** Authors' telephone interview with Kecia Carter, granddaughter of Henry Knight, son of Mat and Fannie Knight, April 8, 2008.

315   **"We'll all die guerillas":** "Knight Legend Lives On in Mulatto Offspring," **Clarion-Ledger,** October 6, 1977.

BIBLIOGRAPHY

For more than a hundred years, Newton Knight and his army of Southern Unionists have been seen as stains on the fabric of the white South and its reverence for the Lost Cause. This is because the history of Jones County explodes two central beliefs about the Confederacy: that white Southerners were **united** in their efforts to form a new democratic nation; and that they accepted defeat nobly and heroically. Newton Knight and his comrades reveal a different, darker side of the Confederacy—a deeply divided nation, especially along class lines, that more closely resembled a totalitarian state than a democracy.

From the perspective of Newton and Rachel Knight (and other Southern Unionists), the South **won** the war. Rebels did not surrender at Appomattox in any meaningful way. Instead, they returned home, continued terrorizing their enemies, and thwarted Unionist efforts to remake society in the image of freedom and equality under the law. By 1876, Northerners lost the will to fight, and former rebels preserved an old order that kept blacks unfree for another one hundred years.

In essence, the true history of Newton Knight constituted a nightmare vision for white Southerners. Here was a man who, John Brown–like, forged intimate alliances with blacks, treated them with dignity and respect, and tried to destroy slavery.

As a result, for more than a hundred years, white Southerners have sanitized and revised the story of Newton and Rachel Knight in order to accommodate their faith in a noble Lost Cause.

The first history of Jones County's Unionists, G. Norton Galloway's "A Confederacy Within a Confederacy," **Magazine of American History** 16 (July–December 1886): 387–90, began a tradition that horribly blurred fact and fiction. It contains numerous errors, including Newton's name (whom Galloway refers to as Nathan).

Five years later, in 1891, the Northern-born Harvard historian Albert Bushnell Hart argued with prescient insight that Jones County and other Southern Unionists, together with blacks, contributed to the South's defeat. See Hart, "Why the South Was Defeated in the Civil War," **New England Magazine** 11:3 (November 1891): 363–76.

Lost Cause advocates vigorously refuted Hart's arguments, denying any noteworthy opposition to the Confederacy in Jones County or elsewhere in Mississippi. This historical assault on Newton Knight and his guerrillas persisted throughout the twentieth century, typified by the influential essay by Goode Montgomery, "Alleged Secession of Jones County,"

Publications of the Mississippi Historical Society 8 (1904): 13–22. Montgomery's article is featured on the Jones County Web site at http://www.natchezbelle.org/ahgp-ms/jones/secession1.htm.

In the Great Depression, Newton Knight's son Thomas Knight privately published the first biography of his father and the Jones County Scouts: Thomas J. Knight, **The Life and Activities of Captain Newton Knight and His Company and the Free State of Jones** (Ellisville, Miss.: printed by the Progress Item, © 1934), copies at New York Public Library and Mississippi Department of Archives and History. Thomas characterizes Newton as a Robin Hood who seceded from the state and fought the Confederacy with a band of fellow deserters, but he ignores Newton's relationships with Rachel Knight and other blacks. Nevertheless, neo-Confederates discredited his story.

During World War II, the Mississippi journalist James Street published a novel based on Newton's company of Unionists: **Tap Roots** (New York: The Book League of America, 1942). Street, who grew up in Laurel, Mississippi, read deeply in the available sources and interviewed people from Jones County for his book. He wrote a sympathetic and in some respects stunningly accurate account of Newton and Jones County Unionism.

Street's protagonist Hoab Dabney is loosely based on Newton, while Hoab's adopted daughter, Kyd, resembles Rachel Knight: she is part Indian and black and is treated as an equal member of Hoab's family.

Like Newton, Hoab is a deeply religious "shouting abolitionist" who abstains from alcohol and fights to preserve the Union and end slavery (p. 30). Street casts Hoab as the John Brown of the South, partly as a way to give Southern Unionists credit for their role in ending slavery. "John Brown tried to lead the slaves in armed rebellion. . . . I will free them," Hoab declares (p. 397). He liberates his county of Lebanon, Mississippi, from the Confederacy and establishes "The Free State of Lebanon" (p. 392). But unlike Newton, Hoab is not committed to racial equality: he prohibits blacks from settling in Lebanon and treats his black friends as children rather than equals.

In 1948 **Tap Roots** was adapted into a film starring Susan Hayward and Van Heflin. It is a sanitized version of the novel (and of Newton Knight and the South), ignoring slavery as the cause of the war and purging Hoab of his antislavery sympathies. In the film, Hoab is an educated newspaperman who organizes poor farmers against misguided Confederates. The only non-white character is a Choctaw named Tishomingo, a noble savage who befriends Hoab's family and embodies the Southern ideals of agrarian freedom and individualism.

After Newton and Rachel's great-grandson Davis Knight was put on trial for miscegenation in 1948, it became impossible to ignore blacks in Newton's story. In the wake of the trial, Ethel Knight, Newton's grandniece, published **The Echo of the Black Horn** (1951; reprinted, York, Penn.: The Maple-Vail

Book Manufacturing Group, 2003). She describes how Tom Knight, now "old and shaken with palsy," finally confronts the "horrible truth" about his father. Newton was no Robin Hood but a cowardly deserter, murderer, and madman who disgraced his family and contaminated his bloodline by succumbing to the Jezebel Rachel and treating her as his wife. Ethel dedicates **The Echo of the Black Horn** to "the memory of the Noble Confederates who lived and died for Jones County." Despite its flaws, it constitutes the most extensive oral history of Newton and Rachel Knight.

The following year, a much more reliable though brief account of Newton and Rachel Knight was published by Rachel's granddaughter Anna Knight, who became a renowned Seventh-Day Adventist missionary. Anna describes her childhood in Jones County in her autobiography, **Mississippi Girl** (Nashville: Southern Publishing Association, 1952).

Since the 1980s, two scholarly accounts of Jones County Unionism during the Civil War have been published. Rudy H. Leverett, the great-grandson of Amos McLemore, the Confederate officer killed by Newton and his comrades, vigorously denies that Jones County Scouts communicated with Union soldiers, pledged allegiance to the Union, or aided other farmers. He portrays Newton as a common thief, deserter, and murderer and asserts that although some Jones County farmers remained "loyal to the United States," this did not make them "disloyal to the Confederacy" (p. 125). It is an absurd statement, since loyalty to the Confederacy meant being a traitor to the United States. In his quest to redeem the Confederacy and his ancestor's death, Leverett ignores slavery and blacks. See Rudy H. Leverett, **Legend of the Free State of Jones** (Jackson: University Press of Mississippi, 1984).

Victoria E. Bynum was the first person, in 2001, to write against this neo-Confederate tradition. A descendant of one of Newton's comrades, Bynum spent years researching her book; and her scholarly monograph, **The Free State of Jones: Mississippi's Longest Civil War** (Chapel Hill: University of North Carolina Press, 2001), offers a social history of Jones County from 1820 to Davis Knight's trial in 1948. We have been deeply influenced by Bynum's book and notes and transcripts of interviews at the University of Southern Mississippi, and we are indebted to her research. Given its scope, however, she devotes only about fifty pages to the Civil War and Reconstruction, and she does not connect Jones County to the larger network of deserters and Unionism in Southern Mississippi.

These revisions of Jones County events parallel the histories of the Civil War that continue (often subtly) to redeem the Confederacy by ignoring the role of blacks and Southern Unionists. In a recent popular history of the Confederacy, the distinguished scholar and Southerner Gary W. Gallagher, in **The Confederate War** (Cambridge, Mass.: Harvard University Press, 1997), argued that the vast majority of white Southerners "waged a determined struggle for independence" and "steadfastly supported their nascent republic" (pp. 3 and 17). Another eminent Southern-bred scholar of the Civil War era, David Herbert Donald, asserted in an influential essay that the Confederacy lost because it was **too** democratic. See **"Died of Democracy": Why the North Won the Civil War** (1960; reprint, New York: Simon and Schuster, 1996), pp. 81–92. Though not by any means the **only** interpretations of the Confederacy, Gallagher's and Donald's arguments remain dominant in the American imagination.

The State of Jones is the first comprehensive narrative and popular history of Newton Knight and his band of Unionists in Southern Mississippi during the Civil War and Reconstruction. It draws on a cache of new evidence, including recently discovered depositions, oral interviews with Rachel Knight's descendants, and overlooked wartime documents that capture the lived experience at the time.

Our story focuses on the two areas of Civil War studies that have been among the most neglected by scholars: deserters, and the large numbers of Southern Unionists. In reconstructing the lives of Southern dissidents, and the blacks who fought with them against the Confederacy, we offer an alternative history of the South. Encompassing extraordinary feats of courage, determination, and principled action, it is a story that Americans can be justly proud of.

The historiography of Southern Unionism is comparatively sparse. A few Mississippi historians have drawn attention to Unionism in Jones County: John K. Bettersworth, **Confederate Mississippi: The People and Policies of a Cotton State in Wartime** (Baton Rouge: Louisiana State University Press, 1943); John K. Bettersworth, ed., **Mississippi in the Confederacy: As They Saw It** (Baton Rouge: Louisiana State University Press, 1961); John K. Bettersworth, ed., **Mississippi in the Confederacy: As Seen in Retrospect** (Baton Rouge: Louisiana State University Press, 1961); and M. Shannon Mallard, " 'I Had No Comfort to Give the People': Opposition to the Confederacy in Civil War Mississippi," in **North & South** 6:4 (May 2003): 79–86. Mallard, a doctoral student at Mississippi State University who died tragically before completing his dissertation, argued that by early 1865, Jones County was the center of a Union stronghold extending throughout southern Mississippi, roughly one-third of the state.

For narratives (primary and secondary) of Southern Unionism and desertion outside of the Piney Woods, Mississippi, see William Baxter, **Pea Ridge and Prairie Grove, or, Scenes and Incidents of the War in Arkansas,** ed. William L. Shea (1864; reprint, Fayetteville: University of Arkansas Press, 2000); Thomas Cockrell and Michael B. Ballard, eds., **Chickasaw: A Mississippi Scout for the Union: The Civil War Memoir of Levi H. Naron, as Recounted by R. W. Surby** (1865; reprint, Baton Rouge: Louisiana State University Press, 2005); John H. Aughey, **The Iron**

Furnace: or, Slavery and Secession (1865; reprint, New York: Negro Universities Press, 1969); John H. Aughey, Tupelo (Lincoln, Neb.: E. Journal Company, 1888); Ella Lonn, Desertion During the Civil War (1928; reprint, Lincoln: University of Nebraska Press, 1998); Georgia Lee Tatum, Disloyalty in the Confederacy (1934; reprint, Chapel Hill: University of North Carolina Press, 1999); Charles W. Ramsdell, Behind the Lines in the Southern Confederacy (1944; reprint, Baton Rouge: Louisiana State University Press, 1997); John Roy Lynch, Reminiscences of an Active Life: The Autobiography of John Roy Lynch, ed. John Hope Franklin (Chicago: University of Chicago Press, 1970); Phillip S. Paludan, Victims: A True Story of the Civil War (Knoxville: University of Tennessee Press, 1981); Carl N. Degler, The Other South: Southern Dissenters in the Nineteenth Century (Boston: Northeastern University Press, 1982); Daniel W. Crofts, Reluctant Confederates: Upper South Unionists in the Secession Crisis (Chapel Hill: University of North Carolina Press, 1989); Wayne K. Durrill, War of Another Kind: A Southern Community in the Great Rebellion (New York: Oxford University Press, 1990); Richard N. Current, Lincoln's Loyalists: Union Soldiers from the Confederacy (Boston: Northeastern University Press, 1992); Joseph T. Glatthaar, Forged in Battle: The Civil War Alliance of Black Soldiers and White Officers (Baton Rouge: Louisiana State University Press, 2000); Joseph T. Glatthaar, "Black Glory: The African-American Role in Union Victory," in Why the Confederacy Lost, ed. Gabor S. Boritt (New York: Oxford University Press, 1992); Jon L. Wakelyn, ed., Southern Unionist Pamphlets and the Civil War (Columbia: University of Missouri Press, 1999); John C. Inscoe and Robert C. Kenzer, eds., Enemies of the Country: New Perspectives on Unionists in the Civil War South (Athens: University of Georgia Press, 2001); William C. Davis, Look Away! A History of the Confederate States of America (New York: The Free Press, 2002); Margaret M. Storey, Loyalty and Loss: Alabama's Unionists in the Civil War and Reconstruction (Baton Rouge: Louisiana State University Press, 2004); William W. Freehling, The South vs. the South: How Anti-Confederate Southerners Shaped the Course of the Civil War (New York: Oxford University Press, 2001); William W. Freehling, The Road to Disunion, vol. 2: Secessionists Triumphant, 1854–1861 (New York: Oxford University Press, 2007); James M. McPherson, This Mighty Scourge: Perspectives on the Civil War (New York: Oxford University Press, 2007), pp. 43–50.

On accounts suggesting or implying that the South won the war, see John Richard Dennett, The South as It Is, 1865–1866 (1866; reprint, New York: Compass Books, 1967); Albert T. Morgan, Yazoo; or, On the Picket Line of Freedom in the South: A Personal Narrative (1884; reprint, Columbia: University of South Carolina Press, 2000); John Roy Lynch, The Facts of Reconstruction (1913; reprint, New

York: Arno Press, 1968); W. E. B. Du Bois, **Black Reconstruction: An Essay Toward a History of the Part Which Black Folk Played in the Attempt to Reconstruct Democracy in America, 1861–1880** (New York: Russell and Russell, 1935); Eric Foner, **Reconstruction: America's Unfinished Revolution, 1863–1877** (New York: Harper and Row, 1988); Steven Hahn, **A Nation Under Our Feet: Black Political Struggles in the Rural South from Slavery to the Great Migration** (Cambridge, Mass.: Harvard University Press, 2003); Storey, **Loyalty and Loss;** Nicholas Lemann, **Redemption: The Last Battle of the Civil War** (New York: Farrar, Straus and Giroux, 2006); and especially Stephen Budiansky, **The Bloody Shirt: Terror After Appomattox** (New York: Viking, 2008).

On interracial romance and alliance in the South, see Harriet A. Jacobs, **Incidents in the Life of a Slave Girl, Written by Herself,** ed. Jean Fagan Yellin (1861; reprint, Cambridge, Mass.: Harvard University Press, 1987); Morgan, **Yazoo;** Eugene D. Genovese, **Roll, Jordan, Roll: The World the Slaves Made** (New York: Vintage Books, 1974), pp. 413–31; Deborah Gray White, **Ar'n't I a Woman: Female Slaves in the Plantation South** (New York: W. W. Norton, 1985); Stephanie M. H. Camp, **Closer to Freedom: Enslaved Women and Everyday Resistance in the Plantation South** (Chapel Hill: University of North Carolina Press, 2004); Thavolia Glymph, **Out of the House of Bondage: The Transformation of** the Plantation Household (New York: Cambridge University Press, 2008); Catherine Clinton, **Tara Revisited: Women, War, and the Plantation Legend** (New York: Abbeville Press, 1995); Marie Jenkins Schwartz, **Born in Bondage: Growing Up Enslaved in the Antebellum South** (Cambridge, Mass.: Harvard University Press, 2000); Virginia Elise Lemire, **"Miscegenation": Making Race in America** (Philadelphia: University of Pennsylvania Press, 2002); Annette Gordon-Reed, **The Hemingses of Monticello: An American Family** (New York: W. W. Norton, 2008); David J. Libby et al., eds., **Affect and Power: Essays on Sex, Slavery, Race, and Religion in Appreciation of Winthrop D. Jordan** (Jackson: University Press of Mississippi, 2005); Randall Kennedy, **Interracial Intimacies: Sex, Marriage, and Adoption** (New York: Pantheon, 2003); Carl Plasa and Betty J. Ring, eds., **The Discourse of Slavery: Aphra Behn to Toni Morrison** (New York: Routledge, 1994); Martha Hodes, ed., **Sex, Love, Race: Crossing Boundaries in North America** (New York: New York University Press, 1999); and Martha Hodes, **White Women, Black Men: Illicit Sex in the Nineteenth-Century South** (New Haven: Yale University Press, 1997).

On the memory of the Civil War, see Hugh Tulloch, **The Debate on the American Civil War Era** (Manchester: Manchester University Press, 1999); David W. Blight, **Race and Reunion: The Civil War in American Memory** (Cambridge, Mass.:

Harvard University Press, 2001); Matthew J. Grow, "The Shadow of the Civil War: A Historiography of Civil War Memory," in **American Nineteenth Century History** 4:2 (Summer 2003): 77–103; Wolfgang Schivelbusch, **The Culture of Defeat: On National Trauma, Mourning, and Recovery** (New York: Picador, 2004); Alice Fahs and Joan Waugh, eds., **The Memory of the Civil War in American Culture** (Chapel Hill: University of North Carolina Press, 2004); W. Fitzhugh Brundage, **The Southern Past: A Clash of Race and Memory** (Cambridge, Mass.: Harvard University Press, 2005); David B. Sachsman, S. Kittrell Rushing, and Roy Morris Jr., eds., **Memory and Myth: The Civil War in Fiction and Film from Uncle Tom's Cabin to Cold Mountain** (West Lafayette, Ind.: Purdue University Press, 2007); and Gary W. Gallagher, **Causes Won, Lost, and Forgotten: How Hollywood and Popular Art Shape What We Know About the Civil War** (Chapel Hill: University of North Carolina Press, 2008).

INDEX

INSERT CREDITS

Page 1

Top left: From the collection of Herman Welborn, courtesy of Martha Welborn and Barbara Blackledge

Top middle: From the collection of Herman Welborn, courtesy of Martha Welborn and Barbara Blackledge

Top right: From the collection of Herman Welborn, courtesy of Martha Welborn and Barbara Blackledge

Center: Library of Congress

Bottom: Library of Congress

Page 2

Top left: Alabama Department of Archives and History, Montgomery, AL

Top middle: Library of Congress

Top right: Alabama Department of Archives and History, Montgomery, AL

Bottom: The New York Public Library/Art Resource, NY

Page 3
Top: Harper's Weekly
Bottom: Library of Congress

Page 4
Top: Library of Congress
Bottom: Library of Congress

Page 5
Top: Courtesy of Jim Kelly
Bottom: Library of Congress

Page 6
Top left: Library of Congress
Top right: Library of Congress
Bottom: Library of Congress

Page 7
Top: Library of Congress
Bottom: Library of Congress

Page 8
Top left: Library of Congress
Top right: From the collection of Herman Welborn, courtesy of Martha Welborn and Barbara Blackledge
Bottom: Library of Congress

SALLY JENKINS is an award-winning journalist for the **Washington Post** and the author of **The Real All Americans,** as well as the legendary **New York Times** bestseller **It's Not About the Bike** with Lance Armstrong. She lives in New York City.

JOHN STAUFFER is chair and professor of the History of American Civilization at Harvard University and the award-winning author of **The Black Hearts of Men** and other books on the Civil War era, including **Giants: The Parallel Lives of Frederick Douglass and Abraham Lincoln.** He lives in Cambridge, Massachusetts.